Voyages of Discovery

Voyages of Discovery

JAMES ARMSTRONG

*For us the voyage signifies the
exploration of the self and the
world, of potential essences.*

—W. H. Auden
The Enchafed Flood

John Wiley & Sons, Inc.

New York • *London* • *Sydney* • *Toronto*

~

Library of Congress Catalog Card Number: 70-37931
ISBN 0-471-03330-8

Printed in the United States of America.

10 9 8 7 6 5 4 3 2 1

For Becky, Patty, Susan, and Tom:
may their voyages bring them joy

Preface

There it is. *"Saturday, 19 June 71,"* the entry reads. *"Mediterranean Palace Boutique (advice fm Englishman). Lakones—Bella Vista. Paleocastritsa. Kanoni—Nafsikas rest."*

Five short lines in my pocket notebook. And the whole day comes flooding back on me. A rich day, a day so full I had no time to make my usual logbook entry. And I had thought those names were lost. *Lakones. Bella Vista.* I'd forgotten completely the visit to the Mediterranean Palace Boutique; the English owner of the shop had told me to turn right at Kanones to reach the Bella Vista cafe. And then the gin and tonic at Kanoni before dinner at the Nafsikas.

Nafsikas. *Nausicaa*, she's usually called in the English translations of the *Odyssey*: "the white-armed Nausicaa." The daughter of the king of this island—Odysseus met her when he was washed ashore here, closer to home than he realized after that incredible ten-year voyage all over the Mediterranean.

Closer to home than I was at that point in my own odyssey. Ithaca lay only a few kilometers to the south of Kerkira, the country of the Phoeacians, as Homer called it. California lay on the other side of the world from me, although I had only been away for two months.

I remember thinking about Odysseus that afternoon at the Bella Vista. A thousand feet or more below me lay the green coves of Paleocastritsa, and the surf breaking on the most gorgeous coastline I've ever seen. It reminded me of the view from the Nepenthe restaurant on the Big Sur coast of California, but I was much higher and the shoreline was much more irregular, with five or six shallow, sandy-bottomed coves holding water so clear that a few anchored boats seemed to be floating in mid-air.

Well, so it's not lost—the memory of the owner of the Mediterranean Palace Boutique snorting about Lawrence Durrell (for a moment I'd imagined that he might *be* Lawrence Durrell) and telling me about the view from the Bella Vista. The whole day is gradually filling in—coffee and ice cream under the arcade that faces the cricket green a block or so south of the Mediterranean Palace, the fantastic winding drive through terraced olive groves from Lakones up to the Bella Vista; much more. I'm glad. I was feeling sad and guilty about neglecting my logbook at that time, but I did manage to get a few words down after all.

And the little irony of it pleases me now, because I was thinking that afternoon about this preface, and how I had wanted to say something about the absolute urgency of writing things down so you don't lose them forever. There were stretches in Yugoslavia that seemed to have vanished completely, many other days there and in Greece safely memorialized in my red spiral-bound notebook.

I'm pleased with what I've brought home from that trip: not the gifts and souvenirs, but the memories in my head and the words in my logbook and in that pocket notebook. Those are the really precious things, the things I'll be sharing for years with my children, my friends, my students. Some of them will undergo the kind of transformation that those five lines did in becoming this preface. Some of them may become longer essays, articles, even books. A few are perhaps perfect as they are, little gems I'll use somewhere just as I wrote them in the logbook. Many will stay in that logbook, seen by no one but me, unless some day my children find them, or someone else inherits my miscellaneous papers. But they'll give me pleasure in the meantime, because once in a while I'll look back over them and remember those days when they were written. And I'll remember more richly than I could without them.

Voyages and logbooks go together. I can't imagine making a voyage without one. That's the idea behind this book, as the reader will see. Voyages and discoveries are meant to be written about, communicated, shared. We are all outward bound, to destinations we don't yet know, perhaps; we can't know how significant our voyages will be, any more than Columbus could. But some day the records we keep may seem infinitely precious. Like some of the records represented in this book, they may save from oblivion certain moments in which the spirit of man, in its dark voyage through time and space, glowed brightly and beautifully before it vanished.

Laguna Beach　　　　　　　　　　　　　　　　　　*James Armstrong*
December 1971

Acknowledgements

Throughout the preparation of this book I have been impelled and inspired by the memory of Ray Livingston, himself a courageous voyager, who first taught me the importance and the pervasiveness of the voyage theme. I am grateful to Edward J. Corbett, Winston Weathers, and Raymond D. Liedlich for valuable advice about many aspects of the book, and to Mary Ellen Vlietstra and Mary Millard for their superb typing.

Contents

Contents

Casting Off Moorings

Contents

Voyages of Discovery

ROBERT FROST

Neither Out Far nor In Deep

The people along the sand
All turn and look one way.
They turn their back on the land.
They look at the sea all day.

As long as it takes to pass
A ship keeps raising its hull;
The wetter ground like glass
Reflects a standing gull.

The land may vary more;
But wherever the truth may be—
The water comes ashore,
And the people look at the sea.

They cannot look out far.
They cannot look in deep.
But when was that ever a bar
To any watch they keep?

Voyages and Discoveries: An Introduction

Why a book about journeys and voyages?

Because we are all voyagers, travelers upon a mysterious journey from nowhere to somewhere, peering eagerly into the mists ahead, sometimes looking back at the way we've come, but mostly occupied with keeping our vessels afloat and ourselves as comfortable as possible from day to day.

A part of man has always been a traveler, a wanderer, an explorer, ready to abandon the little comfort and security he has in order to search for something else, eternally discontented, eternally hopeful, paradoxically never quite at home in the homes he builds for himself. Yet from all the evidence we can gather, it appears that the majority of men have always preferred to stay at home, at least for several hundred centuries, admiring or envying the few explorers and adventurers among them, but unwilling for some reason to leave what little they have secured for themselves in order to explore the other side of the mountain or the other side of the sea.

That the stay-at-homes have not been entirely content with their lot, and that they have been nearly as curious about what lies beyond as the travelers is amply attested by the perennial popularity of travel stories throughout history. From the ancient epics of Beowulf and Odysseus through the wondrous tales of Marco Polo and Robinson Crusoe to the televised exploits of today's moon voyagers, stories of travel and exploration have the widest and strongest appeal of all our literature. Perhaps our appetite for the accounts of these wanderers is primarily the reflection of the fact that they can go and we cannot, or dare not, though we would like to. But travelers' tales are not merely a safer or cheaper or easier way for us to travel; they feed our insatiable curiosity, they extend our experience many times over, they show us more alternatives, more possibilities for life, and they make us wiser and more worldly than we would otherwise be.

For the mind is the greatest traveler of all. The human imagination has always reached distant places long before the feet have followed—if they have. Sometimes the mental voyage is enough, but often the mind has been the pioneer, the trail blazer for the body which struggles more cumbrously behind. And books, or spoken tales, have almost always been the stimulus to those journeys, and frequently the vehicle as well. We go—in body or in imagination—because we have learned a little about those far shores, but not enough. We will see for ourselves, or we will find out from someone who has been there.

The traveler himself is a fascinating person. What made him do it? Is he different from us? We admire his freedom, his independence, his self-reliance, and we like to believe that we might have as much. Maybe we will

4

go, too; maybe he has only shown us the way. And maybe we will go farther, or set off in some entirely different direction, a direction that corresponds to our own needs, our own dreams. Whatever discoveries are made, by ourselves or by those adventurers in whose footsteps we mentally follow, they have a double value. They not only enrich the discoverer—whether by wealth, or fame, or new knowledge, or pride of achievement—but they also enrich the community to which he returns, or sends back reports. However personal or selfish the traveler's motives, it is a rare voyage of discovery that does not in some way benefit the world at large.

But what of the motives of voyagers? Are they similar? Are they significant, even if known? Whether or not they are significant, they are the object of our most intense curiosity, unless the voyage happens to be our own. Then we are likely to admit cheerfully, even insistently, that we haven't the faintest idea why we are going, or why we went. And if that doesn't discourage our questioners, we may invent some plausible reasons to put them off.

Human motivation is fantastically complex, and while some psychologists will tell you that behind every action lies either love or hate, sex or aggression, others will insist that nobody really knows why anybody does anything. It is easy enough to concede, however, that no matter how complicated men's motives may be, they often have at least one clear reason for doing something. They know it, and perhaps admit it, and almost anyone else with a little interest can discover it. Coronado searched for gold, Henry Morton Stanley for fame; to such voyagers we easily assign motives like "greed" or "ambition," and then we are satisfied.

We know, too, that many travelers seek to escape from something unpleasant—an incident, a situation, a memory. New surroundings offer them the chance to forget what they have left behind and begin again, or at least find a temporary relief from trouble. Our folk wisdom deplores running away and applauds staying to battle adversity, but experience tells us that real wisdom is sometimes a matter of knowing when we've had enough. No one argues that the Pilgrims should have stayed in England.

But what about all those other voyages where motives aren't so clear? Why do men like Slocum and Chichester and Rose sail single-handedly around the world? Why does David Livingstone tramp endlessly through the swamps and jungles of Africa? Why does an Australian nurse decide to go around the world by motorbike? "Wanderlust," we say, or "the desire for adventure." But what does that explain? Why does anyone desire adventure (whatever that is)?

Psychologists have only recently turned their attention to a methodical study of what has been called "exploratory behavior," and their conclusions so far have not been very helpful. In fact, as one of them has wryly observed, the laboratory psychology of the future, if it plunges courageously ahead, may some day catch up with the conclusions of common sense. These conclusions—or speculations—are many, and they are offered by laymen as well as psychologists. We do know that the impulse to explore is characteristic of nearly all living things, that it seems to be a quality of life itself. The urge has been called "primitive" and "instinctive," and it has been observed to be especially strong in infants and children; in fact, in the young of nearly all species. It is not a search for food, or comfort, or wealth, or any tangible reward. Perhaps it arises from boredom—boredom with the familiar, the easy, the comfortable. Perhaps all the species that have survived on this planet have done so because of an innate need to overcome obstacles, to be challenged, to use all their strength and skill and cunning—"to strive, to seek, to find, and not to yield," as Ulysses says.

So there is perhaps a need to exercise our faculties, keep our minds and bodies fit by using them, test what we can do. There is often an element of play involved. "What if . . .?" we ask ourselves. The imagination frisks and capers; it turns the world upside down. Why? How? Where? But it is not only that we like to use what we have, what we are, what is within us; there is also that world *out there*. We want to make it part of ourselves, or at least subject to our command. We want to control our environment—primarily to keep it from hurting us, but also because we take pleasure in making it jump through our hoops. Man is a manipulator. And in order to manipulate what is out there—behind the trees, over the hill, beyond the horizon—in order to protect himself against it, or to make it work for him, turn it into a tool or a weapon, he needs to know what it is.

Curiosity, then, leads to knowledge, and knowledge to the possibility of control of ourselves or our environment or each other. This is not a pat formula to summarize all the complexities we have been considering; there is no such formula. But there does seem to be an almost inevitable relationship between travel and knowledge, or more specifically, between voyages and discoveries. To risk a generalization, every voyage—actual or imaginary, physical or mental—is a means to the discovery of something; the traveler can scarcely *not* discover something, significant at least to himself. On the other hand, every discovery, momentous or trivial, is the consequence of some kind of voyage, some act of getting away from or outside of one's usual frame of reference, physical or mental or both. Herbert Butterfield has abundantly documented this thesis in *The Origins of Modern Science*. Every important scientific discovery he examines was the result of the discoverer's freeing himself from the beliefs or attitudes or preconceptions of his own time and place—not only those of his fellow

6

men, but his own—and for a brief time, at least, getting outside himself and his environment. But the change in perspective is the important thing. Often the scientist found no new facts, no information not available to everyone else. But he found a new way of looking at those facts, and saw new relationships between them.

So this is the value of change, and perhaps another answer to the question of motivation: a change of location, or perspective, or point of view, gives us a new world to consider. Not necessarily a better world, but certainly a different one. And when we come to consider the *kinds* of movements our discoverers undertake to change their perspectives, we sometimes find some strange and paradoxical things. We find them going west in order to go east (Columbus and Magellan), backward in order to go forward (Darwin and Leakey), or down in order to go up (Dante). And we find also that it is sometimes difficult to decide whether the physical or mental component of a voyage is the more important—sometimes, in fact, difficult to distinguish between the two, or to decide whether the voyage is "real" or imaginary.

In selecting the various accounts that this book comprises, I have aimed at many things. My motives—even the known ones—are multiple. But one consideration has always been stronger than the others. I have tried to create the kind of anthology, and ask the kind of questions, that would keep the meanings of "voyage" and "discovery" as broad and as varied as possible. Certainly Columbus made a voyage of discovery. But this is only one sort of voyage and one sort of discovery. (In fact, he made more than one voyage and discovery.) Many of us find it difficult to think nonliterally, that is, metaphorically, or to develop that flexibility of thought that enables us to shift easily and naturally from the literal to the metaphorical and back again, or to think sometimes in both modes at once. To some readers, the metaphorical or figurative (or "imaginary") will seem to be the opposite of the "real," and therefore less important, or less interesting, or less true. But to think that way is to be mentally musclebound.

The readings in this book should raise some interesting questions: What is the relationship between fact and metaphor? Between the concrete and the abstract, the particular and the general? Between the actual and the imaginary? (It is *not*, in any case, that one is true and the other false, or one is right and the other wrong.) Many accounts will raise this question: Is *x* fact or metaphor? (Or both?) If metaphor, to what fact(s) does it point? If fact, for what might it become a metaphor? The possibilities of this kind of thinking will become more evident as the readings are encountered. At this point, there is one vital thing to remember: *voyage* has more than one meaning. So does *discovery*.

"The road of life" is a cliché, or a dead metaphor, though it was once a live one. And however hard we work to keep from speaking such a cliché, or writing it, we keep thinking it. Or perhaps the image is "the river of life," or "the ocean of life." But there it is, and it keeps cropping up in one form or another, and quite naturally, because it's a natural metaphor. Our progress through life (do we really go "through"?) *is* like a journey or voyage—or at least it's easy to think of it so. Both are essentially *process*; the metaphor suggests the ongoing nature of life, the continual change, the quests, the goals, the leave-takings and homecomings, the storms and the clear sailing, the struggle, the loneliness, the discoveries. When we think in these terms, it becomes clear that not only are we embarked upon the great voyage of life, but our lives are full of an infinite variety of lesser voyages— so much so that it would often be difficult to say whether we are beginning or ending or at some point en route. And we are often on several voyages at once.

The age of exploration is not yet over. We are all voyagers in some sense, in many senses: hurtling through space aboard spaceship earth, for instance. All the important discoveries are not yet made. Someone will discover the cause and cure of cancer. Someone will make it possible for us to live longer. Perhaps someone will find a way to prevent war, or to banish poverty and starvation from the earth. But the discoveries most important to *you* only you can make. You are already embarked. *Bon voyage!*

Voyages of Discovery

~~~~~~

Promptings and Preparations

*... Whenever I find myself
growing grim about the mouth;
whenever it is a damp, drizzly
November in my soul; whenever
I find myself involuntarily pausing before coffin warehouses,
and bringing up the rear of every
funeral I meet; and especially
whenever my hypos get such an
upper hand of me, that it requires
a strong moral principle to prevent
me from deliberately stepping
into the street, and methodically
knocking people's hats off—then,
I account it high time to get to
sea as soon as I can.*

—Herman Melville
Moby Dick

Like countless other voyagers before and since, Kenichi Horie, the 23-year-old Japanese who sailed single-handed from Osaka to San Francisco in 1962, was asked many times, "Why did you do it?" Here is his response.

KENICHI HORIE

"What Made You Want to Cross the Pacific?"

"What made you want to cross the Pacific? Why did you do it? What did you expect to get out of it?"

I must have been asked these same questions hundreds of times since my trans-Pacific cruise. Maybe even thousands of times. Writers, newspaper reporters, and all kinds of other people came to see me, always with these same questions. I guess they expected me to say something that would sound nice or startling or convincing or exceptional. Each time I was asked these questions, I had a rough time trying to think of something that would satisfy them, but I always ended up with "Well, I crossed it just because I wanted to." Honestly, I didn't have any purpose or motive other than that when I decided to sail across the Pacific. But none of these people were able to understand this.

"*But,*" they always continued, "you *must* have had a *reason*, you know, something special that made you set out to sea in a tiny sailboat." Some of these people even thought up their own explanations and then tried to prove to me that they were right.

From KODOKU by Kenichi Horie. Reprinted by permission of Charles E. Tuttle Co., Inc., Tokyo, Japan & Rutland, Vermont.

Why? Why couldn't they accept what I told them? It was just that simple. I soon got tired of answering all their questions, and finally I couldn't stand them any longer. Some of the fellows at my club started ribbing me when they saw that these questions were bothering me, but others felt sorry for me and were just as disgusted with the writers as I was. Being yachtsmen too, they understood. One of them said to me: "Forget it! They really can't understand what you mean. They won't believe that there is no damn reason for it, not a *damn* reason," and he was right. Nearly everyone of us yachtsmen at one time or another has dreamed, and seriously dreamed, of the day when he might take the chance and sail across the Pacific. But if you ask him why, he won't know, any more than I did. . .

What motivates men to great adventures? I wonder how accurately these motives can be analyzed, even by the participants themselves. When I think of my own flights in the early years of aviation, I realize that my motives were as obvious, as subtle and as intermixed as the waves on oceans I flew over. But I can say quite definitely that they sprang more from intuition than from rationality; and that the love of flying outweighed practical purposes—important as the latter often were.

—Charles Lindbergh

Why did I choose to sail around the world? Everyone asks me that the instant we meet. First of all, I want to see the world, and not on a tourist's itinerary with a passport stamped full of one-day visas. No, my passport must be imprinted with memories of landfalls where foreigners seldom set foot. Sailing my own boat to small, sparsely settled atolls or rarely visited snug harbors on the continents—that's what appeals to me. Not for just a day, but for months at a time, I planned to hole up among other peoples, eat their bread, and dance to their pipers.

—Robin Lee Graham
"A Teen-ager Sails the World Alone"
National Geographic, October, 1968

... as for me, I am tormented with an everlasting itch for things remote. I love to sail forbidden seas and land on barbarous coasts.

—Herman Melville
Moby Dick

12

REFLECTIONS (1)

REFLECTIONS

Why is it so difficult for travelers and adventurers to explain their motivations? Are they sincere in claiming that the urge to leave home, to travel, to go to sea, is inexplicable? Or are they concealing something from others—or from themselves?

Do you remember the reasons—the *real* reasons—for any trips or adventures you have undertaken? Did you understand your true motivation before you left, or only afterwards—or not at all?

Do you know why you're going to school? Is it an active choice you've made, or are you there because of circumstances beyond your control? Is it worthwhile trying to understand your motives, or doesn't it matter?

*John Steinbeck, a much older and far more
seasoned traveler than Kenichi Horie, is
equally ambiguous about his reasons for
journeying around the United States
in a camper in 1960.*

JOHN STEINBECK

The Urge to Be
Someplace Else

When I was very young and the urge to be someplace else was on me, I was
assured by mature people that maturity would cure this itch. When years
described me as mature, the remedy prescribed was middle age. In middle
age I was assured that greater age would calm my fever and now that I am
fifty-eight perhaps senility will do the job. Nothing has worked. Four
hoarse blasts of a ship's whistle still raise the hair on my neck and set my
feet to tapping. The sound of a jet, an engine warming up, even the clop-
ping of shod hooves on pavement brings on the ancient shudder, the dry
mouth and vacant eye, the hot palms and the churn of stomach high up
under the rib cage. In other words, I don't improve; in further words, once
a bum always a bum. I fear the disease is incurable. I set this matter down
not to instruct others but to inform myself.

When the virus of restlessness begins to take possession of a wayward
man, and the road away from Here seems broad and straight and sweet,
the victim must first find in himself a good and sufficient reason for going.
This to the practical bum is not difficult. He has a built-in garden of reasons

14

to choose from. Next he must plan his trip in time and space, choose a direction and a destination. And last he must implement the journey. How to go, what to take, how long to stay. This part of the process is invariable and immortal. I set it down only so that newcomers to bumdom, like teen-agers in new-hatched sin, will not think they invented it.

Once a journey is designed, equipped, and put in process; a new factor enters and takes over. A trip, a safari, an exploration, is an entity, different from all other journeys. It has personality, temperament, individuality, uniqueness. A journey is a person in itself; no two are alike. And all plans, safeguards, policing, and coercion are fruitless. We find after years of struggle that we do not take a trip; a trip takes us.* Tour masters, schedules, reservations, brass-bound and inevitable, dash themselves to wreckage on the personality of the trip. Only when this is recognized can the blown-in-the-glass bum relax and go along with it. Only then do the frustrations fall away. In this a journey is like marriage. The certain way to be wrong is to think you control it. I feel better now, having said this, although only those who have experienced it will understand it.

My plan was clear, concise, and reasonable, I think. For many years I have traveled in many parts of the world. In America I live in New York, or dip into Chicago or San Francisco. But New York is no more America than Paris is France or London is England. Thus I discovered that I did not know my own country. I, an American writer, writing about America, was working from memory, and the memory is at best a faulty, warpy reservoir. I had not heard the speech of America, smelled the grass and trees and sewage, seen its hills and water, its color and quality of light.† I knew the

---

*Whatever reasons the traveler offers to the tidy-minded who stay at home, his journey is always its own excuse. "Comes over one," wrote D. H. Lawrence, "an absolute necessity to move." It is an escape, above all, from the self, since travel is always a two-way process: you may go to observe the strange customs of a strange country, but in the process you yourself become a stranger; it is you who do the wrong things, eat in the wrong way, speak with the wrong accent. In the end, you may have found out less about the others than about yourself. The change of scene is a prelude to a change of heart.

—A. Alvarez
"Travel as a Passport to Freedom"
Saturday Review, January 2, 1971, p. 17

†We are acquainted with a mere pellicle of the globe on which we live. Most have not delved six feet beneath the surface, nor leaped as many above it. We know not where we are.

—Henry David Thoreau
Walden

changes only from books and newspapers. But more than this, I had not felt the country for twenty-five years. In short, I was writing of something I did not know about, and it seems to me that in a so-called writer this is criminal. My memories were distorted by twenty-five intervening years.

Once I traveled about in an old bakery wagon, double-doored rattler with a mattress on its floor. I stopped where people stopped or gathered, I listened and looked and felt, and in the process had a picture of my country the accuracy of which was impaired only by my own shortcomings.

So it was that I determined to look again, to try to rediscover this monster land. Otherwise, in writing, I could not tell the small diagnostic truths which are the foundations of the larger truth. One sharp difficulty presented itself. In the intervening twenty-five years my name had become reasonably well known. And it has been my experience that when people have heard of you, favorably or not, they change; they become, through shyness or the other qualities that publicity inspires, something they are not under ordinary circumstances. This being so, my trip demanded that I leave my name and my identity at home. I had to be peripatetic eyes and ears, a kind of moving gelatin plate. I could not sign hotel registers, meet people I knew, interview others, or even ask searching questions. Furthermore, two or more people disturb the ecologic complex of an area. I had to go alone and I had to be selfcontained, a kind of casual turtle carrying his house on his back.

With all this in mind I wrote to the head office of a great corporation which manufactures trucks. I specified my purpose and my needs. I wanted a three-quarter-ton pick-up truck, capable of going anywhere under possibly rigorous conditions, and on this truck I wanted a little house built like the cabin of a small boat. A trailer is difficult to maneuver on mountain roads, is impossible and often illegal to park, and is subject to many restrictions. In due time, specifications came through, for a tough, fast, comfortable vehicle, mounting a camper top—a little house with double bed, a four-burner stove, a heater, refrigerator and lights operating on butane, a chemical toilet, closet space, storage space, windows screened against insects—exactly what I wanted. It was delivered in the summer to my little fishing place at Sag Harbor near the end of Long Island. Although I didn't want to start before Labor Day, when the nation settles back to normal living, I did want to get used to my turtle shell, to equip it and learn it. It arrived in August, a beautiful thing, powerful and yet lithe. It was almost as easy to handle as a passenger car. And because my planned trip had aroused some satiric remarks among my friends, I named it Rocinante, which you will remember was the name of Don Quixote's horse.

Since I made no secret of my project, a number of controversies arose

16

among my friends and advisers. (A projected journey spawns advisers in schools.) I was told that since my photograph was as widely distributed as my publisher could make it, I would find it impossible to move about without being recognized. Let me say in advance that in over ten thousand miles, in thirty-four states, I was not recognized even once. I believe that people identify things only in context. Even those people who might have known me against a background I am supposed to have, in no case identified me in Rocinante.

I was advised that the name Rocinante painted on the side of my truck in sixteenth-century Spanish script would cause curiosity and inquiry in some places. I do not know how many people recognized the name, but surely no one ever asked about it.

Next, I was told that a stranger's purpose in moving about the country might cause inquiry or even suspicion. For this reason I racked a shotgun, two rifles, and a couple of fishing rods in my truck, for it is my experience that if a man is going hunting or fishing his purpose is understood and even applauded. Actually, my hunting days are over. I no longer kill or catch anything I cannot get into a frying pan; I am too old for sport killing. This stage setting turned out to be unnecessary.

It was said that my New York license plates would arouse interest and perhaps questions, since they were the only outward identifying marks I had. And so they did—perhaps twenty or thirty times in the whole trip. But such contacts followed an invariable pattern, somewhat as follows:

Local man: "New York, huh?"

Me: "Yep."

Local man: "I was there in nineteen thirty-eight—or was it thirty-nine? Alice, was it thirty-eight or thirty-nine we went to New York?"

Alice: "It was thirty-six. I remember because it was the year Alfred died."

Local man: "Anyway, I hated it. Wouldn't live there if you paid me."

There was some genuine worry about my traveling alone, open to attack, robbery, assault. It is well known that our roads are dangerous. And here I admit I had senseless qualms. It is some years since I had been alone, nameless, friendless, without any of the safety one gets from family, friends, and accomplices. There is no reality in the danger. It's just a very lonely, helpless feeling at first—a kind of desolate feeling. For this reason I took one companion on my journey—an old French gentleman poodle known as Charley. Actually his name is Charles le Chien. He was born in Bercy on the outskirts of Paris and trained in France, and while he knows a little poodle-English, he responds quickly only to commands in French. Other-

17

wise he has to translate, and that slows him down. He is a very big poodle, of a color called *bleu,* and he is blue when he is clean. Charley is a born diplomat. He prefers negotiation to fighting, and properly so, since he is very bad at fighting. Only once in his ten years has he been in trouble—when he met a dog who refused to negotiate. Charley lost a piece of his right ear that time. But he is a good watch dog—has a roar like a lion, designed to conceal from night-wandering strangers the fact that he couldn't bite his way out of a *cornet du papier.* He is a good friend and traveling companion, and would rather travel about than anything he can imagine. If he occurs at length in this account, it is because he contributed much to the trip. A dog, particularly an exotic like Charley, is a bond between strangers. Many conversations en route began with "What degree of a dog is that?"

The techniques of opening conversation are universal. I knew long ago and rediscovered that the best way to attract attention, help, and conversation is to be lost. A man who seeing his mother starving to death on a path kicks her in the stomach to clear the way, will cheerfully devote several hours of his time giving wrong directions to a total stranger who claims to be lost.

Under the big oak trees of my place at Sag Harbor sat Rocinante, handsome and self-contained, and neighbors came to visit, some neighbors we didn't even know we had. I saw in their eyes something I was to see over and over in every part of the nation—a burning desire to go, to move, to get under way, anyplace, away from any Here. They spoke quietly of how they wanted to go someday, to move about, free and unanchored, not toward something but away from something. I saw this look and heard this yearning everywhere in every state I visited.‡ Nearly every American hungers to move. One small boy about thirteen years old came back every day. He stood apart shyly and looked at Rocinante; he peered in the door, even lay on the ground and studied the heavy-duty springs. He was a silent, ubiquitous small boy. He even came at night to stare at Rocinante. After a week he could stand it no longer. His words wrestled their way hell-bent through his shyness. He said, "If you'll take me with you, why, I'll do anything. I'll

‡Every mail to me was burdened with the letters of applicants who were suffocating in the "man-stifled towns," and it soon dawned upon me that a twentieth century Ulysses required a corps of stenographers to clear his correspondence before setting sail.

—Jack London
The Cruise of the Snark

cook, I'll wash all the dishes, and do all the work and I'll take care of you."**

Unfortunately for me I knew his longing. "I wish I could," I said. "But the school board and your parents and lots of others say I can't."

"I'll do anything," he said. And I believe he would. I don't think he ever gave up until I drove away without him. He had the dream I've had all my life, and there is no cure.

Equipping Rocinante was a long and pleasant process. I took far too many things, but I didn't know what I would find. Tools for emergency, tow lines, a small block and tackle, a trenching tool and crowbar, tools for making and fixing and improvising. Then there were emergency foods. I would be late in the northwest and caught by snow. I prepared for at least a week of emergency. Water was easy; Rocinante carried a thirty-gallon tank.

I thought I might do some writing along the way, perhaps essays, surely notes, certainly letters. I took paper, carbon, typewriter, pencils, notebooks, and not only those but dictionaries, a compact encyclopedia, and a dozen other reference books, heavy ones. I suppose our capacity for self-delusion is boundless. I knew very well that I rarely make notes, and if I do I either lose them or can't read them. I also knew from thirty years of my profession that I cannot write hot on an event. It has to ferment. I must do what a friend calls "mule it over" for a time before it goes down. And in spite of this self-knowledge I equipped Rocinante with enough writing material to take care of ten volumes. Also I laid in a hundred and fifty pounds of those books one hasn't got around to reading—and of course those are the books one isn't ever going to get around to reading. Canned goods, shotgun shells, rifle cartridges, tool boxes, and far too many clothes, blankets and pillows, and many too many shoes and boots, padded nylon sub-zero underwear, plastic dishes and cups and a plastic dishpan, a spare tank of bottled gas. The overloaded springs sighed and settled lower and lower. I judge now that I carried about four times too much of everything. . .

~~~~~~

**They were so earnest, these boys, they wanted so much to go. "I am sixteen but large for my age," said one; and another, "Seventeen but large and healthy." "I am as strong at least as the average boy of my size," said an evident weakling. . . "I have no one who cares whether I go or not," was the pathetic note sounded by another.

—Jack London
The Cruise of the Snark

19

JOHN MASEFIELD

Sea-Fever

I must go down to the seas again, to the lonely sea and the sky,
And all I ask is a tall ship and a star to steer her by,
And the wheel's kick and the wind's song and the white sail's
    shaking,
And a grey mist on the sea's face and a grey dawn breaking.

I must go down to the seas again, for the call of the running tide
Is a wild call and a clear call that may not be denied;
And all I ask is a windy day with the white clouds flying,
And the flung spray and the blown spume, and the sea-gulls
    crying.

I must go down to the seas again to the vagrant gypsy life,
To the gull's way and the whale's way where the wind's like a
    whetted knife;
And all I ask is a merry yarn from a laughing fellow-rover,
And quiet sleep and a sweet dream when the long trick's over.

Reprinted with permission of The Macmillan Company from POEMS by John Masefield. Copyright © 1912 by The Macmillan Company, renewed 1940 by John Masefield.

ARTHUR GUITERMAN

Sea-Chill

When Mrs. John Masefield and her husband, the author of "I Must Go Down to the Seas Again," arrived here on a liner, she said to a reporter, 'It was too uppy-downy, and Mr. Masefield was ill.'

—*News item*

I must go down to the seas again, where the billows romp and reel,
So all I ask is a large ship that rides on an even keel,
And a mild breeze and a broad deck with a slight list to leeward,
And a clean chair in a snug nook and a nice, kind steward.

I must go down to the seas again, the sport of wind and tide,
As the gray wave and the green wave play leapfrog over the side.
And all I want is a glassy calm with a bone-dry scupper,
A good book and a warm rug and a light, plain supper.

I must go down to the seas again, though there I'm a total loss,
And can't say which is worst, the pitch, the plunge, the roll, the
    toss.
But all I ask is a safe retreat in a bar well tended,
And a soft berth and a smooth course till the long trip's ended.

From GAILY THE TROUBADORS re-published by permission of Vida Lindo Guiterman.

REFLECTIONS (2)

REFLECTIONS

Most travelers, like John Steinbeck, enjoy explaining their supplies and equipment. Sir Francis Chichester, in *Gypsy Moth Circles the World*, devotes 24 pages to a minutely detailed list of "Stores and Stowage." Is this kind of information as interesting to anyone else as it is to the traveler himself?

What would you pack, to be carried . . .
1. on your back, for a week's hiking in the wilderness?
2. in your car, for a six-week trip around the country?
3. in your suitcase, for a two-week trip to . . .
    a. Tahiti?   b. Alaska?   c. Rome?   d. Moscow?

If you had three months to go anywhere in the world you wanted to, by any means, at no expense to yourself, what would be your itinerary?

*In the passage that follows, the author offers
another sort of motivation for his journey—
the need to "find himself." The* Commedia
*(or "Divine Comedy") of Dante Alighieri
(1265–1321) is the reflection of a supreme
spiritual crisis in the life of its author.
Even though the story he tells in three parts
(the* Inferno, Purgatorio, *and* Paradiso*)
is a deliberately contrived work of art rather
than a personal confession, the Dante who
moves through its 100 cantos is not greatly
different from the historical Dante we know.
And however distant some of his conclusions and doctrines may be from our own
beliefs, the essential psychic experience he
dramatizes here is remarkable in its universality. Dante's poem needs to be read not as a
body of specific religious teachings, but as
a metaphorical rendering of a common and
crucial human experience. At the beginning,
Dante describes his mental confusion, his
sense of being "lost in a dark wood,"
wandering in bewilderment and fright; he
knows he has somehow missed "the True
Way." He can see ahead of him the good
he desires, but he finds that reaching his goal
is not as easy as it appears: his way is blocked
by three fierce beasts. The guide who
appears to advise him is, quite fittingly,
Virgil, the master poet whose example he
has studied and followed. Illustrating the
paradox that "the way down is the way up,"
Virgil explains that Dante cannot proceed
directly to the "Mount of Joy"; he must first
descend into the underworld—a symbolic
dying to his old life—before he can proceed
in his upward journey toward a spiritual
rebirth. Dante's symbolism is intricate and
complex, but its major elements are clear.
The descent into the underworld, for example, is (among other things) an exploration of the unconscious part of his own mind.
Such an exploration has its dangers and its
terrors, but a successful passage will provide*

23

*the inner voyager with the self-understanding
he needs to reconcile his conflicting desires
and to integrate the fragmented elements
of his personality into a successfully functioning whole—a "new life" better than the
old. "The Dark Wood," then, is Dante's
starting point: the recognition of his need
for a spiritual journey, and from this point
he departs.*

DANTE ALIGHIERI
Translated by John Ciardi

The Dark Wood
Canto I of The Inferno

Midway in our life's journey, I went astray
    from the straight road and woke to find myself
    alone in a dark wood. How shall I say

what wood that was! I never saw so drear,
    so rank, so arduous a wilderness!
    Its very memory gives a shape to fear.

Death could scarce be more bitter than that place!
    But since it came to good, I will recount
    all that I found revealed there by God's grace.

From DANTE'S INFERNO, translated by John Ciardi. © 1954 by John Ciardi. Reprinted by permission of the translator.

How I came to it I cannot rightly say,
    so drugged and loose with sleep had I become
    when I first wandered there from the True Way.

But at the far end of that valley of evil
    whose maze had sapped my very heart with fear!
    I found myself before a little hill

and lifted up my eyes. Its shoulders glowed
    already with the sweet rays of that planet
    whose virtue leads men straight on every road,

and the shining strengthened me against the fright
    whose agony had wracked the lake of my heart
    through all the terrors of that piteous night.

Just as a swimmer, who with his last breath
    flounders ashore from perilous seas, might turn
    to memorize the wide water of his death—

so did I turn, my soul still fugitive
    from death's surviving image, to stare down
    that pass that none had ever left alive.

And there I lay to rest from my heart's race
    till calm and breath returned to me. Then rose
    and pushed up that dead slope at such a pace

each footfall rose above the last. And lo!
    almost at the beginning of the rise
    I faced a spotted Leopard, all tremor and flow

and gaudy pelt. And it would not pass, but stood
    so blocking my every turn that time and again
    I was on the verge of turning back to the wood.

This fell at the first widening of the dawn
    as the sun was climbing Aries with those stars
    that rode with him to light the new creation.

Thus the holy hour and the sweet season
    of commemoration did much to arm my fear
    of that bright murderous beast with their good omen.

Yet not so much but what I shook with dread
    at sight of a great Lion that broke upon me
    raging with hunger, its enormous head

held high as if to strike a mortal terror
   into the very air. And down his track,
    a She-Wolf drove upon me, a starved horror

ravening and wasted beyond all belief.
   She seemed a rack for avarice, gaunt and craving.
    Oh many the souls she has brought to endless grief!

She brought such heaviness upon my spirit
   at sight of her savagery and desperation,
    I died from every hope of that high summit.

And like a miser—eager in acquisition
   but desperate in self-reproach when Fortune's wheel
    turns to the hour of his loss—all tears and attrition

I wavered back; and still the beast pursued,
   forcing herself against me bit by bit
    till I slid back into the sunless wood.

And as I fell to my soul's ruin, a presence
   gathered before me on the discolored air,
    the figure of one who seemed hoarse from long silence.

At sight of him in that friendless waste I cried:
   "Have pity on me, whatever thing you are,
    whether shade or living man." And it replied:

"Not man, though man I once was, and my blood
   was Lombard, both my parents Mantuan.
    I was born, though late, *sub Julio*, and bred

in Rome under Augustus in the noon
   of the false and lying gods. I was a poet
    and sang of old Anchises' noble son

who came to Rome after the burning of Troy.
   But you—why do *you* return to these distresses
    instead of climbing that shining Mount of Joy

which is the seat and first cause of man's bliss?"
   "And are you then that Virgil and that fountain
    of purest speech?" My voice grew tremulous:

"Glory and light of poets! now may that zeal
   and love's apprenticeship that I poured out
    on your heroic verses serve me well!

For you are my true master and first author,
    the sole maker from whom I drew the breath
    of that sweet style whose measures have brought me honor.

See there, immortal sage, the beast I flee.
    For my soul's salvation, I beg you, guard me from her,
    for she has struck a mortal tremor through me."

And he replied, seeing my soul in tears:
    "He must go by another way who would escape
    this wilderness, for that mad beast that fleers

before you there, suffers no man to pass.
    She tracks down all, kills all, and knows no glut,
    but, feeding, she grows hungrier than she was.

She mates with any beast, and will mate with more
    before the Greyhound comes to hunt her down.
    He will not feed on lands nor loot, but honor

and love and wisdom will make straight his way.
    He will rise between Feltro and Feltro, and in him
    shall be the resurrection and new day

of that sad Italy for which Nisus died,
    and Turnus, and Euryalus, and the maid Camilla.
    He shall hunt her through every nation of sick pride

till she is driven back forever to Hell
    whence Envy first released her on the world.
    Therefore, for your own good, I think it well

you follow me and I will be your guide
    and lead you forth through an eternal place.
    There you shall see the ancient spirits tried

in endless pain, and hear their lamentation
    as each bemoans the second death of souls.
    Next you shall see upon a burning mountain

souls in fire and yet content in fire,
    knowing that whensoever it may be
    they yet will mount into the blessed choir.

To which, if it is still your wish to climb,
    a worthier spirit shall be sent to guide you.
    With her shall I leave you, for the King of Time,

who reigns on high, forbids me to come there
   since, living, I rebelled against his law.
   He rules the waters and the land and air

and there holds court, his city and his throne.
   Oh blessed are they he chooses!" And I to him:
   "Poet, by that God to you unknown,

lead me this way. Beyond this present ill
   and worse to dread, lead me to Peter's gate
   and be my guide through the sad halls of Hell."

And he then: "Follow." And he moved ahead
in silence ,and I followed where he led.

Again, for poets, the physical world has usually been not only a cyclical world but a "middle earth," situated between an upper and a lower world. These two worlds reflect in their form the heavens and hells of the religions contemporary with the poet, and are normally thought of as abodes of unchanging being, not as cyclical. The upper world is reached by some form of ascent, and is a world of gods or happy souls. The most frequent images of ascent are the mountain, the tower, the winding staircase or ladder, or a tree of cosmological dimensions. The upper world is often symbolized by the heavenly bodies, of which the one nearest us is the moon. The lower world, reached by descent through a cave or under water, is more oracular and sinister, and as a rule is or includes a place of torment and punishment. It follows that there would be two points of particular significance in poetic symbolism. One is the point, usually the top of a mountain just below the moon, where the upper world and this one come into alignment, where we look up to the heavenly world and down on the turning cycle of nature. The other is the point, usually in a mysterious labyrinthine cave, where the lower world and this one come into alignment, where we look down to a world of pain and up to the turning cycle of nature. This upward perspective sees the same world, though from the opposite pole, as the downward perspective in the vision of ascent, and hence the same cyclical symbols may be employed for it.

—Northrop Frye,
"New Directions from Old," in *Myth and Mythmaking*,
edited and with an introduction by Henry A. Murray
(New York: George Braziller, 1960), p. 123.

In the vision of descent, where we enter a world of darkness and mystery, there is more emphasis on initiation, on learning the proper rites, on acquiring effective talismans like the golden bough. . . At the top of the winding stair one normally attains direct knowledge or vision, but the reward of descent is usually oracular or esoteric knowledge, concealed or forbidden to most people, often the knowledge of the future.

—Northrop Frye
Ibid, p. 127

As Joseph Campbell points out in The Hero with a Thousand Faces, *the pattern of "the hero's journey" occurs repeatedly not only in the legends, myths, folk-tales, and literature of the world, but in our dreams and visions as well. From this he concludes that the pattern in its generalized form represents the basic development of an almost universal experience. Not every voyage, physical or mental, embodies all the elements of the archetypal hero's journey; many are partial or include the elements in a different order. Yet familiarity with the basic pattern makes it easier to see what many voyages have in common, and to understand something of the significance of the various characters and events. This does not mean that only what fits the pattern is significant or valid. We have here a principle rather than a law, a tool rather than a master. The pattern is not experience itself, but an attempt to see experience in a significant perspective.*

JOSEPH CAMPBELL

The Hero's Journey

The adventure can be summarized in the following diagram:

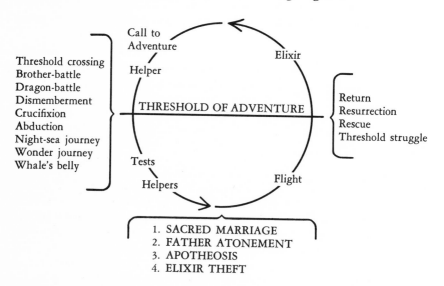

The mythological hero, setting forth from his commonday hut or castle, is lured, carried away, or else voluntarily proceeds, to the threshold of adventure. There he encounters a shadow presence that guards the passage. The hero may defeat or conciliate this power and go alive into the kingdom of the dark (brother-battle, dragon-battle; offering, charm), or be slain by the opponent and descend in death (dismemberment, crucifixion). Beyond

From THE HERO WITH A THOUSAND FACES, by Joseph Campbell, Bollingen Series XVII (copyright © 1949 by Bollingen Foundation), Princeton University Press: quote pp. 245–247.

the threshold, then, the hero journeys through a world of unfamiliar yet strangely intimate forces, some of which severely threaten him (tests), some of which give magical aid (helpers). When he arrives at the nadir of the mythological round, he undergoes a supreme ordeal and gains his reward. The triumph may be represented as the hero's sexual union with the goddess-mother of the world (sacred marriage), his recognition by the father-creator (father atonement), his own divinization (apotheosis), or again— if the powers have remained unfriendly to him—his theft of the boon he came to gain (bride-theft, fire-theft); intrinsically it is an expansion of consciousness and therewith of being (illumination, transfiguration, freedom). The final work is that of the return. If the powers have blessed the hero, he now sets forth under their protection (emissary); if not, he flees and is pursued (transformation flight, obstacle flight). At the return threshold the transcendental powers must remain behind; the hero re-emerges from the kingdom of dread (return, resurrection). The boon that he brings restores the world (elixir).

The changes rung on the simple scale of the monomyth defy description. Many tales isolate and greatly enlarge upon one or two of the typical elements of the full cycle (test motif, flight motif, abduction of the bride), others string a number of independent cycles into a single series (as in the Odyssey). Differing characters or episodes can become fused, or a single element can reduplicate itself and reappear under many changes.

The outlines of myths and tales are subject to damage and obscuration. Archaic traits are generally eliminated or subdued. Imported materials are revised to fit local landscape, custom, or belief, and always suffer in the process. Furthermore, in the innumerable retellings of a traditional story, accidental or intentional dislocations are inevitable. To account for elements that have become, for one reason or another, meaningless, secondary interpretations are invented, often with considerable skill.

REFLECTIONS (3)

REFLECTIONS

Dante's experience may be a vision, a dream, or a metaphorical description of a conscious train of thought. Are there any indications of which way we are meant to understand it? Is it important to know?

To what stories that you know does Campbell's scheme apply? For example, how about Jack and the Beanstalk?

Thor Heyerdahl undoubtedly stands foremost among the voyager-explorers of the twentieth century, even in the face of the fantastic achievements of the astronauts. Heyerdahl is the epitome of the man who stands alone against the expert opinions of his age, scoffed at rather than supported by his fellow men, and yet he succeeds almost single-handedly in carrying through his designs and proving himself right and the experts wrong. Since 1947 Heyerdahl's name has been linked with Kon-Tiki, *the balsa-wood raft with which he dramatically demonstrated the validity of his theory of east-to-west trans-Pacific migrations. But he has not rested on his laurels. What his* next *voyage will be we can only guess, but his most recent one carried him across the Atlantic in a paper boat—or wicker basket, if you prefer. John Lear, the science editor of* Saturday Review, *wrote the following article as Heyerdahl was preparing to embark aboard the bundle of papyrus reeds he had christened* Ra, *and to sail with a multinational crew of six from Africa to America.*

JOHN LEAR

Thor Heyerdahl's Next Voyage

Gizeh, Egypt
May 3, 1969

A big reed basket designed to carry seven men across the Atlantic Ocean is being put together here in the sands of the Sahara, at the edge of Cairo, behind the third pyramid of Gizeh.

Shaped like a swan with a pointed tail taller than its undulant neck, this frail craft belongs to Thor Heyerdahl, whose raft of balsa logs, *Kon-Tiki*, drifted over 4,300 miles of the Pacific Ocean nearly a quarter century ago.

While the *Kon-Tiki* was being lashed together, experts on balsa wood said the logs in the raft would become saturated with seawater and would sink before the *Kon-Tiki* was under way a month. The *Kon-Tiki,* however, remained intact after plunging over a Polynesian reef 101 days out from the harbor of Callao, Peru.

Today, experts on papyrus—the reed Heyerdahl's new boat, *Ra,* consists of—are betting that the reeds will become water-soaked, and that the basket will go to the bottom within two weeks of its launching. Nevertheless, Heyerdahl is confidently proceeding with plans for a voyage to start in mid-May, off the coast of Morocco, and to end in July, hopefully on the coast of Yucatan.

Heyerdahl is gambling his life on his disagreement with those who are supposed to know, for he will skipper the voyage of the *Ra*. He is also gambling the lives of six other men: five whites from nations other than his native Norway, and a black African tribesman from the Republic of Chad.

The black member of the *Ra*'s crew will be one of three blacks who are actually building the *Ra*. Heyerdahl doesn't yet know which one he will choose. All three have put on occasional shows of temperament, as genuine artists will when a patron offers unwelcome suggestions about their work. For generations past, it has been the tradition of Lake Chad reed boatmen to shape their boats like ducks, with low-slung necks and almost flat tails. Heyerdahl says that shape is fine for an inland waterway like mid-African Chad, but it just won't do for the open ocean. Since the *Ra* is going to depend on the equatorial current of the Atlantic as well as on the wind for propulsion, Heyerdahl argues that the boat must have a high tail bound tightly at the end like the tip of a tusk, so that the stern of the boat will be lifted by waves coming up from the rear before the waves can break and inundate the reed basket.

Whether he is right or wrong in his high-tail judgment, Heyerdahl isn't being whimsical. He must do what the Egyptians of 4,000 to 5,000 years ago did, in precisely the way they did it, in order to discover whether it was physically possible for people from Africa to have reached the shores of America ages before Christopher Columbus.

Only if an Atlantic crossing proves to be feasible in a boat built of Nile reeds can he go on to consider other arguments favoring the proposition that ancient Egyptians were the *viracochas*, or bearded white men, who legend says were the highly civilized precursors of the Incas of Peru, the Mayas of Mexico, the mound-builders of North America, and the stone-head sculptors of Easter Island.

Whether or not the Heyerdahl expedition succeeds, it is worth serious attention as an example of the broad, interdisciplinary study of living nature that current trends in ecology suggest will dominate the long future of science. If we are genuinely trying to learn where man as an evolutionary creature is going, we need to understand the role of his environment in having brought him where he is now. How did the currents of wind and water move him about, with what consequences?

Heyerdahl asks questions like these from an eminence rare among anthropologists and geographers. He holds the only honorary degree ever awarded to a Norwegian by the University of Oslo. He has won the Vega Gold Medal of the Royal Swedish Society of Anthropology and Geography, and the Patron's (that is, Queen Elizabeth II's) Gold Medal of the Royal Geographical Society of Great Britain. He is a Commander of the Norwegian Order of St. Olaf, an elected member of the Norwegian Academy of Sciences, an honorary member of the Academy of Sciences of the U.S.S.R., and a Fellow of the New York Academy of Sciences. Geographical societies of Belgium, Brazil, Peru, and Scotland have honored him either with memberships or with medals, and he is a Great Officer in the distinguished service orders of Italy and Peru.

His now enormous prestige was not easily come by. As a young man, even into his early years as a world-famous figure, Heyerdahl endured the ridicule of scientific colleagues. They dismissed him as a daredevil dilettante. His privileged boyhood in the family of a wealthy brewer gave him opportunities for unusual experiences which less fortunate people can be forgiven for misinterpreting. Most of that phase of Heyerdahl's life is related in Arnold Jacoby's biography, *Señor Kon-Tiki*. It is enough to note here that any youth who chooses to go native on a South Sea island for a year to test whether his bride can appreciate Stone Age paradise is not likely to be hailed as the possessor of a profound mind. If he quits school before graduating in order to exercise this choice, any theory emerging from the holiday will not easily command scientific respect, especially if the theory demolishes long-cherished beliefs.

Yet, Heyerdahl's year as an academic dropout on the tropical island of Fatu Hiva, in the Marquesas, gave him time for on-the-spot observations that he had not expected to make: observations that the wind and water always moved toward Fatu Hiva from the east. Any approach to the island from the west would be neither easy nor natural; certainly it could never have been achieved accidentally by primitive men. Suddenly it was obvious to Heyerdahl that original colonization of Fatu Hiva's volcano cone had not occurred from Polynesia, despite the then almost universal teaching that it had.

Heyerdahl's later crossing of the Pacific from Peru to Polynesia on a raft of balsa logs had such a romantic impact on the public mind of 1947 that the long chain of scientific reasoning leading to the exploit was obscured. That a twentieth century man would risk his life and the lives of companions in brute struggle with the wind and water was all that came through. Who cared for the why behind the gamble? What mattered was raw human courage in the raging face of nature.

Actually, in Heyerdahl's mind the voyage of the *Kon-Tiki* (so named for the Andean altiplano white-faced gods who were revered on islands thousands of miles *west* of the South American continent) hadn't much risk in it. Even his fling on Fatu Hiva had not been as fantastically wild as it seemed to outsiders. Heyerdahl had gone to the Marquesas under the informal sponsorship of Bjarne Kroepelien, a prosperous Oslo businessman who had lived on Tahiti years earlier, and who had drawn together an enormous library of books and papers on Polynesian life, with special emphasis on the origins and evolution of that life in its isolated context. Kroepelien was a friend of the great Tahitian tribal chief, Teriieroo a Teriierooterai, who saw to it that a native copra schooner plying between Tahiti and Fatu Hiva made occasional inquiry about the two young Norwegian volunteers for service in the Stone Age.

There were giant stone images on Fatu Hiva, and Heyerdahl wrote about them in 1938, in a book titled *In Search of Paradise*, after his return to Oslo from the South Seas. The book threw him into the company of Iver Fougner, a Norwegian farmer who had spent some time in Bella Coola Valley, British Columbia, and who (along with many others) had noticed the Asiatic character of the Indians native to Bella Coola. Heyerdahl mentally collated all these events and gradually evolved a theory about trans-Pacific migration. The theory held that the first wave of migrants to Polynesia had come from South America by way of the Humboldt Current. The second wave had come from the opposite direction, having originated somewhere in the Malay Peninsula and having traveled northward on the Malay Current into the Japan Current, then eastward below the Aleutians to the British Columbian coast, and, finally, southwestward to Hawaii and beyond.

Heyerdahl's theory reached formal publication for the first time in 1941 in a war refugee journal, *International Science*. It appeared under the interrogative title, "Did Polynesian Culture Originate in America?"

After a period of rough life around Bella Coola and another period of still rougher life in the Norwegian resistance to Adolf Hitler's occupation of Norway, Heyerdahl tried to market a manuscript that wrapped up all his ideas on human migration across the Pacific. He titled it, "Polynesia and America—a Study of Prehistoric Relations." He took it to a scientist he respected very much: Dr. Herbert Spinden, president of the Explorers Club and director of the Brooklyn Museum.

"It is quite true that South America was the home of some of the most curious civilizations of antiquity, and we know neither who they were nor where they vanished to when the Incas came into power," Spinden told Heyerdahl after hearing the Norwegian's summary of the manuscript on the desk before them. "But one thing we do know for certain—that none of the peoples of South America got over to the islands in the Pacific. Do you know why? They had no boats!"

"They had rafts," Heyerdahl objected. "You know, balsa wood rafts."

"Well," said Spinden, "you can try a trip from Peru to the Pacific islands on a balsa wood raft!"

To anyone else, such a venture would have been madness. But not to Heyerdahl. Rafts of balsa under skilled navigation at sea had been seen by the Spaniards who invaded Peru in the sixteenth century. The buoyancy of the logs enabled the rafts to carry very heavy cargoes. Botanists knew that someone from South America had carried the bottle gourd, the sweet potato, the chili pepper, the small pineapple, the papaya, and the husk-tomato to Polynesia and transplanted them there, for those plants can't be reroduced from seeds. What could be more logical than the assumption that the planters had crossed the water on balsa logs?

So Heyerdahl literally followed Spinden's advice.

Before the *Kon-Tiki* adventure, Heyerdahl had periods of wondering how his next meal would be paid for. His book, *Kon-Tiki*, and motion pictures of the anachronistic Pacific crossing freed him financially and eventually let him buy and rehabilitate the ruins of a small medieval village on the Italian Riviera where he and his second wife, Yvonne, and their three children live in a bipolar setting: the warm Mediterranean in front and snow-capped Alps behind. Landlord Heyerdahl is home, however, only between expeditions. For the *Kon-Tiki* voyage was not the end but the beginnig of a quest.

Having shown that the Pacific islands could have been peopled from America long before the days of Columbus, Heyerdahl set out to learn how the colonizing process had proceeded. Why was there no record of anyone stopping at the Galápagos Islands? They lay far closer to the Peruvian coast than any other Pacific islands and directly in the path of the Humboldt Current as it swung west off the South American continent. An archaeological survey of the Galápagos in 1951 revealed to Heyerdahl that the Peruvians had indeed visited the Galápagos before the Norsemen had gone to Iceland.

During this research, Heyerdahl accidentally discovered from South American Indian seafarers off the southern coast of Ecuador how to guide a balsa raft by simultaneously manipulating the rudder and the sail. His *Kon-Tiki* had carried a rudder, but Heyerdahl had not been able to figure out how to use it during the *Kon-Tiki* voyage. Now, four years after the completion of that hazardous expedition, he at last had the knowledge that would allow him to sail the *Kon-Tiki* into as well as before the wind.

Shortly after achieving total mastery of the balsa raft, he noted some things that caused him to wonder whether the ancient westward crossing of the Pacific had actually been accomplished on rafts. In 1952, in the Bolivian Andes, he came upon another type of boat with much cleaner lines and several times the raft's speed. This was a 120-foot reed boat in daily use on Lake Titicaca, home of the Tiahuanaco culture that preceded the Incas and left behind it the legend of the *viracochas*. Tiahuanacan engineers had built stepped pyramids and huge stone men. Even more significant to Heyerdahl than these was his discovery of drawings of crescent-shaped reed boats decorating buried pottery of the pre-Inca period.

Three years after watching the reed boats on Lake Titicaca, Heyerdahl chartered a Scandinavian ocean-going vessel and fitted it out for a year's stay on Easter Island, the next large island in the Pacific beyond the Galápagos. For the full flavor of that expedition readers are referred to *Aku-Aku*, Heyerdahl's personal account of a fabulous adventure. Adequate background for the story of the *Ra* requires here only the notation that on Easter Island Heyerdahl saw drawings of reed boats on the ceiling of caves, stone models of reed boats under sail, and rough sketches of three-masted reed boats on the chests of great stone men. The bodies of the statues were hewn from gray volcanic rock, but the heads were crowned with red stone quarried at a different site than that of the gray stone. The red crowns reminded Heyerdahl of red-haired mummies in Peruvian tombs. The drawings and models of the reed boats prompted him to ask whether anyone on Easter Island knew how such boats were made. A family of four old brothers, fishermen, built two boats for him: one a *pora*, a sort of surfboard to be managed by a lone swimmer; the other a crescent-shaped craft 12 feet in length with a carrying capacity of two or more men and stability sufficient to allow diving from either side of the boat without inviting capsize.

The particular reed the old men chose for the boatmaking was growing in a swampy lake in the caldera of a dead volcano. The plant's botanical name was *Scirpus tatora*. It was the identical reed that went into the boats on Lake Titicaca. It did not grow from seeds but only from transplanted root stock. Who had brought the transplants to the lake in the volcano cone? South Americans, obviously. When? Bore holes drilled in the caldera floor beside the lake gave up *Scirpus tatora* pollen dating as far back as the earliest particles of carbon found in the same holes. The carbon must have come from forest fires, presumably set after the first men colonized the island.

Just when the data that had been accumulating for so many years finally set Heyerdahl to tracing the reed boats and the stepped pyramids eastward beyond the Polynesia-Easter Island-South American axis is not clear. But the 1966 session of the biennial International Americanist Congress in Argentina undoubtedly marked a watershed in his thought. Shortly before that meeting, an eminent American anthropologist published a paper citing the reed boats in support of the widely held theory that advanced technological concepts appear simultaneously in far-separated places without bearing any relation to each other. The reed boats, this anthropologist declared, just could not have been sailed over the great stretches of water providing the sites of the boats existing today. His arguments were repeated and amplified at the Argentinian symposium with apparent acceptance.

Heyerdahl's immediate reaction was to fly from Buenos Aires to La Paz for another, longer look at the reed boats on Lake Titicaca. Living with

Indians who inhabit the lake shores, he made long sailing trips with them, and again the carrying capacity and speed of the boats impressed him.

Almost automatically, he reviewed the parallels that run all the way across Africa to Central and South America and on into the Pacific: sun-worshiping peoples with enough knowledge of astronomy to cut calendars out of the native rock and to watch for the rise of particular constellations of stars in the sky; ruling castes whose male members always married their sisters; the writing of script—hieroglyphics in the tombs of the Pharaohs, *rongo-rongo* on Easter Island; trepanning of the skull for surgical purposes; a massive construction technology based not only on the cutting and polishing of huge stones but the subsequent fitting together of those stones without mortar or cement; terraced irrigation; entombment in stepped pyramids; skilled navigation of intricately constructed reed boats.

A photograph in the *National Geographic* triggered Heyerdahl into action. Illustrating an article about the former French colonies in Africa, it showed reed boats under sail on Lake Chad. After poring over this picture, Heyerdahl decided to go to Lake Chad and see what differences there were between the Chad boats and the reed boats he had seen on Lake Titicaca and on Easter Island. With visual documentation in mind, he hired two free-lance photographers—a Frenchman and an Italian—and flew them with him to the capital of the Republic of Chad, Fort Lamy. From there, he organized a jeep caravan overland to the lake, stopping at the village of Bol. Bol is peopled by the Buduma tribe, a once piratical family of blacks who make reed boats for the Lake Chad traffic.

Heyerdahl's first discovery in Bol was that the Chad boats are made of the papyrus reed, from which the ancient Egyptians made the first known writing paper. Heyerdahl's second discovery in Bol was a pair of brothers, Mussa Bulumi and Omar M'Bulu. While Heyerdahl was struggling to communicate with Mussa and Omar in French, a third Chad tribesman appeared beside them and resolved the confusion. All the talk thereafter passed through him, for he could speak French and Arabic. He gave his name as Abdoulaye Djibrine and described himself as a "Chad Arab."

Mussa Bulumi knew only the language of his tribe, Buduma. So Mussa spoke Buduma to his brother, Omar. Omar, at home in Arabic as well as in Buduma, told Abdoulaye in Arabic what Mussa had said in Buduma. Abdoulaye then told Heyerdahl in French what Omar had said in Arabic.

On an impulse, Heyerdahl asked Abdoulaye to ask Mussa and Omar if they would be willing to build a reed boat for Heyerdahl in Egypt. Abdoulaye reported that Mussa and Omar would be happy to build the boat. Abdoulaye then added, on his own account, "I will come, too, to be your translator." Although none of the parties realized it then, the *Ra* boat-building project had begun.

From the practical point of view, there was only one place on the Mediterranean suitable for the construction of a papyrus reed boat intended to sail the Atlantic Ocean from Africa. That place was Cairo. But papyrus reeds were no longer grown around Cairo, or, indeed, anywhere else in Egypt. The reeds did grow in profusion along the shores of Lake Chad. However, to carry the reed makings of a boat from Lake Chad to Cairo within any reasonable span of time would require the chartering of a couple of large cargo airplanes. The cost of that would be prohibitive.

In search of an alternate source of reeds, Heyerdahl went from Lake Chad to Ethiopia, where the papyrus reed grows wild around Lake Tana, source of the Blue Nile, and around Lake Zwai, to the south of Addis Ababa. In Ethiopia, he found an Italian settler who was willing to contract with a local band of black monks and some lake fishermen to harvest twelve tons of reeds of a standard variation in length: from 14 to 18 feet. These are very long papyrus reeds. But the Italian guaranteed their delivery by truck across Ethiopia's 10,000-foot-high mountains to the western shore of the Red Sea. Heyerdahl next consulted a Greek shipowner, who agreed to carry the reeds north on the Red Sea to the port of Suez. Suez lay in the zone of active conflict between the Arabs and the Israelis. Since Heyerdahl intended to fly the U.N. flag on the *Ra* to symbolize the global nature of his expedition, he figured he could if necessary appeal to the belligerents to pass his cargo unmolested under a momentary truce. And he suspended his negotiating in Africa to return to his adopted home in the medieval village on the Italian Riviera.

There it occurred to Heyerdahl that a neighbor of his, Angelo Corio, a high school teacher of French, had the ideal temperament and command of languages to boss the boat-building job. Would Corio spend six months in Cairo? He would, if the Italian school authorities would grant him a sabbatical. They did, and by Christmas 1968, Corio had set up headquarters in the Mena House Hotel here in Gizeh, virtually across the street from the three great pyramids.

When Heyerdahl applied to the Egyptian Government for permission to rope off a stretch of sand behind the third great pyramid to serve him as a workshop, out of the way of tourists—and, significantly for his purpose, within plain sight of a line of smaller pyramids with stepped terraces reminiscent of pyramids in Yucatan, Lake Titicaca, Easter Island, and Fatu Hiva—he encountered his first difficulties. Everyone in the antiquarian community denied existence of any evidence whatever that ancient Egyptians

43

had sailed reed boats on the Mediterranean, let alone on the Atlantic. Reed boat traffic, so far as anyone with an opinion worth respecting knew, had been confined to the Nile, where reed boats are still seen today. If Egypt were to provide the site for the building of Heyerdahl's *Ra,* would the Government thereby risk becoming accessory to an attempted suicide? Egypt's foremost authority on papyrus reeds was called in: Hassin Ragab, president of the Papyrus Institute of Egypt. He cited contemporary experience in Ethiopia to support his conviction that salt water would saturate the reeds within two weeks' time. He soaked some reeds in his bathtub to prove the point. Before the two-week deadline was up, the water in the tub began filling with bubbles, due to fermentation of the papyrus.

Heyerdahl protested that Ragab's test had two flaws. First, the reeds in the bathtub remained continually in the same water, which thus became chemically polluted, whereas the water beneath the *Ra* would be constantly changing as the boat moved over the surface of the sea. Second, an individual reed, when cut for the boat, was like an empty bottle without a cork. If cast on the water, the bottle would sooner or later fill and sink. If the bottle were tightly corked before being floated, the bottle would stay on the sea surface as long as the cork kept out the water. The reeds in the boat would be like the corked bottle, because of the upraised tusk-like tips at either end of the *Ra's* design. Heyerdahl asked to be judged by an actual trial run over an extended period with a small reed boat on the Red Sea. When the Arab-Israeli war ruled that out, the Nasser regime capitulated and gave Heyerdahl his pyramid-side permit in January 1969.

By February the boat-building site had been roped off, and 500 bales of papyrus reeds had been stacked there under canvas. The reeds had reached Suez just in time to come under one of the periodic cross-canal bombardments that punctuate the Arab-Israeli dispute. Cargo handlers had panicked in the midst of unloading the papyrus, but some inventive person had told them the noise they had heard was only the bumping together of boats stranded in the idle canal, and all the reeds were landed.

Heyerdahl originally had planned to return to Lake Chad to pick up his boatbuilders. But while he awaited the arrival of the reeds, an unexpected letter came from Abdoulaye Djibrine. Unable to write in any language, that alert black tribesman had dictated his message to a friendly Protestant missionary, who had set it down and mailed it. "Mussa and Omar and I are ready to make the boat for you," Abdoulaye's letter said. "When are you coming to get us?"

Surprised by this display of initiative, Heyerdahl decided to see how far it might extend. He needed to go back to Lake Titicaca in the Bolivian Andes for a final check on the staying power of the reed boats there. Perhaps he could save time by making the trip to America while Abdoulaye brought Mussa and Omar to Cairo.

A return letter to Lake Chad by way of the friendly missionary produced a quick reply—Abdoulaye would be happy to accept responsibility for the appearance of Mussa and Omar in Cairo if Heyerdahl would only send three airplane tickets and some travel expense money. Relieved by this news, Heyerdahl put the tickets and the money in the mail to Chad, and took a plane for Lake Titicaca.

It was at this point that I stumbled into the story of the *Ra*. In the air-mail edition of the *Manchester Guardian,* I read a Norwegian reporter's brief account of Heyerdahl's intent: ACROSS THE ATLANTIC IN A PAPER BOAT. The *Guardian* headline writer had been not only witty but almost accurate.

By appealing to Rand McNally, American publishers of Heyerdahl's books, I located the explorer on the telephone in Washington, D.C. Only the night before, I discovered, he had dined in New York with the editor of *Saturday Review* and had sought the editor's help in obtaining the intervention of U.N. Secretary General U Thant. A crisis had developed over-night and nothing less than a letter from U Thant could prevent the *Ra* from becoming the focus of an international incident.

The trouble had started in Chad when the postman delivered to Abdoulaye the money and the plane tickets that Heyerdahl had sent. When Abdoulaye could offer no better explanation for this extravagant attention than a vague and fuzzy story about making a reed boat in Egypt to cross the Atlantic, he had been put in jail.

With U Thant's letter of recommendation in his briefcase, Heyerdahl flew from New York to Fort Lamy. Just before boarding the plane, he told me that if he could clear Abdoulaye's up-to-then spotless police record, I would be invited to come to Cairo to watch the *Ra* abuilding. Several weeks of silence followed before I found on my desk one morning a cable from Gizeh: YOU ARE WELCOME ANY TIME.

I was greeted at the Cairo airport by an ebullient young Arab female agent of the Egyptian Tourist Office. She whisked me to the money exchange window, then to the visa desk, then through customs, and at last to a taxicab in the street outside. In return for her efficient help, she asked only that I give one of her girl friends a lift into town.

I was two hours behind schedule because one of my fellow passengers on a TWA through-flight from New York via Rome and Athens had disappeared in Athens, and had to be rounded up. In sixteen-and-a-half hours I had napped for perhaps twenty minutes, but I felt wide awake after un-shuttering the windows of my room above Heyerdahl's hotel headquarters and seeing the pyramids looming in the night. In the clear desert air they seemed close enough to touch.

At 6:30 o'clock next morning, the ringing of the telephone wakened me to an awareness of Heyerdahl's enthusiasm for the *Ra*. I breakfasted at 7 in a glass patio inhabited by a flock of small brown birds which flew about as I ate, and quarreled quietly over pecking rights at the marmalade dish on my table. I noticed that they seemed to have assigned themselves to particular tables, as waiters do. At 7:30, Heyerdahl and I were off in a hired motorcar for the third pyramid. His jeep had broken down the day before.

Within less than half an hour, we had left the car on the narrow macadam road that carries tourists around the pyramids. We trudged unevenly through jeep-wheel ruts in the sand for perhaps a hundred yards before I glimpsed, at the bottom of a depression in the earth, one of the loneliest sights of my life—a little colony of small canvas tents as gray as the sand on which they were pitched. At an acute angle in the distance, my eye next caught a crescent shape that reminded me of drawings I had seen from the tombs of the Pharaohs. That, I thought, would be the *Ra*.

It was. By the time we reached it, Mussa and Omar and Abdoulaye were already hard at work. Heyerdahl gravely approached them, smiled broadly, shook hands, spoke a few words, and introduced me as someone who had "come all the way from America to see what we are doing." As the boat-builders turned back to their job, he took me aside and explained how U Thant's letter had saved the day in Chad.

Being in charge of one of the newest nations on the planet, officials of the Republic of Chad are rightfully concerned about protecting their citizens from abuse. The slave trade is one of the most unpleasant memories of Africa's past. When Abdoulaye suddenly flourished what in local terms was a small fortune, he was not unnaturally suspected of complicity in a slave-trading ring. His story about needing Mussa and Omar to make a reed boat in Cairo for crossing the Atlantic Ocean contributed nothing to his credibility. By the time he got word of his dilemma out through the missionary to Heyerdahl, Abdoulaye had regained his freedom through the local equivalent of paying expensive talent to argue legal technicalities. All the money that Heyerdahl had sent was exhausted in these appeals.

Even after Heyerdahl arrived with U Thant's letter and cleared the air, arrangements still had to be made to allow the three blacks to leave their homeland. The process was more complicated than usual, but not because of Abdoulaye. Mussa and Omar insisted that (1) both were twenty-nine years old, and (2) Mussa was four years older than Omar. This interesting situation had to be described explicitly in their passports. That those documents, once issued, passed unchallenged is a tribute to Heyerdahl's persuasiveness. It is a tribute both to his patience and to the intelligence and adaptability of the Chad tribesmen that he quickly taught Abdoulaye, Mussa, and Omar to eat with knives, forks, and spoons instead of with their fingers, and to walk up and down flights of stairs and to ride elevators, automobiles, and airplanes fearlessly.

The three blacks wear marvelously colored ceremonial costumes at appropriate times. When working on the *Ra,* Mussa and Abdoulaye dress in flowing white robes, Mussa with a rich plum-hued sweater under his. Omar prefers a sweater over his robe and is often bareheaded; Mussa wears a subdued plaid turban; Abdoulaye sports a gaily-banded knit skullcap. Heyerdahl works with them in jodhpurs and boots, a turtleneck sweater-shirt, and a battered white sailcloth hat with a center peak.

Primitive craftsmanship is notoriously difficult to fit to any arbitrarily timed rhythm. Heyerdahl has managed it on the *Ra* project by splitting up the responsibility. Several unskilled Arab boys chop the papyrus reeds at both ends with machetes. Several others dip the shortened reeds in a concrete tank of cold water. After the reeds have been soaked for several hours —to make them pliable for what follows—other boys carry the dripping reeds to the boat, where the three Chad blacks take over.

The actual boat building is done as one might try to build a swan by stuffing individual feathers tightly together. The process begins with only four reeds. These are bound firmly at one end with a circlet of rope. Next, a second rope circlet is looped around the reeds a short distance away from the original circlet. Then as many reeds as possible are thrust through the second circlet into the tiny opening formed within the tip of the first four reeds. After the second circlet is gorged with reeds, a third loop of rope is thrown around the reed bundle at some proportionate distance from the second circlet, and the prior performance is repeated. When the third circlet can hold no more reeds, a fourth circlet is placed at a distance proportional to the progression of the distances between the preceding circlets. When the fourth circlet is stuffed, a fifth is added, and so on until there is a thin, banana-like crescent bound tightly at each end.

As the core crescent is woven, other crescents are knitted onto it, giving the finished whole some semblance of a huge bunch of bananas in which the shape of each banana can be discerned without being distinguished from any other banana in the bunch.

Although precious time was lost because of the episode in Chad and because of five days of sandstorms (there was also a small earthquake, which swung the hotel chandeliers and moved the floor of the library in which I was writing at the time, but which was not felt at the building site of the *Ra*), Heyerdahl, by keeping his assembly line moving from dawn to dusk every day of the week, hopes to put the *Ra* into the water in the Moroccan port of Safi (where traditions, which run back to the days of the Phoenicians, include legends of Atlantic crossings long before Columbus) around May 15.

By then, the big crescent basket of reeds will be just under 50 feet long and just over 16 feet wide, with a bottom 4.5 feet thick. The closest approach to solid flooring in the craft will be a plaited 9-by-15-foot wicker mat—the bottom of a domed wicker hut that will ride on the crescent basket and provide quarters for the crew (currently listed for it, in addition to Norwegian Heyerdahl and the Chad black, are an Egyptian, an Italian, a Mexican, a Russian, and an American—one of them to be always on deck duty while the others rotate use of six bunks in the cabin). The hut is a handsome piece of handmade furniture, thatched on top, with an open storage space forward to hold packages of simple foods like those available to the ancient Egyptians and a battery of clay pots filled with drinking water. Also housed beneath the thatched roof will be three navigating necessities: an inflatable rubber raft, an electric generator to power lights for underwater photography, and a portable radio. All the gear will be stowed with the seven men behind a trapezoidal cotton sail strung from a wishbone mast about 30 feet tall.

According to Heyerdahl's theory, the reeds of the boat will drain off water as fast as the waves can pour the water in. Won't the sea rise through the boat bottom just as easily? Heyerdahl says not as long as the papyrus reeds retain any appreciable fraction of their normal buoyancy. I was skeptical of this last point before coming to Cairo, but here I have been seeing incredible demonstrations in its favor. To amuse me during my visits to the *Ra* building site, the young Arab reed cutters have taken individual reeds and shoved them one by one, broad end down, into the water of the concrete soaking pit, then let the reeds go. Every one of the papyrus shafts has bounded out of the water with a great splash, like a fighting fish.

In the face of virtually unanimous professional Egyptologist opinion that the *Ra* cannot possibly survive an Atlantic crossing, Heyerdahl maintains utterly unruffled confidence in what he is doing. This other-worldly quality —if it can be correctly so described—never intrudes into his conversation phrases customary to mystics. If you don't feel it, it isn't there. Someone asked him what he would do if the *Ra* began to settle. "Oh," he said, "You know we will have a rubber life raft aboard." "The raft is big enough to carry seven safely?" "Yes. But it only needs to hold six." "You mean you would stay on the *Ra*?" "I think so. You know that one of the oldest laws of the sea says. . ." "Says the captain goes down with his ship?" "Says that anyone who finds an abandoned vessel at sea has the right to board and seize it."

As long as the reeds stay afloat after leaving Safi, the water and wind will carry them westward. For it was from these very same coastal waters of Morocco that Columbus set sail; the sea and air currents carried him as far west as present-day Puerto Rico. . .

Epilogue*

The *Ra* left Safi on May 25, 1969. Fifty-six days and 2,700 miles later, only 600 miles from Barbados in the West Indies, Heyerdahl and his crew were forced to abandon their craft after heavy seas had aggravated a weakness in the construction of the stern and put most of the deck awash. Repairs had been attempted, but sharks made work on the sagging hull impossible, and the crew reluctantly transferred to a coast guard vessel summoned by radio.

Heyerdahl was satisfied that the distance they had covered successfully had fully proved the two basic points of his theory: that a papyrus vessel is capable of traveling great distances at sea, and that it would indeed have been possible for ancient peoples to have sailed from Africa to America. Nevertheless, Heyerdahl wanted to prove that he could go all the way. Hiring a new boat-building crew of four Aymara Indians from Bolivia, he immediately began construction of his second "paper boat." Less than a year after the launching of *Ra*, on May 17, 1970, Heyerdahl and his crew again set forth from Safi aboard *Ra II*. After a voyage of fifty-seven days, they stepped happily ashore in Bridgetown, Barbados.

*Editorial note.

49

REFLECTIONS (4)

REFLECTIONS

Does *adventurer* accurately describe Thor Heyerdahl? Does the word have connotations that may be as important as the denotations? If *adventurer* seems inappropriate, what term would you use to describe Heyerdahl? What about John Steinbeck? Kenichi Horie?

Heyerdahl's most evident motive for undertaking the voyages of both *Kon-Tiki* and *Ra* was that he wanted to prove something—the validity of a theory. Does every voyager, in a sense, hope to prove something?

Do you have a theory or belief that is not accepted by most of your acquaintances? If so, how could you test the truth of your idea in such a way that success would compel others to agree that you are right?

Truth sometimes hides behind a facade of nonsense. Edward Lear's Jumblies are as delightfully absurd a crew of voyagers as ever put to sea; yet the similarities between their leaky vessel and the Ra, *and between their success and Heyerdahl's, is remarkable. The voyages have not only parallel histories but a common moral.*

EDWARD LEAR

The Jumblies

I

They went to sea in a Sieve, they did,
   In a Sieve they went to sea:
In spite of all their friends could say,
On a winter's morn, on a stormy day,
   In a Sieve they went to sea!
And when the Sieve turned round and round,
And every one cried, 'You'll all be drowned!'
They called aloud, 'Our Sieve ain't big,
But we don't care a button! we don't care a fig!
   In a Sieve we'll go to sea!'
     Far and few, far and few,
      Are the lands where the Jumblies live;
     Their heads are green, and their hands are blue,
     And they went to sea in a Sieve.

II

They sailed away in a Sieve, they did,
  In a Sieve they sailed so fast,
With only a beautiful pea-green veil
Tied with a riband by way of a sail,
  To a small tobacco-pipe mast;
And every one said, who saw them go,
'O won't they be soon upset, you know!
For the sky is dark, and the voyage is long,
And happen what may, it's extremely wrong
  In a Sieve to sail so fast!'
    Far and few, far and few,
      Are the lands where the Jumblies live;
      Their heads are green, and their hands are blue,
      And they went to sea in a Sieve.

III

The water it soon came in, it did,
  The water it soon came in;
So to keep them dry, they wrapped their feet
In a pinky paper all folded neat,
  And they fastened it down with a pin.
And they passed the night in a crockery-jar,
And each of them said, 'How wise we are!
Though the sky be dark, and the voyage be long,
Yet we never can think we were rash or wrong,
  While round in our Sieve we spin!'
    Far and few, far and few,
      Are the lands where the Jumblies live;
      Their heads are green, and their hands are blue,
      And they went to sea in a Sieve.

IV

And all night long they sailed away;
   And when the sun went down,
They whistled and warbled a moony song
To the echoing sound of a coppery gong,
   In the shade of the mountains brown.
'O Timballo! How happy we are,
When we live in a sieve and a crockery-jar,
And all night long in the moonlight pale,
We sail away with a pea-green sail,
   In the shade of the mountains brown!'
     Far and few, far and few,
       Are the lands where the Jumblies live;
       Their heads are green, and their hands are blue,
       And they went to sea in a Sieve.

V

They sailed to the Western Sea, they did,
   To a land all covered with trees,
And they bought an Owl, and a useful Cart,
And a pound of Rice, and a Cranberry Tart,
   And a hive of silvery Bees.
And they bought a Pig, and some green Jack-daws,
And a lovely Monkey with lollipop paws,
And forty bottles of Ring-Bo-Ree,
   And no end of Stilton Cheese.
     Far and few, far and few,
       Are the lands where the Jumblies live;
       Their heads are green, and their hands are blue,
       And they went to sea in a Sieve.

VI

And in twenty years they all came back,
   In twenty years or more,
And every one said, 'How tall they've grown!
For they've been to the Lakes, and the Torrible Zone,
   And the hills of the Chankly Bore;
And they drank their health, and gave them a feast
Of dumplings made of beautiful yeast;
And every one said, 'If we only live,
We too will go to sea in a Sieve,—
   To the hills of the Chankly Bore!'
    Far and few, far and few,
     Are the lands where the Jumblies live;
    Their heads are green, and their hands are blue,
    And they went to sea in a Sieve.

Voyages of Discovery

~~~~~~

The Logbook

Everyone had to know something, and what they said
About that, the thing they'd learned by curious heart,
They said well.
 That was what he wanted to hear,
Something you had done too exactly for words,
Maybe, but too exactly to lie about either.

—William Meredith
"In Memory of Robert Frost"

The Logbook

Every seaman who has taken a voyage of any length knows about the log-book, in which a record of the voyage is kept. Sea travelers of all times and places have jotted down the factual details of their progress—the speed of their vessels, the weather conditions, the sighting of important landfalls—and most have added their own personal touch to these routine notations, describing the beauty of the night sky at sea or the awesome power of a storm, commenting on the numerous little shipboard duties that keep them occupied every waking minute, remarking sometimes on their sense of loneliness and insignificance.

Most logbooks become more than dull listings of nautical data: they become highly individual records of the mariners' lives during those weeks and months at sea. They gain value and importance in proportion to the amount of material that is entered into them and the intelligence and per-ception of the ones who keep them. Not only historians and oceanographers and map-makers have profited from them, but the keepers of the logs them-selves have afterwards found them of inestimable value.

Now everyone's life is a voyage, in a sense, as storytellers have recog-nized since the earliest times, and many of our best-loved tales, *The Sea-farer, The Odyssey, The Rime of the Ancient Mariner,* are both stories of adventure and metaphors of human life. The metaphor is a natural one, for each new undertaking is like an embarkation upon a voyage to a destination known or unknown, or like a particular stage in the longer voyage that is our life.

And so it is also natural that many persons have kept logbooks—or journals or diaries—of the voyages they have taken without ever going to sea. Writers, of course, are particularly faithful logkeepers or journalists, for their whole lives depend upon their ability to turn the raw stuff of their observations and experiences and reflections into the written words that will preserve their thoughts and feelings and communicate them to others. But even ordinary men and women keep journals and diaries, for themselves or for their children, or for no one in particular, but only be-cause they want to leave behind some record of their days upon this earth.

Since your progress through this book and this course is a kind of voyage, your own logbook is the appropriate place to record your day-to-day reactions and observations. In keeping such a record, you will find yourself writing more—much more—than you ordinarily do. There is value in this, for like any other skill, writing improves with practice.

Some of your logbook writing will be assigned by your instructor. Beyond that, the contents are up to you. Students sometimes feel limited or restricted by the assigned writing in a course, knowing that they could write better if they were free to write what they chose. So your voluntary entries are a chance not only to impress and please your instructor, but to please and satisfy yourself.

There are many ways to think of your logbook. One has already been suggested: think of it as a record of your travels—mental and physical—as you go through this course, through college, through life. There are countless curious and important things to be noted, beyond those your instructor assigns.

Here are three other ways to think of your logbook:

1. Think of it as a mirror of your life—or better yet, as a vast canvas upon which you are painting, day by day, a great mural which will eventually be an image of you and your life. Your medium will be words instead of paint (although you might wish to add pictures to make a collage), and your aim will be to try to represent as complete and honest a reflection of your life as possible.

2. Think of it as a psychologist's or philosopher's notebook in which, day by day, you question and probe yourself to try to learn what you really think and feel about the things that matter most to you. (What do you really think about your plans for the future, for example? Do they reflect your own honest interests and desires, or are you allowing yourself to be influenced against your better judgment by someone else's notion of what you should be and do?)

3. Think of it as an "idea" book, into which you put all the strange new ideas that you encounter every day in your looking, listening, and reading. Capture the things that impress or startle you, the things that make you laugh or wonder, the things you're always wishing you had at hand with which to liven your conversation.

There are many other possible ways to think of your logbook; the important thing is that the way, or ways, you choose should be interesting to you. Don't limit yourself merely to charting your daily activities and moods ("Tom took me to a movie tonight, but he was upset about losing his job and we didn't have a very good time."); explore all the dimensions of your experience and look for fresh ways to capture some part of your life. For starters, here are a few suggestions:

1. *Anecdotes, jokes, quotations.* Sometimes a brief story or joke or quotation you come across seems so "right" to you—such a true statement of the way things are—that you just have to save it and remember it. Your logbook is the place.

2. *Words.* You may have become aware of the value of working deliberately to increase your vocabulary, and your logbook can serve as a permanent record of new words you hear or come across in your reading, along with definitions from your dictionary, and examples of the words used in context.

3. *Verbal sketches.* Like an artist, you may enjoy doing brief sketches of what interests you—friends, pets, relatives, places—word-portraits that capture the unique character of someone or something.

4. *Clippings, cartoons, pictures, and other "scrapbook" items.* Not all of what interests you can be easily reduced to words; sometimes a graphic representation is better. Or some of your written entries may need illustration; or, on the other hand, you may want to write something about a picture. (Rubber cement is the best adhesive to use when you want to include a picture in your logbook.)

Sample Entries

Here are some entries from the logbooks and journals of a number of people, including several college students. Perhaps they will give you a clearer idea of some of the possibilities that exist for you. And as you read the selections in the chapters that follow, remember that many of them, too, are partly or entirely derived from journals and logbooks.

If you already have your own ideas, fine! Don't feel bound to follow someone else's lead. But when the well of inspiration runs dry and your daily life seems too ordinary for words, something here may provide the priming you need.

Feb. 2—It's still being Michigan outside—the mercury in all the thermometers hid. I headed all the way across campus in the sleet for my 12:40, and after twenty minutes I just wanted to bag it and crawl back into bed. (Why, oh *why* did I go to a school where some buildings are over a mile apart?) I tromped up the stairs into Social Stratification and found out that M., the prof, hadn't shown—he was sick, poor baby. That really ticked me off; you'd think that with all the facilities on this campus, they could notify students if a class were to be cancelled; WMSN could broadcast every hour on the hour. It would save a lot of grief. . . . (Kate Haracz) *

*From THE EDUCATION OF KATE HARACZ. Reprinted by permission of Change Magazine, May–June, 1970.

58

Sept. 14—Watched The Endless Summer instead of doing my homework. It was beautiful. I am amazed at the friendliness of the people Mike & Robert became friends with, that is how the world should be. Again I felt a yearning to go away; maybe I should avoid movies such as this. (Nancy Way)

I saw yesterday, Sunday, whilst at dinner, my neighbor Hosmer creeping into my barn. At once it occurred, "Well, men are lonely, to be sure, and here is this able, social, intellectual farmer under this grim day, as grimly, sidling into my barn, in the hope of some talk with me, showing me how to husband my cornstalks. Forlorn enough!" (Ralph Waldo Emerson)

I liked an aphorism of C. G. Lichtenberg, quoted by W. H. Auden in *The Dyer's Hand*: "A book is a mirror: if an ass peers into it, you can't expect an apostle to look out." (JA)

My mother—she can't stand anything phony. She refuses to go to teas, prefers young people to older. She works in the garden, making flowers come up out of the dirt. She wears her hair long, down her back, when she's at home, and up in a braided roll when she goes out. Her back is strong and her hands are gnarly and full of veins. I think she must have worked very hard when she was little to have such hands. Her eyes are huge, frightened, deep, and magnificent; her forehead almost always in a worry design; her mouth too tight and her chin tense. Yet there is an overwhelming strength in her face, and she is one of about five women I can think of who are in her category of beauty. Her figure is excellent. When she runs, on the beach, dressed in blue jeans and a T-shirt, with her hair all down, she looks nineteen. She is fifty-four. . . . (Joan Baez) *

Observed during Christmas vacation, in a locked Chrysler Imperial parked overlooking Crescent Bay in Laguna Beach, a smartly dressed gray-haired lady reading *Playboy*. (JA)

Oct. 19—One of the greatest thrills I've ever had was when I was on a 90' yacht just off Newport Beach and we suddenly found ourselves in the middle of a school of porpoises. There were about 50 of them jumping along side the boat and riding in the wake. It seemed that if I jumped into the water they would take me down to some undersea utopia. They were so beautiful and intelligent looking also. Someday I will be working with them, learning how man and the porpoise can best help each other. (Nancy Way)

The elevator boy in my hotel, after he has shut the grilled gate and started the car, always slips his hand through the bars of the gate so that as he passes each floor the sill-plate will give him a dangerous little kiss on the end of his finger. It is the only record he keeps of his fabulous travels. A doctor could probably tell him why he does it; but for that matter a doctor could probably tell me why when I pass through a long corridor I always kick lightly sideways with one foot so that it ticks the baseboard. A doctor *could,* but a doctor isn't going to. There are things about my life I don't wish to pry into, and that is one of them. (E. B. White) *

Feb. 4—The Funny Things that Go On in a Dorm Department: Janie just knocked at my door and said, "Jersey, come here quick." As I made my way out the door, I looked up and saw a guy braced between the two walls of the hall, nine feet up. He slid down one wall and said, "Hi." I said, "Great." It really thrills me to know that the people around here have refused to be impressed with the sanctity of the dorm and use it as it's meant to be—as a toy. (Kate Haracz) †

May 7—I can't understand all this I hear about cats being so terribly proud, aristocratic, and independent, how they will tolerate your company but can do perfectly well without it. My cat's not like that.

Now Zorba may be an exception, I admit—perhaps a sub-normal sort of cat. But still, in the interests of Truth, he has to be considered. He's quite an ordinary cat, as far as his family and social background is concerned. No one knows who his father is, probably not even his mother, so technically he's a bastard; but bastardy apparently doesn't carry quite the stigma among cats that it does among humans. I mean, I've seen some rather stuffy people play with illegitimate kittens without the least indication of disapproval.

But the point about Zorba's heritage is that it's perhaps just the thing that keeps him from being haughty. Now these other cats that the cat-fanciers are always gloating about, don't you suppose they're pretty aristocratic cats? I mean with proper pedigrees and all that—good fam'ly, y'know. And aren't most aristocratic and socially prominent people likely to be snobbish and stand-offish, too?

Well, Zorba's certainly not like that, whatever the cause. He's very gregarious and affectionate. He sidles up to anyone who comes in, and in two minutes he's lying in their lap, licking their fingers. And he's always climb-

*From ONE MAN'S MEAT by E. B. White. Reprinted by permission of Harper & Row, Publishers, Inc.

†From THE EDUCATION OF KATE HARACZ. Reprinted by permission of Change Magazine, May–June, 1970.

ing all over me, or sitting on my desk, or meowing at me to stroke him or scratch his head.

Not only that, but he follows me around and tries to get in on whatever I'm doing. Now I've resented this for quite a while, and when he comes poking his nose in the way when I'm washing dishes, or sitting on my notebook and chewing my pen when I'm trying to write, I generally give him the old heave-ho. Out you go, buddy-boy, I've got work to do. I've attributed this kind of interference to various things—a demand for attention, interest in some moving object, or just that general curiosity cats are supposed to have.

But do you know what I think it really is? I think it's a genuine desire to participate, to help out, to do whatever I'm doing. I've often noticed that domestic animals seem to think they can do everything their masters do, and of course the poor things get a lot of lumps for it. But I think dogs and cats aren't very aware that they're different from us. And the longer they live with us, the more likely they are to adopt our habits, or try. I've heard of dogs, for instance, who have taken to smoking pipes and wearing slippers. Well, they're fortunate enough to have understanding masters. After all, if we're going to coop these animals up and do everything we can to keep them from acting like animals, why should we be surprised when they try to act like us?

So I'm going to be more indulgent with Zorba in the future. If he wants to socialize, we'll socialize; if he wants to help, I'll let him help. Next time he comes prowling around when I'm washing dishes, I'll hand him a towel. The writing, I'm afraid, will be a bit too much for him. But I don't want to discourage him. Maybe he'd be happy if I got him some colored chalk and a chalk board. (JA)

I am always reminded, and now again by reading last night in Rousseau's *Confessions,* that it is not in the events in one's life, but in the faculty of selecting and reporting them, that the interest lies. (Ralph Waldo Emerson)

Jan. 30—Fair Haven pond is *scored* with the trails of foxes, and you may see where they have gambolled and gone through a hundred evolutions, which testify to a singular listlessness and leisure in nature.

Suddenly, looking down the river, I saw a fox some sixty rods off, making across to the hills on my left. As the snow lay five inches deep, he made but slow progress, but it was no impediment to me. So, yielding to the instinct of the chase, I tossed my head aloft and bounded away, snuffing the air like a fox-hound, and spurning the world and Humane Society at each bound. It seemed the woods rang with the hunter's horn, and Diana and all the satyrs joined in the chase and cheered me on. Olympian and Elean youths were waving palms on the hills. In the meanwhile I gained rapidly on the fox; but he showed a remarkable presence of mind, for, instead of keeping up the face of the hill, which was steep and unwooded in that part, he kept along the slope in the direction of the forest, though he lost ground by it. Notwithstanding his fright, he took no step which was not beautiful. The course on his part was a series of most graceful curves. It was a sort of leopard canter, I should say, as if he were no-wise impeded by the snow, but were husbanding his strength all the while. When he doubled I wheeled and cut him off, bounding with fresh vigor, and Antaeus-like, recovering my strength each time I touched the snow. Having got near enough for a fair view, just as he was slipping into the wood, I gracefully yielded him the palm. He ran as though there were not a bone in his back, occasionally dropping his muzzle to the snow for a rod or two, and then tossing his head aloft when satisfied of his course. When he came to a declivity he put his fore feet together and slid down it like a cat. He trod so softly that you could not have heard it from any nearness, and yet with such expression that it would not have been quite inaudible at any distance. So, hoping this experience would prove a useful lesson to him, I returned to the village by the highway of the river. (Henry David Thoreau)

The Chabot College librarian reports a note found in a returned book: "Remind Henry not to climb the tree with his skates on." (JA)

Sept. 27—Why is it that I'm so gullible? I can't be that stupid. Even teachers who tell fantastic scientific phenomena get me to believe them. When I tell anyone the same thing they laugh. Maybe I just leave out some of the vitals. I'm also the one that stands with a blank look on my face when a joke has been told. Is innocence supposed to be rewarding? (Nancy Way)

Transformation of the Log

Keeping a logbook may be an end in itself; much of what is written there may go no further and serve no other purpose. Yet things written down tend to become more firmly fixed in the memory and recalled—perhaps with surprise—on some later occasion. More deliberately, the keeper of a log may return to certain entries with an eye to expanding and developing them into something better, more substantial. Henry James, for example, seems to have gotten the idea for his famous ghost story, *The Turn of the Screw,* from a story told to him one evening by the Archbishop of Canterbury—"the mere vague, undetailed, faint sketch of it"—which

James recorded in rough outline in a notebook entry of about 200 words on January 12, 1895. From this germ nearly three years later came a story of 36,000 words.

Such a degree of expansion is unusual, of course; a more typical proportion between a logbook entry and a developed version of it is seen in this example from *Kodoku,* Kenichi Horie's account of his solo voyage from Osaka to San Francisco. The original logbook entry comes first:

65TH DAY OUT: JULY 14TH, SATURDAY*

Wind continues without shifting, but it's not very strong.
Wish it would freshen up. The Mermaid *isn't perky these days.*
It may be because of her foul[1] bottom.
It's another scorcher, and no relief.
But it's a beautiful, clear, moonlit night. The Mermaid *silently gliding along the dark sea.*
She and I with my cup of hot Lipton tea—these, my worldly goods.

That was really a great night. The *Mermaid* was putting on a grand performance. She was moving ahead through the seas in strong, steady strides, not just gliding on the surface but riding the waves. Each time she shoved ahead, I could feel the rush of the seas under her bottom. She wasn't just moving, she was picking up momentum with each stride, cutting through the water. A truly great performance!

With the sliding hatch wide open, I lay on my berth staring into the clear, starlit sky. And soon the moon, nearly full, shone high in the sky. Polaris, the Big Dipper, Andromeda, Cassiopeia—all so familiar to the navigator—filled the northern skies. There was a special lyric beauty to the sea and sky—breathtaking and mystic almost. Even my daily cup of hot Lipton tea had a special fragrance, a special delicate flavor. It seemed a pity to gulp it down. I sipped it quietly, listening to the water rushing past the *Mermaid.* I was happy. The surging boat, the twinkling stars, the delicious tea—all this and good health, and knowing that we were well on the way to fulfilling our plans. Life is well worth living for moments like this.

The difference is enormous; some mysterious transformation has occurred between those jotted notes in the log and the vivid, dramatic recreation of that happy evening. A few written words awakened memories, and the whole experience was re-lived and shared. Notice the details that

---

[1] Overgrown with marine organisms, such as barnacles.

*From KODOKU by Kenichi Horie. Reprinted by permission of Charles E. Tuttle Co., Inc., Tokyo, Japan & Rutland, Vermont.

have been added; notice, too, that there seems to be a contradiction: in Horie's expanded account the *Mermaid* sails better than she did according to the logbook! Who knows which is truer. The writer controls his material, the story becomes what he wants it to be. There is no need to be slavishly faithful to the original notes. Dozens of considerations may dictate changes, omissions, additions.

Henry David Thoreau, who kept a journal almost daily for 24 years, mining from it *Walden, Civil Disobedience,* and numerous other works, explained why two versions of a thing are often better than one:

> If you are describing any occurrence, or a man, make two or more distinct reports at different times. Though you may think you have said all, you will tomorrow remember a whole new class of facts which perhaps interested most of all at the time, but did not present themselves to be reported. If we have recently met and talked with a man, and would report our experience, we commonly make a very partial report at first, failing to seize the most significant, picturesque, and dramatic points; we describe only what we have had time to digest and dispose of in our minds, without being conscious that there were other things really more novel and interesting to us, which will not fail to recur to us and impress us suitably at last.

And so journals and logbooks continue to engender themes, essays, stories, poems, and books.

Richard Henry Dana, author of the classic voyage narrative *Two Years Before the Mast,* says of his book in the preface:

> It is written out from a journal which I kept at the time, and from notes which I made of most of the events as they happened. . . .

On the first page of *Kon-Tiki,* Thor Heyerdahl describes himself "on a wooden raft with a parrot and five companions," as one morning he "sat writing in a dew-drenched logbook:

> May 17. Norwegian Independence Day. Heavy sea. Fair wind. I am cook today and found seven flying fish on deck, one squid on the cabin roof, and one unknown fish in Torstein's sleeping bag. . . ."

And here is the French mountain-climber Maurice Herzog talking about his thrilling best-seller, *Annapurna*:

> The basis of the narrative is, of course, my memory of all that happened. In so far as the record is comprehensive and exact, that is due to

the Expedition's log which Marcel Ichac so faithfully kept—an essential document, sometimes written up at the very moment of action. . . .

And he sometimes quotes from the log in the book.

Your own logbook will undoubtedly be put to similar use and undergo its own transformations. As you read the selections that follow, new ideas will occur to you. You will often be aware of the other writer's journal or logbook, either obviously in the foreground or behind the scenes. Speculate when you read the journals of Lewis and Clark what changes might have been made had the explorers re-written them. Consider what such materials might become in the hands of a good novelist. And then surprise and delight yourself by drawing from your own logbook better themes than you knew you could write.

Format

Shipboard logbooks are usually kept in sturdily-bound volumes resembling ledgers, with several ruled columns to facilitate the orderly recording of various nautical data such as latitude and longitude, wind velocity, etc. Daily entries may follow one another immediately or be spaced one to a page. Sometimes daily entries are confined to the right-hand pages, and the left-hand pages are used for sketches, maps, etc. The format is mostly a matter of the writer's convenience, except on naval vessels or the ships of large companies, where a standard format is prescribed.

If your instructor specifies a format, follow that; otherwise, suit yourself. You may wish to obtain a ledger book at a stationery or variety store, or you may prefer to use a simple spiral-bound notebook. Be wary of loose-leaf notebooks and notebooks in which the sheets are affixed to a glued backing, since in both cases the pages are easily torn out and damaged or lost.

Two final reminders: write in ink, and date your entries.

65

~~~~~~

An Exemplary Voyage

*Why is almost every robust
healthy boy with a robust healthy
soul in him, at some time or other
crazy to go to sea?*

—Herman Melville
Moby Dick

*Joseph Conrad's "Youth" is an adventure
story, the story of a twenty-year-old second
mate's voyage through an almost incredible
series of disasters to the Far East. It is also a
richly comic story, partly because of the
piling up of one absurd catastrophe after
another and partly because of the wry, ironic
manner in which Marlow, the old salt who
tells the story, recalls the youthful cheerful-
ness and naiveté with which he faced each
new calamity. "Youth" is one of the finest
voyage stories we have. The voyage itself
might almost be called "archetypal," so much
does it seem a kind of model or pattern upon
which all other voyages are based. It has
mythic qualities, it deals with fundamental
themes—time and transience, youth and age,
illusion and reality—and it contains nearly
all the usual elements of any extended
voyage. For this reason it makes an ideal
"first" voyage story; the pattern can be clearly
seen, and the various parts of the pattern can
be easily recognized elsewhere. For Marlow,
the voyage is certainly one of discovery, but
though he reaches his goal, the romantic and
mysterious East, the important discovery is
the one he makes about himself. There are
several discoveries, in fact—for the reader
as well as for Marlow.*

JOSEPH CONRAD

Youth

This could have occurred nowhere but in England, where men and sea interpenetrate, so to speak—the sea entering into the life of most men, and the men knowing something or everything about the sea, in the way of amusement, of travel, or of bread-winning.

We were sitting round a mahogany table that reflected the bottle, the claret-glasses, and our faces as we leaned on our elbows. There was a director of companies, an accountant, a lawyer, Marlow, and myself. The director had been a *Conway* boy,[1] the accountant had served four years at sea, the lawyer—a fine crusted Tory, High Churchman, the best of old fellows, the soul of honour—had been chief officer in the P. & O.[2] service in the good old days when mail-boats were square-rigged at least on two masts, and used to come down the China Sea before a fair monsoon with stun'sails set alow and aloft. We all began life in the merchant service. Between the five of us there was the strong bond of the sea, and also the fellowship of the craft, which no amount of enthusiasm for yachting, cruising, and so on can give, since one is only the amusement of life and the other is life itself.

Marlow (at least I think that is how he spelt his name) told the story, or rather the chronicle, of a voyage:—

"Yes, I have seen a little of the Eastern seas; but what I remember best is my first voyage there. You fellows know there are those voyages that seem ordered for the illustration of life, that might stand for a symbol of existence. You fight, work, sweat, nearly kill yourself, sometimes do kill yourself, trying to accomplish something—and you can't. Not from any fault of yours. You simply can do nothing, neither great nor little—not a

[1] That is, learned seamanship aboard the training ship *Conway* in the Mersey River near Liverpool.
[2] Pacific and Orient—a ship company.

thing in the world—not even marry an old maid, or get a wretched 600-ton cargo of coal to its port of destination.

"It was altogether a memorable affair. It was my first voyage to the East, and my first voyage as second mate; it was also my skipper's first command. You'll admit it was time. He was sixty if a day; a little man, with a broad, not very straight back, with bowed shoulders and one leg more bandy than the other, he had that queer twisted-about appearance you see so often in men who work in the fields. He had a nut-cracker face—chin and nose trying to come together over a sunken mouth—and it was framed in iron-gray fluffy hair, that looked like a chin-strap of cotton-wool sprinkled with coal-dust. And he had blue eyes in that old face of his, which were amazingly like a boy's, with that candid expression some quite common men preserve to the end of their days by a rare internal gift of simplicity of heart and rectitude of soul. What induced him to accept me was a wonder. I had come out of a crack Australian clipper, where I had been third officer, and he seemed to have a prejudice against crack clippers as aristocratic and high-toned. He said to me, 'You know, in this ship you will have to work.' I said I had to work in every ship I had ever been in. 'Ah, but this is different, and you gentlemen out of them big ships; . . . but there! I dare say you will do. Join to-morrow.'

"I joined to-morrow. It was twenty-two years ago; and I was just twenty. How time passes! It was one of the happiest days of my life. Fancy! Second mate for the first time—a really responsible officer! I wouldn't have thrown up my new billet for a fortune. The mate looked me over carefully. He was also an old chap, but of another stamp. He had a Roman nose, a snow-white, long beard, and his name was Mahon, but he insisted that it should be pronounced Mann. He was well connected; yet there was something wrong with his luck, and he had never got on.

"As to the captain, he had been for years in coasters,[3] then in the Mediterranean, and last in the West Indian trade. He had never been round the Capes. He could just write a kind of sketchy hand, and didn't care for writing at all. Both were thorough good seamen of course, and between those two old chaps I felt like a small boy between two grandfathers.

"The ship also was old. Her name was the *Judea*. Queer name, isn't it? She belonged to a man Wilmer, Wilcox—some name like that; but he has been bankrupt and dead these twenty years or more, and his name don't matter. She had been laid up in Shadwell basin for ever so long. You may imagine her state. She was all rust, dust, grime—soot aloft, dirt on deck. To me it was like coming out of a palace into a ruined cottage. She was

---

[3] Vessels that sail along the coast, rather than on long overseas voyages.

about 400 tons, had a primitive windlass,[4] wooden latches to the doors, not a bit of brass about her, and a big square stern. There was on it, below her name in big letters, a lot of scrollwork, with the gilt off, and some sort of a coat of arms, with the motto 'Do or Die' underneath. I remember it took my fancy immensely. There was a touch of romance in it, something that made me love the old thing—something that appealed to my youth!

"We left London in ballast[5]—sand ballast—to load a cargo of coal in a northern port for Bankok. Bankok! I thrilled. I had been six years at sea, but had only seen Melbourne and Sydney, very good places, charming places in their way—but Bankok!

"We worked out of the Thames under canvas, with a North Sea pilot on board.[6] His name was Jermyn, and he dodged all day long about the galley drying his handkerchief before the stove. Apparently he never slept. He was a dismal man, with a perpetual tear sparkling at the end of his nose, who either had been in trouble, or was in trouble, or expected to be in trouble—couldn't be happy unless something went wrong. He mistrusted my youth, my common-sense, and my seamanship, and made a point of showing it in a hundred little ways. I dare say he was right. It seems to me I knew very little then, and I know not much more now; but I cherish a hate for that Jermyn to this day.

"We were a week working up as far as Yarmouth Roads, and then we got into a gale—the famous October gale of twenty-two years ago. It was wind, lightning, sleet, snow, and a terrific sea. We were flying light,[7] and you may imagine how bad it was when I tell you we had smashed bulwarks and a flooded deck. On the second night she shifted her ballast into the lee bow,[8] and by that time we had been blown off somewhere on the Dogger Bank. There was nothing for it but go below with shovels and try to right her, and there we were in that vast hold, gloomy like a cavern, the tallow dips stuck and flickering on the beams, the gale howling above, the ship tossing about like mad on her side; there we all were, Jermyn, the captain, every one, hardly able to keep our feet, engaged on that grave-digger's work, and trying to toss shovelfuls of wet sand up to windward. At every tumble of the ship you could see vaguely in the dim light men falling down with a great flourish of shovels. One of the ship's boys (we

[4] Machine used to weigh (lift) the anchor.
[5] Heavy material placed in the bottom of the hold to keep the ship steady.
[6] The voyage begins in London; the ship proceeds north up the coast through the North Sea toward Newcastle, to pick up a cargo of coal to be delivered to Bankok.
[7] Sailing with only a small part of the total amount of sail surface available.
[8] The ballast of sand, sliding off center in the storm, unbalances the ship.

71

had two), impressed by the weirdness of the scene, wept as if his heart would break. We could hear him blubbering somewhere in the shadows.

"On the third day the gale died out, and by and by a north-country tug picked us up. We took sixteen days in all to get from London to the Tyne![9] When we got into dock we had lost our turn for loading, and they hauled us off to a tier[10] where we remained for a month. Mrs. Beard (the captain's name was Beard) came from Colchester to see the old man. She lived on board. The crew of runners[11] had left, and there remained only the officers, one boy and the steward, a mulatto who answered to the name of Abraham. Mrs. Beard was an old woman, with a face all wrinkled and ruddy like a winter apple, and the figure of a young girl. She caught sight of me once, sewing on a button, and insisted on having my shirts to repair. This was something different from the captains' wives I had known on board crack clippers. When I brought her the shirts, she said: 'And the socks? They want mending, I am sure, and John's—Captain Beard's—things are all in order now. I would be glad of something to do.' Bless the old woman. She overhauled my outfit for me, and meantime I read for the first time *Sartor Resartus* and Burnaby's *Ride to Khiva*. I didn't understand much of the first then; but I remember I preferred the soldier to the philosopher at the time; a preference which life has only confirmed. One was a man, and the other was either more—or less. However, they are both dead and Mrs. Beard is dead, and youth, strength, genius,[12] thoughts, achievements, simple hearts—all die. . . . No matter.

"They loaded us at last. We shipped a crew. Eight able seamen and two boys. We hauled off one evening to the buoys at the dock-gates, ready to go out, and with a fair prospect of beginning the voyage next day. Mrs. Beard was to start for home by a late train. When the ship was fast we went to tea. We sat rather silent through the meal—Mahon, the old couple, and I. I finished first, and slipped away for a smoke, my cabin being in a deck-house just against the poop.[13] It was high water, blowing fresh with a drizzle; the double dock-gates were opened, and the steam-colliers[14] were going in and out in the darkness with their lights burning bright, a great plashing of propellers, rattling of winches, and a lot of hailing on the pier-heads. I watched the procession of head-lights gliding high and of green

[9] River on which Newcastle, a coal port, is located, a distance of about 300 miles from London.
[10] Row of anchorages or mooring places.
[11] Smugglers (jokingly).
[12] Talent.
[13] Deck near the stern.
[14] Coal-carrying steamships.

lights gliding low in the night, when suddenly a red gleam flashed at me, vanished, came into view again, and remained. The fore-end of a steamer loomed up close. I shouted down the cabin, 'Come up, quick!' and then heard a startled voice saying afar in the dark, 'Stop her, sir.' A bell jingled. Another voice cried warningly, 'We are going right into that barque,[15] sir.' The answer to this was a gruff 'All right,' and the next thing was a heavy crash as the steamer struck a glancing blow with the bluff of her bow about our fore-rigging. There was a moment of confusion, yelling, and running about. Steam roared. Then somebody was heard saying, 'All clear, sir.' . . . 'Are you all right?' asked the gruff voice. I had jumped forward to see the damage, and hailed back, 'I think so.' 'Easy astern,' said the gruff voice. A bell jingled. 'What steamer is that?' screamed Mahon. By that time she was no more to us than a bulky shadow manoeuvring a little way off. They shouted at us some name—a woman's name, Miranda or Melissa —or some such thing. 'This means another month in this beastly hole,' said Mahon to me, as we peered with lamps about the splintered bulwarks and broken braces. 'But where's the captain?'

"We had not heard or seen anything of him all that time. We went aft to look. A doleful voice arose hailing somewhere in the middle of the dock, '*Judea* ahoy!' . . . How the devil did he get there? . . . 'Hallo!' we shouted. 'I am adrift in our boat without oars,' he cried. A belated water-man[16] offered his services, and Mahon struck a bargain with him for half-a-crown to tow our skipper alongside; but it was Mrs. Beard that came up the ladder first. They had been floating about the dock in that mizzly cold rain for nearly an hour. I was never so surprised in my life.

"It appears that when he heard my shout 'Come up' he understood at once what was the matter, caught up his wife, ran on deck, and across, and down into our boat, which was fast to the ladder. Not bad for a sixty-year-old. Just imagine that old fellow saving heroically in his arms that old woman—the woman of his life. He set her down on a thwart, and was ready to climb back on board when the painter[17] came adrift somehow, and away they went together. Of course in the confusion we did not hear him shouting. He looked abashed. She said cheerfully, 'I suppose it does not matter my losing the train now?' 'No, Jenny—you go below and get warm,' he growled. Then to us: 'A sailor has no business with a wife—I say. There I was, out of the ship. Well, no harm done this time. Let's go and look at what that fool of a steamer smashed.'

---

[15] Or "bark." A three-masted sailing ship.
[16] Man who operates a small boat for hire.
[17] Rope attached to the bow of a boat or ship.

"It wasn't much, but it delayed us three weeks. At the end of that time, the captain being engaged with his agents, I carried Mrs. Beard's bag to the railway-station and put her all comfy into a third-class carriage. She lowered the window to say, 'You are a good young man. If you see John—Captain Beard—without his muffler at night, just remind him from me to keep his throat well wrapped up.' 'Certainly, Mrs. Beard,' I said. 'You are a good young man; I noticed how attentive you are to John—to Captain——' The train pulled out suddenly; I took my cap off to the old woman: I never saw her again. . . . Pass the bottle.

"We went to sea next day. When we made that start for Bankok we had been already three months out of London. We had expected to be a fortnight or so—at the outside.

"It was January, and the weather was beautiful—the beautiful sunny winter weather that has more charm than in the summer-time, because it is unexpected, and crisp, and you know it won't, it can't, last long. It's like a windfall, like a godsend, like an unexpected piece of luck.

"It lasted all down the North Sea, all down Channel; and it lasted till we were three hundred miles or so to the westward of the Lizards:[18] then the wind went round to the sou'west and began to pipe up. In two days it blew a gale. The *Judea,* hove to,[19] wallowed on the Atlantic like an old candle-box. It blew day after day: it blew with spite, without interval, without mercy, without rest. The world was nothing but an immensity of great foaming waves rushing at us, under a sky low enough to touch with the hand and dirty like a smoked ceiling. In the stormy space surrounding us there was as much flying spray as air. Day after day and night after night there was nothing round the ship but the howl of the wind, the tumult of the sea, the noise of water pouring over her deck. There was no rest for her and no rest for us. She tossed, she pitched, she stood on her head, she sat on her tail, she rolled, she groaned, and we had to hold on while on deck and cling to our bunks when below, in a constant effort of body and worry of mind.

"One night Mahon spoke through the small window of my berth. It opened right into my very bed, and I was lying there sleepless, in my boots, feeling as though I had not slept for years, and could not if I tried. He said excitedly—

" 'You got the sounding-rod[20] in here, Marlow? I can't get the pumps to suck. By God! it's no child's play.'

---

[18] Point near the southwest tip of England.
[19] Brought to a stop.
[20] Iron rod to measure the depth of water.

"I gave him the sounding-rod and lay down again, trying to think of various things—but I thought only of the pumps. When I came on deck they were still at it, and my watch relieved at the pumps. By the light of the lantern brought on deck to examine the sounding-rod I caught a glimpse of their weary, serious faces. We pumped all the four hours. We pumped all night, all day, all the week—watch and watch.[21] She was working herself loose, and leaked badly—not enough to drown us at once, but enough to kill us with the work at the pumps. And while we pumped the ship was going from us piecemeal: the bulwarks went, the stanchions were torn out, the ventilators smashed, the cabin-door burst in. There was not a dry spot in the ship. She was being gutted bit by bit. The long-boat changed, as if by magic, into matchwood where she stood in her gripes. I had lashed her myself, and was rather proud of my handiwork, which had withstood so long the malice of the sea. And we pumped. And there was no break in the weather. The sea was white like a sheet of foam, like a caldron of boiling milk; there was not a break in the clouds, no—not the size of a man's hand—no, not for so much as ten seconds. There was for us no sky, there were for us no stars, no sun, no universe—nothing but angry clouds and an infuriated sea. We pumped watch and watch, for dear life; and it seemed to last for months, for years, for all eternity, as though we had been dead and gone to a hell for sailors. We forgot the day of the week, the name of the month, what year it was, and whether we had ever been ashore. The sails blew away, she lay broadside on under a weathercloth,[22] the ocean poured over her, and we did not care. We turned those handles, and had the eyes of idiots. As soon as we had crawled on deck I used to take a round turn with a rope about the men, the pumps, and the mainmast, and we turned, we turned incessantly, with the water to our waists, to our necks, over our heads. It was all one. We had forgotten how it felt to be dry.

"And there was somewhere in me the thought: By Jove! this is the deuce of an adventure—something you read about; and it is my first voyage as second mate—and I am only twenty—and here I am lasting it out as well as any of these men, and keeping my chaps up to the mark. I was pleased. I would not have given up the experience for worlds. I had moments of exultation. Whenever the old dismantled craft pitched heavily with her counter[23] high in the air, she seemed to me to throw up, like an appeal, like a defiance, like a cry to the clouds without mercy, the words written on her stern: *'Judea,* London. Do or Die.'

---

[21] Changing shifts every other watch (four-hour period).
[22] Covering of canvas or tarpaulin used as protection against wind or spray.
[23] Curved part of the stern.

"O youth! The strength of it, the faith of it, the imagination of it! To me she was not an old rattletrap carting about the world a lot of coal for a freight—to me she was the endeavour, the test, the trial of life. I think of her with pleasure, with affection, with regret—as you would think of someone dead you have loved. I shall never forget her. . . . Pass the bottle.

"One night when tied to the mast, as I explained, we were pumping on, deafened with the wind, and without spirit enough in us to wish ourselves dead, a heavy sea crashed aboard and swept clean over us. As soon as I got my breath I shouted, as in duty bound, 'Keep on, boys!' when suddenly I felt something hard floating on deck strike the calf of my leg. I made a grab at it and missed. It was so dark we could not see each other's faces within a foot—you understand.

"After that thump the ship kept quiet for a while, and the thing, whatever it was, struck my leg again. This time I caught it—and it was a saucepan. At first, being stupid with fatigue and thinking of nothing but the pumps, I did not understand what I had in my hand. Suddenly it dawned upon me, and I shouted, 'Boys, the house on deck is gone. Leave this, and let's look for the cook.'

"There was a deck-house forward, which contained the galley, the cook's berth, and the quarters of the crew. As we had expected for days to see it swept away, the hands had been ordered to sleep in the cabin—the only safe place in the ship. The steward, Abraham, however, persisted in clinging to his berth, stupidly, like a mule—from sheer fright I believe, like an animal that won't leave a stable falling in an earthquake. So we went to look for him. It was chancing death, since once out of our lashings we were as exposed as if on a raft. But we went. The house was shattered as if a shell had exploded inside. Most of it had gone overboard—stove, men's quarters, and their property, all was gone; but two posts, holding a portion of the bulkhead to which Abraham's bunk was attached, remained as if by a miracle. We groped in the ruins and came upon this, and there he was, sitting in his bunk, surrounded by foam and wreckage, jabbering cheerfully to himself. He was out of his mind; completely and for ever mad, with this sudden shock coming upon the fag-end of his endurance. We snatched him up, lugged him aft, and pitched him head-first down the cabin companion. You understand there was no time to carry him down with infinite precautions and wait to see how he got on. Those below would pick him up at the bottom of the stairs all right. We were in a hurry to go back to the pumps. That business could not wait. A bad leak is an inhuman thing.

"One would think that the sole purpose of that fiendish gale had been to make a lunatic of that poor devil of a mulatto. It eased before morning, and next day the sky cleared, and as the sea went down the leak took up.

76

When it came to bending²⁴ a fresh set of sails the crew demanded to put back—and really there was nothing else to do. Boats gone, decks swept clean, cabin gutted, men without a stitch but what they stood in, stores spoiled, ship strained. We put her head for home, and—would you believe it? The wind came east right in our teeth. It blew fresh, it blew continuously. We had to beat up²⁵ every inch of the way, but she did not leak so badly, the water keeping comparatively smooth. Two hours' pumping in every four is no joke—but it kept her afloat as far as Falmouth.

"The good people there live on casualties of the sea, and no doubt were glad to see us. A hungry crowd of shipwrights sharpened their chisels at the sight of that carcass of a ship. And, by Jove! they had pretty pickings off us before they were done. I fancy the owner was already in a tight place. There were delays. Then it was decided to take part of the cargo out and caulk her topsides. This was done, the repairs finished, cargo reshipped; a new crew came on board, and we went out—for Bankok. At the end of a week we were back again. The crew said they weren't going to Bankok— a hundred and fifty days' passage—in a something hooker that wanted pumping eight hours out of the twenty-four; and the nautical papers inserted again the little paragraph: '*Judea*. Barque. Tyne to Bankok; coals; put back to Falmouth leaky and with crew refusing duty.'

"There were more delays—more tinkering. The owner came down for a day, and said she was as right as a little fiddle. Poor old Captain Beard looked like the ghost of a Geordie²⁶ skipper—through the worry and humiliation of it. Remember he was sixty, and it was his first command. Mahon said it was a foolish business, and would end badly. I loved the ship more than ever, and wanted awfully to get to Bankok. To Bankok! Magic name, blessed name. Mesopotamia wasn't a patch on it. Remember I was twenty, and it was my first second-mate's billet, and the East was waiting for me.

"We went out and anchored in the outer roads²⁷ with a fresh crew—the third. She leaked worse than ever. It was as if those confounded shipwrights had actually made a hole in her. This time we did not even go outside. The crew simply refused to man the windlass.

"They towed us back to the inner harbour, and we became a fixture, a feature, an institution of the place. People pointed us out to visitors as 'That 'ere barque that's going to Bankok—has been here six months—put

²⁴ Fastening (the sails) to a spar.
²⁵ Tack into the wind.
²⁶ Coal-carrying ship.
²⁷ Anchorage area.

back three times.' On holidays the small boys pulling about in boats would hail, '*Judea,* ahoy!' and if a head showed above the rail shouted, 'Where you bound to?—Bankok?' and jeered. We were only three on board. The poor old skipper mooned in the cabin. Mahon undertook the cooking, and unexpectedly developed all a Frenchman's genius for preparing nice little messes. I looked languidly after the rigging. We became citizens of Falmouth. Every shopkeeper knew us. At the barber's or tobacconist's they asked familiarly, 'Do you think you will ever get to Bankok?' Meantime the owner, the underwriters, and the charterers squabbled amongst themselves in London, and our pay went on. . . . Pass the bottle.

"It was horrid. Morally it was worse than pumping for life. It seemed as though we had been forgotten by the world, belonged to nobody, would get nowhere; it seemed that, as if bewitched, we would have to live for ever and ever in that inner harbour, a derision and a byword to generations of long-shore loafers and dishonest boatmen. I obtained three months' pay and a five days' leave, and made a rush for London. It took me a day to get there and pretty well another to come back—but three months' pay went all the same. I don't know what I did with it. I went to a music-hall, I believe, lunched, dined, and supped in a swell place in Regent Street, and was back to time, with nothing but a complete set of Byron's works and a new railway rug to show for three months' work. The boat-man who pulled me off to the ship said: 'Hallo! I thought you had left the old thing. *She* will never get to Bankok.' 'That's all *you* know about it,' I said scornfully —but I didn't like that prophecy at all.

"Suddenly a man, some kind of agent to somebody, appeared with full powers. He had grog-blossoms[28] all over his face, an indomitable energy, and was a jolly soul. We leaped into life again. A hulk came alongside, took our cargo, and then we went into dry dock to get our copper[29] stripped. No wonder she leaked. The poor thing, strained beyond endurance by the gale, had, as if in disgust, spat out all the oakum[30] of her lower seams. She was recaulked, new coppered, and made as tight as a bottle. We went back to the hulk and reshipped our cargo.

"Then, on a fine moonlight night, all the rats left the ship.

"We had been infested with them. They had destroyed our sails, consumed more stores than the crew, affably shared our beds and our dangers, and now, when the ship was made seaworthy, concluded to clear out. I

---

[28] Red spots or pimples caused by excessive drinking. (Grog is a mixture of liquor and water.)

[29] Copper sheathing covering a ship's sides and bottom.

[30] Loose fibers from untwisted ropes, used for caulking seams to make them watertight.

called Mahon to enjoy the spectacle. Rat after rat appeared on our rail, took a last look over his shoulder, and leaped with a hollow thud into the empty hulk. We tried to count them, but soon lost the tale. Mahon said: 'Well, well! don't talk to me about the intelligence of rats. They ought to have left before, when we had that narrow squeak from foundering. There you have the proof how silly is the superstitution about them. They leave a good ship for an old rotten hulk, where there is nothing to eat, too, the fools! . . . I don't believe they know what is safe or what is good for them, any more than you or I.'

"And after some more talk we agreed that the wisdom of rats had been grossly overrated, being in fact no greater than that of men.

"The story of the ship was known, by this, all up the Channel from Land's End to the Forelands, and we could get no crew on the south coast. They sent us one all complete from Liverpool, and we left once more—for Bankok.

"We had fair breezes, smooth water right into the tropics, and the old *Judea* lumbered along in the sunshine. When she went eight knots every-thing cracked aloft, and we tied our caps to our heads; but mostly she strolled on at the rate of three miles an hour. What could you expect? She was tired—that old ship. Her youth was where mine is—where yours is—you fellows who listen to this yarn; and what friend would throw your years and your weariness in your face? We didn't grumble at her. To us aft, at least, it seemed as though we had been born in her, reared in her, had lived in her for ages, had never known any other ship. I would just as soon have abused the old village church at home for not being a cathedral.

"And for me there was also my youth to make me patient. There was all the East before me, and all life, and the thought that I had been tried in that ship and had come out pretty well. And I thought of men of old who, centuries ago, went that road in ships that sailed no better, to the land of palms, and spices, and yellow sands, and of brown nations ruled by kings more cruel than Nero the Roman, and more splendid than Solomon the Jew. The old bark lumbered on, heavy with her age and the burden of her cargo, while I lived the life of youth in ignorance and hope. She lumbered on through an interminable procession of days; and the fresh gilding flashed back at the setting sun, seemed to cry out over the darkening sea the words painted on her stern, '*Judea*, London. Do or Die.'

"Then we entered the Indian Ocean and steered northerly for Java Head. The winds were light. Weeks slipped by . She crawled on, do or die, and people at home began to think of posting us as overdue.

"One Saturday evening, I being off duty, the men asked me to give them an extra bucket of water or so—for washing clothes. As I did not wish to screw on the fresh-water pump so late, I went forward whistling, and with a key in my hand to unlock the forepeak scuttle,[31] intending to serve the water out of a spare tank we kept there.

"The smell down below was as unexpected as it was frightful. One would have thought hundreds of paraffin-lamps had been flaring and smoking in that hole for days. I was glad to get out. The man with me coughed and said, 'Funny smell, sir.' I answered negligently, 'It's good for the health they say,' and walked aft.

"The first thing I did was to put my head down the square of the midship ventilator. As I lifted the lid a visible breath, something like a thin fog, a puff of faint haze, rose from the opening. The ascending air was hot, and had a heavy, sooty, paraffiny smell. I gave one sniff, and put down the lid gently. It was no use choking myself. The cargo was on fire.

"Next day she began to smoke in earnest. You see it was to be expected, for though the coal was of a safe kind, that cargo had been so handled, so broken up with handling, that it looked more like smithy coal than anything else. Then it had been wetted—more than once. It rained all the time we were taking it back from the hulk, and now with this long passage it got heated, and there was another case of spontaneous combustion.

"The captain called us into the cabin. He had a chart spread on the table, and looked uphappy. He said, 'The coast of West Australia is near, but I mean to proceed to our destination. It is the hurricane month, too; but we will just keep her head for Bankok, and fight the fire. No more putting back anywhere, if we all get roasted. We will try first to stifle this 'ere damned combustion by want of air.'

"We tried. We battened down everything, and still she smoked. The smoke kept coming out through imperceptible crevices; it forced itself through bulkheads and covers; it oozed here and there and everywhere in slender threads, in an invisible film, in an incomprehensible manner. It made its way into the cabin, into the forecastle; it poisoned the sheltered places on the deck, it could be sniffed as high as the mainyard.[32] It was clear that if the smoke came out the air came in. This was disheartening. This combustion refused to be stifled.

"We resolved to try water, and took the hatches off. Enormous volumes of smoke, whitish, yellowish, thick, greasy, misty, choking, ascended as high as the trucks. All hands cleared out aft. Then the poisonous cloud blew away, and we went back to work in a smoke that was no thicker now than that of an ordinary factory chimney.

[31] Hole or hatch in the deck.
[32] Cross-piece fastened in the middle to the mainmast and used to spread the mainsail.

"We rigged the force-pump, got the hose along, and by and by it burst. Well, it was as old as the ship—a prehistoric hose, and past repair. Then we pumped with the feeble head-pump, drew water with buckets, and in this way managed in time to pour lots of Indian Ocean into the main hatch. The bright stream flashed in sunshine, fell into a layer of white crawling smoke, and vanished on the black surface of coal. Steam ascended mingling with the smoke. We poured salt water as into a barrel without a bottom. It was our fate to pump in that ship, to pump out of her, to pump into her; and after keeping water out of her to save ourselves from being drowned, we frantically poured water into her to save ourselves from being burnt.

"And she crawled on, do or die, in the serene weather. The sky was a miracle of purity, a miracle of azure. The sea was polished, was blue, was pellucid, was sparkling like a precious stone, extending on all sides, all around to the horizon—as if the whole terrestrial globe had been one jewel, one colossal sapphire, a single gem fashioned into a planet. And on the lustre of the great calm waters the *Judea* glided imperceptibly, enveloped in languid and unclean vapours, in a lazy cloud that drifted to leeward, light and slow; a pestiferous cloud defiling the splendour of sea and sky.

"All this time of course we saw no fire. The cargo smouldered at the bottom somewhere. Once Mahon, as we were working side by side, said to me with a queer smile: 'Now, if she only would spring a tidy leak—like that time when we first left the Channel—it would put a stopper on this fire. Wouldn't it?' I remarked irrelevantly, 'Do you remember the rats?'

"We fought the fire and sailed the ship too as carefully as though nothing had been the matter. The steward cooked and attended on us. Of the other twelve men, eight worked while four rested. Everyone took his turn, captain included. There was equality, and if not exactly fraternity, then a deal of good feeling. Sometimes a man, as he dashed a bucketful of water down the hatchway, would yell out, 'Hurrah for Bankok!' and the rest laughed. But generally we were taciturn and serious—and thirsty. Oh! how thirsty! And we had to be careful with the water. Strict allowance. The ship smoked, the sun blazed. . . . Pass the bottle.

"We tried everything. We even made an attempt to dig down to the fire. No good, of course. No man could remain more than a minute below. Mahon, who went first, fainted there, and the man who went to fetch him out did likewise. We lugged them out on deck. Then I leaped down to show how easily it could be done. They had learned wisdom by that time, and contented themselves by fishing for me with a chainhook tied to a broom-handle, I believe. I did not offer to go and fetch up my shovel, which was left down below.

"Things began to look bad. We put the long-boat into the water. The

81

second boat was ready to swing out. We had also another, a 14-foot thing, on davits[33] aft, where it was quite safe.

"Then, behold, the smoke suddenly decreased. We redoubled our efforts to flood the bottom of the ship. In two days there was no smoke at all. Everybody was on the broad grin. This was on a Friday. On Saturday no work, but sailing the ship of course, was done. The men washed their clothes and their faces for the first time in a fortnight, and had a special dinner given them. They spoke of spontaneous combustion with contempt, and implied *they* were the boys to put out combustions. Somehow we all felt as though we each had inherited a large fortune. But a beastly smell of burning hung about the ship. Captain Beard had hollow eyes and sunken cheeks. I had never noticed so much before how twisted and bowed he was. He and Mahon prowled soberly about hatches and ventilators, sniffing. It struck me suddenly poor Mahon was a very, very old chap. As to me, I was as pleased and proud as though I had helped to win a great naval battle. O! Youth!

"The night was fine. In the morning a homewardbound ship passed us hull down[34]—the first we had seen for months; but we were nearing the land at last, Java Head being about 190 miles off, and nearly due north.

"Next day it was my watch on deck from eight to twelve. At breakfast the captain observed, 'It's wonderful how that smell hangs about the cabin.' About ten, the mate being on the poop, I stepped down on the main-deck for a moment. The carpenter's bench stood abaft[35] the mainmast: I leaned against it sucking at my pipe, and the carpenter, a young chap, came to talk to me. He remarked, 'I think we have done very well, haven't we?' and then I perceived with annoyance the fool was trying to tilt the bench. I said curtly, 'Don't Chips,' and immediately became aware of a queer sensation, of an absurd delusion,—I seemed somehow to be in the air. I heard all round me like a pent-up breath released—as if a thousand giants simultaneously had said Phoo!—and felt a dull concussion which made my ribs ache suddenly. No doubt about it—I was in the air, and my body was describing a short parabola. But short as it was, I had the time to think several thoughts in, as far as I can remember, the following order: 'This can't be the carpenter—What is it?—Some accident—Submarine volcano?—Coals, gas!—By Jove! we are being blown up—Everybody's dead—I am falling into the after-hatch—I see fire in it.'

"The coal-dust suspended in the air of the hold had glowed dull-red at

---

[33] Supports to hold a small boat over a ship's side or stern.
[34] Below the horizon so that sails and masts, but not hull, can be seen.
[35] Behind; on the stern side of.

the moment of the explosion. In the twinkling of an eye, in an infinitesimal fraction of a second since the first tilt of the bench, I was sprawling full length on the cargo. I picked myself up and scrambled out. It was quick like a rebound. The deck was a wilderness of smashed timber, lying cross-wise like trees in a wood after a hurricane; an immense curtain of soiled rags waved gently before me—it was the mainsail blown to strips. I thought, The masts will be toppling over directly; and to get out of the way bolted on all-fours towards the poop-ladder. The first person I saw was Mahon, with eyes like saucers, his mouth open, and the long white hair standing straight on end round his head like a silver halo. He was just about to go down when the sight of the main-deck stirring, heaving up, and changing into splinters before his eyes, petrified him on the top step. I stared at him in unbelief, and he stared at me with a queer kind of shocked curiosity. I did not know that I had no hair, no eyebrows, no eyelashes, that my young moustache was burnt off, that my face was black, one cheek laid open, my nose cut, and my chin bleeding. I had lost my cap, one of my slippers, and my shirt was torn to rags. Of all this I was not aware. I was amazed to see the ship still afloat, the poop-deck whole—and, most of all, to see anybody alive. Also the peace of the sky and the serenity of the sea were distinctly surprising. I suppose I expected to see them convulsed with horror. . . . Pass the bottle.

"There was a voice hailing the ship from somewhere—in the air, in the sky—I couldn't tell. Presently I saw the captain—and he was mad. He asked me eagerly, 'Where's the cabin-table?' and to hear such a question was a frightful shock. I had just been blown up, you understand, and vi-brated with that experience,—I wasn't quite sure whether I was alive. Mahon began to stamp with both feet and yelled at him, 'Good God! don't you see the deck's blown out of her?' I found my voice, and stammered out as if conscious of some gross neglect of duty, 'I don't know where the cabin-table is.' It was like an absurd dream.

"Do you know what he wanted next? Well, he wanted to trim the yards.[36] Very placidly, and as if lost in thought, he insisted on having the foreyard squared. 'I don't know if there's anybody alive,' said Mahon, al-most tearfully. 'Surely,' he said, gently, 'there will be enough left to square the foreyard.'

"The old chap, it seems, was in his own berth winding up the chronom-eters, when the shock sent him spinning. Immediately it occurred to him —as he said afterwards—that the ship had struck something, and he ran out into the cabin. There, he saw, the cabin-table had vanished somewhere.

[36] Adjust the sails with reference to the wind.

The deck being blown up, it had fallen down into the lazarette[37] of course. Where we had our breakfast that morning he saw only a great hole in the floor. This appeared to him so awfully mysterious, and impressed him so immensely, that what he saw and heard after he got on deck were mere trifles in comparison. And, mark, he noticed directly the wheel deserted and his barque off her course—and his only thought was to get that miserable, stripped, undecked, smouldering shell of a ship back again with her head pointing at her port of destination. Bankok! That's what he was after. I tell you this quiet, bowed, bandylegged, almost deformed little man was immense in the singleness of his idea and in his placid ignorance of our agitation. He motioned us forward with a commanding gesture, and went to take the wheel himself.

"Yes; that was the first thing we did—trim the yards of that wreck! No one was killed, or even disabled, but everyone was more or less hurt. You should have seen them! Some were in rags, with black faces, like coal-heavers, like sweeps, and had bullet heads that seemed closely cropped, but were in fact singed to the skin. Others, of the watch below, awakened by being shot out from their collapsing bunks, shivered incessantly, and kept on groaning even as we went about our work. But they all worked. That crew of Liverpool hard cases had in them the right stuff. It's my experience they always have. It is the sea that gives it—the vastness, the loneliness surrounding their dark stolid souls. Ah! Well! we stumbled, we crept, we fell, we barked our shins on the wreckage, we hauled. The masts stood, but we did not know how much they might be charred down below. It was nearly calm, but a long swell ran from the west and made her roll. They might go at any moment. We looked at them with apprehension. One could not foresee which way they would fall.

"Then we retreated aft and looked about us. The deck was a tangle of planks on edge, of planks on end, of splinters, of ruined woodwork. The masts rose from that chaos like big trees above a matted undergrowth. The interstices of that mass of wreckage were full of something whitish, sluggish, stirring—of something that was like a greasy fog. The smoke of the invisible fire was coming up again, was trailing, like a poisonous thick mist in some valley choked with dead wood. Already lazy wisps were beginning to curl upwards amongst the mass of splinters. Here and there a piece of timber, stuck upright, resembled a post. Half of a fife-rail[38] had been shot through the foresail, and the sky made a patch of glorious blue in the ignobly soiled canvas. A portion of several boards holding together had fallen across the rail, and one end protruded overboard, like a gangway

---

[37] Space between decks, used as a storeroom.
[38] Rail around a mast, fitted with belaying pins for securing lines.

leading upon nothing, like a gangway leading over the deep sea, leading to death—as if inviting us to walk the plank at once and be done with our ridiculous troubles. And still the air, the sky—a ghost, something invisible was hailing the ship.

"Someone had the sense to look over, and there was the helmsman,[39] who had impulsively jumped overboard, anxious to come back. He yelled and swam lustily like a merman, keeping up with the ship. We threw him a rope, and presently he stood amongst us streaming with water and very crestfallen. The captain had surrendered the wheel, and apart, elbow on rail and chin in hand, gazed at the sea wistfully. We asked ourselves, What next? I thought, Now, this is something like. This is great. I wonder what will happen. O youth!

"Suddenly Mahon sighted a steamer far astern. Captain Beard said, 'We may do something with her yet.' We hoisted two flags, which said in the international language of the sea, 'On fire. Want immediate assistance.' The steamer grew bigger rapidly, and by and by spoke with two flags on her foremast, 'I am coming to your assistance.'

"In half an hour she was abreast, to windward, within hail, and rolling slightly, with her engines stopped. We lost our composure, and yelled all together with excitement, 'We've been blown up'. A man in a white helmet, on the bridge, cried, 'Yes! All right! all right!' and he nodded his head, and smiled, and made soothing motions with his hand as though at a lot of frightened children. One of the boats dropped in the water, and walked towards us upon the sea with her long oars. Four Calashes pulled a swinging stroke. This was my first sight of Malay seamen. I've known them since, but what struck me then was their unconcern: they came alongside, and even the bowman standing up and holding to our main-chains with the boat-hook did not deign to lift his head for a glance. I thought people who had been blown up deserved more attention.

"A little man, dry like a chip and agile like a monkey, clambered up. It was the mate of the steamer. He gave one look, and cried, 'O boys—you had better quit.'

"We were silent. He talked apart with the captain for a time,—seemed to argue with him. Then they went away together to the steamer.

"When our skipper came back we learned that the steamer was the *Somerville,* Captain Nash, from West Australia to Singapore *via* Batavia with mails, and that the agreement was she should tow us to Anjer or Batavia, if possible, where we could extinguish the fire by scuttling,[40] and then proceed on our voyage—to Bankok! The old man seemed excited.

[39] Man who steers the ship.
[40] Boring holes in the ship to let in water.

'We will do it yet,' he said to Mahon, fiercely. He shook his fist at the sky. Nobody else said a word.

"At noon the steamer began to tow. She went ahead slim and high, and what was left of the *Judea* followed at the end of seventy fathom of tow-rope,—followed her swiftly like a cloud of smoke with mast-heads protruding above. We went aloft to furl[41] the sails. We coughed on the yards,[42] and were careful about the bunts.[43] Do you see the lot of us there, putting a neat furl on the sails of that ship doomed to arrive nowhere? There was not a man who didn't think that at any moment the masts would topple over. From aloft we could not see the ship for smoke, and they worked carefully, passing the gaskets with even turns. 'Harbour furl—aloft there!' cried Mahon from below.

"You understand this? I don't think one of those chaps expected to get down in the usual way. When we did I heard them saying to each other, 'Well, I thought we would come down overboard, in a lump—sticks and all—blame me if I didn't.' 'That's what I was thinking to myself,' would answer wearily another battered and bandaged scarecrow. And, mind, these were men without the drilled-in habit of obedience. To an onlooker they would be a lot of profane scallywags without a redeeming point. What made them do it—what made them obey me when I, thinking consciously how fine it was, made them drop the bunt of the foresail twice to try and do it better? What? They had no professional reputation—no examples, no praise. It wasn't a sense of duty; they all knew well enough how to shirk, and laze, and dodge—when they had a mind to it—and mostly they had. Was it the two pounds ten a-month that sent them there? They didn't think their pay half good enough. No; it was something in them, something inborn and subtle and everlasting. I don't say positively that the crew of a French or German merchantman wouldn't have done it, but I doubt whether it would have been done in the same way. There was a completeness in it, something solid like a principle, and masterful like an instinct—a disclosure of something secret—of that hidden something, that gift of good or evil that makes racial difference, that shapes the fate of nations.

"It was that night at ten that, for the first time since we had been fighting it, we saw the fire. The speed of the towing had fanned the smouldering destruction. A blue gleam appeared forward, shining below the wreck of the deck. It wavered in patches, it seemed to stir and creep like the light of a glowworm. I saw it first, and told Mahon. 'Then the game's up,' he said. 'We had better stop this towing, or she will burst out suddenly fore

[41] Roll up (sails) snugly on yards or booms, and secure them.
[42] Cross-pieces on the masts, by which the sails are fully spread.
[43] Middle parts of the sails.

and aft before we can clear out.' We set up a yell; rang bells to attract their attention; they towed on. At last Mahon and I had to crawl forward and cut the rope with an axe. There was no time to cast off the lashings. Red tongues could be seen licking the wilderness of splinters under our feet as we made our way back to the poop.

"Of course they very soon found out in the steamer that the rope was gone. She gave a loud blast of her whistle, her lights were seen sweeping in a wide circle, she came up ranging close along-side, and stopped. We were all in a tight group on the poop looking at her. Every man had saved a little bundle or a bag. Suddenly a conical flame with a twisted top shot up forward and threw upon the black sea a circle of light, with the two vessels side by side and heaving gently in its centre. Captain Beard had been sitting on the gratings still and mute for hours, but now he rose slowly and advanced in front of us, to the mizzen-shrouds.[44] Captain Nash hailed: 'Come along! Look sharp. I have mail-bags on board. I will take you and your boats to Singapore.'

" 'Thank you! No!' said our skipper. 'We must see the last of the ship.'

" 'I can't stand by any longer,' shouted the other, 'Mails—you know.'

" 'Ay! ay! We are all right.'

" 'Very well! I'll report you in Singapore. . . Good-bye!'

"He waved his hand. Our men dropped their bundles quietly. The steamer moved ahead, and passing out of the circle of light, vanished at once from our sight, dazzled by the fire which burned fiercely. And then I knew that I would see the East first as commander of a small boat. I thought it fine; and the fidelity to the old ship was fine. We should see the last of her. Oh, the glamour of youth! Oh, the fire of it, more dazzling than the flames of the burning ship, throwing a magic light on the wide earth, leaping audaciously to the sky, presently to be quenched by time, more cruel, more pitiless, more bitter than the sea—and like the flames of the burning ship surrounded by an impenetrable night.

•   •   •

"The old man warned us in his gentle and inflexible way that it was part of our duty to save for the underwriters as much as we could of the ship's gear. Accordingly we went to work aft, while she blazed forward to give us plenty of light. We lugged out a lot of rubbish. What didn't we save? An old barometer fixed with an absurd quantity of screws nearly cost me my life: a sudden rush of smoke came upon me, and I just got away in time. There were various stores, bolts of canvas, coils of rope; the poop

---

44 Lines supporting the mizzen-mast (mast nearest the stern).

looked like a marine bazaar, and the boats were lumbered to the gunwales.[45] One would have thought the old man wanted to take as much as he could of his first command with him. He was very, very quiet, but off his balance evidently. Would you believe it? He wanted to take a length of old steam-cable and a kedge-anchor with him in the long-boat. We said, 'Ay, ay, sir,' deferentially, and on the quiet let the things slip overboard. The heavy medicine-chest went that way, two bags of green coffee, tins of paint—fancy, paint!—a whole lot of things. Then I was ordered with two hands into the boats to make a stowage and get them ready against the time it would be proper for us to leave the ship.

"We put everything straight, stepped the long-boat's mast[46] for our skipper, who was to take charge of her, and I was not sorry to sit down for a moment. My face felt raw, every limb ached as if broken, I was aware of all my ribs, and would have sworn to a twist in the backbone. The boats, fast astern, lay in a deep shadow, and all around I could see the circle of the sea lighted by the fire. A gigantic flame arose forward straight and clear. It flared fierce, with noises like the whirr of wings, with rumbles as of thunder. There were cracks, detonations, and from the cone of flame the sparks flew upwards, as man is born to trouble, to leaky ships, and to ships that burn.

"What bothered me was that the ship, lying broadside to the swell and to such wind as there was—a mere breath—the boats would not keep astern where they were safe, but persisted, in a pig-headed way boats have, in getting under the counter and then swinging alongside. They were knocking about dangerously and coming near the flame, while the ship rolled on them, and, of course, there was always the danger of the masts going over the side at any moment. I and my two boat-keepers kept them off as best we could, with oars and boat-hooks; but to be constantly at it became exasperating, since there was no reason why we should not leave at once. We could not see those on board, nor could we imagine what caused the delay. The boat-keepers were swearing feebly, and I had not only my share of the work but also had to keep at it two men who showed a constant inclination to lay themselves down and let things slide.

"At last I hailed, 'On deck there,' and someone looked over. 'We're ready here,' I said. The head disappeared, and very soon popped up again. 'The captain says, All right, sir, and to keep the boats well clear of the ship.'

"Half an hour passed. Suddenly there was a frightful racket, rattle, clanking of chain, hiss of water, and millions of sparks flew up into the

[45] Filled to the brim.
[46] Erected the mast; that is, placed the heel, or butt, of the mast into a block secured to the keel.

shivering column of smoke that stood leaning slightly above the ship. The cat-heads[47] had burned away, and the two red-hot anchors had gone to the bottom, tearing out after them two hundred fathom of red-hot chain. The ship trembled, the mass of flame swayed as if ready to collapse, and the fore top-gallant-mast[48] fell. It darted down like an arrow of fire, shot under, and instantly leaping up within an oar's-length of the boats, floated quietly, very black on the luminous sea. I hailed the deck again. After some time a man in an unexpectedly cheerful but also muffled tone, as though he had been trying to speak with his mouth shut, informed me, 'Coming directly, sir,' and vanished. For a long time I heard nothing but the whirr and roar of the fire. There were also whistling sounds. The boats jumped, tugged at the painters, ran at each other playfully, knocked their sides together, or, do what we would, swung in a bunch against the ship's side. I couldn't stand it any longer, and swarming up a rope, clambered aboard over the stern.

"It was as bright as day. Coming up like this, the sheet of fire facing me was a terrifying sight, and the heat seemed hardly bearable at first. On a settee cushion dragged out of the cabin Captain Beard, his legs drawn up and one arm under his head, slept with the light playing on him. Do you know what the rest were busy about? They were sitting on deck right aft, round an open case, eating bread and cheese and drinking bottled stout.

"On the background of flames twisting in fierce tongues above their heads they seemed at home like salamanders, and looked like a band of desperate pirates. The fire sparkled in the whites of their eyes, gleamed on patches of white skin seen through the torn shirts. Each had the marks as of a battle about him—bandaged heads, tied-up arms, a strip of dirty rag round a knee—and each man had a bottle between his legs and a chunk of cheese in his hand. Mahon got up. With his handsome and disreputable head, his hooked profile, his long white beard, and with an uncorked bottle in his hand, he resembled one of those reckless sea-robbers of old making merry amidst violence and disaster. 'The last meal on board,' he explained solemnly. 'We had nothing to eat all day, and it was no use leaving all this.' He flourished the bottle and indicated the sleeping skipper. 'He said he couldn't swallow anything, so I got him to lie down,' he went on; and as I stared, 'I don't know whether you are aware, young fellow, the man had no sleep to speak of for days—and there will be dam' little sleep in the boats.' 'There will be no boats by-and-by if you fool about much longer,' I said, indignantly. I walked up to the skipper and shook

[47] Projecting timbers for supporting the anchors.
[48] Mast supporting the third sail above the deck.

him by the shoulder. At last he opened his eyes, but did not move. 'Time to leave her, sir,' I said quietly.

"He got up painfully, looked at the flames, at the sea sparkling round the ship, and black, black as ink farther away; he looked at the stars shining dim through a thin veil of smoke in a sky black, black as Erebus.[49]

" 'Youngest first,' he said.

"And the ordinary seaman, wiping his mouth with the back of his hand, got up, clambered over the taffrail,[50] and vanished. Others followed. One, on the point of going over, stopped short to drain his bottle, and with a great swing of his arm flung it at the fire. 'Take this!' he cried.

"The skipper lingered disconsolately, and we left him to commune alone for a while with his first command. Then I went up again and brought him away at last. It was time. The ironwork on the poop was hot to the touch.

"Then the painter of the long-boat was cut, and the three boats, tied together, drifted clear of the ship. It was just sixteen hours after the explosion when we abandoned her. Mahon had charge of the second boat, and I had the smallest—the 14-foot thing. The long-boat would have taken the lot of us; but the skipper said we must save as much property as we could—for the underwriters—and so I got my first command. I had two men with me, a bag of biscuits, a few tins of meat, and a breaker of water. I was ordered to keep close to the long-boat, that in case of bad weather we might be taken into her.

"And do you know what I thought? I thought I would part company as soon as I could. I wanted to have my first command all to myself. I wasn't going to sail in a squadron if there were a chance for independent cruising. I would make land by myself. I would beat the other boats. Youth! All youth! The silly, charming, beautiful youth.

"But we did not make a start at once. We must see the last of the ship. And so the boats drifted about that night, heaving and setting on the swell. The men dozed, waked, sighed, groaned. I looked at the burning ship.

"Between the darkness of earth and heaven she was burning fiercely upon a disc of purple sea shot by the blood-red play of gleams; upon a disc of water glittering and sinister. A high, clear flame, an immense and lonely flame, ascended from the ocean, and from its summit the black smoke poured continuously at the sky. She burned furiously; mournful and imposing like a funeral pile kindled in the night, surrounded by the sea, watched over by the stars. A magnificent death had come like a grace, like a gift, like a reward to that old ship at the end of her laborious days. The

[49] Mythical region of darkness, between Earth and Hades.
[50] Rail around a ship's stern.

surrender of her weary ghost to the keeping of stars and sea was stirring like the sight of a glorious triumph. The masts fell just before daybreak, and for a moment there was a burst and turmoil of sparks that seemed to fill with flying fire the night patient and watchful, the vast night lying silent upon the sea. At daylight she was only a charred shell, floating still under a cloud of smoke and bearing a glowing mass of coal within.

"Then the oars were got out, and the boats forming in a line moved round her remains as if in procession—the long-boat leading. As we pulled across her stern a slim dart of fire shot out viciously at us, and suddenly she went down, head first, in a great hiss of steam. The unconsumed stern was the last to sink; but the paint had gone, had cracked, had peeled off, and there were no letters, there was no word, no stubborn device that was like her soul, to flash at the rising sun her creed and her name.

"We made our way north. A breeze sprang up, and about noon all the boats came together for the last time. I had no mast or sail in mine, but I made a mast out of a spare oar and hoisted a boat-awning for a sail, with a boat-hook for a yard. She was certainly over-masted,[51] but I had the satisfaction of knowing that with the wind aft I could beat the other two. I had to wait for them. Then we all had a look at the captain's chart, and, after a sociable meal of hard bread and water, got our last instructions. These were simple: steer north, and keep together as much as possible. 'Be careful with that jury-rig,[52] Marlow,' said the captain; and Mahon, as I sailed proudly past his boat, wrinkled his curved nose and hailed, 'You will sail that ship of yours under water, if you don't look out, young fellow.' He was a malicious old man—and may the deep sea where he sleeps now rock him gently, rock him tenderly to the end of time!

"Before sunset a thick rain-squall passed over the two boats, which were far astern, and that was the last I saw of them for a time. Next day I sat steering my cockle-shell—my first command—with nothing but water and sky around me. I did sight in the afternoon the upper sails of a ship far away, but said nothing, and my men did not notice her. You see I was afraid she might be homeward bound, and I had no mind to turn back from the portals of the East. I was steering for Java—another blessed name —like Bankok, you know. I steered many days.

"I need not tell you what it is to be knocking about in an open boat. I remember nights and days of calm, when we pulled, we pulled, and the boat seemed to stand still, as if bewitched within the circle of the sea horizon. I remember the heat, the deluge of rainsqualls that kept us baling for

---

51 Having too high a mast for the size of the boat.
52 Temporary, make-shift mast and sail.

dear life (but filled our water-cask), and I remember sixteen hours on end with a mouth dry as a cinder and a steering-oar over the stern to keep my first command head on to a breaking sea. I did not know how good a man I was till then. I remember the drawn faces, the dejected figures of my two men, and I remember my youth and the feeling that will never come back any more—the feeling that I could last for ever, outlast the sea, the earth, and all men; the deceitful feeling that lures us on to joys, to perils, to love, to vain effort—to death; the triumphant conviction of strength, the heat of life in the handful of dust, the glow in the heart that with every year grows dim, grows cold, grows small, and expires—and expires, too soon, too soon—before life itself.

"And this is how I see the East. I have seen its secret places and have looked into its very soul; but now I see it always from a small boat, a high outline of mountains, blue and afar in the morning; like faint mist at noon; a jagged wall of purple at sunset. I have the feel of the oar in my hand, the vision of a scorching blue sea in my eyes. And I see a bay, a wide bay, smooth as glass and polished like ice, shimmering in the dark. A red light burns far off upon the gloom of the land, and the night is soft and warm. We drag at the oars with aching arms, and suddenly a puff of wind, a puff faint and tepid and laden with strange odours of blossoms, of aromatic wood, comes out of the still night—the first sigh of the East on my face. That I can never forget. It was impalpable and enslaving, like a charm, like a whispered promise of mysterious delight.

"We had been pulling this finishing spell for eleven hours. Two pulled, and he whose turn it was to rest sat at the tiller. We had made out the red light in that bay and steered for it, guessing it must mark some small coasting port. We passed two vessels, outlandish and high-sterned, sleeping at anchor, and, approaching the light, now very dim, ran the boat's nose against the end of a jutting wharf. We were blind with fatigue. My men dropped the oars and fell off the thwarts[53] as if dead. I made fast to a pile. A current rippled softly. The scented obscurity of the shore was grouped into vast masses, a density of colossal clumps of vegetation, probably— mute and fantastic shapes. And at their foot the semicircle of a beach gleamed faintly, like an illusion. There was not a light, not a stir, not a sound. The mysterious East faced me, perfumed like a flower, silent like death, dark like a grave.

"And I sat weary beyond expression, exulting like a conqueror, sleepless and entranced as if before a profound, a fateful enigma.

"A splashing of oars, a measured dip reverberating on the level of water, intensified by the silence of the shore into loud claps, made me jump up.

---

[53] Seats across the boat, on which the oarsmen sit.

A boat, a European boat, was coming in. I invoked the name of the dead; I hailed: *Judea* ahoy! A thin shout answered.

"It was the captain. I had beaten the flagship by three hours, and I was glad to hear the old man's voice again, tremulous and tired. 'Is it you, Marlow?' 'Mind the end of that jetty, sir,' I cried.

"He approached cautiously, and brought up with the deep-sea lead-line which we had saved—for the underwriters. I eased my painter and fell alongside. He sat, a broken figure at the stern, wet with dew, his hands clasped in his lap. His men were asleep already. 'I had a terrible time of it,' he murmured. 'Mahon is behind—not very far.' We conversed in whispers, in low whispers, as if afraid to wake up the land. Guns, thunder, earthquakes would not have awakened the men just then.

"Looking round as we talked, I saw away at sea a bright light travelling in the night. 'There's a steamer passing the bay,' I said. She was not passing, she was entering, and she even came close and anchored. 'I wish,' said the old man, 'you would find out whether she is English. Perhaps they could give us a passage somewhere.' He seemed nervously anxious. So by dint of punching and kicking I started one of my men into a state of somnambulism, and giving him an oar, took another and pulled towards the lights of the steamer.

"There was a murmur of voices in her, metallic hollow clangs of the engine-room, footsteps on the deck. Her ports shone, round like dilated eyes. Shapes moved about, and there was a shadowy man high up on the bridge. He heard my oars.

"And then, before I could open my lips, the East spoke to me, but it was in a Western voice. A torrent of words was poured into the enigmatical, the fateful silence; outlandish, angry words, mixed with words and even whole sentences of good English, less strange but even more surprising. The voice swore and cursed violently; it riddled the solemn peace of the bay by a volley of abuse. It began by calling me Pig, and from that went crescendo into unmentionable adjectives—in English. The man up there raged aloud in two languages, and with a sincerity in his fury that almost convinced me I had, in some way, sinned against the harmony of the universe. I could hardly see him, but began to think he would work himself into a fit.

"Suddenly he ceased, and I could hear him snorting and blowing like a porpoise. I said—

" 'What steamer is this, pray?'

" 'Eh? What's this? And who are you?'

" 'Castaway crew of an English barque burnt at sea. We came here to-night. I am the second mate. The captain is in the long-boat, and wishes to know if you would give up a passage somewhere.'

93

" 'Oh, my goodness! I say. . . . This is the *Celestial* from Singapore on her return trip. I'll arrange with your captain in the morning, . . . and, . . . I say, . . . did you hear me just now?'

" 'I should think the whole bay heard you.'

" 'I thought you were a shore-boat. Now, look here—this infernal lazy scoundrel of a caretaker has gone to sleep again—curse him. The light is out, and I nearly ran foul of the end of this damned jetty. This is the third time he plays me this trick. Now, I ask you, can anybody stand this kind of thing? It's enough to drive a man out of his mind. I'll report him. . . . I'll get the Assistant Resident to give him the sack, by . . . ! See—there's no light. It's out, isn't it? I take you to witness the light's out. There should be a light, you know. A red light on the——'

" 'There was a light,' I said, mildly.

" 'But it's out, man! What's the use of talking like this? You can see for yourself it's out—don't you? If you had to take a valuable steamer along this God-forsaken coast you would want a light, too. I'll kick him from end to end of his miserable wharf. You'll see if I don't. I will——'

" 'So I may tell my captain you'll take us?' I broke in.

" 'Yes, I'll take you. Good-night,' he said, brusquely.

"I pulled back, made fast again to the jetty, and then went to sleep at last. I had faced the silence of the East. I had heard some of its language. But when I opened my eyes again the silence was as complete as though it had never been broken. I was lying in a flood of light, and the sky had never looked so far, so high, before. I opened my eyes and lay without moving.

"And then I saw the men of the East—they were looking at me. The whole length of the jetty was full of people. I saw brown, bronze, yellow faces, the black eyes, the glitter, the colour of an Eastern crowd. And all these beings stared without a murmur, without a sigh, without a movement. They stared down at the boats, at the sleeping men who at night had come to them from the sea. Nothing moved. The fronds of palms stood still against the sky. Not a branch stirred along the shore, and the brown roofs of hidden houses peeped through the green foliage, through the big leaves that hung shining and still like leaves forged of heavy metal. This was the East of the ancient navigators, so old, so mysterious, resplendent and sombre, living and unchanged, full of danger and promise. And these were the men. I sat up suddenly. A wave of movement passed through the crowd from end to end, passed along the heads, swayed the bodies, ran along the jetty like a ripple on the water, like a breath of wind on a field— and all was still again. I see it now—the wide sweep of the bay, the glitter- ing sands, the wealth of green infinite and varied, the sea blue like the sea of a dream, the crowd of attentive faces, the blaze of vivid colour—the

94

water reflecting it all, the curve of the shore, the jetty, the high-sterned outlandish craft floating still, and the three boats with the tired men from the
West sleeping, unconscious of the land and the people and of the violence
of sunshine. They slept thrown across the thwarts, curled on bottom-boards,
in the careless attitudes of death. The head of the old skipper, leaning back
in the stern of the long-boat, had fallen on his breast, and he looked as
though he would never wake. Farther out old Mahon's face was upturned
to the sky, with the long white beard spread out on his breast, as though
he had been shot where he sat at the tiller; and a man, all in a heap in the
bows of the boat, slept with both arms embracing the stem-head and with
his cheek laid on the gunwale. The East looked at them without a sound.

"I have known its fascination since; I have seen the mysterious shores,
the still water, the lands of brown nations, where a stealthy Nemesis[54] lies
in wait, pursues, overtakes so many of the conquering race, who are proud
of their wisdom, of their knowledge, of their strength. But for me all the
East is contained in that vision of my youth. It is all in that moment when
I opened my young eyes on it. I came upon it from a tussle with the sea—
and I was young—and I saw it looking at me. And this is all that is left
of it! Only a moment; a moment of strength, of romance, of glamour—of
youth! . . . A flick of sunshine upon a strange shore, the time to remember,
the time for a sigh, and—good-bye!—Night—Good-bye . . . !"

He drank.

"Ah! The good old time—the good old time. Youth and the sea.
Glamour and the sea! The good, strong sea, the salt, bitter sea, that could
whisper to you and roar at you and knock your breath out of you."

He drank again.

"By all that's wonderful it is the sea, I believe, the sea itself—or is it
youth alone? Who can tell? But you here—you all had something out of
life: money, love—whatever one gets on shore—and, tell me, wasn't that
the best time, that time when we were young at sea; young and had nothing, on the sea that gives nothing, except hard knocks—and sometimes a
chance to feel your strength—that only—what you all regret?"

And we all nodded at him: the man of finance, the man of accounts, the
man of law, we all nodded at him over the polished table that like a still
sheet of brown water reflected our faces, lined, wrinkled; our faces marked
by toil, by deceptions, by success, by love; our weary eyes looking still,
looking always, looking anxiously for something out of life, that while it
is expected is already gone—has passed unseen, in a sigh, in a flash—together with the youth, with the strength, with the romance of illusions.

---

[54] Retribution, destruction. (Greek goddess of vengeance or retributive justice.)

"Youth" is a feat of memory. It is a record of experience; but that experience, in its facts, in its inwardness and in its outward colouring, begins and ends in myself.

—Joseph Conrad

But initiation is so closely linked to the mode of being of human existence that a considerable number of modern man's acts and gestures continue to repeat initiatory scenarios. Very often the "struggle for life," the "ordeals" and "difficulties" that stand in the way of a vocation or a career, in some sort reiterate the ordeals of initiation; it is after the "blows" that are dealt him, the moral and even physical "suffering" and "torture" he undergoes, that a young man "proves himself," knows his possibilities, grows conscious of his powers, and finally becomes himself, spiritually adult and creative (the spirituality is, of course, what is understood as such in the modern world.) For every human existence is formed by a series of ordeals, by repeated experience of "death" and "resurrection." And this is why, in a religious perspective, existence is established by initiation; it could almost be said that, in so far as human existence is fulfilled, it is itself an initiation.

—Mircea Eliade
The Sacred and the Profane: The Nature of Religion
trans. Willard R. Trask
New York: Harcourt, Brace and World, Inc., 1959, pp. 208–209.

In Conrad's Wake:
The Reader as Voyager

Perhaps it is just as well to begin by establishing an understanding about the assumptions underlying the relationship between writer and reader. What can they legitimately expect of each other? The reader can expect that the writer knows his craft and will use it to communicate something entertaining or informative; he cannot legitimately expect the writer to write for him alone. The writer's audience is not one reader. The writer, on the other hand, can expect that his readers have enough experience in life to understand various common human situations, and enough experience in literature to understand common ways of portraying these situations; he is not entitled to expect his readers to be familiar with a particular part of the world or a particular style of living. (These are the very things, more often than not, that he is trying to communicate to them—the unfamiliar in terms of the familiar.)

The writer's expectations about his readers lead him to take certain things for granted: that he need not explain, for example, each time he writes a story, what approach or techniques or devices he has decided to use. He assumes that his readers will have encountered these or similar methods in other stories and will know how to understand them here. He himself has become an experienced reader before he has turned to writing, and he supposes (unless he is writing children's stories) that he may justly address his readers as equals, as fellow voyagers on a parallel course, or only a short distance in his wake.

In this discourse among equals, much is taken for granted, and a novice voyager, at sea for the first time or new to this particular area, may for a time find certain terms and practices puzzling. When he does, he turns naturally to the experienced voyager for explanations—that is, to the experienced reader. In reading, as in every other area of human activity, experience counts for much. The difference between an experienced reader and an inexperienced one may be as great as the difference between a yachtsman who has sailed for thirty years on the open seas in all weather and the weekend sailor who enjoys sailing his twelve-foot catboat around a nearby lake when the weather is good. The weekend sailor may some day go to sea in a bigger boat; but if he hasn't "learned the ropes" from veteran seamen before he sets out, he should not be surprised if he runs aground on the first reef.

Experience in literature means reading widely, of course; it also means reading closely, thoughtfully. It means reading what other readers have thought about various pieces of literature. It means reading what writers have said about their own work. It may mean doing some writing oneself. The experienced reader, then, is in the position to make some generalizations about literature—some conclusions about the kinds of things that have gone on in what he has read in the past, and some assumptions about what is likely to go on in what he reads next. These conclusions and assumptions are as valid and as useful as the laws and hypotheses of science. However, since literary people—writers, readers, teachers, critics—are likely to be impatient with a rigid methodology, the principles by which they operate are not very often found neatly expressed in a formula (as, for example, "The period covered by the action of a play should be no more than twenty-four hours"). True, criticism has sometimes codified such rules, but writers have generally been as anxious to break them as to follow them. Besides, the rules change from generation to generation, and there are often several sets of rules being used concurrently. So reading is partly a matter of perceiving what sort of rules, or "conventions," a particular writer is following.

Most of the conventions that Conrad accepts are fairly simple and familiar ones—for example, the convention that the narrator of the story is an actual person, and that the events he is relating are true. This is a fiction that we agree to accept in order to "believe in" the story and enjoy it more fully. Children sometimes have trouble understanding how this convention works: they may insist on the literal reality of giants and talking animals, or they may simply reject a story because it's "not true." But adults usually don't have much trouble with what Coleridge called "the willing suspension of disbelief," or with distinguishing between actual fact and realistic fiction. There are, however, conventions that are less familiar and less generally acceptable. Some readers, of course, dislike all fiction. ("If it isn't true, why read it?") Others like realistic fiction, but reject fantasy. ("Who can care about hobbits?") Many readers reject the notion that a writer would say one thing and mean another—that he would use metaphor or symbol. ("That story means just what it says, and nothing more.") Here, then, is where we need to have an understanding.

98

The fact is that Joseph Conrad is one writer who often writes metaphorically, or symbolically. There are other conventions common to his stories, but this is the one most likely to cause trouble. Not to every reader, of course. To some readers what Conrad is doing is perfectly obvious; there is no question about it. To others, any meaning beyond the literal one is "put in" by the reader. There are two good reasons for thinking that certain nonliteral, metaphorical meanings were intended by Conrad, however. In the first place, they "work"; they make sense; they are consistent with the literal meaning, and they make the story a richer experience. In the second place, Conrad says that he believes literature has a symbolic character:

> I wish at first to put before you a general proposition: that a work of art is very seldom limited to one exclusive meaning and not necessarily tending to a definite conclusion. And this for the reason that the nearer it approaches art, the more it acquires a symbolic character. . . . All the great creations of literature have been symbolic, and in that way have gained in complexity, in power, in depth, and in beauty. . . . (Letter to Barrett H. Clark)

So here is a dimension of "Youth" the reader needs to be aware of. Not that the symbolic meanings are very difficult to see; Conrad's symbols are natural and obvious ones, and some he even calls to our attention: "You fellows know there are those voyages that seem ordered for the illustration of life, that might stand for a symbol of existence." To ignore such symbols as this is to miss most of Conrad's meaning.

The next assumption we need to agree upon is that Conrad as a writer exercises a certain artistry in the way he presents his narrative; he doesn't just say, "Hello; I'm Joseph Conrad and I'd like to tell you about a sea voyage I took as a young man." No, he's more subtle than that. Elsewhere he tells us that "Youth" is about himself ("*Youth* is a feat of memory. It is a record of experience. . . ."), but here he disguises himself as Marlow, as he also does in another story based on his own experience, *Heart of Darkness*. The "I" who introduces "Youth," however, is not Marlow. Who is he, then? Another of Conrad's alter egos? An anonymous and insignificant fiction? It doesn't matter, really. What does matter is *why* Conrad begins the story in this way. And here we come upon the question of strategy. Once we see that a writer has alternatives, that there were other ways he might have done a thing, then we begin to see the artist at work. Now perhaps this is no concern of yours; perhaps you are content to enjoy the story for its own sake and not pry behind the scenes. Very well; you have much already. Only you're stopping at the surface. And one of Conrad's ideas in the story is that surface appearances may be illusory. Since we've embarked together on a voyage of discovery, let's dive below the surface a little—not to catalog in exhaustive detail everything that we can see, but only to note how some of the meanings emerge from the story; or rather, how Conrad the writer makes things happen.

To some extent a writer knows where he's going when he writes a story or poem; but to some extent he always discovers or invents things as he goes along.[1] He is a pathfinder, a trailblazer, making the way clear for the reader who comes after him. Suppose we retrace our route—and Conrad's —once more.

Conrad's Craft

The story-within-a-story device that Conrad uses is not original, but it is useful. It sets between Marlow and the reader another personality— apparently a mature, successful, thoughtful man, who himself has had considerable experience at sea. And he seems to find Marlow's story both instructive and believable; what he does, then, is to function as an advocate for the authenticity of the story and as a guide for our reactions. He influences us by the way he behaves, like a more experienced member of the audience at a theater performance. He helps to create the sober, reflective mood—as do the three other friends of Marlow on the boat. And yet we never hear him (or the others) laughing at the more comical episodes. Why not? Here we have to exercise our judgment. Does Conrad expect us to see the humor unaided? Are we to imagine that Marlow's four listeners never do more than smile quietly? Should Conrad have had this first narrator report his amused reactions to Marlow's tale? We are involved in a matter that touches both our interpretation (understanding) of the story and our critical evaluation of Conrad's craftsmanship.

One thing is clear: Conrad uses his first narrator for certain effects. Exactly how and how well those effects are achieved is a matter for discussion.

The principal narrator, of course, is Marlow. He has been introduced to us by the first narrator, but we haven't been told much about him. We learn what kind of a man he is as he tells his story. Marlow's storytelling manner is quiet, deliberate, reflective, dry—almost monotonous. Exclamation points appear at moments of excitement or wonder, but we can't imagine the pitch or volume of his voice changing very much. Even the comical moments are presented in a poker-faced manner. (Doesn't Marlow

[1] See Robert Frost, "The Figure a Poem Makes," page 273.

see the humor in them, or is he only pretending not to?) A tone of nostalgia envelops the story, a nostalgia arising from Marlow's conviction that "these were the best times" and that they lie far in the past.

Time, which is an important theme in the story, creates a double point of view: that of Marlow, now forty-two, and that of Youth, Marlow at twenty (or Marlow as he remembers himself at twenty). The Youth's view is one of involvement in the trials of life, and it is romantic. Marlow's view is one of detachment from those adventurous times, and his attitude is definitely anti-romantic. Is Marlow's view now better, wiser, more desirable than that of his Youth? This is one of the fascinating questions Conrad raises by creating this complex point of view. Consider the difference if we were to read the account of the voyage as recorded in the Youth's journal. Does distance (in time) lend enchantment?

Another effect of the double point of view is the tragi-comic tone of the story. Marlow's detachment from his youthful enthusiasm enables him to relate the absurdities of his behavior with dry wit, as when he describes the attempts to fight the smoldering fire in the hold:

> Mahon, who went first, fainted there, and the man who went to fetch him out did likewise. We lugged them out on deck. Then I leaped down to show how easily it could be done. They had learned wisdom by that time, and contented themselves by fishing for me with a chain-hook tied to a broomhandle, I believe. I did not offer to go and fetch up my shovel, which was left down below.

There is danger here, and suffering, but for Marlow and for us the experience has been transformed into comedy. Even tragedy is purged of its pain, and we regard it with a mixture of amusement and awe. When Abraham, the steward, goes mad from fright and shock as the deck house is swept from around him by the storm, there is something comical about the picture Marlow describes:

> The house was shattered as if a shell had exploded inside. Most of it had gone overboard—stove, men's quarters, and their property, all was gone; but two posts, holding a portion of the bulkhead to which Abraham's bunk was attached, remained as if by a miracle. We groped in the ruins and came upon this, and there he was, sitting in his bunk, surrounded by foam and wreckage, jabbering cheerfully to himself. He was out of his mind; completely and for ever mad, with this sudden shock coming upon the fag-end of his endurance. We snatched him up, lugged him aft, and pitched him head-first down the cabin companion. You understand there was no time to carry him down with infinite precau-

tions and wait to see how he got on. Those below would pick him up at the bottom of the stairs all right.

And yet the scene is not so hilarious that we forget that such madness is tragic; we may smile, but we feel sympathy for Abraham.

Marlow is both in the situation and above it; and so are we. It is this Olympian detachment that allows us to see humor where the participant can feel only the immediately relevant emotions—fright, anxiety, elation, etc. When Marlow re-boards the burning ship to learn why the captain and crew are delaying so long, he can only feel exasperation and incredulity at the scene that meets his eyes:

> It was as bright as day. Coming up like this, the sheet of fire facing me was a terrifying sight, and the heat seemed hardly bearable at first. On a settee cushion dragged out of the cabin Captain Beard, his legs drawn up and one arm under his head, slept with the light playing on him. Do you know what the rest were busy about? They were sitting on deck right aft, round an open case, eating bread and cheese and drinking bottled stout. . . . Mahon got up. . . . "The last meal on board," he explained solemnly.

But free as Marlow now is from the peril of the situation, we can relish its wild absurdity.

Comedy and irony come from another kind of doubleness—between what is appropriate to a given situation and what actually happens. When the rats leave the ship, for example, it is only after the leaks have been patched and the ship completely recaulked. When Marlow receives his "first command," it is not a ship the size of the *Judea,* but a 14-foot rowboat. And another kind of irony results when Marlow wryly observes that to save the ship during the gale, the crew had to pump water out of it, while to save it from the fire in the hold, they have to pump water into it.

Conrad the storyteller practices his craft as skillfully as Marlow the sailor, and like the middle-aged Marlow, he is aware that human experience is full of significance. He reviews his own experience not only to entertain us for a few moments, but to encourage us to see and to share certain truths with him. Conrad the craftsman merges into Conrad the philosopher.

Conrad's Themes

The themes that emerge from the experiences of "Youth" are themes that have occupied many writers and philosophers—the romantic illusions of youth, the swiftness of passing time, the brevity of youth and strength—and of life, the frustrations of expending effort futilely in impossible tasks, the sometimes menacing and sometimes sympathetic face of nature, the comradeship, the discipline, and the heroism of man.

The central theme, suggested by the title of the story, is strongly and clearly stated, but it develops only after a couple of other themes have been introduced—themes against which the central one is more sharply defined. The first of these related themes has to do with the feelings of frustration and futility as inevitable qualities of life. "You fight, work, sweat, nearly kill yourself, sometimes do kill yourself, trying to accomplish something—and you can't," says Marlow. "Not from any fault of yours. You simply can do nothing, neither great nor little—not a thing in the world—not even marry an old maid, or get a wretched 600-ton cargo of coal to its port of destination." Obviously Marlow is speaking about his own experience, but he is also generalizing: this is the human situation, this is life, this is the way it is. (Which is why Marlow doesn't consider himself either especially unfortunate or especially heroic, why his four friends nod with understanding and agreement as they listen, and why the story has significance for us as readers. It is about not just one man's experience, but all men's.)

"How time passes!" says Marlow, and another theme begins. Occasionally it intertwines with the first, as in the series of delays that prevent the *Judea* from getting under way for Bankok; time passes—an inordinate amount of time—but still the job can't be completed. The inexorable passage of time only makes the frustration more intense. Time holds a special significance for Marlow as he relates his tale. Those events took place twenty-two years ago; was it really so long? And those people are gone now, along with his youth: "However, they are both dead [Carlyle and Burnaby, whose books he was reading] and Mrs. Beard is dead, and youth, strength, genius, thoughts, achievements, simple hearts—all die. . . ."

And while time passes, men labor in futility. Images of futile work abound: the crew in the hold, endlessly flinging shovelfuls of wet sand uphill, trying to restore the balance of the ship, falling down, getting nowhere; and later, as the ship is in danger of foundering in a gale, pumping "all night, all day, all the week. . . . We pumped watch and watch, for dear life, and it seemed to last for months, for years, for all eternity, as though we had been dead and gone to a hell for sailors. We forgot the day of the week, the name of the month, what year it was, and whether we had ever been ashore. . . . We turned those handles, and had the eyes of idiots. . . ."

Marlow reminds us that "man is born to trouble, to leaky ships, and to ships that burn." And yet in spite of the frequency and the insistence with which these themes are reiterated, the effect is not a gloomy one. The conclusion is not pessimistic. For Marlow shows us time and again that men are not overwhelmed by these frustrations and disasters; they sweat and curse and suffer, but their spirits are not crushed. They fight on. And the younger they are, of course, the more enthusiastically they fight on. The young Marlow responds with exultation:

> And there was somewhere in me the thought: By Jove! this is the deuce of an adventure—something you read about; and it is my first voyage as second mate—and I am only twenty—and here I am lasting it out as well as any of these men, and keeping my chaps up to the mark. I was pleased. I would not have given up the experience for worlds.

But the rest of the crew, and the captain as well, respond to adversity with courage and good humor. As they labor to put out the smoldering fire in the hold,

> Everyone took his turn, captain included. There was equality, and if not exactly fraternity, then a deal of good feeling. Sometimes a man, as he dashed a bucketful of water down the hatchway, would yell out, "Hurrah for Bankok!" and the rest laughed.

Marlow's romantic enthusiasm remains undiminished even after the cargo explodes and he is blown head over heels into the hold; but he is impressed to find the whole crew carrying on undaunted, scrambling aloft to trim the sails of the disabled ship in spite of their injuries and in spite of the knowledge that the masts might topple over at any moment and plunge them into the sea to be drowned, entangled among the rigging. "What made them do it?" Marlow puzzles. It is not youth, for the old respond as doggedly as the young. There is no answer; it is something in human beings, in life itself, that refuses to quit, refuses to accept defeat. And this is why there is no pessimism in Marlow; only a bemused nostalgia for those days when he was younger and stronger, when he knew less and expected more, and a contentment that life has given him a chance to prove himself and to experience the fullness and exhilaration of living at the highest pitch he was capable of.

This is what the central theme of youth is about: not simply sadness and regret that youth is past, but the happy memory of its richness, amusement at its naiveté, and wonder at its energy, along with the wistful acceptance of the realization that it is gone and will never return. It is a wise story—wise in the way that youth itself can never be wise because youth knows nothing other than youth. It is only by contrast that the quality of a thing appears clearly; it is only to the person who has been young and is now old that the true character and the value of youth become clear.

Marlow's tone is one of wonder and admiration as he recalls his youth: "The strength of it, the faith of it, the imagination of it!" He speaks of the "glamour" of youth: not that youth appears glamorous to the old, but that youth sees the world and life as glamorous, that the "ignorance and hope" of youth protect it from the weariness and resignation of experienced maturity. This sense of glamor and romance, says Marlow, is an illusion; it is killed by experience, which cannot confirm it. It is a feeling "that will never come back any more—the feeling that I could last forever, outlast the sea, the earth, and all men; the deceitful feeling that lures us on to joys, to perils, to love, to vain effort—to death; the triumphant conviction of strength, the heat of life in a handful of dust, the glow in the heart that with every year grows dim, grows cold, grows small, and expires—and expires, too soon, too soon—before life itself." It has expired in Marlow now, as it had already expired in Mahon and in Captain Beard. Its loss does not mean the loss of courage or strength: Captain Beard is still able to impress the young Marlow by saving his wife when the *Judea* is struck by a steamer in the dark:

> It appears that when he heard my shout "Come up" he understood at once what was the matter, caught up his wife, ran on deck, and across, and down into our boat, which was fast to the ladder. Not bad for a sixty-year old.

And Beard, Mahon, and the entire crew show themselves as able to endure adversity as the youthful Marlow. The difference is the attitude with which they endure it—wearily and with resignation. They carry on because they are men and they have a job to do; they have accepted the terms of the job—and of life—and they are bound to complete it or die trying.

But Marlow never simply grits his teeth and endures; he exults in every new calamity. Here is another chance to test himself, to prove himself. "Now, this is something like," he crows after the explosion of coal-gas and coal-dust has blown up the ship. "This is great. I wonder what will happen." Nothing that does happen dismays him. He welcomes the worst.

But that was twenty-two years ago. The middle-aged Marlow is no longer susceptible to "the romance of illusions"; he has come to the point in his life when he realizes that the best is already behind him. He and his four companions have outlived their youthful hopes and dreams. They sit reminiscing together, as Marlow describes them,

> . . . our faces marked by toil, by deceptions, by success, by love; our

105

weary eyes looking still, looking always, looking anxiously for something out of life, that while it is expected is already gone. . . .

Illusions die hard, and the last one to go is the belief that somewhere ahead lies the goal of all their striving, the achievement, the discovery that will make all their struggles worthwhile; somewhere ahead lies each man's Bankok, each man's East. To lose this illusion is truly to lose one's youth. And so perhaps youth is not a period of time in one's life after all: youth is a state of mind—or a state of feeling. Youth is a hopeful quest.

This is a generalization. Conrad's story is also a generalization—an assertion that what holds true for Marlow holds true for all of us. Conrad is interested in the particulars of Marlow's experience (Conrad's experience) because he believes that by looking closely enough at particulars we see universals. We see truths that apply to all our lives. These are the mythic dimensions of "Youth": there are patterns of human life here, patterns that hold true around the world and across the ages. Myths in this sense are not lies but truths—the universal truths of human experience.

Conrad's Mythmaking

At least four mythic elements are apparent in "Youth," and their interrelationship suggests the unity of Conrad's story. The first element, the idea that a person's life is a kind of voyage through time, is implied in Marlow's opening statement: "You fellows know there are those voyages that seem ordered for the illustration of life, that might stand for a symbol of existence." If a voyage can represent life, then life is like a voyage. The metaphor is a natural and obvious one, and so common that it is familiar to all of us. But a myth is first of all a narrative, a story, and a metaphor becomes a myth only as it is extended in time. Conrad's myth of life embodied in the voyage of "Youth" is not a very complex or a very profound one. It says mainly that "life is just one damned thing after another," that life is a series of frustrations and disasters. Perhaps Conrad's real view of life is not as simple as this—certainly he acknowledges many other dimensions in his other writings—but he is not really concerned here with the development of a philosophical position; he is concerned with dramatizing (with the aid of some exaggeration) one statement about life, and the statement, as far as it goes, seems to be a true one. Certainly most of us feel this way about life at one time or another—perhaps many times.

But the myth can be read another way. The adversities of life need not be merely a series of painful and dangerous and exasperating things that make one's life miserable; one can see them as a challenge, a test, an opportunity to try out one's courage and resourcefulness and strength, a chance to prove to oneself and others that he is a man, capable of taking whatever life can dish out. This is the youthful Marlow's response. For him, the voyage of the *Judea* "was the endeavor, the test, the trial of life." It is his way of proving himself to be a man among men, a leader, a potential first mate or even captain. He succeeds, of course; his behavior is exemplary, even heroic. Through one crisis after another he cheerfully shepherds the men he is responsible for, and when the ship finally sinks he is ready and eager to take charge of his first vessel—even though it is only a 14-foot boat with a jury-rigged mast and a crew of two.

The truth of this myth is clear: to prove himself worthy of acceptance as an adult or as a leader, a man must not only endure a good deal of pain and trouble, but he must do so without complaining. Furthermore, he must be active, not passive; he must take the initiative, and find ways to overcome obstacles. The trial, the ordeal of initiation into adulthood is a familiar myth because it is a fact of life: whatever the variations in difficulty and danger, every human culture has always demanded that its youths undergo some form of initiation before they are accepted as adults. The myth has countless variations. It appears in ancient fairy tales as well as in contemporary novels, and what it shows us is always the same: how one youth faced the trials of his initiation. What we learn is not how to overcome the ordeals of our own initiations; we learn simply that it can be done. If he can do it, so can we.

Sometimes the transition from youth to adulthood takes the form of a quest—a search for some valued object or goal. The tests and ordeals of the initiation myth are always part of the quest myth (even though the quest need not always involve initiation). The dragons, evil sorcerers, and other perils that the wandering knight must overcome in his quest for the Holy Grail are counterparts of the obstacles that face anyone who undertakes a quest. Difficulties of some kind always stand between the quester and his goal. The protagonist of "youth" has two goals, actually; there are two quests undertaken concurrently. One is the quest for his manhood, and for his right to command a ship. The other, which he openly acknowledges, is his quest for the East, for Bankok. It is clear from the beginning that Bankok's value for Marlow is primarily symbolic: it is a place of romance, of mystery, a strange foreign place that only the farthest travelers go to, a land that is literally on the other side of the earth. Marlow doesn't get to Bankok, but he gets to Java. It's all the same to him; it's "the East." And he is content. The East is nothing so very extraordinary, but he is not disappointed. Since the romance of the East is the creation of his own mind, he projects it onto the scene that meets his eyes—the line of mountains that rises from the sea as his small boat approaches Java, the warm air filled with odors of blossoms and aromatic wood, ". . . like a whispered promise of mysterious delight." When the angry curses of a British sea captain break the silence of the dark harbor (". . . the East spoke to me, but it was in a Western voice"), the contrast only intensifies the silent mystery of the exotic night, and of the quiet faces that peer down at him from the wharf the next morning. The harbor in daylight is as full of beauty and romance as it was at night. "This was the East of the ancient navigators, so old, so mysterious, resplendent and sombre, living and unchanged, full of danger and promise." Marlow later learned enough of the reality of the East to disillusion him, but that first romantic vision still persists like a vivid dream, almost stronger than reality: ". . . for me all the East is contained in that vision of my youth." The quest has been fulfilled.

While young Marlow's eyes drink in the splendor of the East, his shipmates lie slumbering in their boats, "unconscious of the land and the people and of the violence of sunshine." This contrast between Marlow's response to the beauty or the terror of the moment and the doggedness of the others has been typical of the entire voyage. The others, after all, are not youths; their eyes don't see the same romantic illusions. Another mythic dimension of the story has to do with what Shakespeare called "the seven ages of Man," which Conrad here reduces to three: youth, maturity, and old age. We see the attitudes and the reactions of each age in every situation, for each is embodied in a character. Beard, of course, represents Age; Mahon (pronounced "Man") represents Manhood; and Marlow is Youth. (The identification of Meaning here is perhaps a little heavy-handed, but Conrad doesn't labor it.[2]) On the other hand, Conrad does not go out of his way to obscure his meanings, because they are natural meanings, not forced or manipulated. For example, in speaking of Mahon, he makes a statement about Man: "He was well connected; yet there was something wrong with his luck, and he had never got on." This may be a purely gratuitous bit of wry humor, yet it does reinforce the theme that "man is born to trouble, to leaky ships, and to ships that burn."

Seen in the perspective of general humanity, Mahon and Beard are not truly representative of Manhood and Age; most men simply don't lead such dangerous lives. And though the Captain and First Mate groan and grumble under the strain, they never falter, they never give up. Ordinary men are less resolute; and what about the cowards, the shirkers, the quitters? Conrad is generalizing, of course. There are other types of men, to be sure,

[2] Actually, Conrad is simply exploiting the meaning inherent in reality; Beard and Mahon were the real names of the Captain and First Mate of the *Palestine,* upon which Conrad took the voyage Marlow describes.

and he examines many of them in his other stories and novels. In "Youth" there is simply neither time nor space to deal with the exceptions. We may take it that Conrad's general view of mankind is a benevolent one. On the whole, he seems to say, Man behaves himself very well in outrageously trying circumstances.

The attitudes and behavior of Mahon and Beard (and to some extent, the rest of the crew) serve as foils to emphasize by contrast the romantic optimism and exuberance of Youth. They do their jobs and endure the hardships; they shake their heads in weary resignation and carry on. They are not particularly surprised at each new difficulty; they have seen too much of life to expect anything else. To them, Marlow's enthusiasm is foolish, though Beard (and his wife) show more tolerance of it than Mahon. "Be careful with that jury-rig, Marlow," says Captain Beard as Marlow sails cockily off in his 14-foot boat with an improvised sail. Mahon wrinkles his nose and warns, "You will sail that ship of yours under water, if you don't look out, young fellow." Everything considered, Marlow accomplishes no more than the Captain and the First Mate, but he has more fun doing it.

Finally, there are hints that Conrad sees the *Judea* as a kind of miniature world, sailing through space. This is not an unfamiliar idea in our times, when we have heard references to "this spaceship, Earth." The comparison is reversible; if the earth is like a sailing vessel, then a sailing vessel may be like the earth. Herman Melville plays with this idea in *Moby Dick,* where the *Pequod* becomes a symbol of the earth, with its crew of *isolattoes,* isolated individuals, representing many nations and races. The fate of the ship-world in "Youth," as in *Moby Dick,* is not a happy one, and yet it does not necessarily mean that Conrad is pessimistic. That the world will end some day has been the general belief of most of mankind through the ages. There is a particular timeliness in one image Conrad gives us of the ship, as it sails across the Indian Ocean with its smoldering cargo.

> The sky was a miracle of purity, a miracle of azure. The sea was polished, was blue, was pellucid, was sparkling like a precious stone, extending on all sides, all round to the horizon. . . . And on the lustre of the great calm waters the *Judea* glided imperceptibly, enveloped in languid and unclean vapours, in a lazy cloud that drifted to leeward, light and slow; a pestiferous cloud defiling the splendour of sea and sky.

Newspaper cartoonists in recent years have frequently envisioned our planet in just this way, trailing its cloud of pestilential, polluted air through space. That it does not yet look quite this way to our astronauts is somehow reassuring. Perhaps we are not as near the end as the *Judea* was.

The Relevance of Reading

Becoming aware of the writer as a fellow voyager attempting to share his discoveries and insights opens new dimensions of significance. What we read becomes more than entertainment or information; it becomes an opportunity to watch a craftsman at work, to learn something of his skills and share his wisdom. Writing is seen as a vehicle of exploration, a way of putting familiar things together in new ways to create the relationships we call "meaning," a way of striking out into the unknown.

The relevance of reading and of writing, then, lies in their capacity to impart understanding as well as information—understanding of the ways of the world, of other people, of ourselves. Not complete understanding; rarely do we feel we've achieved that. But a better understanding than we had before. These are ways of knowing—reading, sharing our impressions of what we've read, comparing the experiences and the observations of others with our own.

These comments on Conrad's story are an attempt to demonstrate the richness of meaning that a story (or any piece of writing) may contain. They represent not *the* meaning of the story, but *some* meanings—or rather, some of what seems meaningful to one reader. We take our choices among the meanings of life, at least where we know that meaning exists. It exists in art—in every conscious creation of man—as truly as it exists in nature. And it is discoverable. The discovery is up to us.

~~~~~~

Casting Off Moorings

The moment or hour of leave-taking is one of the pleasantest times in human experience, for it has in it a warm sadness without loss. People who don't ordinarily like you very well are overcome with affection at leave-taking. We said good-by again and again and still could not bring ourselves to cast off the lines and start the engines. It would be good to live in a perpetual state of leave-taking, never to go nor to stay, but to remain suspended in that golden emotion of love and longing; to be missed without being gone; to be loved without satiety.

—John Steinbeck
The Log from the Sea of Cortez

*The voyager's departure is attended not
only by well-wishers, but sometimes by
solemn-faced prophets of disaster, darkly
predicting his destruction by unforeseen
dangers. W. H. Auden, taking as a pattern
an anonymous old nonsense poem, "The
Cutty Wren," dramatically contrasts the dire
warnings of the dissuaders and the cool dis-
dain of the committed voyager.*

W. H. AUDEN

O Where Are You Going?

'O where are you going?' said reader to rider,
'That valley is fatal when furnaces burn,
Yonder's the midden whose odours will madden,
That gap is the grave where the tall return.'

'O do you imagine,' said fearer to farer,
'That dusk will delay on your path to the pass,
Your diligent looking discover the lacking
Your footsteps feel from granite to grass?'

'O what was that bird,' said horror to hearer,
'Did you see that shape in the twisted trees?
Behind you swiftly the figure comes softly,
The spot on your skin is a shocking disease.'

'Out of this house'—said rider to reader,
'Yours never will'—said farer to fearer,
'They're looking for you'—said hearer to horror,
As he left them there, as he left them there.

"Five Songs, V." Copyright 1934 and renewed 1962 by W. H. Auden. Reprinted from
COLLECTED SHORTER POEMS 1927–1957, by W. H. Auden, by permission of Random
House, Inc.

*Loren Eiseley, whose knowledge as a scientist
makes him keenly aware of man's unique position in space and time, transforms the simple
act of floating down a shallow river into a
"tremendous adventure" by an imaginative
awareness that embraces a whole continent
and eons of time. His half-conscious goal as
he shoves off is a thorough immersion in his
"mother element," water—an immersion so
total that sensation and knowledge become
one.*

LOREN EISELEY

Down the River of Time

Once in a lifetime, perhaps, one escapes the actual confines of the flesh. Once in a lifetime, if one is lucky, one so merges with sunlight and air and running water that whole eons, the eons that mountains and deserts know, might pass in a single afternoon without discomfort. The mind has sunk away into its beginnings among old roots and the obscure tricklings and movings that stir inanimate things. Like the charmed fairy circle into which a man once stepped, and upon emergence learned that a whole century had passed in a single night, one can never quite define this secret; but it has something to do, I am sure, with common water. Its substance reaches everywhere; it touches the past and prepares the future; it moves under the poles and wanders thinly in the heights of air. It can assume forms of exquisite perfection in a snowflake, or strip the living to a single shining bone cast up by the sea.

Many years ago, in the course of some scientific investigations in a remote western country, I experienced, by chance, precisely the sort of curious
absorption by water—the extension of shape by osmosis—at which I have
been hinting. You have probably never experienced in yourself the me-
andering roots of a whole watershed or felt your outstretched fingers
touching, by some kind of clairvoyant extension, the brooks of snow-line
glaciers at the same time that you were flowing toward the Gulf over the
eroded debris of worndown mountains. A poet, MacKnight Black, has
spoken of being "limbed . . . with waters gripping pole and pole." He had
the idea, all right, and it is obvious that these sensations are not unique,
but they are hard to come by; and the sort of extension of the senses that
people will accept when they put their ear against a sea shell, they will
smile at in the confessions of a bookish professor. What makes it worse is
the fact that because of a traumatic experience in childhood, I am not a
swimmer, and am inclined to be timid before any large body of water.
Perhaps it was just this, in a way, that contributed to my experience.

As it leaves the Rockies and moves downward over the high plains
towards the Missouri, the Platte River is a curious stream. In the spring
floods, on occasion, it can be a mile-wide roaring torrent of destruction,
gulping farms and bridges. Normally, however, it is a rambling, dispersed
series of streamlets flowing erratically over great sand and gravel fans
that are, in part, the remnants of a mightier Ice Age stream bed. Quicksands and shifting islands haunt its waters. Over it the prairie suns beat
mercilessly throughout the summer. The Platte, "a mile wide and an inch
deep," is a refuge for any heat-weary pilgrim along its shores. This is
particularly true on the high plains before its long march by the cities
begins.

The reason that I came upon it when I did, breaking through a willow
thicket and stumbling out through ankle-deep water to a dune in the
shade, is of no concern to this narrative. On various purposes of science I
have ranged over a good bit of that country on foot, and I know the kinds
of bones that come gurgling up through the gravel pumps, and the arrow-
heads of shining chalcedony that occasionally spill out of water-loosened
sand. On that day, however, the sight of sky and willows and the weaving
net of water murmuring a little in the shallows on its way to the Gulf
stirred me, parched as I was with miles of walking, with a new idea: I was
going to float. I was going to undergo a tremendous adventure.

The notion came to me, I suppose, by degrees. I had shed my clothes
and was floundering pleasantly in a hole among some reeds when a great
desire to stretch out and go with this gently insistent water began to pluck
at me. Now to this bronzed, bold, modern generation, the struggle I waged

114

with timidity while standing there in knee-deep water can only seem farcical; yet actually for me it was not so. A near-drowning accident in childhood had scarred my reactions; in addition to the fact that I was a nonswimmer, this "inch-deep river" was treacherous with holes and quicksands. Death was not precisely infrequent along its wandering and illusory channels. Like all broad wastes of this kind, where neither water nor land quite prevails, its thickets were lonely and untraversed. A man in trouble would cry out in vain.

I thought of all this, standing quietly in the water, feeling the sand shifting away under my toes. Then I lay back in the floating position that left my face to the sky, and shoved off. The sky wheeled over me. For an instant, as I bobbed into the main channel, I had the sensation of sliding down the vast tilted face of the continent. It was then that I felt the cold needles of the alpine springs at my fingertips, and the warmth of the Gulf pulling me southward. Moving with me, leaving its taste upon my mouth and spouting under me in dancing springs of sand, was the immense body of the continent itself, flowing like the river was flowing, grain by grain, mountain by mountain, down to the sea. I was streaming over ancient sea beds thrust aloft where giant reptiles had once sported; I was wearing down the face of time and trundling cloud-wreathed ranges into oblivion. I touched my margins with the delicacy of a crayfish's antennae, and felt great fishes glide about their work.

I drifted by stranded timber cut by beaver in mountain fastnesses; I slid over shallows that had buried the broken axles of prairie schooners and the mired bones of mammoth. I was streaming alive through the hot and working ferment of the sun, or oozing secretively through shady thickets. I *was* water and the unspeakable alchemies that gestate and take shape in water, the slimy jellies that under the enormous magnification of the sun writhe and whip upward as great barbeled fish mouths, or sink indistinctly back into the murk out of which they arose. Turtle and fish and the pinpoint chirpings of individual frogs are all watery projections, concentrations—as man himself is a concentration—of that indescribable and liquid brew which is compounded in varying proportions of salt and sun and time. It has appearances, but at its heart lies water, and as I was finally edged gently against a sand bar and dropped like any log, I tottered as I rose. I knew once more the body's revolt against emergence into the harsh and unsupporting air, its reluctance to break contact with that mother element which still, at this late point in time, shelters and brings into being nine tenths of everything alive.

As for men, those myriad little detached ponds with their own swarming corpuscular life, what were they but a way that water has of going about

115

beyond the reach of rivers? I, too, was a microcosm of pouring rivulets and floating driftwood gnawed by the mysterious animalcules of my own creation. I was three fourths water, rising and subsiding according to the hollow knocking in my veins: a minute pulse like the eternal pulse that lifts Himalayas and which, in the following systole,[1] will carry them away.

Thoreau, peering at the emerald pickerel in Walden Pond, called them "animalized water" in one of his moments of strange insight. If he had been possessed of the geological knowledge so laboriously accumulated since his time, he might have gone further and amusedly detected in the planetary rumblings and eructations which so delighted him in the gross habits of certain frogs, signs of that dark interior stress which has reared sea bottoms up to mountainous heights. He might have developed an acute inner ear for the sound of the surf on Cretaceous beaches where now the wheat of Kansas rolls. In any case, he would have seen, as the long trail of life was unfolded by the fossil hunters, that his animalized water had changed its shapes eon by eon to the beating of the earth's dark millennial heart. In the swamps of the low continents, the amphibians had flourished and had their day; and as the long skyward swing—the isostatic response of the crust—had come about, the era of the cooling grasslands and mammalian life had come into being.

---

[1] Rhythmic contraction (usually applied, with *diastole,* to the movements of the heart).

REFLECTIONS (5)

REFLECTIONS

Since the late seventeenth century, science and poetry have generally been considered to be opposed to one another. Scientist Loren Eiseley, however, demonstrates in his poetic prose that they are not. What does poetry, or the poetic imagination, have to contribute to science? What can science contribute to poetry?

Eiseley frankly admits that fear almost kept him from shoving off on his journey; no doubt fear is what usually prevents us from "cutting loose." Are there, however, other feelings or motives that inhibit our impulses to adventure and exploration?

WALT WHITMAN

Beginning My Studies

Beginning my studies the first step pleas'd me so much,
The mere fact consciousness, these forms, the power of motion,
The least insect or animal, the senses, eyesight, love,
The first step I say awed me and pleas'd me so much,
I have hardly gone and hardly wish'd to go any farther,
But stop and loiter all the time to sing it in ecstatic songs.

*The first man ever to sail single-handedly
around the world was Captain Joshua
Slocum, a sea captain of nearly 40 years'
sailing experience when he began his voyage
in 1895 at the age of 51. Slocum was a lucky
man as well as a skillful one, but in spite of
years of hard work he had never managed
to accumulate enough money even to buy a
house. The voyage of the Spray, however,
brought him both fame and money, as he was
invited in port after port to relate his adventures to admiring crowds, and found on
his return home a large and eager audience
for his book about the cruise, which he
called* Sailing Alone Around the World.
*Slocum's book has been a favorite among sea
travelers ever since its publication, and was
even at one time required reading in the
public schools. Slocum's natural reticence
helped to produce a literary style which, in
its understatement, is very much in the long
tradition of English literature. A sly sense of
humor enhances the understatement, so that
Slocum seems perpetually to be amused at
himself and his adventures, whether he is
running aground on the coast of Uruguay or
fighting off Fuegian savages in the Strait of
Magellan. Slocum's exhilaration as he leaves
Boston on his round-the-world voyage is
apparent in the following passage . . .*

JOSHUA SLOCUM

Away from Boston

I spent a season in my new craft fishing on the coast, only to find that I had not the cunning properly to bait a hook. But at last the time arrived to weigh anchor and get to sea in earnest. I had resolved on a voyage around the world, and as the wind on the morning of April 24, 1895, was fair, at noon I weighed anchor, set sail, and filled away from Boston, where the *Spray* had been moored snugly all winter. The twelve-o'clock whistles were blowing just as the sloop shot ahead under full sail. A short board was made up the harbor on the port tack, then coming about she stood seaward, with her boom well off to port, and swung past the ferries with lively heels. A photographer on the outer pier at East Boston got a picture of her as she swept by, her flag at the peak throwing its folds clear. A thrilling pulse beat high in me. My step was light on deck in crisp air. I felt that there could be no turning back, and that I was engaging in an adventure the meaning of which I thoroughly understood. I had taken little advice from any one, for I had a right to my own opinions in matters pertaining to the sea. That the best of sailors might do worse than even I alone was borne in upon me not a league from Boston docks, where a great steamship, fully manned, officered, and piloted, lay stranded and broken. This was the *Venetian*. She was broken completely in two over a ledge. So in the first hour of my lone voyage I had proof that the *Spray* could at least do better than this full-handed steamship, for I was already farther on my voyage than she. "Take warning, *Spray*, and have a care," I uttered aloud to my bark, passing fairylike down the bay.

The wind freshened, and the *Spray* rounded Deer Island light, going at the rate of seven knots. Passing it, she squared away direct for Gloucester, where she was to procure some fishermen's stores. Waves dancing joyously

from SAILING ALONE AROUND THE WORLD by Capt. Joshua Slocum, Dover Publications, Inc.

across Massachusetts Bay met the sloop coming out, to dash themselves instantly into myriads of sparkling gems that hung about her breast at every surge. The day was perfect, the sunlight clear and strong. Every particle of water thrown into the air became a gem, and the *Spray,* making good her name as she dashed ahead, snatched necklace after necklace from the sea, and as often threw them away. We have all seen miniature rainbows about a ship's prow, but the *Spray* flung out a bow of her own that day, such as I had never seen before. Her good angel had embarked on the voyage; so I read it in the sea.

Probably few exploratory ventures are embarked upon with such joyous anticipation as sexual ones. In "Going to Bed," John Donne, a seventeenth-century poet, expresses a lover's impatience and delight as he watches his lady undress and then welcomes her to bed.

JOHN DONNE

Going to Bed
(Elegy XIX)

Come, Madam, come, all rest my powers defy;
Until I labour, I in labour lie.
The foe oft-times having the foe in sight,
Is tir'd with standing though he never fight.
Off with that girdle, like heaven's zone glittering,
But a far fairer world encompassing.
Unpin that spangled breastplate which you wear,
That th'eyes of busy fools may be stopt there.
Unlace yourself, for that harmonious chime
Tells me from you that now it is bed time.
Off with that happy busk, which I envy,
That still can be, and still can stand so nigh.
Your gown going off, such beauteous state reveals,
As when from flowry meads th'hills' shadow steals.
Off with that wirey coronet and show
The hairy diadem which on you doth grow:
Now off with those shoes, and then safely tread
In this love's hallow'd temple, this soft bed.
In such white robes, heaven's angels us'd to be
Received by men; thou, angel, bring'st with thee
A heaven like Mahomet's Paradise; and though
Ill spirits walk in white, we easily know

By this, these angels from an evil sprite:
Those set our hairs, but these our flesh upright.

License my roving hands, and let them go
Before, behind, between, above, below.
O my America! my new-found-land,
My kingdom, safeliest when with one man man'd,
My mine of precious stones, my empery,
How blest am I in this discovering thee!
To enter in these bonds is to be free;
Then where my hand is set, my seal shall be.

Full nakedness! All joys are due to thee;
As souls unbodied, bodies uncloth'd must be,
To taste whole joys. Gems which you women use
Are like Atlanta's balls, cast in men's views,
That when a fool's eye lighteth on a gem,
His earthly soul may covet theirs, not them.
Like pictures, or like books' gay coverings made
For lay-men, are all women thus array'd;
Themselves are mystick books, which only we
(Whom their imputed grace will dignify)
Must see reveal'd. Then since that I may know,
As liberally as to a midwife show
Thyself: cast all, yea, this white linen hence;
There is no penance due to innocence.

To teach thee, I am naked first; why then,
What need'st thou have more covering than a man?

. . . Zorba shook his head.

"No, you're not free," he said. "The string you're tied to is perhaps longer than other people's. That's all. You're on a long piece of string, boss; you come and go, and think you're free, but you never cut the string in two. And when people don't cut that string . . ."

"I'll cut it some day!" I said defiantly, because Zorba's words had touched an open wound in me and hurt.

"It's difficult, boss, very difficult. You need a touch of folly to do that; folly, d'you see? You have to risk everything! . . ."

—Nikos Kazantzakis
Zorba the Greek

Voyages of Discovery

~~~~~~

Alone on Earth

*Loneliness does not come from
having no people about one, but
from being unable to communicate the things that seem important to oneself, or from holding
certain views which others find
inadmissible.*

C. G. Jung
Memories, Dreams, Reflections

*Loneliness is one of the great problems of
the voyager. Spending days, sometimes weeks
without speaking to another soul, often
knowing himself to be miles from help
should he need it, the lone traveler comes
face to face with the fact of his isolation. It
can be an unnerving, even terrifying experience. Most travelers, however, soon learn
or invent techniques for dealing with it. They
know they have to. The problem of loneliness is not confined to voyagers, of course;
it is part of the human condition, and most
of us are intermittently lonely a good part
of our lives. Solitude is an objective fact, but
the feeling of loneliness is subjective and
relative: it is not uncommon to be lonely in
a crowd. We are interested, therefore, to
watch how others grapple with their loneliness; we sympathize, we understand, and
perhaps we learn something about facing our
own loneliness. Listen to Robin Lee Graham
as his sloop slices northward through the
south Atlantic on the homeward leg of his
solo round-the-world voyage:*

*But each day was like the next. Loneliness began to take
hold of me like a pain that wouldn't go away. I fought
it every way I could. You have to, or it will drive you
crazy. It's slow torture, not like the sharp stab of fear a
bad storm brings. But I think it's worse.*

*Sleeping helps. I think sleep is kind of neat. It's the
only real escape there is. I wanted to stay in that bunk
until one day I'd wake up and find myself in port. That*

126

was only a dream, but now that the ships had disappeared, I did begin sleeping at night—or trying to. . . .
Keeping busy helps, too—or at least keeping distracted. I'd wake up at dawn every morning and read for a while (I never could have stayed sane without books). That was a nice time, because the rising sun felt cheerful after the darkness and the cabin wasn't hot yet. . . .

—Robin Lee Graham
"World-roaming Teen-ager Sails On"
National Geographic, April, 1969

Does an old sea dog become immune to the
pangs of loneliness? Joshua Slocum had
almost 40 years' sailing experience when he
set out on his globe-circling voyage. Yet here
he is only two months out from Gloucester. . .

JOSHUA SLOCUM

I Heard All the Voices

of the Past

On the evening of July 5 the *Spray,* after having steered all day over a
lumpy sea, took it into her head to go without the helmsman's aid.[1] I had
been steering southeast by south, but the wind hauling forward a bit, she
dropped into a smooth lane, heading southeast, and making about eight
knots,[2] her very best work. I crowded on sail to cross the track of the liners
without loss of time, and to reach as soon as possible the friendly Gulf
Stream. The fog lifting before night, I was afforded a look at the sun just
as it was touching the sea. I watched it go down and out of sight. Then I
turned my face eastward, and there, apparently at the very end of the bowsprit, was the smiling full moon rising out of the sea. Neptune himself
coming over the bows could not have startled me more. "Good evening,
sir," I cried; "I'm glad to see you." Many a long talk since then I have had
with the man in the moon; he had my confidence on the voyage.

[1] Without Slocum's steering.
[2] Nautical miles per hour; eight knots is just over nine miles per hour (statute
miles).

from SAILING ALONE AROUND THE WORLD by Capt. Joshua Slocum, Dover Publications, Inc.

About midnight the fog shut down again denser than ever before. One could almost "stand on it." It continued so for a number of days, the wind increasing to a gale. The waves rose high, but I had a good ship. Still, in the dismal fog I felt myself drifting into loneliness, an insect on a straw in the midst of the elements. I lashed the helm, and my vessel held her course, and while she sailed I slept.

During these days a feeling of awe crept over me. My memory worked with startling power. The ominous, the insignificant, the great, the small, the wonderful, the commonplace—all appeared before my mental vision in magical succession. Pages of my history were recalled which had been so long forgotten that they seemed to belong to a previous existence. I heard all the voices of the past laughing, crying, telling what I had heard them tell in many corners of the earth.

The loneliness of my state wore off when the gale was high and I found much work to do. When fine weather returned, then came the sense of solitude, which I could not shake off. I used my voice often, at first giving some order about the affairs of a ship, for I had been told that from disuse I should lose my speech. At the meridian altitude of the sun I called aloud, "Eight bells," after the custom on a ship at sea. Again from my cabin I cried to an imaginary man at the helm, "How does she head, there?" and again, "Is she on her course?" But getting no reply, I was reminded the more palpably of my condition. My voice sounded hollow on the empty air, and I dropped the practice. However, it was not long before the thought came to me that when I was a lad I used to sing; why not try that now, where it would disturb no one? My musical talent had never bred envy in others, but out on the Atlantic, to realize what it meant, you should have heard me sing. You should have seen the porpoises leap when I pitched my voice for the waves and the sea and all that was in it. Old turtles, with large eyes, poked their heads up out of the sea as I sang "Johnny Boker," and "We'll Pay Darby Doyl for his Boots," and the like. But the porpoises were, on the whole, vastly more appreciative than the turtles; they jumped a deal higher. One day when I was humming a favorite chant, I think it was "Babylon's a-Fallin'," a porpoise jumped higher than the bowsprit. Had the *Spray* been going a little faster she would have scooped him in. The sea-birds sailed around rather shy.

Another thing I caught myself doing, that was really bugging me, is that I started answering myself. I'd ask a question, then I'd answer it. It's all right to talk to yourself, but when you start answering—that's bad.

—Robin Lee Graham

Then, breaking the water as though they swam in an obscure mirror, the porpoises surrounded us. They really came to us. We have seen them change course to join us, these curious animals. The Japanese will eat them, but rarely will Occidentals touch them. Of our crew, Tiny and Sparky, who loved to catch every manner of fish, to harpoon any swimming thing, would have nothing to do with porpoises. "They cry so," Sparky said, "when they are hurt, they cry to break your heart." This is rather a difficult thing to understand; a dying cow cries too, and a stuck pig raises his protesting voice piercingly and few hearts are broken by those cries. But a porpoise cries like a child in sorrow and pain. And we wonder whether the general seaman's real affection for porpoises might not be more complicated than the simple fear of hearing them cry. The nature of the animal might parallel certain traits in ourselves—the outrageous boastfulness of porpoises, their love of play, their joy in speed. We have watched them for many hours, making designs in the water, diving and rising and then seeming to turn over to see if they are watched. In bursts of speed they hump their backs and the beating tails take power from the whole body. Then they slow down and only the muscles near the tails are strained. They break the surface, and the blow-holes, like eyes, open and gasp in air and then close like eyes before they submerge. Suddenly they seem to grow tired of playing; the bodies hump, the incredible tails beat, and instantly they are gone.

—John Steinbeck
The Log from the Sea of Cortez

*There is no more amazing sea voyager than
William Willis, who first went to sea at the
age of fifteen, and at seventy sailed a raft
single-handedly 11,000 miles across the
Pacific from Peru to Australia in 204 days.
The raft drifted rudderless most of the way
and was twice driven on reefs and nearly
capsized and wrecked; Willis fought off
death from a strangulated hernia by hoisting
himself feet first off the deck and hanging
upside down for hours; a back injury left him
lying helpless on deck for six days, paralyzed
from the waist down; yet Willis not only survived but survived victoriously and joyfully.
Two years later he was back at sea, heading
from New York to England in a tiny eleven-
and-a-half-foot sloop. Twice he failed, first
when his hernia got the better of him, the
next year when a Polish fishing boat picked
him up while in a trance from excessive deep
breathing. In May of 1968, in his seventy-
fifth year, he was off again. "The trip will
keep me young for another 25 years," he
said. A few weeks later his empty boat,
dismasted and half swamped, was found
drifting 400 miles off Ireland. The title of
his last book was a fitting epitaph for
William Willis:* Whom the Sea Has Taken.
*Willis knew solitude more than most of us,
and concluded that it is not a condition we
can long endure.*

WILLIAM WILLIS

Man Belongs to Man

Man forever tries to master the solitude to help him solve the riddle of life but always falls back, for he cannot live in isolation for any length of time and remain sane. He is born of flesh and needs the companionship of flesh to keep alive. Every moment of his life he takes from his fellow beings and in return gives. A continuous exchange takes place—has taken place since the beginning—which binds all men into an insoluble mass. Even a hermit hiding in a cave lives on men, for his thoughts can only be of men or of a god formed like a man.

Man with man beside him can face death easier than if alone. A condemned man stands firmer on the gallows if the hangman whispers a kind word or a cry of courage rings out from an onlooker. He will even smile at a joke. If a friendly hand touches his shoulder, he feels all mankind in his heart and annihilation does not appear final. Perhaps a few hours before, while in the awful emptiness of his cell awaiting the fateful opening of the door, he screamed in terror at the very thought of what was to come or tried to smash his head against the wall. Man belongs to man, and if he ever reaches the stars, all must go together. There is no salvation for one— Nirvana is the escape of the weak. That is the lesson taught out here, on the threshold of the infinite.

REFLECTIONS (6)

REFLECTIONS

Someone says, "I was so lonely," and we understand. But do we? What is it like to be lonely? Is it the same for everyone? When you are lonely, what does it feel like? What do you think about? What do you do?

Singing, sleeping, doing physical chores—there are various ways to fight loneliness or try to escape from it. What works best for you?

Writing about one's loneliness is very personal, almost confessional. Is it in bad taste to do so? Is there any justification for writing such personal things to be read by others?

*For some, perhaps, the real terror of being
alone is the necessity of making choices,
making one's own decisions, with no one else
to turn to, no certified authority to consult,
and one's life in the balance. Freedom.
Freedom to choose: perhaps to choose
wrongly. A terrible responsibility. But there
are those who exult in this freedom, who
love the responsibility and the choice, the
uncertainty and the possibility of error. To
choose is to be alive. And here we have the
odd phenomenon of an expert technician,
Richard Bach, celebrating imprecision and
uncertainty and joy and beauty. Shall we have
labels or meanings? You choose.*

RICHARD BACH

Let Us Mean Joy

Adventures begin with the sun. By the time the mist is gone, and the mud dry on the wings, the biplane and I begin our first full day together. The only sounds in the field are the unusual ones of cylinders 1–3–5–2–4 slowly, over and again while the bright blade flickers around.

I pace the field in front of the plane, moving blown tree branches and occasional stones aside, marking the holes that could give difficulty. This first part of the takeoff is critical, before the weight has gone from the wheels into the wings.

The 1–3–5–2–4 comes fainter and fainter as I pace, a soft sewing machine stitching quietly away to itself. If someone wanted, he could dash to the bi-

From pp. 22–28 in BIPLANE by Richard Bach. Copyright © 1966 by Richard D. Bach.
Reprinted by permission of Harper & Row, Publishers, Inc.

plane, push the throttle forward, and be gone. I know that the field is deserted, but still I am glad to return and work closer to the biplane.

Sleeping bag stowed in its tight fluffy cylinder and strapped in the front cockpit, giant fan-wind whirring past once again to establish a pattern of familiar, we are ready to say goodbye to a field that has been friend and tutor.

The thought flag comes down, checkered, and a single word: Go. Center of a roaring hemisphere of 1–3–5–2–4 round and round 1750 times a minute, moving slowly at first on heavy wheels, jouncing. Then faster. Then skipping from peak to tiny peak. Splashing mud in the first second, then spattering it, then spraying it hard, then skimming it, then leaving it smooth and untouched, casting down a shuddering black shadow.

Goodbye, field.

A railroad track points east, and so does the nose of the Parks. For the decision to fly from coast to coast, for the poor human frailty of wanting to tie things in neat packages with colorful bows just so, we fly east on our journey west. Because of an intangible unseen whim, a most seen and quite tangible old biplane whirs and thrashes through the sky, above a railroad track, reaching for the Atlantic Ocean.

Ahead, the sun rises from a golden sea. I need railroad tracks no longer, and shift my navigation from dull rails to a blinding star.

Sometimes there are so many symbols about me in the air that it is surprising I can see to fly. I become a symbol, myself. Which is a glorious sort of feeling, for there are so many meanings for me that I can inspect the meaning-bin and carefully select the one that looks best and feels best for this day and this hour. And all good meanings, and real.

What shall I be, this moment? For that part of me that keeps a cautious and uneasy distance from meanings, I am the holder of Commercial Airman's Certificate 1393604, with the privileges of flight instructor, rated for instrument flying and to control single- and multi-engine land airplanes through the air and along the ground as necessary to accomplish the mission of flight. For that part of me, I am 5.27 miles from the Wilmington Omnirange, on the 263-degree radial, at 2,176 feet pressure altitude at 1118 hours Greenwich Mean Time on the 27th day of April in the 1,964th year of the Gregorian Calendar, New Style.

The fuselage of the airplane I fly is painted Stearman Vermilion, Randolph stock number 1918, the wings and tail are Champion Yellow, Randolph stock number unknown but very definitely and precisely listed somewhere in the dusty records of a forgotten drawer in a lost attic away over the horizon. A very precise airplane, every bolt and joint and stitch of it. Not only Detroit-Ryan Speedster, Model Parks P-2A, but serial number

135

101, registration number N499H, built December, 1929, and licensed January, 1930, under Aircraft Type Certificate 276.

Divorced from meanings, with labels only attached, the airplane and I become very complex and forbidding machines. Every bolt and wire of the engine and the airplane has a stock number, a serial number, a lot number. Take a magnifying glass, scrape away the varnish, and there are our numbers, stamped. And meaningless. When one surrounds oneself with meanings there are conflicts and shades of meanings and meanings whose holes are not drilled to line up and can't be bolted together. One can be safe, with serial numbers, in a land of utter quiet. No disputes. Nothing moves.

But I am moving now, and so would carefully select a tailored meaning to outfit my airplane and one to slip about my own shoulders.

Since it is a bright day, biplane, and promising fair, let us mean joy. How does that fit? Look: joy seeks the sun, and the early of the mornings. Joy moves with delight, hasting to where the ocean is golden and the air crisp and cold. Joy tastes the liquid air spraying back onto leather helmet and lowered goggles. It delights in the freedom that is only found and won away up in the sky, from which there is no falling if one only keeps moving. And in the moving, we gain, and joy is precious even in Stearman Vermilion number 1918.

Here, here, son. The practical self speaking, uneasy with symbols, the rein-holding, solemn self. Here, here. All we want to do is get this thing out over the Atlantic a foot or two, so you can say you've done it, and then we have to get along on west. Engine, you know. It *could* fail.

How is it possible, I wonder, for me to be so sure, so self-centered certain that I am in control? I do not know, but the fact remains that I am, when I fly. Those clouds, for instance. Others may pass through them, but I am the one who lends them to the world. The patterns now in the sunlight on the sea, the streaks of fire in the sunrise, the cool breeze and the warm, all of these. Mine. For surely there can be in the world no one who knows and loves these as I. There, the source of the confidence and the power. I am sole heir to these, who can lift an airplane into the sky and feel, as the cloud wheels beneath him, that he has come truly home once again.

Look up, of a morning when the sun rises through the clouds, or of an evening as it sets. A thousand slanting shafts of gold, aren't there? A brilliance, a sort of molten fire hidden? These are just the sights of my land seen from the ground, so bright and so warm and with beauty filled that the cloud cannot contain it all and splashes its overflow onto the earth as just a hint of the brilliance and the gold that exists above.

That little sound of four cylinders or five or seven, above the cloud, comes from a winged machine that is immersed in bright wonder. To be up there and fly alongside this creature is to see a vision, for the wings of an airplane in the sunrise are of beaten gold, going bright silver if you catch the proper angle, and on the canopy and along the windscreen dance the sparkle of diamonds. And within, a pilot, watching. What can you say, seeing this? You say nothing, and you share with another man in another cockpit a time of silence.

For when he sees this, when the magnificence floods over an airplane and the man who guides it, there is no speaking. Enchanted in the high land, to mention of beauty and joy in the mundane surroundings of earth and city and wall and polite society is to feel gawkish and out of place. Even to his best beloved, a pilot cannot speak of the wonder of the sky.

After the sun is high and the spell fades, one's fuel is gone. The white needle is at the E, the little indicator cork ceases its bobbing, a red low-level-warning light glares above a fuel counter. And in a minute or five or ten, the tires thud again onto the grass or scream a bluesmoke cry against the concrete of a once-forgotten runway. Mission done, flight over. Chalk up another hour. Pencil and logbook for a moment busy. But though the earth once again spreads beneath our feet, and the unnatural quiet of an engineless world surrounds us, there is new fuel to be hosed into tanks, and another page in the log to be filled.

To a pilot, the most important thing in the world is flight. To share it is the gift without price. Therein is a key to the sometimes wild acts of young pilots. They fly under bridges, they buzz housetops, they loop and roll their airplane much closer to the ground than is safe. They are a major concern of military flight-training bases, for such action reflects a lack of discipline, and occasionally means the loss of student and airplane. But his thought is to give, to share joy with those he loves, to share a truth. For pilots sometimes see behind the curtain, behind the veil of gossamer velvet, and find the truth behind man, the force behind a universe.

In the bright thread are woven four billion lives. Now and again, a man will see a certain brightness beyond the curtain and go spinning away into the depths of reality. We who remain watch him go, marvel for a moment, and return to our stations at our own crossthreads in the woof and the warp of a sparkling illusion.

For even in an airplane we see too often imperfectly. With advancing invention, with cockpits closed and navigation instruments and radio and new electronics, the problem of flying has become something to be solved more and more within an arm's distance of the pilot. Drifting off course? A needle shows it, points the error, and all the pilot must do to see it is to look within a three-inch face of glass. Concerned about weather ahead? Dial a frequency on the radio, call a meteorologist and ask expert advice.

137

Airplane slowing in the air, approaching a stall? A red light flashes on the instrument panel, a warning horn blares. We look outside to the sky only when we have time to enjoy the view, and if we don't want to be bothered with the view, we needn't look outside from takeoff till touchdown. It is this kind of flight over which the manufacturers of flight simulators can boast, "Impossible to tell our trainer from flight itself!" And so it is. Those who define flight as a series of hours spent in attention to the moving gages of an instrument panel cannot tell the difference. The only thing that is missing is the wind. The heat of the sun. The canyons of cloud and sheer white walls rising solid at each wingtip. The sound and the sting of rain, the freezing cold of altitude, the sea of moonlight in its bed of fog, the stars untwinkling and ice-hard in a midnight sky.

So. The biplane. Is it the better way? If the Parks flies too slowly, there are no warning horns or flashing red lights. Just a shudder in the control stick and it turns into a machine unwilling to be controlled, suddenly aware that it is heavier than the air. One must be careful and alert for the shudder. One must look outside, for outside is flight itself, the moving through the air and knowing it. Especially, knowing it.

Navigation is goggles down, look over the side, down through the churning winds. The railroad: so. The river crossing: so. But the lake, there should be a lake here. Perhaps there are headwinds. . . .

A check on the weather is a constant thing. The clouds mass and grow together, lowering into the hills. Slanting columns of rain, where earlier there was no rain. What to do, pilot, what to do? Beyond the hills, the cloud may thin, or break. But then, beyond the hills, the cloud can lower to brush the grasstops ragged and soak them in rain. Hills are green coffins for the airplanes and pilots who judge wrongly. Beware the hills when the cool grey mist is pulled over your eyes.

Decide, pilot. Land now? Choose the pasture for soft touchdown and certainty of longer living? Or push on, into the grey? This is flight: decisions. And knowing that sooner or later an airplane must always come to rest.

A lonely impulse of delight
Drove to this tumult in the clouds . . .

—W. B. Yeats
"An Irish Airman Foresees His Death"

REFLECTIONS (7)

REFLECTIONS

What is the difference between "labels" and "meanings" as Richard Bach uses the words? Do they overlap, or are they distinctly different? Is one more "true" or "real" than the other? Do they have different kinds of uses?

Does Bach succeed in conveying to you some understanding of his mood? If so, does he do it with labels, meanings, symbols, or something else?

*Like Richard Bach, Anne Morrow Lindbergh
(also a flier, and the wife of a more famous
one) plays with symbols and meanings, and
with questions of freedom and joy. Like Bach,
she sees fear as the enemy of joy, as the
poison of solitude. Solitude is not a condition to be borne with resignation, but a
wholeness and independence to be relished.
The occasion of this essay is a vacation on an
island beach, a time for the author to reflect
upon where she is, where she has been, where
she is going. Exploring in thought her relationships with her husband, her children,
and others, she makes discoveries as she
writes, and the meanings radiate from her
words like ripples from stones dropped
in a pool.*

ANNE MORROW
LINDBERGH

Argonauta

There are in the beach-world certain rare creatures, the "Argonauta"
(Paper Nautilus), who are not fastened to their shell at all. It is actually
a cradle for the young, held in the arms of the mother argonaut who floats
with it to the surface, where the eggs hatch and the young swim away. Then
the mother argonaut leaves her shell and starts another life. I am fascinated
by this image of the argonaut, whose temporary dwelling I have seen only
as the treasure of a specialist's collection. Almost transparent, delicately
fluted like a Greek column, this narcissus-white snail shell is feather light

as some coracle of ancient times, ready to set sail across unknown seas. It was named, the book tells me, for the fabled ships of Jason that went in search of the Golden Fleece. Sailors consider these shells a sign of fair weather and favorable winds.

Lovely shell, lovely image—I am tempted to play with it in my mind. Is this the symbol for another stage in relationships? Can we middle-aged argonauts when we outgrow the oyster bed, look forward to the freedom of the nautilus who has left its shell for the open seas? But what does the open sea hold for us? We cannot believe that the second half of life promises "fair weather and favorable winds." What golden fleece is there for the middle-aged?

In speaking of the argonauta one might as well admit one has left the usual shell collections. A double-sunrise shell, an oyster bed—these are common knowledge to most of us. We recognize them; we know about them; they are part of our daily life and the lives of others around us. But with this rare and delicate vessel, we have left the well-tracked beaches of proven facts and experiences. We are adventuring in the chartless seas of imagination.

Is the golden fleece that awaits us some kind of new freedom for growth? And in this new freedom, is there any place for a relationship? I believe there is, after the oyster bed, an opportunity for the best relationship of all: not a limited, mutually exclusive one, like the sunrise shell; and not a functional, dependent one, as in the oyster bed;[1] but the meeting of two whole fully developed people as persons. It would be, to borrow a definition of the Scottish philosopher, MacMurray, a fully personal relationship, that is, "a type of relationship into which people enter as persons with the whole of themselves." "Personal relationships," he goes on to explain, ". . . have no ulterior motive. They are not based on particular interests. They do not serve partial and limited ends. Their value lies entirely in themselves and for the same reason transcends all other values. And that is because they are relations of persons as persons." This relationship of "persons as persons" was prophetically hinted at by the German poet, Rilke, almost fifty years ago. He foresaw a great change in the relationships between men and women, which he hoped in the future would no longer follow the traditional patterns of submission and domination or of possession and competition. He described a state in which there would be space and freedom for growth, and in which each partner would be the means of releasing the other. "A relation," he concludes, "that is meant to be of one human be-

[1] The author alludes to her other essays in *Gift from the Sea,* each one taking a different shell as a symbol of a kind of human relationship.

ing to another, . . . And this more human love (that will fulfill itself, infinitely considerate and gentle, and good and clear in binding and releasing) will resemble that which we are with struggle and endeavor preparing, the love that consists in this, that two solitudes protect and touch and greet each other."

But this new relationship of persons as persons, this more human love, this two solitudes conception is not something that comes easily. It must have grown, like all firm-rooted growth, slowly. It perhaps can only follow a long development in the history of human civilization and individually in each human being's life. Such a stage in life, it would seem to me, must come not as a gift or a lucky accident, but as part of an evolutionary process, an achievement which could only follow certain important developments in each partner.

It cannot be reached until woman—individually and as a sex—has herself come of age, a maturing process we are witnessing today. In this undertaking she must work alone and cannot count on much help from the outsider, eager as he may be in pointing out the way. There are many signs of interest in the new woman today, chiefly in the form of mechanistic studies of her as a female animal. Of course it is necessary and helpful for woman to understand and accept her sexual needs and habits but it is only one side of a very complex problem. One cannot expect statistics on her physical reactions to add much knowlege or nourishment to her inner life, to her basic relation to herself, or to her long postponed hope and right, as a human being, to be creative in other ways besides the purely physical one.

Woman must come of age by herself. This is the essence of "coming of age"—to learn how to stand alone. She must learn not to depend on another, nor to feel she must prove her strength by competing with another. In the past, she has swung between these two opposite poles of dependence and competition, of Victorianism and Feminism. Both extremes throw her off balance; neither is the center, the true center of being a whole woman. She must find her true center alone. She must become whole. She must, it seems to me, as a prelude to any "two solitudes" relationship, follow the advice of the poet to become "world to oneself for another's sake."

In fact, I wonder if both man and woman must not accomplish this heroic feat. Must not man also become world to himself? Must he not also expand the neglected sides of his personality; the art of inward looking that he has seldom had time for in his active outward-going life; the personal relationships which he has not had as much chance to enjoy; the so-called feminine qualities, aesthetic, emotional, cultural and spiritual, which he has been too rushed to fully develop. Perhaps both men and women in America may hunger, in our material, outward, active, masculine culture, for the sup-

143

posedly feminine qualities of heart, mind and spirit—qualities which are actually neither masculine nor feminine, but simply human qualities that have been neglected. It is growth along these lines that will make us whole, and will enable the individual to become world to himself.

And this greater wholeness in each person, this being "world to oneself," does this not mean greater self-sufficiency and therefore, inevitably, greater separation between man and woman? With growth, it is true, comes differentiation and separation, in the sense that the unity of the tree-trunk differentiates as it grows and spreads into limbs, branches, and leaves. But the tree is still one, and its different and separate parts contribute to one another. The two separate worlds or the two solitudes will surely have more to give each other than when each was a meager half. "A complete sharing between two people is an impossibility," writes Rilke, "and whenever it seems, nevertheless, to exist, it is a narrowing, a mutual agreement which robs either one member or both of his fullest freedom and development. But, once the realization is accepted that, even between the closest human beings, infinite distances continue to exist, a wonderful living side by side can grow up, if they succeed in loving the distance between them which makes it possible for each to see the other whole and against a wide sky!"

This is a beautiful image, but who can achieve it in actual life? Where has one seen such a marriage except in a poet's correspondence? It is true that Rilke's two solitudes or MacMurray's fully personal relationship are as yet somewhat theoretical concepts. But theory precedes exploration; we must use any signposts that exist to help us through the wilderness. For we are, actually, pioneers trying to find a new path through the maze of tradition, convention and dogma. Our efforts are part of the struggle to mature the conception of relationships between men and women—in fact all relationships. In such a light, every advance in understanding has value. Every step, even a tentative one, counts. And though we may seldom come upon a perfect argonauta life cycle, we have all had glimpses of them, even in our own lives for brief periods. And these brief experiences give us insight into what the new relation might be.

On this island I have had such a glimpse into the life of the argonauta. After my week alone I have had a week of living with my sister. I will take from it one day. I shall examine it, set it before me as I have set the shells on my desk. I shall turn it around like a shell, testing and analyzing its good points. Not that my life will ever become like this day—a perfect one plucked out of a holiday week; there are no perfect lives. The relation of two sisters is not that of a man and a woman. But it can illustrate the essence of relationships. The light shed by any good relationship illuminates all relationships. And one perfect day can give clues for a more perfect life—the mythical life, maybe, of the argonauta.

We wake in the same small room from the deep sleep of good children, to the soft sound of wind through the casuarina trees and the gentle sleep-breathing rhythm of waves on the shore. We run bare-legged to the beach, which lies smooth, flat, and glistening with fresh wet shells after the night's tides. The morning swim has the nature of a blessing to me, a baptism, a rebirth to the beauty and wonder of the world. We run back tingling to hot coffee on our small back porch. Two kitchen chairs and a child's table between us fill the stoop on which we sit. With legs in the sun we laugh and plan our day.

We wash the dishes lightly to no system, for there are not enough to matter. We work easily and instinctively together, not bumping into each other as we go back and forth about our tasks. We talk as we sweep, as we dry, as we put away, discussing a person or a poem or a memory. And since our communication seems more important to us than our chores, the chores are done without thinking.

And then to work, behind closed doors neither of us would want to invade. What release to write so that one forgets oneself, forgets one's companion, forgets where one is or what one is going to do next—to be drenched in work as one is drenched in sleep or in the sea. Pencils and pads and curling blue sheets alive with letters heap up on the desk. And then, pricked by hunger, we rise at last in a daze, for a late lunch. Reeling a little from our intense absorption, we come back with relief to the small chores of getting lunch, as if they were lifelines to reality—as if we had indeed almost drowned in the sea of intellectual work and welcomed the firm ground of physical action under our feet.

After an hour or so of practical jobs and errands we are ready to leave them again. Out onto the beach for the afternoon where we are swept clean of duties, of the particular, of the practical. We walk up the beach in silence, but in harmony, as the sandpipers ahead of us move like a corps of ballet dancers keeping time to some interior rhythm inaudible to us. Intimacy is blown away. Emotions are carried out to sea. We are even free of thoughts, at least of their articulation; clean and bare as whitened driftwood; empty as shells, ready to be filled up again with the impersonal sea and sky and wind. A long afternoon soaking up the outer world.

And when we are heavy and relaxed as the seaweed under our feet, we return at dusk to the warmth and intimacy of our cottage. We sip sherry at leisure in front of a fire. We start supper and we talk. Evening is the time for conversation. Morning is for mental work, I feel, the habit of

145

school-days persisting in me. Afternoon is for physical tasks, the out-of-door jobs. But evening is for sharing, for communication. Is it the uninterrupted dark expanse of the night after the bright segmented day, that frees us to each other? Or does the infinite space and infinite darkness dwarf and chill us, turning us to seek small human sparks?

Communication—but not for too long. Because good communication is stimulating as black coffee, and just as hard to sleep after. Before we sleep we go out again into the night. We walk up the beach under the stars. And when we are tired of walking, we lie flat on the sand under a bowl of stars. We feel stretched, expanded to take in their compass. They pour into us until we are filled with stars, up to the brim.

This is what one thirsts for, I realize, after the smallness of the day, of work, of details, of intimacy—even of communication, one thirsts for the magnitude and universality of a night full of stars, pouring into one like a fresh tide.

And then at last, from the immensity of interstellar space, we swing down to a particular beach. We walk back to the lights of the cottage glowing from the dark mist of trees. Small, safe, warm and welcoming, we recognize our pinpoint human match-light against the mammoth chaos of the dark. Back again to our good child's sleep.

What a wonderful day, I think, turning it around in my hand to its starting point again. What has made it so perfect? Is there not some clue here in the pattern of this day? To begin with, it is a pattern of freedom. Its setting has not been cramped in space or time. An island, curiously enough, gives a limitless feeling of both. Nor has the day been limited in kinds of activity. It has a natural balance of physical, intellectual and social life. It has an easy unforced rhythm. Work is not deformed by pressure. Relationship is not strangled by claims. Intimacy is tempered by lightness of touch. We have moved through our day like dancers, not needing to touch more than lightly because we were instinctively moving to the same rhythm.

A good relationship has a pattern like a dance and is built on some of the same rules. The partners do not need to hold on tightly, because they move confidently in the same pattern, intricate but gay and swift and free, like a country dance of Mozart's. To touch heavily would be to arrest the pattern and freeze the movement, to check the endlessly changing beauty of its unfolding. There is no place here for the possessive clutch, the clinging arm, the heavy hand; only the barest touch in passing. Now arm in arm, now face to face, now back to back—it does not matter which. Because they know they are partners moving to the same rhythm, creating a pattern together, and being invisibly nourished by it.

146

The joy of such a pattern is not only the joy of creation or the joy of participation, it is also the joy of living in the moment. Lightness of touch and living in the moment are intertwined. One cannot dance well unless one is completely in time with the music, not leaning back to the last step or pressing forward to the next one, but poised directly on the present step as it comes. Perfect poise on the beat is what gives good dancing its sense of ease, of timelessness, of the eternal. It is what Blake was speaking of when he wrote:

> He who bends to himself a joy
> Doth the wingèd life destroy;
> But he who kisses the joy as it flies
> Lives in Eternity's sunrise.

The dancers who are perfectly in time never destroy "the wingèd life" in each other or in themselves.

But how does one learn this technique of the dance? Why is it so difficult? What makes us hesitate and stumble? It is fear, I think, that makes one cling nostalgically to the last moment or clutch greedily toward the next. Fear destroys "the wingèd life." But how to exorcise it? It can only be exorcised by its opposite, love. When the heart is flooded with love there is no room in it for fear, for doubt, for hesitation. And it is this lack of fear that makes for the dance. When each partner loves so completely that he has forgotten to ask himself whether or not he is loved in return; when he only knows that he loves and is moving to its music—then, and then only, are two people able to dance perfectly in tune to the same rhythm.

But is this all to the relationship of the argonauta—this private pattern of two dancers perfectly in time? Should they not also be in tune with a larger rhythm, a natural swinging of the pendulum between sharing and solitude; between the intimate and the abstract; between the particular and the universal, the near and the far? And is it not the swinging of the pendulum between these opposite poles that makes a relationship nourishing? Yeats once said that the supreme experience of life was "to share profound thought and then to touch." But it takes both.

First touch, intimate touch of the personal and particular (the chores in the kitchen, the talk by the fire) then the loss of intimacy in the great stream of the impersonal and abstract (the silent beach, the bowl of stars overhead). Both partners are lost in a common sea of the universal which absorbs and yet frees, which separates and yet unites. Is this not what the more mature relationship, the meeting of two solitudes, is meant to be? The double-sunrise stage was only intimate and personal. The oyster bed was caught in the particular and the functional. But the argonauta, should

147

they not be able to swing from the intimate and the particular and the functional out into the abstract and the universal, and then back to the personal again?

And in this image of the pendulum swinging in easy rhythm between opposite poles, is there not a clue to the problem of relationships as a whole? Is there not here even a hint of an understanding and an acceptance of the winged life of relationships, of their eternal ebb and flow, of their inevitable intermittency? "The life of the spirit," said Saint-Exupéry, "the veritable life, is intermittent and only the life of the mind is constant. . . . The spirit . . . alternates between total vision and absolute blindness. Here is a man, for example, who loves his farm—but there are moments when he sees in it only a collection of unrelated objects. Here is a man who loves his wife—but there are moments when he sees in love nothing but burdens, hindrances, constraints. Here is a man who loves music—but there are moments when it cannot reach him."

The "veritable life" of our emotions and our relationships also is intermittent. When you love someone you do not love them all the time, in exactly the same way, from moment to moment. It is an impossibility. It is even a lie to pretend to. And yet this is exactly what most of us demand. We have so little faith in the ebb and flow of life, of love, of relationships. We leap at the flow of the tide and resist in terror its ebb. We are afraid it will never return. We insist on permanency, on duration, on continuity; when the only continuity possible, in life as in love, is in growth, in fluidity—in freedom, in the sense that the dancers are free, barely touching as they pass, but partners in the same pattern. The only real security is not in owning or possessing, not in demanding or expecting, not in hoping, even. Security in a relationship lies neither in looking back to what it was in nostalgia, nor forward to what it might be in dread or anticipation, but living in the present relationship and accepting it as it is now. For relationships, too, must be like islands. One must accept them for what they are here and now, within their limits—islands, surrounded and interrupted by the sea, continually visited and abandoned by the tides. One must accept the security of the wingèd life, of ebb and flow, of intermittency.

Intermittency—an impossible lesson for human beings to learn. How can one learn to live through the ebb-tides of one's existence? How can one learn to take the trough of the wave? It is easier to understand here on the beach, where the breathlessly still ebb-tides reveal another life below the level which mortals usually reach. In this crystalline moment of suspense, one has a sudden revelation of the secret kingdom at the bottom of the sea. Here in the shallow flats one finds, wading through warm ripples, great horse-conchs pivoting on a leg; white sand dollars, marble medallions engraved in the mud; and myriads of bright-colored cochina-clams, glistening in the foam, their shells opening and shutting like butter-flies' wings. So beautiful is the still hour of the sea's withdrawal, as beautiful as the sea's return when the encroaching waves pound up the beach, pressing to reach those dark rumpled chains of seaweed which mark the last high tide.

Perhaps this is the most important thing for me to take back from beach-living: simply the memory that each cycle of the tide is valid; each cycle of the wave is valid; each cycle of a relationship is valid. And my shells? I can sweep them all into my pocket. They are only there to remind me that the sea recedes and returns eternally.

I got up early and bathed in the pond; that was a religious exercise, and one of the best things which I did. They say that characters were engraven on the bathing tub of King Tching-thang to this effect: "Renew thyself completely each day; do it again, and again, and forever again."

—Henry David Thoreau
Walden

In any weather, at any hour of the day or night, I have been anxious to improve the nick of time, and notch it on my stick too; to stand on the meeting of two eternities, the past and future, which is precisely the present moment; to toe that line.

—Henry David Thoreau
Walden

In every moment of immediate experience is somewhat absolutely original and novel.

—William James
"A Pluralistic Mystic"

REFLECTIONS (8)

REFLECTIONS

Does a symbol (for example, the argonaut shell) generate a meaning (for example, the fully personal relationship), or does a meaning find a symbol? Which way does your mind work? Or does it work either way?

What would be a good symbol for loneliness? For freedom? For joy? For the end of a love affair? For the beginning of one?

What might be symbolized by a fallen leaf? A cork bobbing in a stream? A soda straw? An egg? A broken cup? A star?

Which of Anne Morrow Lindbergh's symbols or comparisons seem most effective, most meaningful, to you? Can you see other ways to use them, other connections to make?

*For Huckleberry Finn and his friend Jim,
the runaway slave, drifting down the Mississippi River on a raft means freedom, in
two ways. The river is their path to free
territory, where Jim can find safety; and the
solitude and isolation imposed on them by
their fugitive status frees them from the
routine and social convention of everyday
life, creating a sense of ease and receptive-
ness that enables them to become fully awake
to the beauty and variety of their world.*

SAMUEL CLEMENS

It's Lovely to Live on a Raft

Two or three days and nights went by; I reckon I might say they swum by, they slid along so quiet and smooth and lovely. Here is the way we put in the time. It was a monstrous big river down there—sometimes a mile and a half wide; we run nights, and laid up and hid day-times; soon as night was most gone, we stopped navigating and tied up—nearly always in the dead water under a tow-head; and then cut young cottonwoods and willows and hid the raft with them. Then we set out the lines. Next we slid into the river and had a swim, so as to freshen up and cool off; then we set down on the sandy bottom where the water was about knee deep, and watched the daylight come. Not a sound, anywheres—perfectly still—just like the whole world was asleep, only sometimes the bull-frogs a-cluttering, maybe. The first thing to see, looking away over the water, was a kind of dull line—that was the woods on t'other side—you couldn't make nothing else out; then a pale place in the sky; then more paleness, spreading around; then the river softened up, away off, and warn't black any more, but gray; you could see little dark spots drifting along, ever so far away—trading scows, and such things; and long black streaks—rafts; sometimes you could hear a sweep screaking; or jumbled up voices, it was so still, and sounds come so far; and by-and-by you could see a streak on the water which you know by the look of the streak that there's a snag there in a swift current which breaks on it and makes that streak look that way; and you see the mist curl up off of the water, and the east reddens up, and the river, and you make out a log cabin in the edge of the woods, away on the bank on t'other side of the river, being a wood-yard, likely, and piled by them cheats so you can throw a dog through it anywheres; then the nice breeze springs up, and comes fanning you from over there, so cool and fresh, and sweet to smell, on account of the woods and the flowers; but sometimes not that way, because they've left dead fish laying around, gars, and such, and they do get pretty rank; and next you've got the full day, and everything smiling in the sun, and the song-birds just going it!

A little smoke couldn't be noticed, now, so we would take some fish off the lines, and cook up a hot breakfast. And afterwards we would watch the lonesomeness of the river, and kind of lazy along, and by-and-by lazy off to sleep. Wake up, by-and-by, and look to see what done it, and maybe see a steamboat coughing along up stream, so far off towards the other side you couldn't tell nothing about her only whether she was stern-wheel or side-wheel; then for about an hour there wouldn't be nothing to hear nor nothing to see—just solid lonesomeness. Next you'd see a raft sliding by, away off yonder, and maybe a galoot on it chopping, because they're almost always doing it on a raft; you'd see the ax flash, and come down—you don't hear nothing; you see that ax go up again, and by the time it's above the man's head, then you hear the *k'chunk!*—it had took all that time to come over the water. So we would put in the day, lazying around, listening to the stillness. Once there was a thick fog, and the rafts and things that went by was beating tin pans so the steamboats wouldn't run over them. A scow or a raft went by so close we could hear them talking and cussing and laughing—heard them plain; but we couldn't see no sign of them; it made you feel crawly, it was like spirits carrying on that way in the air. Jim said he believed it was spirits; but I says:

"No, spirits wouldn't say, 'dern the dern fog.' "

Soon as it was night, out we shoved; when we got her out to about the middle, we let her alone, and let her float wherever the current wanted her to; then we lit the pipes, and dangled our legs in the water and talked about all kinds of things—we was always naked, day and night, whenever the mosquitoes would let us—the new clothes Buck's folks made for me was too good to be comfortable, and besides I didn't go much on clothes, nohow.

Sometimes we'd have that whole river all to ourselves for the longest time. Yonder was the banks and the islands, across the water; and maybe a spark—which was a candle in a cabin window—and sometimes on the water you could see a spark or two—on a raft or a scow, you know; and maybe you could hear a fiddle or a song coming over from one of them crafts. It's lovely to live on a raft. We had the sky, up there, all speckled with stars, and we used to lay on our backs and look up at them, and discuss about whether they was made, or only just happened—Jim he allowed they was made, but I allowed they happened; I judged it would have took too long to *make* so many. Jim said the moon could a *laid* them; well, that looked kind of reasonable, so I didn't say nothing against it, because I've seen a frog lay most as many, so of course it could be done. We used to watch the stars that fell, too, and see them streak down. Jim allowed they'd got spoiled and was hove out of the nest.

Once or twice of a night we would see a steamboat slipping along in the dark, and now and then she would belch a whole world of sparks up out of her chimbleys, and they would rain down in the river and look awful pretty; then she would turn a corner and her lights would wink out and her pow-wow shut off and leave the river still again; and by-and-by her waves would get to us, a long time after she was gone, and joggle the raft a bit, and after that you wouldn't hear nothing for you couldn't tell how long, except maybe frogs or something. . .

Voyages of Discovery

~~~~~~

A Sea of Troubles

*In time of peace in the modern world, if one is thoughtful
and careful, it is rather more difficult to be killed or
maimed in the outland places of the globe than it is in the
streets of our great cities, but the atavistic urge toward
danger persists and its satisfaction is called adventure.
However, your adventurer feels no gratification in crossing
Market Street in San Francisco against the traffic. Instead
he will go to a good deal of trouble and expense to get
himself killed in the South Seas. In reputedly rough water,
he will go in a canoe; he will invade deserts without
adequate food and he will expose his tolerant and
uninoculated blood to strange viruses. This is adventure.
It is possible that his ancestor, wearying of the humdrum
attacks of the saber-tooth, longed for the good old
days of pterodactyl and triceratops.*

—John Steinbeck
The Log from the Sea of Cortez

*Odysseus, King of the island of Ithaca and
hero of Homer's great epic poem,* The
Odyssey, *is the classical archetype of the sea
wanderer. After participating for ten years in
the Achaean seige of the walled city of Troy
and devising the famous trick of the wooden
horse by which Troy was finally vanquished,
Odysseus sailed homeward with his men. A
mishap, however, aroused the anger of
Poseidon, the great god of earthquakes and
oceans, whose enmity produced an astonishing succession of obstacles which kept
Odysseus sailing about the Mediterranean
Sea for another ten years before he finally
reached Ithaca and reclaimed his throne. In
all his adventures, Odysseus is the perfect
leader, yet thoroughly independent and as
courageous alone as with his men. He is endlessly resourceful and inventive in difficulties,
and usually succeeds in turning adverse situations to his advantage. Through all his trials
he never gives in to despair or self-pity.
Perhaps his most impressive quality is his
balance: he takes reasonable precautions, but
never shrinks from trouble; he repeatedly
defies Poseidon, yet he is almost always re-
spectful towards the gods; and though he
manages to enjoy life as much as anyone, he
never loses his cool self-control.* The Odyssey *is
the story of a man trying to get home and
being continually thwarted; yet it is also the
story of a man who finds enjoyment in pitting
himself against the worst adversities that
nature or the gods can offer. Near the end of
his long journey at last, having lost all his
companions, Odysseus is welcomed at the
court of King Alcinous, to the shores of
whose country he has drifted after the
destruction of his boat. At the king's request,
he relates for the court the tale of his adventures. In the portion that follows, which
forms Book XII of* The Odyssey, *Odysseus
tells how, after coping with the sorcery of
Circe who turns men into animals, and en-*

156

listing her assistance in making a visit to
Hades, he and his mariners faced harrowing
encounters with the Sirens, Scylla, and
Charybdis.

HOMER
Translated by Albert Cook

The Perils of Odysseus

"And when the ship had left the stream of the river
Oceanos, and reached the wave of the wide-pathed sea
And the island Aiaia, where the home and the dancing floors
Of the early-born dawn are, and the risings of the sun;
When we arrived there, we beached the ship on the sands
And got out ourselves beside the surf of the sea.
We fell asleep there and awaited the godly dawn.
And when the early-born, rosy-fingered dawn appeared,
I sent my companions off to the halls of Circe
To bring the body of Elpenor, who had died.
At once we cut logs where the shore jutted highest out,
And we buried him, lamenting and shedding a swelling tear.
When his dead body had been burned, and the gear of his body,
We heaped up a mound, dragged a grave marker up on it,
And set up his well-shaped oar on top of the mound.
We talked out the details, nor did we escape the notice
Of Circe as we came from Hades, but very swiftly
She adorned herself and came. Servants with her carried
Bread, many pieces of meat, and sparkling red wine.

Reprinted from Homer/THE ODYSSEY, A New Verse Translation by Albert Cook. By permission of W. W. Norton & Company, Inc. Copyright © 1967 by Albert Cook.

157

The divine goddess took her stand in our midst and spoke:
'Rash you are, who have gone alive into the hall of Hades,
Dying twice, when other men die a single time:
Well, come, eat of the provisions and drink wine
All day long in this place, and as soon as dawn appears
You shall set sail. I shall show you the way and point out
All the details, lest by some troublesome complication
You be hurt and suffer pain on land or on the sea.'
So she said, and the bold heart was persuaded within us.
So then for the entire day till the setting of the sun
We sat there dining on the endless meat and sweet wine.
But when the sun went down and the darkness came on
The men lay down by the stern cable of the ship.
She took me by the hand aside from my dear companions,
Sat me down, lay next to me, and asked me the details,
And I told everything to her in its due order.
Then the queenly Circe addressed a speech to me:
'So all this has been brought to an end. Now listen
To what I tell you; a god himself shall remind you.
First you will come to the Sirens, who enchant
All men, whenever anyone comes upon them.
Whoever in ignorance nears them and hears the voice
Of the Sirens—for that man, his wife and infant children
Do not stand by or rejoice at his homeward return,
But the Sirens enchant him with their clear-toned song,
Seated in a meadow. About is a large heap of bones,
Of men rotting, and the skin is shrinking around them.
But go on past; soften honey-sweet wax and smear it
In the ears of your companions lest any of the rest
Should listen. And if you yourself desire to listen,
Let them bind you upon the swift ship hand and foot
Erect at the mast; and let the rope ends be made fast from it,
So that you may hear and enjoy the Sirens' song.
If you implore your companions and call on them to free you,
Then have them bind you in further fastenings.
And when your companions have got on past those women,
At that point I shall no longer tell you in full detail
Which one of two ways will be yours, but you yourself
Must decide in your heart. I will tell you the alternatives:
In one place there are overhanging rocks; and against them

The great wave of dark blue-eyed Amphitrite[1] roars.
Those, indeed, do the blessed gods call the Wandering Rocks,
Where nothing that flies can get by, not even the timid
Doves that carry ambrosia to father Zeus.
And the sheer rock always takes away one of them,
But the Father sends another to make up the number.
No ship of men that arrives there ever escapes,
But sea waves and storms of destructive fire carry off
The timbers of the ships and the bodies of the men alike.
One seafaring ship alone did sail past the place,
The Argo, known to all men, as it sailed from Aietes,[2]
And it would swiftly have been dashed there on the great rocks
But Hera sent it past, since Jason was dear to her.
The other way there are two crags; one reaches to broad heaven
With its sharp peak, and a dark blue cloud surrounds it
That never recedes, nor ever does a clear sky
Hold the peak of it, either in summer or in autumn.
No mortal man could ever climb it or get on top,
Not even if he had twenty hands and twenty feet,
For the rock is sheer, as though polished all around,
And in the middle of the crag is a murky cave
Turned facing to the dusk toward Erebos,[3] and there,
Noble Odysseus, you should steer your hollow ship.
Nor could a vigorous man shooting with a bow
From the hollow ship reach to the open cave.
There within dwells Scylla, who barks dreadfully,
And her voice comes as loud as that of an unweaned puppy,
But she herself is an evil monster, nor would anyone
Take pleasure to see her, not if a god should confront her.
There are twelve feet on her, all dangling in air;
She has six very long necks, and on each one
A terrible head, and on it three rows of teeth
Thick-set and in a cluster, and full of black death.
She is withdrawn to her middle down in the hollow cave;
She holds her heads outside of the dreadful abyss,

---

[1] A sea goddess, wife of Poseidon.
[2] King of Colchis, from whose land Jason took the Golden Fleece with the help of
Colchis' daughter Medea, a sorceress. The *Argo* was Jason's ship.
[3] A region of darkness.

And there she fishes and reaches all around the crag
For dolphins and dogfish and whatver larger sea creature
She may catch that roaring Amphitrite feeds by the thousands.
There no sailors may ever claim to have escaped past
Unharmed with their ship. She carries off in each head
A mortal she has snatched up from a dark blue-prowed ship.
The second crag you will see lying lower, Odysseus,
Close to the other. And you could shoot an arrow across it.
Upon it is a large wild fig tree blooming with leaves;
There divine Charybdis sucks black water back under.
Three times daily she sends it up, three times sucks back
Terribly. Do not happen to be there when she sucks,
For not even the earth-shaker could save you from evil then,
But sail to the crag of Scylla very rapidly
And drive your ship on past, since it is better by far
To miss six companions on the ship than all at once.'
So she said, and I spoke out to her in answer:
'Come now, goddess, tell me this unerringly,
May I get away from destructive Charybdis somehow
And ward off the other, once she has despoiled my companions?'
So I said, and the divine goddess answered at once:
'You rash man, do the works of war concern you again
And toil? Will you not yield to the immortal gods?
She is not mortal for you, but an immortal evil,
Dreadful, oppressive, wild, and not to be fought.
And there is no defense. It is best to flee from her.
But if you linger and helm yourself beside the rock,
I fear that she may search and light on you again
And take away as many mortals as she has heads.
No, drive very strongly on, cry aloud for Cratais,
The mother of Scylla, who bore her as a bane for mortals.
Then she will stop her from reaching out a second time.
You will arrive at the isle of Thrinacria. There many
Oxen of the Sun and goodly sheep are pasturing,
Seven herds of cattle and as many lovely flocks of sheep,
Fifty in each. No offspring are born from them,
Nor do they ever wane. Goddesses and shepherds over them,
The fair-braided nymphs, Phaethusa and Lampetie,
Whom divine Neaira bore to Hyperion, the Sun.
When their queenly mother had borne them and raised them,
She sent them to the isle of Thrinacria to live far off,

To guard the sheep and crumple-horned cattle of their father.
If you let them go unmolested and think of your return,
You may get to Ithaca, though you do suffer ills.
But if you molest them, then I prophesy destruction
For your ship and companions. And even if you escape yourself
You will return late and ill, having lost all your companions.'
So she said, and at once the golden-throned Dawn came on.
The divine goddess herself returned then up the island,
But I went on to the ship and urged my companions
To go on board themselves and to undo the stern cables.
At once they got on and took their seats at the oarlocks.
Seated in order, they beat the hoary sea with their oars.
A driving wind full in the sails, a fine companion,
Did the fair-braided Circe, dread god with a singing voice,
Send on for us from behind the dark blue-prowed ship.
At once when we had tended to the gear through the ship piece by piece
We took our seats. The wind and a pilot steered her.
Then, grieving in my heart, I spoke to my companions:
'My friends, not one person or two alone need to know
The prophecies that the divine goddess Circe told me.
But I will tell them, so you may know whether we
Shall die or might avoid death and escape fate.
She ordered us first to avoid the voice of the marvelous
Sirens, and also their meadow full of flowers.
Me alone she ordered to hear their voice; but bind me
In hard bonds so that I may stay firm in my place
Erect at the mast. And let the rope-ends be fastened from it.
And if I implore you and call you to untie me
Then constrain me yourselves in further fastenings.'
So I declared, and made known the details to my companions.
Meanwhile the well-made ship arrived speedily
At the isle of the Sirens. A fair breeze drove it on.
Then at that point the wind died down, and there was
A windless calm, and some god put the waves to sleep.
My companions stood up and furled the sails on the ship.
They threw them in the hollow ship; then, seated at the oars,
They made the water white with the blades of smooth fir.
But I cut up a great disc of wax with a sharp sword
Into small pieces and kneaded it with my stout hands.
At once the wax softened when my great force had compelled it,
And the gleam of the Sun, Hyperion's lordly child.

161

I smeared it in all my companions' ears one by one,
And they bound me on the ship by my hands and feet
Erect on the mast and fastened rope ends from it.
Taking their seats, they beat the hoary sea with their oars.
But when it was as far off as a man's shout would carry,
While we pushed swiftly on, the fast-sailing ship did not get past
The Sirens—as it drew near, they struck up their clear-toned song:
'Come near, much-praised Odysseus, the Achaians' great glory;
Bring your ship in, so you may listen to our voice.
No one ever yet sped past this place in a black ship
Before he listened to the honey-toned voice from our mouths,
And then he went off delighted and knowing more things.
For we know all the many things that in broad Troy
The Argives and the Trojans suffered at the will of the gods.
We know all that comes to be on the much-nourishing earth.'
So they said, sending their lovely voice out. My heart
Desired to listen, and I told my companions to free me,
Signaling with my eyebrows. Falling to it, they rowed.
Standing up at once, Perimedes and Eurylochos
Bound me in further bonds and constrained me more,
And when we had got on past them and could no longer
Listen to the cry of the Sirens or their voice,
At once my trusty companions took out the wax
I had smeared in their ears and freed me from my bonds.
But when we had left the island, then at once
I saw smoke and a great wave and heard a noise.
As the men were afraid, the oars flew from their hands;
They all splashed down on the current. And the ship held
In place, since they could no longer drive the sharp-bladed oars with their
  hands.
But I went on through the ship, urging my companions
With soothing speeches, standing close to each man;
'Friends, so far we are not unacquainted with evils,
And this is really no greater evil upon us than when the Cyclops
Penned us in his hollow cave by his powerful force.
Yet even from there, through my prowess and my plan and thought,
We escaped; and I think perhaps we shall remember this too.
Come now, do as I tell you, let us all obey.
Beat the deep breakers of the sea with your oars,
Seated at the oarlocks, so that Zeus somehow
May grant that we escape and avoid this destruction.

To you, pilot, I give this command. And put it
In your heart as you tend the rudder of the hollow ship.
Keep the ship on the outside of this smoke and this wave,
And make for the crag lest the ship get away from you
As it rushes out there and you plunge us all into evil.'
So I said, and they obeyed my words right away.
I said no more of Scylla, the unavoidable danger,
Lest somehow in their fear over me my companions
Should cease from the rowing and crowd themselves within.
And then I forgot the hard injunction of Circe
When she ordered me in no way to arm myself.
I put on my famous armor, took two long spears
In my hands, and went up on the deck of the ship
At the prow, for from that place I expected rocky Scylla
First to be sighted, who bore me woe for my companions.
I could not discern her anywhere. My eyes were tired
As I peered everywhere out toward the murky rock.
And we sailed on through the narrow passage, lamenting.
There was Scylla, and on the other side godly Charybdis
Sucked back terribly the salt water of the sea.
Whenever she disgorged, like a basin in a large fire,
She seethed, all stirred up. And from overhead, foam
Fell down on both sides of the peaks of the crags,
And when she swallowed down the salt water of the sea
She appeared all stirred up within, and the rock roared
Terribly about, and the earth appeared underneath
In dark blue sand. Sallow fear seized the men.
We looked toward her in fear of our destruction.
Meanwhile Scylla snatched off of the hollow ship
Six of my companions, who were mightiest in strength.
But when I looked into the swift ship toward my companions
I saw already their hands and their feet from above
As they were lifted on high. They called to me with a cry,
Calling me then by name for the last time, grieving in heart.
As a fisher on a promontory with a very long rod
Throws down morsels as a lure for the little fish
And sends down into the ocean the horn of a field ox;
Then when he catches one writhing, throws it ashore;
So they, writhing, were raised up toward the rocks.
There at the entrance she ate them as they shrieked,
Reaching their hands toward me in their dread struggle.

163

That was the most piteous thing I saw with my eyes
Of all that I suffered as I sought out the paths of the sea.
But when we had fled the rocks and terrible Charybdis
And Scylla, we arrived at once at the blameless island
Of the god, where the beautiful broad-browed cattle were,
And the many goodly flocks of Hyperion, the Sun.
Then, while I was still on the ocean in the black ship,
I heard a lowing of cattle coming to the fold
And a bleating of sheep. Then there fell on my heart the speech
Of the blind prophet Theban Tiresias,
And of Aiaian Circe, who enjoined me many times
To avoid the isle of the Sun, who delights mortal men.
So then I addressed my companions, grieving in my heart:
'Hear my speech, though you have suffered ills, my companions,
So I may tell you the prophecies of Tiresias
And of Aiaian Circe, who enjoined me many times
To avoid the isle of the Sun, who delights mortal men.
They said a most dreadful evil would come on us there.
So let us drive the black ship on past that island.'
So I said, and their own hearts were shattered within them.
Eurylochos answered me at once with a hateful speech:
'You are tough, Odysseus, with your superior strength; your limbs
Do not get tired, but they are made all of iron for you
Who will not let your companions, worn out with fatigue
And sleepiness, set foot on land, where, moreover,
On the flood-circled island we might make a pleasant dinner,
But you bid us to wander as we are through the sudden night,
Carried away from the island upon the murky ocean.
And hard winds come up out of the night, the destroyers
Of ships. Where might one escape sheer destruction
If suddenly a storm of wind by chance came on,
Of the South Wind or the hard-blowing West Wind, that most
Tear ships to pieces beyond the will of the ruling gods?
No, but indeed, let us now give in to the black night.
Let us prepare dinner as we stay by the swift ship.
At dawn we shall get in and proceed on the broad ocean.'
So Eurylochos said, and my other companions agreed.
Then I knew that some god had devised evils,
And I spoke out to him, uttering winged words:
'Eurylochos, indeed you compel me, single as I am.
Come then, all of you, and swear me a mighty oath.

If we find some herd of cattle or a great flock
Of sheep, that no one in evil recklessness
Will slaughter any cow or sheep. But be secure
And eat the provisions that immortal Circe gave.'
So I said, and they at once swore an oath as I bid them.
And when they had sworn the oath and completed it,
They set the well-fashioned ship in a hollow harbor
Near sweet water. My companions got out and away
From the ship and then prepared dinner skillfully.
But when they had taken their fill of food and drink,
They then remembered and wept for our dear companions
Whom Scylla had snatched out of the hollow ship and eaten.
Balmy sleep came upon them as they were weeping.
When it was the third part of night and the stars had gone by,
Cloud-gathering Zeus raised a wind to blow against them
In a tremendous storm, and he covered land and ocean alike
Over with clouds. And night rose up out of heaven.
And when the early-born, rosy-fingered dawn appeared,
We beached the ship, dragging her into a hollow cave
Where the fair dancing-floors and the haunts of the nymphs were.
And then I made an assembly and addressed them a speech:
'My friends, since there is food and drink in the swift ship,
Let us hold off from the cattle, lest we suffer something.
These are the cattle and goodly sheep of a dreadful god,
The Sun, who sees everything and hears everything.'
So I said, and the bold spirit was persuaded in them.
The South Wind blew steadily a whole month; no other
Wind came up then except the East Wind and the South.
So long as they possessed grain and red wine
They held off from the cattle in their desire for life.
But when all the provisions had been used up from the ship,
They went out on the hunt, roving from necessity
For fish and birds, with bent hooks, for whatever came
Into their own hands. Hunger wore down their bellies.
Then I went away, up into the island so that I might pray
To the gods, for one to show me the way to return.
When I had gone through the island and got clear of my companions,
I washed my hands where there was shelter from the wind,
And I prayed to all of the gods who possess Olympos.
But they poured sweet sleep on me over my eyelids.
And Eurylochos unfolded a bad plan to my companions:

'Hear my speech, companions, though you have suffered ills.
There are all kinds of hateful deaths for wretched mortals,
But most piteous is to die and meet one's fate by hunger.
Come then, let us drive the best of the cattle of the Sun
And sacrifice them to the immortals who hold broad heaven,
And if we ever get to Ithaca, our fatherland,
We shall at once build a rich temple to Hyperion,
The Sun, and put in it many noble ornaments.
But if he is at all enraged for his straight-horned cattle
And wishes to destroy the ship, and the other gods follow,
I would rather gasp once into a wave and lose my life
Then to be starved a long time on a desert island.'
So Eurylochos said, and the other companions agreed.
At once they drove the best of the cattle of the Sun
From nearby. For not far away from the dark blue-prowed ship
Did the fine crumple-horned, broad-browed cattle pasture.
They surrounded them and made prayers to the gods,
When they had plucked tender leaves from an oak with high foliage,
For they did not have white barley on the well-timbered ship.
But when they had prayed and had slaughtered and flayed them,
They cut out the thighs and covered them over with fat.
They made two folds and lay the raw flesh upon them,
Nor did they have wine to pour on the burning sacrifices,
But used water for libation and roasted all the entrails.
And when the thighs were burned and they had eaten the inward parts,
They cut the rest in pieces and pierced it on spits.
And then balmy sleep flew away from my eyelids.
I went down to the swift ship and the strand of the sea.
And when I got up close to the bobbing ship,
The sweet aroma of roasting came over to me.
Then I groaned and cried out to the immortal gods:
'Father Zeus, and you other blessed, ever-living gods,
To my ruin, indeed, have you lulled me in relentless sleep;
And my companions, while waiting, have devised an enormous deed.'
Then a messenger came swiftly to Hyperion the Sun,
Long-gowned Lampetie, to say we had killed his cattle.
At once he addressed the immortals, angered in his heart:
'Father Zeus, and you other blessed, ever-living gods,
Take vengeance on the companions of Laertes' son Odysseus,
Who have presumptuously killed my cattle, in which I
Took delight when I went into the starry heaven

166

And when I turned back again from heaven to earth.
If they do not pay fitting recompense for the cattle,
I will go down to the place of Hades and shine among the dead.'
Cloud-gathering Zeus spoke out to him in answer:
'O Sun, do indeed shine among the immortals
And among mortal men on the grain-giving earth.
I shall smite their swift ship soon with a gleaming bolt
Into small pieces, and burn it in the middle of the wine-faced ocean.'
I heard these things from Calypso of the fair hair,
Who said she had heard them herself from the runner Hermes.
And when I had got down to the ship and the sea,
I rebuked them one after another on the spot. Nor could we
Find any remedy. The cattle were already dead.
Then at once the gods showed forth portents to the men;
The skins were creeping, meat lowed upon the spits,
Both roast and raw, and there came up the voice as of cattle.
And so for six days did my trusty companions
Feast on the fine cattle of the Sun they had driven off.
But when Zeus, son of Cronos, had added the seventh day,
At that point the wind ceased raging in a tempest.
We boarded at once and set out upon the broad ocean,
When we had set the mast up and hoisted the white sails.
And when we had left the island behind, no other land
Appeared at all, but only heaven and the sea.
Then the son of Cronos halted a dark blue cloud
Over the hollow ship, and the ocean darkened beneath it.
She ran on not too long a time. For at once there came
The shrieking West Wind raging in a great tempest,
And a storm of wind broke the forestays of the mast,
Both of them, and the mast fell backward, and all the tackle
Was thrown into the hold. On the stern of the ship
It hit the pilot's head. And in an instant it crushed
All the bones of his head together. Like a diver
He dropped down from the deck, and the bold spirit left his bones.
Zeus at that instant thundered and threw a bolt on the ship.
It whirled all around, struck by Zeus's thunderbolt,
And was filled with brimstone. My companions fell from the ship,
And they resembled sea crows around the black ship
As they were borne on the waves; a god took away their return.
I wandered through my ship until the surge had loosed
The planks from the keel, and the wave carried it stripped.

It broke the mast off the keel, and then the backstay,
Which had been made out of oxhide, was flung up on it.
Then I bound both the keel and the mast together.
Seated on them, I was carried by the destructive winds.
And then the West Wind ceased raging in a tempest
And the South Wind came quickly, bearing pains for my heart,
That I should still remeasure my course to destructive Charybdis.
All night long I was carried, and with the rising sun
I came to the crag of Scylla and to dreadful Charybdis.
And she had sucked back the salty water of the sea,
But I raised myself high up against the tall wild fig tree
And held myself fastened to it like a bat. Nor anywhere
Could I plant my feet firmly or climb up on it,
For its roots held far off and its branches were high swaying,
Tall and great, and they shadowed Charybdis over.
I held there steadily, till she should disgorge back
The mast and keel again. I longed for them, but they came late.
At the time when a man gets up from the assembly for dinner,
One who judges many quarrels of youthful adversaries,
At that time did the timber appear out of Charybdis.
I let my hands and feet be brought down from above
And plunged right on in the midst of the lengthy timbers.
Seated upon them, I rowed on with my hands.
The father of men and gods no longer let Scylla
See me, or I would not have escaped sheer destruction.
Nine days I was borne thence, and on the tenth night
The gods brought me near the island of Ogygia, where lives
Fair-braided Calypso, dread god with a singing voice.
She befriended me and cared for me. Why tell this story?
Already I have told it in your house yesterday
To you and your goodly wife. It is hateful to me
To tell over again a story that has been clearly told."

We might suppose that in thirty centuries
sailors would improve upon Odysseus' solu-
tion to the problem of the Sirens. John
Manifold's modern Odysseus is surely as well
protected against their allure as his ancient
namesake; but is he better off?

JOHN MANIFOLD

The Sirens

Odysseus heard the sirens; they were singing
Music by Wolf and Weinberger and Morley
About a region where the swans go winging,
Vines are in colour, girls are growing surely

Into nubility, and pylons bringing
Leisure and power to farms that live securely
Without a landlord. Still, his eyes were stinging
With salt and seablink, and the ropes hurt sorely.

Odysseus saw the sirens; they were charming,
Blonde, with snub breasts and little neat posteriors,
But could not take his mind off the alarming

Weather report, his mutineers in irons,
The radio failing; it was bloody serious.
In twenty minutes he forgot the sirens.

REFLECTIONS (9)

REFLECTIONS

Could any of Odysseus' adventures serve as symbols (or metaphors, or parables) to illustrate truths of human experience?

Aristotle, in his *Poetics,* argued that poetry is superior to either history or philosophy because it combines the virtues of both; that is, it teaches us both by precept, like philosophy, and by example, like history. Is Aristotle's idea relevant to this portion of *The Odyssey* or not?

On their voyage north up the Missouri River in the summer and fall of 1804, Lewis and Clark's Corps of Discovery awaited with apprehension their first encounter with the fierce Teton Sioux, one of the most feared and respected tribes of the northern plains. The Sioux had regularly terrorized French and Spanish trading parties heading upriver, either demanding tribute of outrageous quantities of goods before permitting further passage, or stopping the parties altogether and confiscating their merchandise. Lewis and Clark were in no mood to be bullied and robbed, and determined to call the Sioux's bluff at the risk of provoking an attack that would quickly have wiped out their small party. But familiar with Indian tactics and psychology, they were aware that confidence and boldness would be respected, while any sign of fear or indecision would provoke further aggression. They also suspected that the Sioux were not willing to risk unnecessarily the loss of many of their warriors, and preferred to gain what they could by bluster and guile. The Corps' strategy put tremendous pressure on every man, and Clark in particular shows the tension in his journal entries. At the same time, however, he is busily recording an impressively perceptive and detailed account of the appearance and behavior of his adversaries.

171

WILLIAM CLARK & ~~~~
JOHN ORDWAY ~~~~

At Odds with
the Teton Sioux

[Clark]   25TH SEPT.—[1804]

all well, raised a Flag Staff & made a orning or Shade on a Sand bar in the
mouth of Teton River,[1] for the purpose of Speeking with the Indians
under,   the Boat Crew on board at 70 yards Distance from the bar
The 5 Indians which we met last night Continued,   about 11 OClock
the It & 2d Chief Came we gave them Some of our Provisions to eat, they
gave us great Quantitis of Meet Some of which was Spoiled   we feel
much at a loss for the want of an interpreter the one we have can Speek
but little.

Met in Council at 12 oClock and after Smokeing, agreeable to the useal
Custom, Cap. Lewis proceeded to Deliver a Speech which we [were] ob-
lige[d] to Curtail for want of a good interpreter   all our party paraded.
gave a Medal to the Grand Chief Calld. in Indian *Un ton gar Sar bar* in
French *Beeffe nure* Black Buffalow. Said to be a good Man,   2nd
Chief *Torto hon gar* or the *Parti sin* or Partizan *bad*   the 3rd is the Beffe
De Medison [Beuffe de Medecine] his name is *Tar ton gar Wa ker*   1st
Considerable Man, *War zing go.* 2nd Considerable Man   *Second Bear*
—*Mato co que par.*

Envited those Cheifs on board to Show them our boat[2] and such Curiossi-

---

[1] Now called the Bad River, which enters the Missouri near Pierre, South Dakota.

[2] The *Discovery,* a 55-foot keelboat with 22 oars, a small swivel cannon at the bow,
and a cabin at the stern. The Corps took it as far as Fort Mandan, then sent it back
to St. Louis with a small party in the spring.

THE JOURNALS OF LEWIS AND CLARK. Copyright, 1953, by Bernard DeVoto. Reprinted by permission of the publisher, Houghton Mifflin Company.

ties as was Strange to them, we gave them ¼ a glass of whiskey which they appeared to be verry fond of, Sucked the bottle after it was out & Soon began to be troublesom, one the 2d Cheif assumeing Drunkness, as a Cloake for his rascally intentions I went with those Cheifs *(in one of the Perogues with 5 men—3 & 2 Inds.)* (which left the boat with great reluctiance) to Shore with a view of reconsileing those men to us, as Soon as I landed the Perogue three of their young Men Seased the Cable of the Perogue, *(in which we had pressents &c)* the Chiefs Soldr. Huged the mast, and the 2d Chief was verry insolent both in words & justures *(pretended Drunkenness & staggered up against me)* declareing I should not go on, Stateing he had not received presents sufficent from us, his justures were of Such a personal nature I felt My self Compeled to Draw my Sword *(and Made a Signal to the boat to prepare for action)* at this Motion Capt. Lewis ordered all under arms in the boat, those with me also Showed a Disposition to Defend themselves and me, the grand Chief then took hold of the roap & ordered the young Warrers away, I felt My Self warm & Spoke in verry positive terms.

Most of the Warriers appeared to have ther Bows strung and took out their arrows from the quiver. as I *(being surrounded)* was not permited to return, I Sent all the men except 2 Inps. [Interpreters] to the boat, the perogue Soon returned with about 12 of our determined men ready for any event. this movement caused a no: of the Indians to withdraw at a distance, Their treatment to me was verry rough & I think justified roughness on my part, they all lift [left] my Perogue, and Councild. with themselves the result I could not lern and nearly all went off after remaining in this Situation Some time I offered my hand to the 1. & 2. Chiefs who refusd. to receve it. I turned off & went with my men on board the perogue, I had not prosd. more the [than] 10 paces before the 1st Cheif 3rd & 2 Brave Men Waded in after me. I took them in & went on board

We proceeded on about 1 Mile & anchored out off a Willow Island placed a guard on Shore to protect the Cooks & a guard in the boat, fastened the Perogues to the boat, I call this Island bad humered Island as we were in a bad humer.

[Sgt. John Ordway][3]   TUESDAY 25TH SEPT. 1804.

a clear and pleasant morning. al things made ready to receive the Band of the Souix nation of Indians, Called the Tribe of Tetons. about 10 o.C. A.M.

---

[3] Third in command of the expedition. Ordway's journal gives more detail and a different perspective on the incident described by Clark.

they Came flocking in from boath Sides of the River. when 30 odd was selected under the american Collours Capt Lewis & Capt Clark went out to Speak and treat with them. Gave the 3 Chiefs 3 niew meddals & 1 american flag Some knives & other Small articles of Goods & Gave the head chief the Black Buffalow a red coat & a cocked hat & feather &.C. likewise Some Tobacco. We had no good interpreter but the old frenchman could make them understand tollarable well. but they did not appear to talk much untill they had got the goods, and then they wanted more, and Said we must Stop with them or leave one of the pearogues with them as that was what they expected. Capt Lewis Shewed them the air Gun.[4] Shot it several times. then the Captains brought the 3 chiefs and one warrier they had with them. Gave the warrier a Sertifficate. then Shewed the chiefs Some curiousities. Gave them a draghm. they brought a quantity of fat Buffaloe meat and offered us   the Captains accepted of Some of it. & Gave them pork in return. then the Captains told them that we had a great ways to goe & that we did not wish to be detained any longer. they then began to act as if they were Intoxicated   with Some difficulty Capt Clark got them to Shore. they then began to Show Some Signs of Stopping or attempting to Stop us. one of them Stayed on board the pearogue when Capt Clark & the chiefs went out of it. the head chief the Black Buffaloe, Seized hold of the cable of the pearogue and Set down. Capt Clark Spoke to all the party to Stand to their arms   Capt Lewis who was on board ordered every man to his arms. the large Swivel [was] loaded immediately with 16 Musquet Ball in it the 2 other Swivels loaded well with Buck Shot [and] each of them manned. Capt Clark used moderation with them told them that we must and would go on and would go. that we were not Squaws. but warriers. the chief Sayed he had warriers too and if we were to go on they would follow us and kill and take the whole of us by degrees or that he had another party or lodge above this [and] that they were able to destroy us. then Capt Clark told them that we were Sent by their great father the president of the U.S. and that if they misused us that he or Capt Lewis could by writing to him have them all distroyed as it were in a moment. they then requested that their women and children See the Boat as they never Saw Such a one, the Capt told them that we could not go far as the day was far Spent, but we would let them see that they Should not Stop us and that we Should go a Short distance and can Camp for the night. the chief then let go the Cable and Sayed that he was Sorry to have us Go for his women and children were naked and poor and wished to Git

---

[4] A newly-designed rifle powered by compressed air, which could fire 40 shots at one loading.

174

Some Goods, but he did not think we were Marchants, nor that we were loaded with Goods, but he was Sorry to have us leave them So Soon—they wished to come on board   Capt Clark took the chief and warriers on bord to Stay all night with them. we then Set off and proceeded on about 1 mile and Camped ankered out. the Guard and cooks on Shore &.C. the Indians Camped on s. s.   our Camp was on a willow Isl in the middle of the river, at our Starbord Side.

[Clark]   26TH OF SEPTEMBER WEDNESDAY 1804

Set out early   proceeded on and Came to by the Wish of the Chiefs for to let their Squars [squaws] & boys see the Boat and Suffer them to treat us well   great numbers of men womin & children on the banks viewing us,   these people Shew great anxiety,   they appear Spritely, Genrally ill looking & not well made their legs [& *arms*] Small generally,   they Grese & Black themselves when they dress make use of a hawks feathers about their heads. the men [wear] a robe & each a polecats Skin, for to hold ther *Bawe roley*[5] for Smoking,   fond of Dress & Show badly armed with fusees, &c.   The Squaws are Chearfull fine look'g womin not handsom, High Cheeks Dressed in Skins a Peticoat and roab which foldes back over ther Sholder, with long wool,   do all their laborious work & I may Say perfect Slaves to the Men, as all Squars of Nations much at War, or where the Womin are more noumerous than the men. after Comeing too Capt. Lewis & 5 men went on Shore with the Cheifs, who appeared disposed to make up & be friendly,   after Captain Lewis had been on Shore about 3 hours I became uneasy for fear of Deception & Sent a Serjeant to See him and know his treatment which he reported was friendly, & they were pre-pareing for a Dance this evening   The[y] made frequent Selicitiations for us to remain one night only and let them Show their good disposition towards us, we deturmined to remain,   after the return of Capt. Lewis, I went on Shore   on landing I was receved on a elegent painted B.[uffalo] Robe & taken to the Village by 6 Men & was not permited to touch the ground untill I was put down in the grand Concill house on a White dressed Robe. I saw Several Maha Prissners and Spoke to the Chiefs it was necessary to give those prisoners up & become good friends with the Mahas if they wished to follow the advice of their great father   I was in Several Lodges neetly formed as before mentioned as to the Baureily *(Bois brulé—Yankton)* Tribe. I was met by about 10 Well Dressd. young

---

[5] *Bois roulé*, the French name for kinnikinnic, a tobaccolike mixture of dried leaves and bark.

Men who took me up in a roabe Highly adecrated and Set me Down by the Side of their Chief on a Dressed Robe in a large Council House, this house formed a ¾ Circle of Skins Well Dressed and Sown together under this Shelter about 70 Men Set forming a Circle   in front of the Cheifs a plac of 6 feet Diameter was Clear and the pipe of peace raised on Sticks under which there was swans down scattered,   on each Side of this Circle two Pipes, the *(two)* flags of Spain[6] & the Flag we gave them in front of the Grand Chief   a large fire was near in which provisions were Cooking, in the Center about 400 lbs. of excellent Buffalo Beef as a present for us. Soon after they Set me Down, the Men went for Capt. Lewis brought him in the same way and placed him also by the Chief   in a fiew minits an old man rose & Spoke aproveing what we had done & informing us of their situation requesting us to take pity on them & which was answered. The great Chief then rose with great State [speaking] to the Same purpote as far as we Could learn & then with Great Solemnity took up the pipe of Peace & after pointing it to the heavins the 4 quarters of the Globe & the earth, he made Some disertation, lit it and presented the Stem to us to Smoke,   when the Principal Chief Spoke with the Pipe of Peace he took in one hand some of the most Delicate parts of the Dog which was prepared for the fiest & made a Sacrefise to the flag. after A Smoke had taken place, & a Short Harange to his people, we were requested to take the Meal *(& then put before us the dog which they had been cooking, & Pemitigon [pemmican] & ground potato in Several platters Pemn. is Buffa meat dried or jerked pounded & mixed with grease raw. Dog Sioux think great dish used on festivals eat little of dog—pemn. & pote good.)*[7] We Smoked for an hour *(till)* Dark & all was Cleared away   a large fire made in the Center, about 10 Musitions playing on tambereens *(made of hoops & Skin stretched),* long Sticks with Deer & Goats Hoofs tied so as to make a gingling noise, and many others of a Similer Kind,   those Men began to Sing, & Beet on the Tamboren,   the Women Came forward highly Deckerated in their Way, with Scalps and Tropies of War of their fathers Husbands Brothers or near Connections & proceeded to Dance the War Dance which they done with great Chearfullness untill about 12 oClock when we informed the Cheifs that they were fatigued &c.   they

---

[6] Spain still claimed much of the land west of the Mississippi and had been carrying on trade there for many years.

[7] The parenthetical additions are by the first editor of the journals, Nicholas Biddle, who had the assistance of the journals of Sergeants John Ordway and William Gass, and the personal presence of Private George Shannon, the best-educated member of the expedition.

then retired & we Accompd. by 4 Cheifs returned to our boat, they Stayed with us all night. Those people have Some brave men[8] which they make use of as Soldiers   those men attend to the police of the Village   Correct all errors   I saw one of them to day whip 2 Squars, who appeared to have fallen out,   when he approachd. all about appeared to flee with great turrow [terror]. at night they keep two 3, 4 5 men at different Distances walking around Camp Singing the accurrunces of the night

All the Men on board 100 paces from Shore   Wind from the S. E. moderate   one man verry sick on board with a Dangerass Abscess on his Hip. All in [good] Spirits this evening.

In this Tribe I saw 25 Squars and Boys taken 13 days ago in a battle with the Mahars   in this battle they Destroyd 40 Lodges, Killed 75 Men, & som boys & Children, & took 48 Prisoners Womin & boys which they promis both Capt. Lewis and my self Shall be Delivered up to Mr. Durion at the Bous rulie Tribe,   those are a retched and Dejected looking people   the Squars appear low & Corse but this is an unfavourable time to judge of them

We gave our Mahar inteptr. some fiew articles to give those Squars in his name Such as Alls, needles &c. &c.

I saw & eat Pemitigon the Dog, Groud. potatoe made into a Kind of homney, which I thought but little inferior. I also Saw a Spoon Made of a horn of an Animell of the Sheep Kind [Rocky Mountain sheep] the Spoon will hold 2 quarts.

27TH OF SEPT. THURSDAY 1804

I rose early after a bad nights Sleep   found the Chief[s] all up, and the bank as useal lined with Spectators   we gave the 2 great Cheifs a Blanket a peace, or rether they took off agreeable to their Custom the one they lay on and each one Peck of corn. after Brackfast Capt. Lewis & the Cheifs went on Shore, as a verry large part of their nation was comeing in, the Disposition of whome I did not know   one of us being sufficent on Shore, I wrote a letter to Mr. P. Durion & prepared a meadel & Some Comsns. *(Certifiates)* & Sent to Cap Lewis   at 2 oClock Capt. Lewis Returned with 4 Chiefs & a Brave Man named *War cha pa* or on his Guard when the friends of those people die they run arrows through their flesh above and below their elbows as a testimony of their Greaf.

after Staying about half an hour, I went with them on Shore, Those men left the boat with reluctience,   I went first to the 2d Cheifs Lodge,

---

[8] Members of secret, ritualistic military societies within the tribe.

177

where a croud came around   after Speeking on various Subjects I went to a princpal mans lodge from them to the grand Chiefs lodge,   after a fiew minits he invited me to a lodge within the Circle in which I Stayed with all their principal Men untill the Dance began, which was Similer to the one of last night performed by their women with poles on which Scalps of their enemies were hung, Some with the Guns Spears & War empliments of their husbands in their hands.

Capt. Lewis Came on Shore and we Continued untill we were Sleepy & returned to our boat,   the 2nd Chief & one principal Man accompanied us,   Those two Indians accompanied me on board in the Small Perogue; Capt. Lewis with a guard Still on Shore   the man who Steered not being much acustomed to Steer, passed the bow of the boat & the peroge Came broad Side against the Cable & broke it which obliged me to order in a loud voice all hands up & at their ores,   my preemptry order to the men and the bustle of their getting to their ores allarmd. the Cheifs, together with the appearance of the Men on Shore, as the boat turnd.   The Cheif hollowaed & allarmed the Camp or Town informing them that the Mahars was about attacking us *(them)*. In about 10 minits the bank was lined with men armed the 1st Cheif at their head,   about 200 men appeared and after about ½ hour returned all but about 60 men who continued on the bank all night,   the Cheifs Contd. all night with us. This allarm I as well as Capt. Lewis Considered as the Signal of their intentions (which was to Stop our proceeding on our journey and if Possible rob us)   we were on our Guard all night,   the misfortune of the loss of our Anchor obliged us to Lay under a falling bank much exposd. to the accomplishment of their hostile intentions. P. C. [Cruzatte] our Bowman who cd. Speek Mahar informed us in the night that the Maha Prisoners informed him we were to be Stoped. we Shew as little Sighns of a Knowledge of their intentions as possible   all prepared on board for any thing which might hapen we kept a Strong guard all night in the boat, no Sleep

28TH OF SEPTEMBER 1804 FRIDAY

Made many attempts in different ways to find our anchor, but Could not, the Sand had Covered it,   from the Misfortune of last night our boat was laying at Shore in a verry unfavourable Situation,   after finding that the anchor Could not be found we deturmined to proceed on,   with great difficuelty got the Chiefs out of our boat, and when we was about Setting out the Class Called the Soldiers took possession of the Cable the 1st Cheif which was still on board, & intended to go a Short distance up with us. I told him the men of his nation Set on the Cable,   he went out

178

& told Capt. Lewis who was at the bow the men Who Set on the roap was Soldiers, and wanted Tobacco   Capt. Lewis would not agree to be forced into any thing,   the 2d Chief [The Partisan] Demanded a flag & Tobacco which we refusd. to Give Stateing proper reasons to them for it   after much Dificuelty—which had nearly reduced us to necessity to hostilities I threw a Carrot of Tobacco to 1st Chief   took the port fire from the gunner. Spoke so as to touch his pride   The Chief gave the Tobacco to his Soldiers & he jurked the rope from them and handed it to the bowsman we then Set out under a Breeze from the S. E.   about 2 miles up we observed the 3rd Chief on Shore beckining to us   we took him on board he informed us the roap was held by the order of the 2d Chief who was a Double Spoken man,   Soon after we Saw a man Comeing full Speed, thro: the plains left his horse & proceeded across a Sand bar near the Shore   we took him on board & observed that he was the Son of the Chief we had on board   we Sent by him a talk to the nation Stateint [stating] the cause of our hoisting the red flag undr. the white,   if they were for peace Stay at home & do as we had Directed them, if the[y] were for war or were Deturmined to stop us we were ready to defend our Selves, we halted one houre & ½ on the S. S. & made a Substitute of Stones for a ancher, refreshed our men and proceeded on about 2 Miles higher up & Came to a verry Small Sand bar in the middle of the river & Stayed all night,   I am verry unwell for want of Sleep   Deturmined to Sleep to night if possible,   the Men Cooked & we rested well.

The first publication of the journals of the Lewis and Clark expedition was in the 1814 edition edited by Nicholas Biddle, a young Philadelphia attorney and magazine editor, who later became president of the Bank of the United States. It is interesting to compare the transcript of the original journals with Biddle's polished version. Here is the Biddle text based on Clark's journal entry for September 25, 1804.

TUESDAY, SEPTEMBER 25TH, 1804

The morning was fine, and the wind continued from the southeast. We raised a flagstaff and an awning, under which we assembled at twelve o'clock, with all the party parading under arms. The chiefs and warriors from the camp two miles up the river, met us, about fifty or sixty in number, and after smoking delivered them a speech; but as our Sioux interpreter, Mr. Durion, had been left with the Yanktons, we were obliged to make use of a Frenchman who could not speak fluently, and therefore we curtailed our harangue. After this we went through the ceremony of acknowledging the chiefs, by giving to the grand chief a medal, a flag of the United States, a laced uniform coat, a cocked hat and feather: to the two other chiefs a medal and some small presents; and to two warriors of consideration certificates. The name of the great chief is Untongasabaw, or Black Buffalo; the second Tortohonga, or the Partisan; the third Tartongawaka, or Buffalo Medicine: the name of one of the warriors was Wawzinggo; that of the second Matocoquepa, or Second Bear.

We then invited the chiefs on board, and showed them the boat, the airgun, and such curiosities as we thought might amuse them: in this we succeeded too well; for after giving them a quarter of a glass of whiskey, which they seemed to like very much, and sucked the bottle, it was with much difficulty that we could get rid of them. They at last accompanied captain Clark on shore in a periogue with five men; but it seems they had formed a design to stop us; for no sooner had the party landed than three of the Indians seized the cable of the periogue, and one of the soldiers of the chief put his arms round the mast: the second chief who affected intoxication, then said, that we should not go on, that they had not received presents enough from us: captain Clark told him that he would not be prevented from going on; that we were not squaws, but warriors; that we were sent by our great father, who could in a moment exterminate them: the chief replied, that he too had warriors, and was proceeding to offer personal violence to captain Clark, who immediately drew his sword, and made a signal to the boat to prepare for action. The Indians who surrounded him, drew their arrows from their quivers and were bending their bows, when the swivel in the boat was instantly pointed towards them, and twelve of our most determined men jumped into the periogue and joined captain Clark. This movement made an impression on them, for the grand chief ordered the young men away from the periogue, and they withdrew and held a short council with the warriors. Being unwilling to irritate them, captain Clark then went forward and offered his hand to the first and second chiefs, who refused to take it. He then turned from them and got into the periogue, but had not gone more than ten paces when both the chiefs and two of the warriors waded in after him, and he brought them on board. We then proceeded on for a mile and anchored off a willow island, which from the circumstances which had just occurred, we called Badhumoured island.

REFLECTIONS (10)

REFLECTIONS

Most of our impressions of the Plains Indians come from the movies and television. Are there any significant differences between these fictional Indians and the Indians described by Clark and Ordway?

What details reveal Clark's attitude toward the Indians? Is his description of them fair or prejudiced?

Comparing the transcript of Clark's original journal for September 25 with the edited version prepared by Biddle for publication, which do you prefer? Why? Was the editing necessary or desirable?

*The incredible horrors of the African slave
trade in the 18th and 19th centuries were for
some souls a hell on earth; for others, they
were an inconvenience, unpleasant only if
they happened to touch the slave-traders
themselves. Several different voices speak in
the poem that follows. The events they
describe actually happened—but on a far
vaster scale than the poem suggests.*

ROBERT HAYDEN

Middle Passage

I

Jesús, Estrella, Esperanza, Mercy:[1]

Sails flashing to the wind like weapons,
sharks following the moans the fever and the dying;
horror the corposant and compass rose.

Middle Passage:
    voyage through death
        to life upon these shores.

"10 April 1800—
Blacks rebellious. Crew uneasy. Our linguist says
their moaning is a prayer for death,
ours and their own. Some try to starve themselves.
Lost three this morning leaped with crazy laughter
to the waiting sharks, sang as they went under."

Desire, Adventure, Tartar, Ann:

---

[1] The names of slave ships.

Standing to America, bringing home
black gold, black ivory, black seed.

Deep in the festering hold thy father lies,
of his bones New England pews are made,
those are altar lights that were his eyes.

Jesus Saviour Pilot Me
Over Life's Tempestuous Sea

We pray that Thou wilt grant, O Lord,
safe passage to our vessels bringing
heathen souls unto Thy chastening.

Jesus Saviour

"8 bells. I cannot sleep, for I am sick
with fear, but writing eases fear a little
since still my eyes can see these words take shape
upon the page & so I write, as one
would turn to exorcism. 4 days scudding,
but now the sea is calm again. Misfortune
follows in our wake like sharks (our grinning
tutelary gods). Which one of us
has killed an albatross? A plague among
our blacks—Ophthalmia: blindness—& we
have jettisoned the blind to no avail.
It spreads, the terrifying sickness spreads.
Its claws have scratched sight from the Capt.'s eyes
& there is blindness in the fo'c'sle
& we must sail 3 weeks before we come
to port."

What port awaits us, Davy Jones'
or home? I've heard of slavers drifting, drifting,
playthings of wind and storm and chance, their crews
gone blind, the jungle hatred
crawling up on deck.

183

Thou Who Walked On Galilee

"Deponent further sayeth *The Bella J*
left the Guinea Coast
with cargo of five hundred blacks and odd
for the barracoons[2] of Florida:

"That there was hardly room 'tween-decks for half
the sweltering cattle stowed spoon-fashion there;
that some went mad of thirst and tore their flesh
and sucked the blood:

"That Crew and Captain lusted with the comeliest
of the savage girls kept naked in the cabins,
that there was one they called The Guinea Rose
and they cast lots and fought to lie with her:

"That when the Bo's'n piped all hands, the flames
spreading from starboard already were beyond
control, the negroes howling and their chains
entangled with the flames:

"That the burning blacks could not be reached,
that the Crew abandoned ship,
leaving their shrieking negresses behind,
that the Captain perished drunken with the wenches:

"Further Deponent sayeth not."

Pilot Oh Pilot Me

II

Aye, lad, and I have seen those factories,
Gambia, Rio Pongo, Calabar;
have watched the artful mongos baiting traps
of war wherein the victor and the vanquished

---

2 Slave barracks.

Were caught as prizes for our barracoons.
Have seen the nigger kings whose vanity
and greed turned wild black hides of Fellatah,
Mandingo, Ibo, Kru to gold for us.

And there was one—King Anthracite we named him—
fetish face beneath French parasols
of brass and orange velvet, impudent mouth
whose cups were carven skulls of enemies:

He'd honor us with drum and feast and conjo
and palm-oil-glistening wenches deft in love,
and for tin crowns that shone with paste,
red calico and German silver trinkets

Would have the drums talk war and send
his warriors to burn the sleeping villages
and kill the sick and old and lead the young
in coffles to our factories.

Twenty years a trader, twenty years,
for there was wealth aplenty to be harvested
from those black fields, and I'd be trading still
but for the fevers melting down my bones.

III

Shuttles in the rocking loom of history,
the dark ships move, the dark ships move,
their bright ironical names
like jests of kindness on a murderer's mouth;
plough through thrashing glister toward
fata morgana's[3] lucent melting shore,
weave toward New World littorals[4] that are
mirage and myth and actual shore.

---

[3] Italian name for Morgan le Fay, creator of mirages.
[4] Shores, coasts.

Voyage through death,

voyage whose chartings are unlove.

A charnel stench, effluvium of living death
spreads outward from the hold,
where the living and the dead, the horribly dying,
lie interlocked, lie foul with blood and excrement.

Deep in the festering hold thy father lies,
the corpse of mercy rots with him,
rats eat love's rotten gelid eyes.

But, oh, the living look at you
with human eyes whose suffering accuses you,
whose hatred reaches through the swill of dark
to strike you like a leper's claw.

You cannot stare that hatred down
or chain the fear that stalks the watches
and breathes on you its fetid scorching breath;
cannot kill the deep immortal human wish,
the timeless will.

"But for the storm that flung up barriers
of wind and wave, *The Amistad*, señores,
would have reached the port of Príncipe in two,
three days at most; but for the storm we should
have been prepared for what befell.
Swift as the puma's leap it came. There was
that interval of moonless calm filled only
with the water's and the rigging's usual sounds,
then sudden movement, blows and snarling cries
and they had fallen on us with machete
and marlinspike. It was as though the very
air, the night itself were striking us.
Exhausted by the rigors of the storm,
we were no match for them. Our men went down

before the murderous Africans. Our loyal
Celestino ran from below with gun
and lantern and I saw, before the cane-
knife's wounding flash, Cinquez,
that surly brute who calls himself a prince,
directing, urging on the ghastly work.
He hacked the poor mulatto down, and then
he turned on me. The decks were slippery
when daylight finally came. It sickens me
to think of what I saw, of how these apes
threw overboard the butchered bodies of
our men, true Christians all, like so much jetsam.
Enough, enough. The rest is quickly told:
Cinquez was forced to spare the two of us
you see to steer the ship to Africa,
and we like phantoms doomed to rove the sea
voyaged east by day and west by night,
deceiving them, hoping for rescue,
prisoners on our own vessel, till
at length we drifted to the shores of this
your land, America, where we were freed
from our unspeakable misery. Now we
demand, good sirs, the extradition of
Cinquez and his accomplices to La
Havana. And it distresses us to know
there are so many here who seem inclined
to justify the mutiny of these blacks.
We find it paradoxical indeed
that you whose wealth, whose tree of liberty
are rooted in the labor of your slaves
should suffer the august John Quincy Adams
to speak with so much passion of the right
of chattel slaves to kill their lawful masters
and with his Roman rhetoric weave a hero's
garland for Cinquez. I tell you that

we are determined to return to Cuba
with our slaves and there see justice done. Cinquez—
or let us say 'the Prince'—Cinquez shall die."

The deep immortal human wish,
the timeless will:

Cinquez its deathless primaveral image,
life that transfigures many lives.

Voyage through death
to life upon these shores.

During the dreaded "Middle Passage" across the Atlantic, whenever the shipmaster had to preserve the safety of the ship, he did not hesitate to jettison his human cargo. Legal definitions to cover such contingencies became a necessity; and for insurance purposes the men, women, and children thrown to the sharks were designated as goods or chattels.

—Lettie J. Austin, Lewis H. Fenderson, and Sophia P. Nelson
The Black Man and the Promise of America

The term Middle Passage arose from the fact that each slaving voyage was made up of three passages—the passage from the home port to the slave coast, the passage from the slave coast to the market, and the passage from that market back to the home port—say, Newport or Liverpool. It was during the middle of the three passages that the slaves were on board.

—John Spears
The American Slave-Trade

. . . the space between the decks where the slaves were to be kept during the time the cargo was accumulating (three to ten months) and while crossing the Atlantic (six to ten weeks) was a room as long and as wide as the ship, but only three feet ten inches high. . . .

—John Spears
The American Slave-Trade

To increase the number of slaves on the deck they were then compelled to lie on their sides, breast to back, "spoon fashion," to use the term then common. Where the 'tween-deck space was two feet high or more the slaves were stowed sitting up in rows, one crowded into the lap of another, and with legs on legs, like riders on a crowded toboggan.

—John Spears
The American Slave-Trade

REFLECTIONS (11)

REFLECTIONS

What use does Mr. Hayden make of irony? What does the irony reveal about the slave-traders?

Presumably Mr. Hayden is sympathetic to the plight of the slaves, yet he shows us nothing from their point of view. Everything is seen from the point of view of the slavers. Why?

Can you imagine any significant *discoveries* being made on the Middle Passage?

*Passing through the strait of Magellan on his
westward course around the world, Joshua
Slocum encountered hazards worthy of
Odysseus. Like Odysseus, however, he met
them with amazing coolness and resolution.
It is impressive to consider how often Slocum
came very near the end of his adventures.*

JOSHUA SLOCUM

Squalls and Savages

It was the 3d of March when the *Spray* sailed from Port Tamar direct for
Cape Pillar,[1] with the wind from the northeast, which I fervently hoped
might hold till she cleared the land; but there was no such good luck in
store. It soon began to rain and thicken in the northwest, boding no good.
The *Spray* neared Cape Pillar rapidly, and, nothing loath, plunged into the
Pacific Ocean at once, taking her first bath of it in the gathering storm.
There was no turning back even had I wished to do so, for the land was
now shut out by the darkness of night. The wind freshened, and I took in
a third reef.[2] The sea was confused and treacherous. In such a time as this
the old fisherman prayed, "Remember, Lord, my ship is small and thy sea is
so wide!" I saw now only the gleaming crests of the waves. They showed
white teeth while the sloop balanced over them. "Everything for an offing,"[3]
I cried, and to this end I carried on all the sail she would bear. She ran all

[1] Slocum is heading northwest out of the Strait of Magellan into the Pacific.
[2] Shortened the sail still further.
[3] Safe distance from shore.

from SAILING ALONE AROUND THE WORLD by Capt. Joshua Slocum, Dover Publications, Inc.

192

night with a free sheet,[4] but on the morning of March 4 the wind shifted to southwest, then back suddenly to northwest, and blew with terrific force. The *Spray,* stripped of her sails, then bore off under bare poles. No ship in the world could have stood up against so violent a gale. Knowing that this storm might continue for many days, and that it would be impossible to work back to the westward along the coast outside of Tierra del Fuego, there seemed nothing to do but to keep on and go east about, after all. Anyhow, for my present safety the only course lay in keeping her before the wind. And so she drove southeast, as though about to round the Horn, while the waves rose and fell and bellowed their never-ending story of the sea; but the Hand that held these held also the *Spray.* She was running now with a reefed forestaysail, the sheets flat amidship. I paid out two long ropes to steady her course and to break combing seas astern, and I lashed the helm amidship. In this trim she ran before it, shipping never a sea. Even while the storm raged at its worst, my ship was wholesome and noble. My mind as to her seaworthiness was put at ease for aye.

When all had been done that I could do for the safety of the vessel, I got to the fore-scuttle,[5] between seas, and prepared a pot of coffee over a wood fire, and made a good Irish stew. Then, as before and afterward on the *Spray,* I insisted on warm meals. In the tide-race off Cape Pillar, however, where the sea was marvelously high, uneven, and crooked, my appetite was slim, and for a time I postponed cooking. (Confidentially, I was seasick!)

The first day of the storm gave the *Spray* her actual test in the worst sea that Cape Horn or its wild regions could afford, and in no part of the world could a rougher sea be found than at this particular point, namely, off Cape Pillar, the grim sentinel of the Horn.

Farther offshore, while the sea was majestic, there was less apprehension of danger. There the *Spray* rode, now like a bird on the crest of a wave, and now like a waif deep down in the hollow between seas; and so she drove on. Whole days passed, counted as other days, but with always a thrill—yes, of delight.

On the fourth day of the gale, rapidly nearing the pitch of Cape Horn, I inspected my chart and pricked off the course and distance to Port Stanley, in the Falkland Islands, where I might find my way and refit, when I saw through a rift in the clouds a high mountain, about seven leagues away on the port beam.[6] The fierce edge of the gale by this time had blown off, and

---

[4] With the wind behind her.

[5] A hatch forward of the cabin. With the wind aft, it would be relatively sheltered.

[6] On the boat's left.

I had already bent a square-sail on the boom in place of the mainsail, which was torn to rags. I hauled in the trailing ropes, hoisted this awkward sail reefed, the forestaysail being already set, and under this sail brought her at once on the wind heading for the land, which appeared as an island in the sea. So it turned out to be, though not the one I had supposed.

I was exultant over the prospect of once more entering the Strait of Magellan and beating through again into the Pacific, for it was more than rough on the outside coast of Tierra del Fuego. It was indeed a mountainous sea. When the sloop was in the fiercest squalls, with only the reefed forestaysail set, even that small sail shook her from keelson to truck[7] when it shivered by the leech.[8] Had I harbored the shadow of a doubt for her safety, it would have been that she might spring a leak in the garboard at the heel of the mast; but she never called me once to the pump. Under pressure of the smallest sail I could set she made for the land like a racehorse, and steering her over the crests of the waves so that she might not trip was nice work. I stood at the helm now and made the most of it.

Night closed in before the sloop reached the land, leaving her feeling the way in pitchy darkness. I saw breakers ahead before long. At this I wore ship[9] and stood offshore, but was immediately startled by the tremendous roaring of breakers again ahead and on the lee bow. This puzzled me, for there should have been no broken water where I supposed myself to be. I kept off a good bit, then wore round, but finding broken water also there, threw her head again offshore. In this way, among dangers, I spent the rest of the night. Hail and sleet in the fierce squalls cut my flesh till the blood trickled over my face; but what of that? It was daylight, and the sloop was in the midst of the Milky Way of the sea, which is northwest of Cape Horn, and it was the white breakers of a huge sea over sunken rocks which had threatened to engulf her through the night. It was Fury Island I had sighted and steered for, and what a panorama was before me now and all around! It was not the time to complain of a broken skin. What could I do but fill away among the breakers and find a channel between them, now that it was day? Since she had escaped the rocks through the night, surely she would find her way by daylight. This was the greatest sea adventure of my life. God knows how my vessel escaped.

The sloop at last reached inside of small islands that sheltered her in smooth water. Then I climbed the mast to survey the wild scene astern. The great naturalist Darwin looked over this seascape from the deck of the

[7] From bottom to top. (Compare "from stem to stern.")
[8] When the wind struck it edge-on.
[9] Changed direction.

Beagle, and wrote in his journal, "Any landsman seeing the Milky Way would have nightmare for a week." He might have added, "or seaman" as well.

The *Spray's* good luck followed fast. I discovered, as she sailed along through a labyrinth of islands, that she was in the Cockburn Channel, which leads into the Strait of Magellan at a point opposite Cape Froward, and that she was already passing Thieves' Bay, suggestively named. And at night, March 8, behold, she was at anchor in a snug cove at the Turn! Every heart-beat on the *Spray* now counted thanks.

Here I pondered on the events of the last few days, and, strangely enough, instead of feeling rested from sitting or lying down, I now began to feel jaded and worn; but a hot meal of venison stew soon put me right, so that I could sleep. As drowsiness came on I sprinkled the deck with tacks, and then I turned in, bearing in mind the advice of my old friend Samblich that I was not to step on them myself. I saw to it that not a few of them stood "business end" up; for when the *Spray* passed Thieves' Bay two canoes had put out and followed in her wake, and there was no disguising the fact any longer that I was alone.

Now, it is well known that one cannot step on a tack without saying something about it. A pretty good Christian will whistle when he steps on the "commercial end" of a carpet-tack; a savage will howl and claw the air, and that was just what happened that night about twelve o'clock, while I was asleep in the cabin, where the savages thought they "had me," sloop and all, but changed their minds when they stepped on deck, for then they thought that I or somebody else had them. I had no need of a dog; they howled like a pack of hounds. I had hardly use for a gun. They jumped pell-mell, some into their canoes and some into the sea, to cool off, I suppose, and there was a deal of free lauguage over it as they went. I fired several guns when I came on deck, to let the rascals know that I was home, and then I turned in again, feeling sure I should not be disturbed any more by people who left in so great a hurry.

The Fuegians, being cruel, are naturally cowards; they regard a rifle with superstitious fear. The only real danger one could see that might come from their quarter would be from allowing them to surround one within bow-shot, or to anchor within range where they might lie in ambush. As for their coming on deck at night, even had I not put tacks about, I could have cleared them off by shots from the cabin and hold. I always kept a quantity of ammunition within reach in the hold and in the cabin and in the fore-peak, so that retreating to any of these places I could "hold the fort" simply by shooting up through the deck.

Perhaps the greatest danger to be apprehended was from the use of fire.

Every canoe carries fire; nothing is thought of that, for it is their custom to communicate by smoke-signals. The harmless brand that lies smoldering in the bottom of one of their canoes might be ablaze in one's cabin if he were not on the alert. The port captain of Sandy Point warned me particularly of this danger. Only a short time before they had fired a Chilean gunboat by throwing brands in through the stern windows of the cabin. The *Spray* had no openings in the cabin or deck, except two scuttles, and these were guarded by fastenings which could not be undone without waking me if I were asleep.

On the morning of the 9th, after a refreshing rest and a warm breakfast, and after I had swept the deck of tacks, I got out what spare canvas there was on board, and began to sew the pieces together in the shape of a peak for my square-mainsail, the tarpaulin. The day to all appearances promised fine weather and light winds, but appearances in Tierra del Fuego do not always count. While I was wondering why no trees grew on the slope abreast of the anchorage, half minded to lay by the sail-making and land with my gun for some game and to inspect a white boulder on the beach, near the brook, a williwaw came down with such terrific force as to carry the *Spray*, with two anchors down, like a feather out of the cove and away into deep water. No wonder trees did not grow on the side of that hill! Great Boreas! a tree would need to be all roots to hold on against such a furious wind.

From the cove to the nearest land to leeward was a long drift, however, and I had ample time to weigh both anchors before the sloop came near any danger, and so no harm came of it. I saw no more savages that day or the next; they probably had some sign by which they knew of the coming williwaws; at least, they were wise in not being afloat even on the second day, for I had no sooner gotten to work at sail-making again, after the anchor was down, than the wind, as on the day before, picked the sloop up and flung her seaward with a vengeance, anchor and all, as before. This fierce wind, usual to the Magellan country, continued on through the day, and swept the sloop by several miles of steep bluffs and precipices overhanging a bold shore of wild and uninviting appearance. I was not sorry to get away from it, though in doing so it was no Elysian shore to which I shaped my course. I kept on sailing in hope, since I had no choice but to go on, heading across for St. Nicholas Bay, where I had cast anchor February 19. It was now the 10th of March! Upon reaching the bay the second time I had circumnavigated the wildest part of desolate Tierra del Fuego. But the *Spray* had not yet arrived at St. Nicholas, and by the merest accident her bones were saved from resting there when she did arrive. The parting of a stay-sail-sheet in a williwaw, when the sea was turbulent and she was plunging into the storm, brought me forward to see instantly a dark cliff ahead and breakers so close under the bows that I felt surely lost, and in my thoughts cried, "Is the hand of fate against me, after all, leading me in the end to this dark spot?" I sprang aft again, unheeding the flapping sail, and threw the wheel over, expecting, as the sloop came down into the hollow of a wave, to feel her timbers smash under me on the rocks. But at the touch of her helm she swung clear of the danger, and in the next moment she was in the lee of the land.

It was the small island in the middle of the bay for which the sloop had been steering, and which she made with such unerring aim as nearly to run it down. Farther along in the bay was the anchorage, which I managed to reach, but before I could get the anchor down another squall caught the sloop and whirled her round like a top and carried her away, altogether to leeward of the bay. Still farther to leeward was a great headland, and I bore off for that. This was retracing my course toward Sandy Point, for the gale was from the southwest.

I had the sloop soon under good control, however, and in a short time rounded to under the lee of a mountain, where the sea was as smooth as a mill-pond, and the sails flapped and hung limp while she carried her way close in. Here I thought I would anchor and rest till morning, the depth being eight fathoms very close to the shore. But it was interesting to see, as I let go the anchor, that it did not reach the bottom before another williwaw struck down from this mountain and carried the sloop off faster than I could pay out cable. Instead of resting, I had to "man the windlass" and heave up the anchor and fifty fathoms of cable hanging up and down in deep water. This was in that part of the strait called Famine Reach. I could have wished it Jericho! On that little crab-windlass I worked the rest of the night, thinking how much easier it was for me when I could say, "Do that thing or the other," than to do it myself. But I hove away on the windlass and sang the old chants that I sang when I was a sailor, from "Blow, Boys, Blow for Californy, O" to "Sweet By and By."

It was daybreak when the anchor was at the hawse. By this time the wind had gone down, and cat's-paws took the place of williwaws. The sloop was then drifting slowly toward Sandy Point. She came within sight of ships at anchor in the roads, and I was more than half minded to put in for new sails, but the wind coming out from the northeast, which was fair for the other direction, I turned the prow of the *Spray* westward once more for the Pacific, to traverse a second time the second half of my first course through the strait.

REFLECTIONS (12)

REFLECTIONS

Reading first-hand accounts of truly dangerous adventures, one is likely to be impressed by the calm courage of the adventurer as he faces possible annihilation. Is this a distortion of reality that occurs in the telling, or do people really behave so well under stress? Is there evidence to support one conclusion or the other?

Comparatively speaking, which storyteller gives the most vivid picture of his disasters or near-disasters—Odysseus, Slocum, or Marlow ("Youth")? What is it that makes the difference?

Considering the kinds of things that our various storytellers *do not* tell us, does there seem to be any principle governing the information that effective narration *omits?*

*In the age-old tradition of the elegy, William
Meredith meditates on the fate of some who
did not survive their encounter with disaster.
How can we reconcile ourselves, he asks, to
this terrible fact we cannot understand?
Though he mourns the victims of a particular
wreck, he reminds us that "this crushing of
people" is a universal occurrence. Is there an
answer, or is there, at the end, only the
question?*

WILLIAM MEREDITH

The Wreck of the Thresher
(Lost at Sea, April 10, 1963)

I stand on the ledge where rock runs into the river
As the night turns brackish with morning, and mourn the drowned.
Here the sea is diluted with river; I watch it slaver
Like a dog curing of rabies. Its ravening over,
Lickspittle ocean nuzzles the dry ground.
(But the dream that woke me was worse than the sea's gray
Slip-slap; there are no such sounds by day.)

This crushing of people is something we live with.
Daily, by unaccountable whim
Or caught up in some harebrained scheme of death,
Tangled in cars, dropped from the sky, in flame,
Men and women break the pledge of breath:
And now under water, gone all jetsam and small
In the pressure of oceans collected, a squad of brave men in a hull.

(Why can't our dreams be content with the terrible facts?
The only animal cursed with responsible sleep,
We trace disaster always to our own acts.
I met a monstrous self trapped in the black deep:
All these years, he smiled, *I've drilled at sea*
For this crush of water. Then he saved only me.)

We invest ships with life. Look at a harbor
At first light: with better grace than men
In their movements the vessels run to their labors
Working the fields that the tide has made green again;
Their beauty is womanly, they are named for ladies and queens,
Although by a wise superstition these are called
After fish, the finned boats, silent and submarine.
The crushing of any ship has always been held
In dread, like a house burned or a great tree felled.

I think of how sailors laugh, as if cold and wet
And dark and lost were their private, funny derision
And I can judge then what dark compression
Astonishes them now, their sunken faces set
Unsmiling, where the currents sluice to and fro
And without humor, somewhere northeast of here and below.

(*Sea-brothers, I lower to you the ingenuity of dreams,*
Strange lungs and bells to escape in; let me stay aboard last—
We amend our dreams in half-sleep. Then it seems
Easy to talk to the severe dead and explain the past.
Now they are saying, *Do not be ashamed to stay alive,*
You have dreamt nothing that we do not forgive.
And gentlier, *Study something deeper than yourselves,*
As, how the heart, when it turns diver, delves and saves.)

Whether we give assent to this or rage
Is a question of temperament and does not matter.
Some will has been done past our understanding,
Past our guilt surely, equal to our fears.
Dullards, we are set again to the cryptic blank page
Where the sea schools us with terrible water.
The noise of a boat breaking up and its men is in our ears.
The bottom here is too far down for our sounding;
The ocean was salt before we crawled to tears.

HOPE ABANDONED FOR 129 ABOARD ATOM SUBMARINE

Navy Board Opens Inquiry in Disappearance of Thresher 220 Miles Off Cape Cod

HUNT PROVES FRUITLESS

Temporary Curb Is Ordered on Diving Operations— Some Debris Found

By JACK RAYMOND

Special to The New York Times

WASHINGTON, April 11—The Navy abandoned hope today for the lost nuclear submarine Thresher and the 129 men aboard.

The Thresher, not armed with Polaris missiles, was the first of her class of swift, deep-diving submersibles designed to attack surface ships and other submarines. She plunged and disappeared in the Atlantic yesterday morning 220 miles east of Cape Cod.

This morning, after 25 hours of a fruitless search by planes, surface ships and submarines, Adm. George W. Anderson, Chief of Naval Operations, said: "This is a sad occasion for me because very reluctantly I have come to the conclusion that the Thresher has indeed been lost."

Korth Visits Search Area

It was the worst submarine disaster in the Navy's history, the Pentagon said. . . .

The New York Times, April 12, 1963

REFLECTIONS (13)
REFLECTIONS

What is the nature of William Meredith's involvement with the loss of the *Thresher* and its crew?

Is there an essential difference between Meredith's poem and the prose account of his subject he might have written instead?

*Our body is a ship that sails on deep blue waters. What
is our goal? To be shipwrecked!*

—Nikos Kazantzakis
The Saviors of God: Spiritual Exercises
tr. Kimon Friar

Full fathom five they father lies;
  Of his bones are coral made;
Those are pearls that were his eyes;
  Nothing of him that doth fade
But doth suffer a sea-change
Into something rich and strange.
Sea nymphs hourly ring his knell:
  Ding-dong.
Hark! now I hear them—ding-dong bell.

—Ariel's song
The Tempest

We have lingered in the chambers of the sea
By sea-girls wreathed with seaweed red and brown
Till human voices wake us and we drown.

—T. S. Eliot
"The Love Song of J. Alfred Prufrock"

~~~~~~

Inner and Outer Space

I sway outside myself
Into the darkening currents,
Into the small spillage of driftwood,
The waters swirling past the tiny headlands.
Was it here I wore a crown of birds for a moment
While on a far point of the rocks
The light heightened,
And below, in a mist out of nowhere,
The first rain gathered?

—Theodore Roethke
"The Rose"

*The moon voyage of the Apollo 11 spacecraft
in July, 1969, was the culmination of
centuries of dreams and speculations: would
man really travel some day to the moon, or
even beyond? Was such a hope insane?
To most people, surely, through the ages, the
idea seemed ridiculous, if not sacrilegious.
The story of Icarus was taken as an object
lesson in the folly of aspiring beyond man's
"natural" limitations. But bold adventurers,
few as they were, still traveled moonward,
carried in their flights of imagination by
winged horses, ethereal sailing ships, magnificent balloons, and even cannon shells.
And at last, in the twentieth century, feet
followed where the mind had often gone.
To children of the space age, the actuality of
landing on the moon is perhaps no more
remarkable than the dozens of other marvels
they have grown up with. But to accept it as
merely ordinary is to fail to comprehend the
vast distances and difficulties involved, or
to understand that for all but the tiniest fraction of human life on earth, such a voyage
has been literally* impossible.
*The history, the complexities, and the
implications of the Apollo 11 journey have
already filled many books, and every one of
us knows the story of that incredible July day;
most of us were "there," in fact, by the
miracle of television. We will read the story
again, though, or watch the films rerun,
many times. Good stories bear repeating.
Here again, then, is the account of those
historic two hours and 21 minutes on the
moon, as it appeared in the pages of one of
the great newspapers of the world,*
The New York Times.

206

JOHN NOBLE WILFORD

On the Moon

At 10:56 P.M., E.D.T., on July 20, 1969, Neil A. Armstrong stepped into history. From the bottom rung of the ladder leading down from Apollo 11's landing craft, he reached out his booted left foot and planted the first human footprint on the moon.

Then he uttered the long-awaited words that are sure to be immortalized: "That's one small step for man, one giant leap for mankind."

There it was, man meeting moon, his first direct contact with another celestial body. For explorers, it was the realization of centuries of dreams. For scientists, it meant an unprecedented opportunity for possible clues to the origin and nature of both the moon and the earth.

Appropriately, Armstrong was able to share the triumphal moment with mankind. As he descended the ladder, he pulled a lanyard that released a fold-down equipment compartment that deployed a television camera. Thus, through the miracle of modern communications, hundreds of millions of people on earth—probably the largest audience ever—witnessed the astronaut's memorable step via TV and heard his words via radio. It required just 1.3 seconds, the time it takes for radio waves to travel the 238,000 miles between moon and earth, for Armstrong's image to appear on home screens. This gave viewers a feeling of "I was there" when history was made.

What was the new environment like, this remote space frontier suddenly invaded by man? Looking through the windows of the landing craft, the astronauts saw a bleak but strangely beautiful world. It was just before dawn over the Sea of Tranquillity, with the sun low over the eastern horizon behind them. The chill of the long lunar night still clung to the boulders, craters and hills before them.

"Magnificent desolation," was the phrase Aldrin used in describing the

207

view. He said that he could see "literally thousands of small craters." But most of all he was impressed initially by the "variety of shapes, angularities, granularities" of the rocks and soil around Tranquillity Base.

At one point, Buzz Aldrin radioed this impression of the general area in which they touched down:

"[There is a] level plain cratered with a fairly large number of craters of the 5- to 50-foot variety. And some ridges, small, 20 to 30 feet high, I would guess. And literally thousands of little one- and two-foot craters around the area. We see some angular blocks out several hundred feet in front of us that are probably two feet in size and have angular edges. There is a hill in view just about on the ground track ahead of us. Difficult to estimate, but might be half a mile or a mile. . . .

"I'd say the color of the local surface is very comparable to that we observed from orbit at this sun angle—about 10 degrees sun angle or that nature. It's pretty much without color. It's gray and it's very white as you look into the zero phase line.[1] And it's considerably darker gray, more like an ashen gray, as you look out 90 degrees to the sun. Some of the surface rocks in close here that have been fractured or disturbed by the rocket engine plume are coated with this light gray on the outside. But where they've been broken, they display a dark, very dark, gray interior and it looks like it could be country basalt."

When Armstrong reached the bottom of the Lunar Module's ladder, he found that the moon was indeed not made of green cheese. Observing that "the LM foot pads are only depressed in the surface about one or two inches," he said: "The surface is fine and powdery. I can pick it up loosely with my toe. It does adhere in fine layers like powdered charcoal to the sole and sides of my boots. I only go in a small fraction of an inch, maybe an eighth of an inch. But I can see the footprints of my boots and the treads in the fine, sandy particles."

Then, while the excited audience watched those first few moments in awe, Armstrong tentatively tested the moon's environment and found it relatively receptive. He found that he could move about easily in his bulky white spacesuit and heavy backpack while under the influence of lunar gravity, which makes everything weigh only one-sixth of what it weighs on earth.

After 19 minutes, Armstrong was joined outside the landing craft by Aldrin, who had been preparing and handing down equipment for the two

[1] That is, toward the sun.

hours of probing and experimenting. The excitement of the moment notwithstanding, Aldrin did not overlook the little necessities. As he emerged through the hatch and started down the ladder, he said, "I want to back up and partially close the hatch, making sure not to lock it on my way out."

"Good thought," Armstrong agreed.

"That's our home for the next couple hours," Aldrin added. "We want to take good care of it."

Then, as Aldrin started his first testing of the surface, Armstrong commented at one point: "Isn't this fun?"

"Right in this area I don't think there's much fine powder," Aldrin noted. "It's hard to tell whether it's a clod or a rock."

"You can pick it up," Armstrong pointed out.

"And it bounces," was Aldrin's reply.

They immediately set up another TV camera away from the craft to give the people on earth a broader look at the Sea of Tranquillity landscape. What was seen during a panoramic camera sweep conformed pretty much with photographs previously transmitted by unmanned satellites: a bleak empty, almost flat, crater-pocked, undulating surface devoid, of course, of vegetation. Yet, Armstrong described the landscape as having "a stark beauty all its own."

"It's like much of the high desert of the United States," he said. "It's different but it's very pretty out here."

One of the first things the astronauts did to embellish that forbidding and monotonous landscape was to plant their three-foot-by-five-foot American flag. It was stiffened with thin wire so as to appear to be flying on the windless lunar surface.

The moon spectacular began earlier than originally scheduled, but a bit later than Armstrong and Aldrin had hoped. The flight plan called for the two astronauts to spend the first 10 hours on the surface inside the Eagle, or Lunar Module, emerging at 2:12 A.M. Monday, E.D.T. They were to devote the time to checking the craft for any damage suffered in the landing, describing what they saw out the window, grabbing a brief snack, sleeping for four hours to rest from their fatiguing descent, eating a leisurely dinner, and then struggling into their spacesuits, visored helmets, boots, and gloves for the EVA, or extra-vehicular activity, outside.

But soon after the landing, upon checking and finding the spacecraft in good condition and feeling chipper themselves, the astronauts decided to open the hatch and venture out earlier than planned. There had been speculation for days before the Apollo 11 flight began that the moon men, anxious to get to the main business at hand, might decide to hold off on their nap. And that's what they did.

"Houston," they radioed to Mission Control. "Our recommendation at this point is planning an EVA with your concurrence starting at about eight o'clock this evening, Houston time. That is about three hours from now. . . . We will give you some time to think about that."

"Tranquillity Base [code name for the LM], Houston," came back the almost immediate reply. "We thought about it. We will support it. We'll go at that time."

Whatever the scientific factors involved, for television viewers in the United States it was a welcome switch. In the East, for example, it meant that the EVA could be seen in almost prime time on Sunday night rather than in the middle of the night. As it turned out, however, the astronauts' departure from the landing craft was delayed for a time when they had trouble depressurizing the cabin so that they could open the hatch. All the oxygen in the cabin had to be vented. The world waited.

Considerable time had to be spent donning the lunar spacesuits and preparing for the alien atmosphere outside. The moon has no air or water. Surface temperatures range from about 250 degrees above zero Fahrenheit in the unfiltered sunlight at lunar midday to about 280 degrees below zero in the depths of the lunar night (the temperature when the astronauts first stepped outside was estimated at 40 or 50 degrees above; in the shadows it was 150 degrees below zero).

For these reasons, the spacesuit, with its portable life support system (PLSS), had to be almost as self-sufficient as a spaceship. It carried its own supply of electricity, water, and oxygen. It had a fan, a refrigeration element, and a sophisticated two-way radio. In addition, it provided protection against total vacuum, the temperature extremes, and the risk of puncture by a hurtling micrometeoroid. At the same time, the suit was flexible enough so that the wearer could walk, climb, dig, and set out instruments on the moon's surface. Altogether, the moon-walk costume weighed 185 pounds—but it seemed like only one-sixth that weight because of the lunar gravity.

The difficulty of maneuvering in the spacesuit in close quarters was demonstrated by the following conversation between Armstrong and Aldrin as Armstrong started to back out the Eagle's Hatch to descend the ladder:

"Okay. Bical pump secondary circuit breaker open. Back to lean—this way. Radar circuit breakers open. Well, I'm looking head-on at it. I'll get it. Okay. My antenna's out. Right. Okay, now we're ready to hook up the LEC. Okay. Now we need to hook this. Your visor. Yep. Your back is up against the perch. Now you're clear. Over toward me. Straight down, to your left a little bit. Plenty of room. You're lined up nicely.

Toward me a little bit. Down. Okay. Now you're clear. You're catching the first hinge. The what hinge? All right, move. Roll to the left. Okay, now you're clear. You're lined up on the platform. Put your left foot to the right a little bit. Okay, that's good. More left. Good. Okay. You're not quite squared away. Roll to the right a little. Now you're even. That's good. You've plenty of room to your left. It's a little close on the. . . . How'm I doing? You're doing fine. Want this bag? Yeah. Got it."

Finally Armstrong announced: "Okay, Houston, I'm on the porch."

The astronauts found walking and working on the moon less taxing than had been forecast. Armstrong once reported he was "very comfortable." They seemed to have a little difficulty in adjusting their vision to the deep shadows, but their perception appeared not to suffer at all. Despite their heavy spacesuits and backpacks, the men bounded about easily in kangaroo, almost floating hops. "You do have to be rather careful to keep track of where your center of mass is," Aldrin observed after testing his agility.

"Sometimes it takes about two or three paces to make sure that you've got your feet underneath you," he explained. "And about two to three, or maybe four, easy paces can bring you to a fairly smooth stop. Like a football player, you just have to put out to the side and cut a little bit. The so-called kangaroo hop—it does work, but it seems the forward ability is not quite as good as it is in the more conventional one foot after another. As far as saying what a safe pace might be—the one that I'm using now could get rather tiring after several hundred. But this may be a function of the suit as well as lack of gravity forces."

Aldrin discussed the adjustment of vision to the shadows:

"I've noticed several times in going from the sunlight into shadow that just as I go in I catch an additional reflection off the LEM that, along with reflection off my face into the visor, makes visibility very poor just at the transition of sunlight into shadow. Since we have so much glare coming onto my visor—shadow—and then it takes a short while for my eyes to adapt to the lighting conditions. Inside the shadow area, visibility is, as we said before is not too great. But with both visors up we can certainly see what sort of footprints we have and the condition of the soil. Then after being out in the sunlight a while it takes . . . watch it, Neil. Neil, you're on a cable. Yeah, lift up your right foot. Right foot. It's still hooked on it. Wait a minute. Okay, you're clear now."

It was an eerie scene, like a throwback to Buck Rogers science fiction. The black-and-white TV pictures of the bug-shaped Lunar Module and the astronauts were so sharp and clear as to seem unreal, more like a toy and toy-like figures than human beings on the most daring and far-reaching expedition thus far undertaken.

Soon after the astronauts came out of the Lunar Module, they checked the outside of the craft to determine whether any damage had occurred in the landing. Here was the discussion:

ALDRIN: I say the jet deflector that's mounted on quad 4 seems to be— the surface of it—seems to be more wrinkled than the one that's on quad 1. Generally the underneath part of the LEM seems to have stood up quite well. We'll get some pictures in the aft part of the LEM that illuminate the thermal effects much better than we could get them up here at the front.

ARMSTRONG: I don't note any abnormalities in the LEM. The pods seem to be in good shape. The primary and secondary struts are in good shape. Antennas are all in place. There's no evidence of any problem underneath the LEM due to either engine exhaust or drainage of any kind.

ALDRIN: It's very surprising, very surprising, the lack of penetration of all four of the foot pads. I'd say if we were to try and determine just how far below the surface they would have penetrated, you'd measure two or three inches, wouldn't you say, Neil?

ARMSTRONG: At the most, yes, Buzz. There is probably less than that.

ALDRIN: We need a picture of the FY strut taken from near the descent stage and I think we'd be able to see a little better what the thermal effects are. They seem to be quite minimal. This one picture taken at the right rear of the spacecraft looking at the skirt of the descent stage, a slight darkening of the surface color, a rather minimal amount of radiating or etching away or erosion of the surface. Now, on descent, both of us remarked that we could see a large amount of very fine dust particles moving out. It was reported beforehand that we would probably see an outgassing from the surface after the actual shutdown, but I recall I was unable to verify that. This is too big an angle, Neil.

ARMSTRONG: Yeah, I think you're right.

ALDRIN: Neil, if you'd take the camera, I'll work on the SEQ base [equipment]. Try to get some closer pictures of that rock.

ARMSTRONG: I was saying, Houston, you stop and take a photograph of something and then want to start moving again sideways, there's quite a tendency to start doing it with just gradual sideways hops.

At one point the astronauts were suddenly interrupted by a summons from Houston. Then President Nixon, to mark the momentous occasion, came on a telephone-radio hook-up to congratulate Armstrong and Aldrin

212

in what, he said, "certainly has to be the most historic telephone call ever made." The conversation was televised at both ends and shown on a split screen, with the president in his oval office at the White House, and the astronauts standing in front of their landing craft.

"Because of what you have done," the president said, "the heavens have become a part of man's world. And as you talk to us from the Sea of Tranquillity, it requires us to redouble our efforts to bring peace and tranquillity to earth. For one priceless moment in the whole history of man, all the people on this earth are truly one—one in their pride in what you have done and one in our prayers that you will return safely to earth."

Armstrong, the Apollo 11 commander, replied: "Thank you, Mr. President. It's a great honor and privilege for us to be here representing not only the United States but men of peace of all nations, men with interests and a curiosity and men with a vision for the future."

The astronauts wasted no time settling down to their chores. Each had a checklist printed on one sleeve of his moonsuit. Aside from providing a televised impression of what the moon is like, they had two primary objectives: (1) to set out three scientific experiments, and (2) to collect up to 60 pounds of lunar rocks and soil.

Because the moon is uncorrupted by the moving gases of an atmosphere and unworn by the erosive pounding of wind and water, as is the earth, scientists hoped that the spacemen's probes would help unlock some of the geological mysteries of the solar system. Unmanned probes during the past five years had provided much information about the moon—through pictures and digging—but the major questions remained unanswered. The ability of astronauts to choose a suitable site to emplace instruments and pick out the rocks of greatest interest was one of the prime justifications for a manned landing.

For the first experiment, Armstrong and Aldrin set up a sheet of aluminum foil a foot wide and a yard long for a solar-wind test. Its purpose was to entrap rare outflowing gases from the sun—such as argon, krypton, xenon, neon, and helium. The captured gases were placed in a vacuum box to be returned to earth for analysis. Scientists hoped this "wind" would throw light on the way in which the sun and planets were formed.

The second experiment used a seismometer to report any tremors caused by falling meteorites or volcanic eruptions. The reports, it was hoped, would provide clues to the composition of the moon.

The third experiment, also left on the moon, was a two-foot-square laser reflector made up of 100 fused-silica prisms. Pointed toward the earth, it was designed to reflect a beam of light directly back to the earth. By measuring the travel time of the pulses to the moon and back, scientists could use the reflector to follow subtle changes in earth-moon distances. These changes might indicate whether gravity was weakening or the continents shifting, and might provide the most sensitive tests to date of Einstein's general theory of relativity.

The astronauts had some discussion about the best location for the experiments:

ALDRIN: Have you got a good area picked out?

ARMSTRONG: Well, I think right out on the rise out there is probably as good as any. Probably stay on the higher ground there.

ALDRIN: Watch at the end of that crater. It's soft.

ARMSTRONG: Yes, that's pretty soft there, isn't it?

ALDRIN: Get a couple of close-ups on these quite rounded, large boulders.

ARMSTRONG: Yeah. About 40 feet out. I'd say to the end of that next part.

ALDRIN: It's going to be a little difficult to find a good level spot here.

ARMSTRONG: The top of that next little ridge there—wouldn't that be a pretty good place?

ALDRIN: All right. I'll put the seismometer about there.

ARMSTRONG: All right.

ALDRIN: I'm going to have to get on the other side of this rock here.

ARMSTRONG: I would go right around that to the left there. Isn't that a level spot there?

ALDRIN: I think this right here is just as level.

ARMSTRONG: Okay. [Observing the ground] Looks like salt and they have probably two-per-cent white minerals in 'em. White crystals. And the thing that I reported before . . . I don't believe that I believe that anymore. I think it's small craters. They look like impact craters where shot —BB shot—has hit the surface.

ALDRIN: Houston, I have the seismometer experiment over now and I'm aligning it with the sun and I'm having a little bit of difficulty getting the feed going to center. It wants to move around and around the outside.

Of all the experimental tasks, however, top priority went to the collection of rocks and soil. After years of inconclusive debate about the origin of the moon, it had become generally apparent that only with a representative collection of samples could the correct answer be determined. The samples taken by Armstrong and Aldrin, both amateur geologists with hours of training, were headed for the Lunar Receiving Laboratory in

214

Houston for initial tests, and then, after a period of quarantine, to other laboratories across the country for more thorough analysis.

Armstrong scooped up the first "contingency" sample and put it in his pants-leg pocket almost as soon as he got out of the Lunar Module. This was even before Aldrin descended, and was done to assure having some lunar material if something suddenly went wrong on the surface and the astronauts had to "abort" the mission.

"Like it's a little difficult to dig through the crust," Armstrong said as he gathered up the sample. "It's very interesting. It's a very soft surface but here and there where I plug with the contingency sample collector I run into very hard surface, but it appears to be very cohesive material of the same sort."

Later, while Aldrin was busy with other tasks, Armstrong went farther from the module and collected more rocks and soil at random. Aldrin then took his turn, making a more selective collection within a radius of up to 100 feet of the craft, while Armstrong took pictures. Since the spacesuits, tightly inflated with oxygen, did not allow the astronauts to bend more than slightly, the men used scoops and tongs with long handles. This first lunar geological prospecting was seen very clearly on home TV screens. As the astronauts walked about, they described by radio what they saw. They put the samples in sealed aluminum boxes for the trip back to earth.

Here is how some of the conversation went:

ARMSTRONG: Now this one's right down front. And I want to know if you can see an angular rock in the foreground.

HOUSTON: Roger, we have a large angular rock in the foreground. And it looks like a much smaller rock a couple of inches to the left.

ARMSTRONG: And beyond it about 10 feet is an even larger rock that's rounded. That rock is about—the closest one to you is about—that one sticking out of the sand—about one foot. It's about a foot and a half long and it's about six inches thick. But it's standing on edge.

ALDRIN: Neil, I've got the table out . . . and the bag deployed.

HOUSTON: Roger. And we see the shadow of the LEM.

ARMSTRONG: The little hill just beyond the shadow of the LEM is a pair of elongated craters, so they appear together as 40 feet long and 20 feet across and they're probably six feet deep. We'll probably get more work in there later.

HOUSTON: Roger. And we see Buzz going about his work.

Armstrong reported that he collected about 50 pounds of soil and rock samples from several areas within the limited excursion sector around the LM. Most of the samples he scooped off the surface, but he went as deep as three inches. There was no significant change in the soil composition at that depth. He did not hit any hard bed. Armstrong said there was a wide variety of rocks, and the boulders were generally about two feet high.

The rocks were coated with surface powder, making them slippery in the deep vacuum that exists on the lunar surface. The astronauts said they found a purple rock. Some of the rocks were described as vesicular; that is, full of cavities. This is characteristic of certain forms of lava, but this does not definitely establish the rock as a lava fragment. Another rock was said to resemble biotite, a dark green or black form of mica that is characteristic of continental rocks on earth. Its presence on the moon could indicate the history of the moon had features in common with that of the earth. However, as the astronauts pointed out, definite identification had to await return and analysis of the rocks.

As one of their last acts on the lunar surface, the moon men drove coring tubes into the surface with a hammer to capture material deep enough to be free of any exposure to exhaust gases from the rocket that lowered the LM. Aldrin said he had no trouble going in about two or three inches, but then had to pound "about as hard as I could." He drove the tube about eight or nine inches into the surface, then he noticed something puzzling.

For some reason, he said, the tube "didn't seem to want to stand upright. I'd keep driving it in and it would dig some sort of a hole, but it wouldn't penetrate in a way that it would support itself." He added that the material in the tube was "quite well packed, a good bit darker, and the way it adhered to the core tube gave me the distinct impression of being moist."

All in all, man's first walk on the moon lasted two hours and 21 minutes. When they had completed their assignments, Armstrong and Aldrin climbed back up into the Eagle, where they continued to radio their impressions to Houston before resting.

As a final description of the landing site, Armstrong reported the following: "We are landed in a relatively clear crater field . . . of circular secondary craters, most of which have rims irrespective of their rays and irrespective of their size. There are a few of the smaller craters around which do not have a discernible rim. The ground mass throughout the area is a very fine sand to a silt. I say the thing that would be most like it on earth is powdered graphite."

Successful completion of the extra-vehicular activity, of course, brought congratulations from around the world and put gleams in the eyes of scientists waiting eagerly for the lunar specimens. But space officials, ever mindful of the complexities of space flight, cautioned about premature cheers. Armstrong and Aldrin still had the risky lift-off to rejoin the orbiting Columbia command ship which Colonel Collins had been piloting all this time. It would be the first launching without the benefit of all the familiar accoutrements, such as concrete bases and steel gantries. Moreover, the two astronauts were completely dependent upon the 3,500-pound-thrust ascent rocket in the upper half of the Lunar Module. If it failed to fire, they would be stranded.

To go places and do things that have never been done be-fore—that's what living is all about.

—Michael Collins

The moon is only the first milestone on the road to the stars.

—Arthur C. Clarke

HERE MEN FROM THE PLANET EARTH
FIRST SET FOOT UPON THE MOON
JULY 1969, A.D.
WE CAME IN PEACE FOR ALL MANKIND

—Plaque left on the moon

In a thousand years there will be few things remembered, but this will be one of them.

—Robert Hofstadter
Nobel-prizewinning physicist

Oh Moon! when I look on they beautiful face,
Careering along through the boundaries of space,
The question has frequently come to my mind,
If ever I'll gaze on thy glorious behind.

—Attributed to Edmund Gosse's serving maid

218

REFLECTIONS (14)

REFLECTIONS

Few of us will ever forget the television image of those ghostly figures "kangaroo-hopping" across the surface of the moon, or the vivid color photographs the Apollo 11 astronauts brought back with them. The camera gives us a strong sense of "presence." Does Wilford's account of the moon exploration suggest that there are any aspects of such an experience accessible to the written word but beyond the reach of the camera?

The descriptions of the moon by Armstrong, Aldrin, and other astronauts are those of scientists and technicians—clear, sometimes graphic, but rarely, if ever, beautiful or poetic. Now that we have had such close contact with the moon, are poetic responses to it no longer possible?

The discoveries of Columbus were hailed by a contemporary as "the most important event since the Creation," a reaction echoed by President Nixon in describing the first moon landing. How valid are these assessments?

Some observers have commented that there are great qualitative differences between earlier discoveries by small groups of explorers (such as those led by Columbus or Lewis and Clark) and the Apollo moon explorations backed by thousands of support personnel and billions of dollars worth of technology—and that there are great differences in the men as well. In short, they say the days of the independent, self-reliant explorer are over, that men like Armstrong and Aldrin can scarcely claim credit for their discoveries. Is this conclusion reasonably accurate?

A favorite device of the satirist is to juxtapose a style and a subject matter that are somehow incongruous. Supposedly serious matters, for example, are burlesqued in a silly style, or more commonly, a trivial subject is treated with mock seriousness by applying to it a style the reader associates with truly momentous affairs. Here James Stevenson shows what happens when the approach of the space voyager is applied to a morning outing in a summer beach resort.

EARTH PROBE: SALTAIRE AVENUE

FRAMES
15-16

DATE: JUNE 13, 1969.

TIME

A.M.

FRAME 14

7.43 APPROACHED EAST BEACH BY VEHICLE (1967 OLDSMOBILE),
PARKED, GOT OUT, AND WALKED UP SALTAIRE AVENUE (WEST

FRAME
17
FRAME
18
TO EAST) CARRYING PAD, PEN, GEOLOGY MAP, CAMERA. SAT ON
CURB OF SIDEWALK NEXT TO BEACH, FACING HOUSES, NEAR
STOP SIGN AND FIRE HYDRANT. EXPERIENCING SLIGHT
NAUSEA, POSSIBLY DUE TO BREAKFAST OF CHOC. CHIP
COOKIES AND WARM TAB.

7.50 UTTER SILENCE, EXCEPT FOR MILD WAVE SOUNDS ON
BEACH TO THE S.E. COOL DAMP AIR COMES FROM THE
WATER BUT TEMP. IS RISING. GOING TO BE SCORCHER. BUGS
ARE BITING.

7.52 STUDIED MAP (SURFICIAL GEOLOGY) ISSUED BY DEPT. OF
INTERIOR, UNITED STATES GEOLOGICAL SURVEY 1961:
SALTAIRE AVENUE (BLACKTOP) RUNS OVER BEACH DEPOSITS
("WELL-SORTED SAND AND PEBBLE GRAVEL DEPOSITED BY
CURRENT AND WAVE ACTION") THEN RISES TOWARD N.E. AND
ENCOUNTERS GLACIAL STREAM DEPOSITS ("GRAVEL, SAND, AND
SILT IN VALLEY FILLS, KAMES, KAME TERRACES, AND
ICE-CHANNEL FILLINGS") FOLLOWED BY END MORAINE
DEPOSITS ("LOOSE TO COMPACT SANDY, STONY TILL WITH
MANY SUBROUNDED BOULDERS") NEAR THE OLD SEA VIEW
HOTEL ON THE HILL NEAR THE WATER TOWER. (SOMEBODY
HAS CLIMBED THE TOWER AND PAINTED THE WORD "BEER"
ON THE SIDE IN HUGE WHITE LETTERS.)

7.59 NO HUMANS IN SIGHT YET. LOTS OF BUGS.
TWINGE OF LONELINESS.
HOUSES SEEM BLANK. IS THERE LIFE — CAN THERE BE
LIFE? — ON SALTAIRE AVE. ?

8.01 STUDIED SURFACE OF BLACKTOP. ROAD IN MEDIOCRE

	SURFACE. NEAR CENTER OF ROAD CRACKS RUN LONGI-
FRAME 23 →	TUDINALLY, BUT BETWEEN FEET, NEAR CURB, CRACKS
	ARE RANDOM, EROSION IS WIDESPREAD, AND SMALL
	MASSES OF BLACKTOP BREAK AWAY — ISLANDS SURROUNDED
	BY SAND.
	FRAME 22
8.05	MILK TRUCK PASSES. DRIVER DOESN'T WAVE.
8.07	LARGE BLACK DOG APPEARS, ROAMS AREA, THEN
	CROSSES BEACH, HEADING EAST. ← **FRAME 29**
◯ 8.11	CONDUCTED EXAMINATION OF AREA IN
	VICINITY OF STOP SIGN. OBSERVED:
	FLORA
	BEACH GRASS CLOVER (NO 4-LEAF)
	THISTLES Q. ANN'G'S LACE
	CRAB GRASS WEEDS OF VARIOUS DESCRIP.
	DAISIES (WHITE)
	BUTTERCUPS
	DISCARDED ITEMS
	BEER CANS (2) POTATO CHIP BAG
	BEER CAN TOPS CIGARETTE PACK
	PAPER PLATE PAPER CUP
◯	GOOD HUMOR STICK MATCHBOOK
8.19	MAN IN SHIRTSLEEVES AND STRAW HAT APPEARS ON
	PORCH OF WHITE HOUSE, LIGHTS CIGAR.
8.20	SECOND MAN — ALSO IN SHIRTSLEEVES AND STRAW HAT —
	BUT ACCOMPANIED BY SMALL BOY — APPEARS ON PORCH
	OF HOUSE NEXT DOOR (YELLOW). "GOT THE OL' CIGAR
	GOING, EH ?" SAYS SECOND MAN, GREETING FIRST.
	GENIAL LAUGHTER. MAN AND BOY WALK DOWN STEPS,
	CROSS SALTAIRE AVE. TO BEACH. FIRST MAN SMOKES
	CIGAR FOR A WHILE, LOOKING AT WATER. THEN WALKS
	DOWN STEPS, GETS INTO CAR, DRIVES AWAY TO E.
8.23	YOUNG MAN AND GIRL - BOTH IN BATHING SUITS — WALK
	TOWARD BEACH FROM W. THEY ARE TALKING
◯	QUIETLY. THEY CROSS SALTAIRE AVE. TO BEACH, SETTLE
	DOWN ON SAND, SITTING ON STRIPED TOWEL NEAR
	WATER.
8.28	LARGE BLACK DOG COMES BACK, CROSSES SAND.
8.31	PICKED UP PAD, PEN, MAP, CAMERA. WALKED BACK
	TO VEHICLE.
8.33	BEGAN RE-ENTRY.

—JAMES STEVENSON

REFLECTIONS (15)

REFLECTIONS

Aside from its humorous effects, does James Stevenson's observation and description have any value?

What other kinds of places would be susceptible to description by Stevenson's approach?

Dr. Jean Houston and Dr. Robert E. L. Masters have for a number of years investigated the uses of psychedelic drugs in psychological research and psychotherapy. Recently they have begun experimenting with various non-drug stimuli, such as multisensory environments and guided meditations to induce "altered states of consciousness," in which the subject becomes highly receptive to uncommon psychic experiences. Clare Mead, a Religion Researcher for Time *magazine, visited the Masters-Houston Foundation for Mind Research in New York City and embarked upon a half-hour-long "inner odyssey," using no drugs or other stimuli except the verbal suggestions of Dr. Houston who served as her "guide," as the spirit of Virgil had been Dante's guide through Hell and Purgatory. Miss Mead's voyage, while briefer and less terrifying than Dante's, nevertheless resulted in a profoundly moving experience and left her an apparently changed young woman.*

224

CLARE MEAD

An Inner Odyssey

I began my journey by following Dr. Houston's instruction to imagine my-self lying in a boat on a wonderfully hot, languid July afternoon, lazily floating past meadows lush with trees and flowers, the whole scene suffused with silence and peace and the prospect of wonderful things to come. I was completely conscious of the chair in which I sat, of the room and its surroundings and of Dr. Houston, but at the same time the experience of being in that boat was as vivid as if I were in a waking dream. Never at any time in the next half-hour did I feel any dulling of consciousness or free will.

After a few minutes, Dr. Houston said that my hands would begin to feel light and to rise. I was aware that I could easily resist this suggestion; yet, when I progressively "let go" of them, my hands did indeed become light and buoyant. At Dr. Houston's suggestion, I began "flying." Not literally, of course, but never except in dreams have I felt so ecstatically the sensation of flight—free, joyous, yet peaceful, ever deeper to the center of my being, until I was conscious of an indescribable unity within myself and with all things. Finally, I felt as if I had flown to the core of life itself.

Dr. Houston then asked me if there was anything I wanted to under-stand better while in this sacred place. I answered that the problem of in-justice was to me the most difficult reality of life to accept. I recalled that as a child I became upset even at the make-believe injustices I saw in Lassie movies or read in Polly Pepper books. Then I had vivid mental images of real-life horrors throughout history, like the Inquisition and the Holocaust of the Jews during World War II. I saw the petty injustices that people commit against each other every day.

I saw New Yorkers choking in smog-filled streets or caged like cattle in screeching subways. I saw the poor strangling in the disease and dirty ugliness of the slums. It became acutely clear to me that no amount of legislation or education will ever dispel completely the force of ingrained racial prejudice and that no degree of virtue among the enlightened will extinguish the evil that breeds wars.

Dr. Houston then told me that I would spend some time contemplating imagery and that I would understand, in a way that would be deep and permanent, something of the problem of injustice. What followed was ineffable, except to say that I became more and more sorrowful at what I envisaged (indeed, tears were streaming down my face); yet increasingly I could "see," in the most profound way I have ever known that the beauty of life far exceeds the sorrow, the injustice.

I was aware of my unity with all the people who have ever suffered, from the victims of petty lies to those killed by untold wars, persecutions and centuries of mistrust and hate. But simultaneously and paradoxically I understood quite vividly that life triumphs over all this misery even though it cannot erase it. Life is indeed "stronger than death"—not just in the religious sense, but quite literally stronger than death's ultimate absurdity. I was aware of smiling and crying at once. An immense resignation and peace flooded my entire being.

At this point Dr. Houston decided that I was able to undergo a psychological "death" and "rebirth." She began by asking me to find within myself the deepest possible self-symbol with which I could identify. I chose a star. My first mental image was of a very black sky with my single star in it, luminous and strong. Slowly it became smaller and smaller, dimmer and dimmer. I knew that it was not going to go out completely unless I allowed it to—and of course I didn't want it to. But Dr. Houston kept insisting, and gradually I was able to relinquish my hold as I watched it disappear, leaving only vast, empty blackness. I felt no panic. I was resigned, but enormously sad. The sorrow increased as I looked into the blackness, and I was aware of tears flowing hard. Eventually I had to restrain myself from sheer bawling. I knew objectively that I was sitting there alive and well in a room in Upper Manhattan, but subjectively the sensation of death was as vivid as if I were looking into my own coffin.

Then, still under Dr. Houston's direction, I made an enormous effort to revive my poor star. At first I thought to myself that this would probably occur as the gradual brightening of a star in the blackness. But instead, and all of a sudden, I saw the black sky suddenly flash into total, blinding white light. And in an inexplicable way I could see thousands of stars everywhere in the blazing whiteness. Quite unexpectedly, the black sky flashed again into my mind, eliminating the light, but the white sky quickly returned, and I was confident that it was going to win out. The struggle between them continued for a brief time, but finally there was just permanent, pure, white light, dense with blazing stars.

The resulting perception can only be understated in words: I knew with incredible clarity that life is the victor in the struggle against death, not in the sense of an afterlife in a faraway heaven, but in the certainty that life is eternal, despite death. I was overcome with the joy of this truth, and I wanted to run out on the street and shout it to the New Yorkers plodding homeward in the gray smog from their dull downtown offices, unaware that a sea of beauty, life and love surrounded and sustained them.

Dr. Houston then told me that I could return from my inner voyage when I wished, and I found myself immediately ready to do so, though the strength of what I had seen has remained with me ever since.

REFLECTIONS (16)

REFLECTIONS

Have you ever had an experience of illumination or understanding as vivid as Clare Mead's? If so, how did it come about?

Are the perceptions or understandings arrived at in such "psychic" voyages as Clare Mead's really trustworthy? Is this as valid an approach to truth as rational analysis?

*Numerous adventuresome people have shared
with us in recent years their accounts of drug
trips, good and bad. But what is it like for
someone who lives on a constant "high" to
come back down for a visit to the square
world? Gordon Cotler tries to imagine.*

GORDON COTLER

Return Trip
(Being an Extract from
the Journal of a Hippy)

I made my decision to venture back into the square world during one of
those inconclusive discussions about the subculture that absorb so much of
our attention these days. A group of us were joined in argument at my
place, or under a bench in St. Mark's Churchyard, or possibly in an old
Rambler American on the Jericho or New Jersey Turnpike.

Instant cries of alarm were sounded by my friends or me: I would do
myself physical or psychological damage beyond repair; I would obscure
my life goals, etc. My reply, scratched by my middle finger in either the
polar white side wall of my refrigerator, the Manhattan schist beneath the
churchyard bench, or the soybean knob of the Rambler's shift lever, was to
the effect that it is the duty of some of the more perceptive among us to
get down there occasionally and bring back the kind of detailed, objective

reports that can be studied by those without the courage to make the trip themselves.

All the considerable reading I had done on the subject cautioned against making the trip in a hostile environment, and so I cozied up in a favorite corner of my pad, settling on, or slightly above, a foam-rubber mattress. My notes indicate that I officially began coming down at 9:15 a.m. in September. Oddly enough, not until near sunup in November did I experience my first symptom. Let me see if I can convey the sense of this. I was reclining on an upper shelf of the linen closet, stroking my cat, when I became aware that something was out of joint. After a moment I perceived with a weird feeling what this was: although the cat was still purring, snapdragons and delphiniums were no longer issuing from its throat. Somewhat giddily, I then observed that the illuminations radiating from the cat's back where I stroked him, which usually remind me of the marquee of Loew's Sheridan, had now dimmed to the point where they seemed nothing more than the aurora borealis through a heavy overcast. When I examined the hand that was doing the stroking, I found myself looking at a palmful of short hairs.

Several minutes or days went by before the next definite sign that I was coming in for a landing. This was a weirdy. It happened while I was lying on the dining table, thoroughly absorbed in an examination of the design on the kitchen floor, which has always been a source of deep satisfaction to me. Gradually, but at an accelerating pace, the central picture on the vinyl, a representation of Laocoön festooned with Russian Easter eggs and wreathed in vapor trails, took on the appearance of a tomato juice stain. No matter how intently I stared, the image persisted. It was now 2:23 p.m. I put on a zippered windbreaker, stuffed pencil and notebook in a pocket, and climbed down three flights of stairs to the street level.

I opened the door on the world at 2:26, almost 2:27 p.m. Immediately, I was assailed by a combination of sights and sounds that lifted me out of myself with a kind of rushing excitement that was almost religious in the way it charged me with a sense of oneness with eternity, a peacefulness as of fulfillment. To hope to convey in words what I experienced would be like trying to put Ravi Shankar in words. But anyway let me set down each sensation as it came to me. As I stepped into the street my ear was struck by the sound of roller skates against sidewalk, a long, rolling rumble broken by the sharp click of skate crossing sidewalk crack and overlaid by the second skate being dragged up even, a sound that went: ro-o-o-ll, click, dra-ag, click, click, ro-o-o-ll, etc. The clicks of course came at random intervals in the rhythm. Looking back over what I have just written, I see that it makes little sense, but there is no question of the sound's profoundly disturbing effect on me—an effect not unlike that of Forster's Malabar Caves on Mrs. Moore.

While I was still ingesting the sound, my eye was being slapped by one coruscating image after another: a sign that hung like a pennant from a storefront and swung the odd message HAND LAUNDRY my way; a motorized refrigerator, marked THIS WEEK'S SPECIAL—FUDGMALLOW RIPPLE, that sounded tiny temple bells as it rolled by; two gnome-like children hopping in and out of cabalistic chalk boxes on the street; a pair of cerise Day-Glo slacks as wide as a sidecar, cradling a woman on a stoop; two boys combing their hair; a jam-packed taxi with a sign on its roof that glowed OFF-DUTY; a man at the corner in a raincoat who took money from passersby and scribbled on scraps of paper that he shoved in his pocket; three girls combing their hair; half a jelly apple clinging to the side of the curbstone. The scene seemed oddly alive and real.

At 2:31 I was walking. I crossed streets, stepped on and off curbs, dodged trucks—vividly aware every instant of the pull and play of muscle, of lungs sucking in air heavy with suspended chemical particles, of a persistent message in my brain that a tightness in my right shoe was developing a dull ache in my little toe. Gloriously sensitive to the stimuli of the "real" world in a way I had never thought possible, I stepped along briskly under a burning sun, my senses sharpening with every step. Music! It had never occurred to me how my sensitivity to, and appreciation of, music might be heightened by "turning off." I passed a music store that chanced to be piping through a loudspeaker the latest album of my favorite San Francisco quintet. The music poured into my very ears, as through a funnel, and I heard the group with a new clarity. The impact was of twelve high school dropouts practicing in a garage. A fresh perspective, and most exciting.

Shop windows flashed by, alive with color and texture. An "Appetizing" store, brilliant concept. The window was of apricots and anchovy cans framed in prunes, the whole sprinkled with hopjes. A window of sneakers came up, softly, and then a window of gypsies. I was buoyed up, and at the same time more than a little apprehensive. Down the avenue eight balls of red in the traffic fixtures popped to green, and the dread was gone.

A great deal has been written, most of it nonsense, about sex among the "turned off." In point of fact, it *is* a different order of experience. It opens surprising new vistas that can profoundly unsettle one's accepted standards of behavior if there are chinks in one's armor of personal security. Let me attempt to explain this in terms of an incident that occurred during my trip. At 2:36 I was fortunate in being hailed in the street by a girl I shall call Joyce, who seemed to know me from some place she called "school." Joyce was a smooth-faced and pleasant-looking girl with brushed hair tied back on her neck and a smile quite impossible to describe to someone with a normal frame of reference. My notes call it "a quick, sunny smile." In the strange, other-worldly state I was in, it seemed quite reasonable for this girl to be asking where I'd been keeping myself and then go on to tell about a position she held in a bio-chemical laboratory while she finished her work on what she called a "doctoral thesis." When I started walking again at 2:47, she said she was going in the same direction and fell in by my side. Now she was rambling on about "the old neighborhood," which hadn't changed except that the elms were "just about gone," and a Mr. Collins had "left to live with his daughter in Illinois" and some people called Perry had bought his house.

The sexual part followed. At 2:51 we arrived at a wide intersection, heavy with rumbling traffic. Crossing, we reached for each other. Joyce's fingertips touched mine. Let me try to describe exactly what I experienced in that instant. An electric, tingly sensation originating under the fleshy pads at the ends of my fingers moved rapidly up my arm and caused a stirring among the short hairs at the back of my neck. There is more. A moment later a swerving taxi caused Joyce to lean her body toward me. Almost as a motor response, my near arm circled her waist. The small neat firmness of it under her coat pervaded my consciousness; the feeling was distinctly pleasurable in a way almost impossible to convey.

On the opposite curb bodily contact between us ceased. Our paths were to diverge here. Joyce prepared to board a bus for home. I found myself nodding agreement to her parting words, a low throaty suggestion—most attractive to listen to—that I call her on the phone one evening. Her eyes were curiously luminescent. At 2:55 she was gone. It would be difficult to explain why, but the encounter is one I would not mind repeating.

At 2:57 I was walking again, taking in sights and sounds, unaccountably buoyed up. I will frankly state that I might still be down there among the "alkali-heads" if not for what happened next. At 3:03 I found myself staring in fascination and terror at a storefront sign: EMPLOYMENT AGENCY. A sense of disorientation began building in me with a frightening roar as I read the smaller signs posted in the window: DISHWASHER WANTED, COMPUTER PROGRAMMER, SPOT WELDER, EXPERIENCED SPACE SALESMAN. I watched men shuffling in and out with briefcases or lunch pails. My heart pounded straight up into my head, and I feared for my sanity. OFFICE MANAGER, STOCK CLERK, COPYING MACHINE REPAIR MAN—the little signs leaped at me, hammering at my face. I felt myself coming apart, body and mind, in the most terrifying few moments I have ever known.

At 3:11 p.m. I was back in my pad, stroking either my cat, my guitar, or this friend of mine, well on my way up. I am not in the least sorry I took my trip. It was in many ways a beautiful and enriching experience. But once is enough.

*The Swiss psychologist Carl Gustav Jung
was a scientist who readily acknowledged the
limitations of science, and spent much of his
life exploring regions where science has yet
to go. He was especially interested in the
unconscious mind, and believed that each of
us could benefit enormously by establishing
conscious contact with the unconscious. The
unconscious, Jung said, has much to tell us,
being the repository of all our psychic
inheritance, primitive and prehistoric as well
as more recent. Through conscious effort,
Jung developed an acute sensitivity to his
own dreams, and in waking moments could
recall many of them in astonishing detail.
Believing that although dreams must be interpreted tentatively, they offer us priceless
insights into our deepest fears and desires,
he insisted that each person is the best interpreter of his own dreams. One of the most
interesting of Jung's own dreams described
in his autobiography,* Memories, Dreams,
Reflections, *occurred during a trip to Africa.
Many Europeans and Americans who have
visited Africa have experienced the sense of
moving backward in time that Jung describes
here. Joseph Conrad's Marlow expresses it
in* Heart of Darkness:

> *Going up that river [the Congo] was
> like traveling back to the earliest begin-
> nings of the world, when vegetation
> rioted on earth and the big trees were
> kings. . . . We were wanderers on a
> prehistoric earth, on an earth that wore
> the aspect of an unknown planet.*

*Marlow's struggle with Kurtz, too, in that
story, bears some remarkable similarities to
the dream struggle related by Jung—as does
the experience of the protagonist in another
Conrad story,* The Secret Sharer. *These
uncanny resemblances would not have surprised Dr. Jung; they would be a confirma-*

234

tion of his belief that the content and the
nature of the unconscious mind in all of us
is very similar, that we share a common
psychic heritage. If Jung is correct, then what
we can learn from the dreams of others may
be of nearly as much value to us as what
we learn from our own.

C. G. JUNG

Travels: North Africa

At the beginning of 1920 a friend told me that he had a business trip to make to Tunis, and would I like to accompany him? I said yes immediately. We set out in March, going first to Algiers. Following the coast, we reached Tunis and from there Sousse, where I left my friend to his business affairs.

At last I was where I had longed to be: in a non-European country where no European language was spoken and no Christian conceptions prevailed, where a different race lived and a different historical tradition and philosophy had set its stamp upon the face of the crowd. I had often wished to be able for once to see the European from outside, his image reflected back at him by an altogether foreign milieu. To be sure, there was my ignorance of the Arabic language, which I deeply regretted; but to make up for this I was all the more attentive in observing the people and their behavior. Frequently I sat for hours in an Arab coffee house, listening to conversations of which I understood not a word. But I studied the people's gestures, and especially their expression of emotions; I observed the subtle change in their gestures when they spoke with a European, and thus learned to see to some extent with different eyes and to know the white man outside his own environment.

What the Europeans regard as Oriental calm and apathy seemed to me a mask; behind it I sensed a restlessness, a degree of agitation, which I could not explain. Strangely, in setting foot upon Moorish soil, I found myself haunted by an impression which I myself could not understand: I kept thinking that the land smelled queer. It was the smell of blood, as though the soil were soaked with blood. This strip of land, it occurred to me, had already borne the brunt of three civilizations: Carthaginian, Roman, and Christian. What the technological age will do with Islam remains to be seen.

When I left Sousse, I traveled south to Sfax, and thence into the Sahara, to the oasis city of Tozeur. The city lies on a slight elevation, on the margin of a plateau, at whose foot lukewarm, slightly saline springs well up profusely and irrigate the oasis through a thousand little canals. Towering date palms formed a green, shady roof overhead, under which peach, apricot, and fig trees flourished, and beneath these alfalfa of an unbelievable green. Several kingfishers, shining like jewels, flitted through the foliage. In the comparative coolness of this green shade strolled figures clad in white, among them a great number of affectionate couples holding one another in close embrace—obviously homosexual friendships. I felt suddenly transported to the times of classical Greece, where this inclination formed the cement of a society of men and of the *polis* based on that society. It was clear that men spoke to men and women to women here. Only a few of the latter were to be seen, nunlike, heavily veiled figures. I saw a few without veils. These, my dragoman explained, were prostitutes. On the main streets the scene was dominated by men and children.

My dragoman confirmed my impression of the prevalence of homosexuality, and of its being taken for granted, and promptly made me offers. The good fellow could have no notion of the thoughts which had struck me like a flash of lightning, suddenly illuminating my point of observation. I felt cast back many centuries to an infinitely more naïve world of adolescents who were preparing, with the aid of a slender knowledge of the Koran, to emerge from their original state of twilight consciousness, in which they had existed from time immemorial, and to become aware of their own existence, in self-defense against the forces threatening them from the North.

While I was still caught up in this dream of a static, age-old existence, I suddenly thought of my pocket watch, the symbol of the European's accelerated tempo. This, no doubt, was the dark cloud that hung threateningly over the heads of these unsuspecting souls. They suddenly seemed to

236

me like game who do not see the hunter but, vaguely uneasy, scent him—
"him" being the god of time who will inevitably chop into the bits and
pieces of days, hours, minutes, and seconds that duration which is still the
closest thing to eternity.

From Tozeur I went on to the oasis of Nefta. I rode off with my dragoman early in the morning, shortly after sunrise. Our mounts were large,
swift-footed mules, on which we made rapid progress. As we approached
the oasis, a single rider, wholly swathed in white, came toward us. With
proud bearing he rode by without offering us any greeting, mounted on a
black mule whose harness was banded and studded with silver. He made
an impressive, elegant figure. Here was a man who certainly possessed no
pocket watch, let alone a wrist watch; for he was obviously and unself-
consciously the person he had always been. He lacked that faint note of
foolishness which clings to the European. The European is, to be sure, convinced that he is no longer what he was ages ago; but he does not know
what he has since become. His watch tells him that since the "Middle Ages"
time and its synonym, progress, have crept up on him and irrevocably taken
something from him. With lightened baggage he continues his journey,
with steadily increasing velocity, toward nebulous goals. He compensates
for the loss of gravity and the corresponding *sentiment d'incomplétitude*
by the illusion of his triumphs, such as steamships, railroads, airplanes, and
rockets, that rob him of his duration and transport him into another reality
of speeds and explosive accelerations.

The deeper we penetrated into the Sahara, the more time slowed down
for me; it even threatened to move backward. The shimmering heat waves
rising up contributed a good deal to my dreamy state, and when we reached
the first palms and dwellings of the oasis, it seemed to me that everything
here was exactly the way it should be and the way it had always been.

Early the next morning I was awakened by the various unfamiliar noises
outside my inn. There was a large open square which had been empty the
night before, but which was now crowded with people, camels, mules, and
donkeys. The camels groaned and announced in manifold variations of
tone their chronic discontent, and the donkeys competed with cacophonous
screams. The people ran around in a great state of excitement, shouting
and gesticulating. They looked savage and rather alarming. My dragoman
explained that a great festival was being celebrated that day. Several desert
tribes had come in during the night to do two days of field work for the
marabout. The marabout was the administrator of poor relief and owned
many fields in the oasis. The people were to lay out a new field and irrigation canals to match.

At the farther end of the square there suddenly rose a cloud of dust; a
green flag unfolded, and drums rolled. At the head of a long procession

of hundreds of wild-looking men carrying baskets and short, wide hoes appeared a white-bearded, venerable old man. He radiated inimitable natural dignity, as though he were a hundred years old. This was the marabout, astride a white mule. The men danced around him, beating small drums. The scene was one of wild excitement, hoarse shouting, dust, and heat. With fanatic purposefulness the procession swarmed by, out into the oasis, as if going to battle.

I followed this horde at a cautious distance, and my dragoman made no attempt to encourage me to approach closer until we reached the spot where the "work" was going on. Here, if possible, even greater excitement prevailed; people were beating drums and shouting wildly; the site of the work resembled a disturbed anthill; everything was being done with the utmost haste. Carrying their baskets filled with heavy loads of earth, men danced along to the rhythm of the drums; others hacked into the ground at a furious rate, digging ditches and erecting dams. Through this wild tumult the marabout rode along on his white mule, evidently issuing instructions with the dignified, mild, and weary gestures of advanced age. Wherever he came, the haste, shouting, and rhythm intensified, forming the background against which the calm figure of the holy man stood out with extraordinary effectiveness. Toward evening the crowd was visibly overcome by exhaustion; the men soon dropped down beside their camels into deep sleep. During the night, after the usual stupendous concert of the dogs, utter stillness prevailed, until at the first rays of the rising sun the invocation of the muezzin—which always deeply stirred me—summoned the people to their morning prayer.

This scene taught me something: these people live from their affects, are moved and have their being in emotions. Their consciousness takes care of their orientation in space and transmits impressions from outside, and it is also stirred by inner impulses and affects. But it is not given to reflection; the ego has almost no autonomy. The situation is not so different with the European; but we are, after all, somewhat more complicated. At any rate the European possesses a certain measure of will and directed intention. What we lack is intensity of life.

Without wishing to fall under the spell of the primitive, I nevertheless had been psychically infected. This manifested itself outwardly in an infectious enteritis which cleared up after a few days, thanks to the local treatment of rice water and calomel.

Overcharged with ideas, I finally went back to Tunis. The night before we embarked from Marseilles I had a dream which, I sensed, summed up the whole experience. This was just as it should be, for I had accustomed myself to living always on two planes simultaneously, one conscious, which attempted to understand and could not, and one unconscious, which wanted to express something and could not formulate it any better than by a dream.

I dreamt that I was in an Arab city, and as in most such cities there was a citadel, a casbah. The city was situated in a broad plain, and had a wall all around it. The shape of the wall was square, and there were four gates.

The casbah in the interior of the city was surrounded by a wide moat (which is not the way it really is in Arab countries). I stood before a wooden bridge leading over the water to a dark, horseshoe-shaped portal, which was open. Eager to see the citadel from the inside also, I stepped out on the bridge. When I was about halfway across it, a handsome, dark Arab of aristocratic, almost royal bearing came toward me from the gate. I knew that this youth in the white burnoose was the resident prince of the citadel. When he came up to me, he attacked me and tried to knock me down. We wrestled. In the struggle we crashed against the railing; it gave way and both of us fell into the moat, where he tried to push my head under water to drown me. No, I thought, this is going too far. And in my turn I pushed his head under water. I did so although I felt great admiration for him; but I did not want to let myself be killed. I had no intention of killing him; I wanted only to make him unconscious and incapable of fighting.

Then the scene of the dream changed, and he was with me in a large vaulted octagonal room in the center of the citadel. The room was all white, very plain and beautiful. Along the light-colored marble walls stood low divans, and before me on the floor lay an open book with black letters written in magnificent calligraphy on milky-white parchment. It was not Arabic script; rather, it looked to me like the Uigurian script of West Turkestan, which was familiar to me from the Manichaean fragments from Turfan. I did not know the contents, but nevertheless I had the feeling that this was *"my* book," that I had written it. The young prince with whom I had just been wrestling sat to the right of me on the floor. I explained to him that now that I had overcome him he must read the book. But he resisted. I placed my arm around his shoulders and forced him, with a sort of paternal kindness and patience, to read the book. I knew that this was absolutely essential, and at last he yielded.

In this dream, the Arab youth was the double of the proud Arab who had ridden past us without a greeting. As an inhabitant of the casbah he was a figuration of the self, or rather, a messenger or emissary of the self. For the casbah from which he came was a perfect mandala: a citadel surrounded by a square wall with four gates. His attempt to kill me was an echo of the motif of Jacob's struggle with the angel; he was—to use the language of the Bible—like an angel of the Lord, a messenger of God who wished to kill men because he did not know them.

Actually, the angel ought to have had his dwelling in me. But he knew only angelic truth and understood nothing about man. Therefore he first came forward as my enemy; however, I held my own against him. In the second part of the dream I was the master of the citadel; he sat at my feet and had to learn to understand my thoughts, or rather, learn to know man.

Obviously, my encounter with Arab culture had struck me with overwhelming force. The emotional nature of these unreflective people who are so much closer to life than we are exerts a strong suggestive influence upon those historical layers in ourselves which we have just overcome and left behind, or which we think we have overcome. It is like the paradise of childhood from which we imagine we have emerged, but which at the slightest provocation imposes fresh defeats upon us. Indeed, our cult of progress is in danger of imposing on us even more childish dreams of the future, the harder it presses us to escape from the past.

On the other hand, a characteristic of childhood is that, thanks to its naïveté and unconsciousness, it sketches a more complete picture of the self, of the whole man in his pure individuality, than adulthood. Consequently, the sight of a child or a primitive will arouse certain longings in adult, civilized persons—longings which relate to the unfulfilled desires and needs of those parts of the personality which have been blotted out of the total picture in favor of the adapted persona.

In traveling to Africa to find a psychic observation post outside the sphere of the European, I unconsciously wanted to find that part of my personality which had become invisible under the influence and the pressure of being European. This part stands in unconscious opposition to myself, and indeed I attempt to suppress it. In keeping with its nature, it wishes to make me unconscious (force me under water) so as to kill me; but my aim is, through insight, to make it more conscious, so that we can find a common modus vivendi. The Arab's dusky complexion marks him as a "shadow," but not the personal shadow, rather an ethnic one associated not with my persona but with the totality of my personality, that is, with the self. As master of the casbah, he must be regarded as a kind of shadow of the self. The predominantly rationalistic European finds much that is human alien to him, and he prides himself on this without realizing that his rationality is won at the expense of his vitality, and that the primitive part of his personality is consequently condemned to a more or less underground existence.

The dream reveals how my encounter with North Africa affected me. First of all there was the danger that my European consciousness would be overwhelmed by an unexpectedly violent assault of the unconscious psyche. Consciously, I was not a bit aware of any such situation; on the contrary, I could not help feeling superior because I was reminded at every step of

240

my Europeanism. That was unavoidable; my being European gave me a certain perspective on these people who were so differently constituted from myself, and utterly marked me off from them. But I was not prepared for the existence of unconscious forces within myself which would take the part of these strangers with such intensity, so that a violent conflict ensued. The dream expressed this conflict in the symbol of an attempted murder.

I was not to recognize the real nature of this disturbance until some years later, when I stayed in tropical Africa. It had been, in fact, the first hint of "going black under the skin," a spiritual peril which threatens the uprooted European in Africa to an extent not fully appreciated. "Where danger is, there is salvation also"—these words of Hölderlin often came to my mind in such situations. The salvation lies in our ability to bring the unconscious urges to consciousness with the aid of warning dreams. These dreams show that there is something in us which does not merely submit passively to the influence of the unconscious, but on the contrary rushes eagerly to meet it, identifying itself with the shadow. Just as a childhood memory can suddenly take possession of consciousness with so lively an emotion that we feel wholly transported back to the original situation, so these seemingly alien and wholly different Arab surroundings awaken an archetypal memory of an only too well known prehistoric past which apparently we have entirely forgotten. We are remembering a potentiality of life which has been overgrown by civilization, but which in certain places is still existent. If we were to relive it naïvely, it would constitute a relapse into barbarism. Therefore we prefer to forget it. But should it appear to us again in the form of a conflict, then we should keep it in our consciousness and test the two possibilities against each other—the life we live and the one we have forgotten. For what has apparently been lost does not come to the fore again without sufficient reason. In the living psychic structure, nothing takes place in a merely mechanical fashion; everything fits into the economy of the whole, relates to the whole. That is to say, it is all purposeful and has meaning. But because consciousness never has a view of the whole, it usually cannot understand this meaning. We must therefore content ourselves for the time being with noting the phenomenon and hoping that the future, or further investigation, will reveal the significance of this clash with the shadow of the self. In any case, I did not at the time have any glimmering of the nature of this archetypal experience, and knew still less about the historical parallels. Yet though I did not then grasp the full meaning of the dream, it lingered in my memory, along with the liveliest wish to go to Africa again at the next opportunity. That wish was not to be fulfilled for another five years.

Now the real treasure, to end our misery and trials, is never far away; it is not to be sought in any distant region; it lies buried in the innermost recess of our own home, that is to say, our own being. And it lies behind the stove, the life-and-warmth giving center of the structure of our existence, our heart of hearts—if we could only dig. But there is the odd and persistent fact that it is only after a faithful journey to a distant region, a foreign country, a strange land, that the meaning of the inner voice that is to guide our quest can be revealed to us. And together with this odd and persistent fact there goes another, namely, that the one who reveals to us the meaning of our cryptic inner message, must be a stranger, of another creed and a foreign race.

—Heinrich Zimmer
Myths and Symbols in Indian Art and Civilization
ed. Joseph Campbell
The Bollingen Series VI (New York: Pantheon Books, 1946), p. 221

The mind of man is capable of anything—because everything is in it, all the past as well as all the future.

—Marlow, in Joseph Conrad's
Heart of Darkness

The images of the unconscious place a great responsibility upon a man. Failure to understand them . . . deprives him of his wholeness and imposes a painful fragmentariness on his life.

—C. G. Jung
Memories, Dreams, Reflections

242

REFLECTIONS (17)

REFLECTIONS

Jung recognizes the limitations of European (and American) rationality and the strength of primitive irrationality, but he is careful not to glamorize the latter by exaggeration or oversimplification. What dangers does he see in seeking or succumbing to the dominance of the irrational?

Recognizing both rational and irrational elements within himself, Jung avoids labeling them "good" or "bad." What does he suggest about their proper relationship to each other?

Have you had dreams that were either particularly mysterious or particularly revealing to you? Are such dreams likely to be manifestations of unresolved inner conflicts?

As a man-of-war that sails through the sea, so this earth that sails through the air. We mortals are all on board a fast-sailing, never-sinking world-frigate, of which God was the shipwright; and she is but one craft in a Milky-Way fleet, of which God is the Lord High Admiral. The port we sail from is forever astern. And though far out of sight of land, for ages and ages we continue to sail with sealed orders, and our last destination remains a secret to ourselves and our officers; yet our final haven was predestinated ere we slipped from the stocks at Creation.

—Herman Melville
White Jacket

Voyages of Discovery

~~~~~~

No Frigate Like a Book

There is no Frigate like a Book
To take us Lands away
Nor any Coursers like a Page
Of prancing Poetry—
This Travers may the poorest take
Without oppress of Toll—
How frugal is the Chariot
That bears the Human soul.

                                    —Emily Dickinson

Reprinted by permission of the publishers and the Trustees of Amherst College from Thomas
H. Johnson, Editor, THE POEMS OF EMILY DICKINSON, Cambridge, Mass.: The Bel-
knap Press of Harvard University Press, Copyright, 1951, 1955, by The President and Fellows of Harvard College.

*In her books and her classes, Elizabeth Drew
has led thousands of readers and students
on fascinating explorations of the world of
poetry, pointing out what we might not have
noticed but for her, communicating her enthusiasm and delight as she shares her
discoveries. Here she leads us into an investigation of poetic inspiration and composition. We become aware that the writing
of a poem is itself a voyage of discovery, that
in fact there are multiple voyages involved:
Keats reading, Keats writing, Drew reading,
Drew writing, ourselves reading. . .*

ELIZABETH DREW

Much Have I Travell'd in the Realms of Gold

On a certain October day in the year 1816, Charles Cowden Clarke told his young friend John Keats that he had been lent a copy of Chapman's translation of Homer, and he asked Keats to come and explore it with him that evening. Keats went, and the two friends read on through the night till dawn, not beginning at the beginning and working through the epics, but picking out what Cowden Clarke calls 'the famousest passages', or 'looking into' it, as Keats himself expressed it. Then the young medical student walked back to his own home in another part of London as the day was breaking. When Cowden Clarke came down to a late breakfast next morning at 10 o'clock he found on the table an envelope in Keats's handwriting. Inside was a sheet of paper containing a sonnet:

> Much have I travell'd in the realms of gold,
> And many goodly states and kingdoms seen;
> Round many western islands have I been
> Which bards in fealty to Apollo hold.
> Oft of one wide expanse had I been told
> That deep-brow'd Homer ruled as his demesne:
> Yet never could I judge what men might mean
> Till I heard Chapman speak out loud and bold:
> Then felt I like some watcher of the skies
> When a new planet swims into his ken;
> Or like stout Cortez, when with wond'ring eyes
> He stared at the Pacific—and all his men
> Look'd at each other with a wild surmise—
> Silent, upon a peak in Darien.

These two young men had had a common experience the night before. They had read a book together. Cowden Clarke has left a description of that evening in prose. Keats has left a poem. We should surely be able to discover something of what is vital to the nature of poetry and the poet by a contrast of the two methods of communication and an examination of the particular character of each.

They have one great point of similarity. With both, the experience has become *words*. It is no longer the actual reading of a book which Charles Cowden Clarke shared with John Keats. Both the prose and the poetry are collections of words, and everything which we as readers receive from reading them, reaches us through the words the writers have chosen.

Cowden Clarke tells us the facts of the matter as they appeared to him.

'A beautiful copy of the folio edition of Chapman's translation of Homer had been lent me. It was the property of Mr. Alsager, the gentleman who for years had contributed no small share of celebrity to the great reputation of the *Times* newspaper by the masterly manner in which he conducted the money-market department of that journal. . . .

'Well, then, we were put in possession of the Homer of Chapman, and to work we went, turning to some of the "famousest" passages, as we had scrappily known them in Pope's version. . . .'

Then follows an account of some of the passages, and arrival of the sonnet next morning.

Now let us read the sonnet again and see how the matter appeared to Keats. Again we are in that world we have already visited.[1] What *is* its peculiar quality? We have said that within it, we are always conscious of two things. First, that the way in which the poet has seen and felt the experience is different from that in which the ordinary man sees and feels experience. It is different, first of all, because instead of being a diffused and general impression of loosely related objects and events, it is a synthesis, in which whatever is significant and eternal in the experience is present, and from which whatever is insignificant and temporal has been excluded. The actual scene and the actual sequence of events in it have been excluded, but the heart and core of its emotional reality to the poet has been seized upon by some mysterious power, revealed in all its riches, and unified into a splendid isolation. And this revelation is made in a particular way. It is not achieved by analysis or argument or statement or description. It is created directly by the poetic vision, and the essence of the poetic vision is that it embodies itself always in the form of symbols. In one complete act of apprehension, Keats embodies the heart and core of that experience with Cowden Clarke into the central symbol of a voyage of discovery. He at once challenges our attention and raises the pitch of the experience which we are to share to a diffcrent level, by the first line:

Much have I travell'd in the realms of gold.

At once we are far away from Mr. Alsager and his masterly conduct of the money-market department in the London *Times:* from Cowden Clarke, too, and the very slightly patronizing way in which he pointed out the finest passages to his young friend. Reading Homer is no longer concerned with a certain copy of the book in a particular time and place. It is part of the adventures of the poet's personality in the whole world of books.

At once, too, we become conscious of the second great difference between the world of poetry and the world of statement. *The words are different.* Just as the poet has seen and felt the experience in a special way, so he uses his medium of interpreting and communicating the experience in a special way. Words are no longer merely the means of *conveying* facts. They are concerned to *suggest the quality* of those facts. They are no longer *practical:* they are *evocative.* Here they are required to communicate the quality which the poet discerns in his beloved world of books and reading, and all the richness, the rareness, the colour, the sovereign power which dwell for him in the atmosphere of that world, he incarnates in the two words he uses to suggest it, *the realms of gold.* All its associations with

[1] That is, the world of poetry.

romance, with poetry, with the medieval flavour he loved, with Greek myth, and Apollo, the Greek God of song and sunrise, he packed into his description of the islands in those golden realms, *which bards in fealty to Apollo hold.*

And now the central symbol of the poet's voyage of discovery among books is enlarged and enriched by the creation of new images and a swelling and intensification of the emotion. The atmosphere of excited exploration is changed to that of triumphant achievement. Words loaded with atmosphere and colour give place to those clear direct monosyllables, *I heard Chapman speak out loud and bold.* And finally we are swept forward to see and feel those two marvellous symbols of the living spirit of discovery, which form the sestet of the sonnet. As we read of Cortez, too, the unity of the imagery throughout is strengthened by the echo of the 'realms of gold' in the first line. For the realms of gold, besides being Keats's creation of a name for the world of reading, is the literal translation of 'el dorado', the mythical land the conquistadors set out to find, and the greatest of the conquistadors was Cortez.[2]

By that act of apprehension, indeed, which the poetic vision of Keats achieved from all the materials which that experience presented to it, and by the language which gave it form, is created in fourteen lines of verse, a new world. A world in which the original experience he shared with Cowden Clarke—the actual experience of spending a night in reading a book, no longer exists. Instead of a scene in which the actors were Charles Cowden Clarke and John Keats and Mr. Alsager's copy of Chapman's Homer, there is a world, contained within the confines of an abstract shape of fourteen lines, in which romance and Eldorado and Greece, Homer and Apollo, Chapman and Cortez and the poet himself, Darien and the empyrean, all harmonize into one exquisite unity of being.

• • •

How poetry comes to the poet is a mystery. The idea of the Muse is an obvious symbol of the fact which all creators have felt to be true—that inspiration is a reality. Something of what Mozart describes in one of his letters happens to every artist.

'When I am feeling well and in good humour . . . thoughts come in swarms and with marvellous ease. . . Once I catch my air, another comes soon to join the first, according to the requirements of the whole composition. . . Then my mind kindles—the work grows—I keep hearing it

[2] See *Studies in Keats.* J. Middleton Murry. [Drew]

and bring it out more and more clearly, and the composition ends by being completely executed in my mind, however long it may be.'

Something, which is usually called the imagination, comes to the poet which not only sharpens and intensifies all the faculties he shares in common with his fellow men, but creates a new function of his mind which they do not possess. It is a function which enables the poet to release his imprisoned and chafing vitality in the particular form it needs to take, that is, in the poetic act. Keats describes himself, when the creative passion is upon him, as living under an everlasting restraint, never relieved except when he was composing. Wordsworth calls it a passion and a power, by which we 'see into the life of things'. This must be what Keats means, too, when he declares that a poet is the most unpoetical thing in existence because he has no identity, he is continually filling some other body, and thus partaking of experience in unfamiliar modes. When he is possessed by the need to write poetry, the poet only exists with great difficulty and distress in the actual and factual world about him. His mind is not functioning in that world: he is a stranger there. For the passion and the power generate in him 'unknown modes of being'. And it is this sense of unknown modes of being, this faculty for revealing things to the mind in relationships which are hidden in normal experience, which is the innermost secret of poetic genius. The poet, as Wordsworth again says, rejoices more than other men in the spirit of life which is in him, but besides the passion of perception which that joy brings him, is that particular power of synthesizing perceptions which other men lack: that power of conceiving experiences in the terms of something else; of seizing and communicating analogies; of creating symbol, image, metaphor; and of associating in this way different levels and kinds of experience (such as exploring and Homer and astronomy and reading books), so that their conjunction, by some mysterious intellectual and emotional chemistry, creates a new quality of experience, a new 'mode of being' which was not there before, and which is unlike anything else.

The working of this power is a mystery. It remains a mystery even when its results have been minutely examined. For instance, it so happens that we have the actual clues to all the associations on which the creative passion of Keats seized, and on which it worked when he was composing the famous sonnet. We can guess why it was that Homer and astronomy and Cortez and Darien thronged his mind together,[3] and it is possible to work

---

[3] See *Essays and Studies of the English Association,* vol. XVI, for a much fuller account of this. [Drew]

out in a small way the same process which has already been recreated so brilliantly by J. Livingston Lowes in regard to *The Ancient Mariner* and *Kubla Khan*.[4]

As Keats walked home through the quiet streets, with the stars fading out into the dawn, he may well have had his imagination kindled to an image of 'a watcher of the skies', but this may have been helped by a particular memory of the past. A few years before, when Keats had left school, he had won a prize. It was an introduction to astronomy by a man called Bonnycastle. One of the chapters is called 'Of the new Planets and other discoveries'. The author was fond of lightening his discourses with passages from the poets, and one of these passages was definitely one of those 'famousest passages' from Homer (in Pope's translation) which Cowden Clarke mentions—the shipwreck of Ulysses in the fifth book. He said Keats gave one of his 'delighted stares' as they read the description together—evidently remembering the stilted version of it quoted by Bonnycastle. And so we get the image of the poet as he discovers the 'demesne' of Homer:

> like some watcher of the skies
> When a new planet swims into his ken.

We can trace, too, something of the working of Keats's mind as it found the famous simile of Cortez and Darien. It is a recollection from a passage in Robertson's *History of America*. The associations of that evening must have made Keats re-live in memory much of his school-days at Enfield. The headmaster of the school was Cowden Clarke's father; the Bonnycastle was a school prize, Keats and Cowden Clarke had made friends over poetry, and we have his direct testimony that Robertson's *History* was one of Keats's favorite books in the school library. It was a small jump, as his mind busied itself with ideas of books and discoveries, from Bonnycastle and astronomy, to Robertson and Darien. In that book he had read

> 'The isthmus of Darien is not above sixty miles in breadth, but this neck of land . . . is stretched by a chain of lofty mountains . . . which render it a barrier of solidity sufficient to resist the impulses of two opposite oceans. . . .
>
> 'At length the Indians assured them, that from the top of the next mountain they should discover the ocean which was the object of their wishes. When, with infinite toil, they had climbed up the greater part of that steep ascent, Balboa commanded his men to halt, and advanced

[4] In *The Road to Xanadn*.

251

alone to the summit, that he might be the first who should enjoy a spectacle which he had so long desired. As soon as he beheld the South Sea stretching in endless prospect below him, he fell on his knees, and lifting up his hands to Heaven, returned thanks to God. . . . His followers, observing his transports of joy, rushed forward to join in his wonder, exultation and gratitude.'

Why Keats confused Cortez and Balboa we do not know, but we can make a guess. It may have been that immediately before the passage in Robertson of Balboa discovering the Pacific, is a description of a Spanish expedition in which Cortez figures: or it may have been that, as we know from Leigh Hunt, Keats had seen the portrait of Cortez by Titian, and had been greatly impressed by the eyes—the 'eagle eyes' which appeared in the later version of the poem.

The only other change Keats made was to alter the line *'Yet did I never judge what men could mean'* to *'Yet did I never breathe its pure serene'*, an echo from Dante which definitely links with the idea of the empyrean and the watcher of the skies.

The picture of Cortez' men owed something to *The Rape of Lucrece:*[5]

Enchanted Tarquin answers with surmise
In silent wonder of still gazing eyes.

. . .

Here we can catch a glimpse of the poetic process; of the unifying harmonizing power over material which the poet possesses. A poem is a synthesis of memoried impressions, which the average liver of life leaves in their original chaotic state. 'Life is like a blind and limitless expanse of sky, for ever dividing into tiny drops of circumstance that rain down, thick and fast, a ceaseless, meaningless drip. Art is like the dauntless plastic force that builds up stubborn amorphous substance cell by cell into the frail geometry of a shell.' Into the deep well of our subconscious memory go all the impressions and reminiscences and facts which fall upon our minds and senses and emotions. And there in general they lie, a huddled sleeping company; or they come out straggling and inchoate, the mere tricks of disconnected association. But the poet, with the fire of his imagination, remints these scraps of memoried litter into new-welded living form, pouring them into a fresh mould, and stamping them with the new bright impress of his own vitality. Poetry and life differ, just as coal and diamonds differ, though the basis of both is exactly the same substance.

[5] A long poem by Shakespeare.

The poet remains a man as other men. He is not a mixture of a prophet, a seer, a priest and a medicine man. He may be any manner of man: as moral as Tennyson, as pagan as Keats; as classic as Housman, as romantic as Swinburne; as optimistic as Browning, as pessimistic as Hardy; as mystic as Blake, as practical as Pope; as subtle as de la Mare, as simple as Herrick. The experience he uses as a starting point may be anything: a story, a mood, a moment, an incident, a character, a comment. It may be high or low, grave or gay, steady or fleeting. But whatever it is, it will begin by stirring within him that ferment of excitement, that mysterious working of the glands or the nerve centres or whatever it is which we call inspiration. The sense of inspiration itself is incommunicable. That passion of 'burning with mental bliss' as a modern poet has called it, cannot be transferred, any more than a love poem can communicate the passion of love. The communicable part of the experience, the part with which criticism can concern itself, is that which can be, and is, embodied in words. *Poetry is a special use of words.*

The ability to relate and to connect, sometimes in odd and yet in striking fashion, lies at the heart of any creative use of the mind, no matter in what field or discipline.

—George J. Seidel
The Crisis in Creativity

How many a man has dated a new era in his life from the reading of a book!

—Henry David Thoreau
Walden

Knowing too well the uncertain and elusive
nature of "secrets" embodied in poetry,
Denise Levertov, herself an accomplished
poet, describes how she felt when she learned
that one of her own poems held an
important secret.

DENISE LEVERTOV

The Secret

Two girls discover
the secret of life
in a sudden line of
poetry.

I who don't know the
secret wrote
the line. They
told me

(through a third person)
they had found it
but not what it was
not even

what line it was. No doubt
by now, more than a week
later, they have forgotten
the secret,

the line, the name of
the poem. I love them
for finding what
I can't find,

and for loving me
for the line I wrote,
and for forgetting it
so that

a thousand times, till death
finds them, they may
discover it again, in other
lines

in other
happenings. And for
wanting to know it,
for

assuming there is
such a secret, yes,
for that
most of all.

REFLECTIONS (18)

REFLECTIONS

Have you ever shared an exciting discovery with someone, as Keats and Clarke did, or Levertov's two girls? How would you *show* a reader the emotional quality of the experience, without merely *telling* him in such abstract words as "exciting" and "wonderful"?

The *synthesis* at the heart of a creative experience depends on making a connection, a mental association, between two (or more) things that are not ordinarily thought of as related. Considering discoveries and inventions you are familiar with, as well as your own experience, what other examples can you cite of creative synthesis?

If it were possible to embody "the secret of life" in a poem, what sort of symbol would be most appropriate?

John Ciardi, poet, translator of poetry, critic,
teacher, lecturer, is also a perceptive reader
whose persistent question as he reads is likely
to be "how?" rather than "what?" or
"why?" He is more interested in how *a poem*
means than in what *it means. The process by*
which the poet's experience becomes the
reader's experience through the medium of a
poem is his concern in the essay that follows.
This process is, he says, among other things,
a matter of discovery—for the poet as well
as for the reader.

JOHN CIARDI

Robert Frost:
The Way to the Poem

ROBERT FROST[1]

Stopping by Woods on a Snowy Evening

Whose woods these are I think I know.
His house is in the village though;
He will not see me stopping here
To watch his woods fill up with snow.

[1] From Complete Poems of Robert Frost. Copyright 1923 by Holt, Rinehart and Winston, Inc. Copyright renewed 1951 by Robert Frost. Reprinted by permission of Holt, Rinehart and Winston, Inc.

258

My little horse must think it queer
To stop without a farmhouse near
Between the wood and frozen lake
The darkest evening of the year.

He gives his harness bells a shake
To ask if there is some mistake.
The only other sound's the sweep
Of easy wind and and downy flake.

The woods are lovely, dark and deep.
But I have promises to keep,
And miles to go before I sleep,
And miles to go before I sleep.

The School System has much to say these days of the virtue of reading widely, and not enough about the virtues of reading less but in depth. There are any number of reading lists for poetry, but there is not enough talk about individual poems. Poetry, finally, is one poem at a time. To read any one poem carefully is the ideal preparation for reading another. Only a poem can illustrate how poetry works.

Above, therefore, is a poem—one of the master lyrics of the English language, and almost certainly the best-known poem by an American poet. What happens in it?—which is to say, not *what* does it mean, but *how* does it mean? How does it go about being a human re-enactment of a human experience? The author—perhaps the thousandth reader would need to be told—is Robert Frost.

Even the TV audience can see that this poem begins as a seemingly simple narration of a seemingly simple incident but ends by suggesting meanings far beyond anything specifically referred to in the narrative. And even readers with only the most casual interest in poetry might be made to note the additional fact that, though the poem suggests those larger meanings, it is very careful never to abandon its pretense to being simple narration. There is duplicity at work. The poet pretends to be talking about one thing, and all the while he is talking about many others.

Many readers are forever unable to accept the poet's essential duplicity. It is almost safe to say that a poem is never about what it seems to be about. As much could be said of the proverb. The bird in the hand, the rolling stone, the stitch in time never (except by an artful double deception) intend any sort of statement about birds, stones, or sewing. The incident of this poem, one must conclude, is at root a metaphor.

Duplicity aside, this poem's movement from the specific to the general illustrates one of the basic formulas of all poetry. Such a grand poem as Arnold's "Dover Beach" and such lesser, though unfortunately better-known, poems as Longfellow's "Village Blacksmith" and Holmes's "Chambered Nautilus" are built on the same progression. In these three poems, however, the generalization is markedly set apart from the specific narration, and even seems additional to the telling rather than intrinsic to it. It is this sense of division one has in mind in speaking of "a tacked-on moral."

There is nothing wrong-in-itself with a tacked-on moral. Frost, in fact, makes excellent use of the device at times. In this poem, however, Frost is careful to let the whatever-the-moral-is grow out of the poem itself. When the action ends the poem ends. There is no epilogue and no explanation. Everything pretends to be about the narrated incident. And that pretense sets the basic tone of the poem's performance of itself.

The dramatic force of that performance is best observable, I believe, as a progression in three scenes.

In scene one, which coincides with stanza one, a man—a New England man—is driving his sleigh somewhere at night. It is snowing, and as the man passes a dark patch of woods he stops to watch the snow descend into the darkness. We know, moreover, that the man is familiar with these parts (he knows who owns the woods and where the owner lives), and we know that no one has seen him stop. As scene one forms itself in the theatre of the mind's-eye, therefore, it serves to establish some as yet unspecified relation between the man and the woods.

It is necessary, however, to stop here for a long parenthesis: Even so simple an opening statement raises any number of questions. It is impossible to address all the questions that rise from the poem stanza by stanza, but two that arise from stanza one illustrate the sort of thing one might well ask of the poem detail by detail.

Why, for example, does the man not say what errand he is on? What is the force of leaving the errand generalized? He might just as well have told us that he was going to the general store, or returning from it with a jug of molasses he had promised to bring Aunt Harriet and two suits of long underwear he had promised to bring the hired man. Frost, moreover, can handle homely detail to great effect. He preferred to leave his motive generalized. Why?

And why, on the other hand, does he say so much about knowing the absent owner of the woods and where he lives? Is it simply that one set of details happened in whereas another did not? To speak of things "happening in" is to assault the integrity of a poem. Poetry cannot be discussed meaningfully unless one can assume that everything in the poem—every last comma and variant spelling—is in it by the poet's specific act of choice. Only bad poets allow into their poems what is haphazard or cheaply chosen.

The errand, I will venture a bit brashly for lack of space, is left generalized in order the more aptly to suggest *any* errand in life and, therefore, life itself. The owner is there because he is one of the forces of the poem. Let it do to say that the force he represents is the village of mankind (that village at the edge of winter) from which the poet finds himself separated (has separated himself?) in his moment by the woods (and to which, he recalls finally, he has promises to keep). The owner is he-who-lives-in-his-village-house, thereby locked away from the poet's awareness of the-time-the-snow-tells as it engulfs and obliterates the world the village man allows himself to believe he "owns." Thus, the owner is a representative of an order of reality from which the poet has divided himself for the moment, though to a certain extent he ends by reuniting with it. Scene one, therefore, establishes not only a relation between the man and the woods, but the fact that the man's relation begins with his separation (though momentarily) from mankind.

End parenthesis one, begin parenthesis two.

Still considering the first scene as a kind of dramatic performance of forces, one must note that the poet has meticulously matched the simplicity of his language to the pretended simplicity of the narrative. Clearly, the man stopped because the beauty of the scene moved him, but he neither tells us that the scene is beautiful nor that he is moved. A bad writer, always ready to overdo, might have written: "The vastness gripped me, filling my spirit with the slow steady sinking of the snow's crystalline perfection into the glimmerless profundities of the hushed primeval wood." Frost's avoidance of such a spate illustrates two principles of good writing. The first, he has stated himself in "The Mowing": "Anything *more* than the truth would have seemed too weak" (italics mine). Understatement is one of the basic sources of power in English poetry. The second principle is to let the action speak for itself. A good novelist does not tell us that a given character is good or bad (at least not since the passing of the Dickens tradition): he shows us the character in action, and then, watching him, we know. Poetry, too, has fictional obligations: even when the characters are ideas and metaphors rather than people, they must be *characterized in action*. A poem does not *talk about* ideas; it *enacts* them. The force of the poem's performance, in fact, is precisely to act out (and thereby to make us act out emphatically, that is, to *feel out*, that is, *to identify with*) the speaker and why he stopped. The man is the principal actor in this little "drama of why," and in scene one he is the only character, though, as noted, he is somehow related to the absent owner.

261

End second parenthesis.

In scene two (stanzas two and three) a *foil* is introduced. In fiction and drama, a foil is a character who "plays against" a more important character. By presenting a different point of view or an opposed set of motives, the foil moves the more important character to react in ways that might not have found expression without such opposition. The more important character is thus more fully revealed—to the reader and to himself. The foil here is the horse.

The horse forces the question. Why did the man stop? Until it occurs to him that his "little horse must think it queer" he had not asked himself for reasons. He had simply stopped. But the man finds himself faced with the question he imagines the horse to be asking: what *is* there to stop for out there in the cold, away from bin and stall (house and village and mankind?) and all that any self-respecting beast could value on such a night? In sensing that other view, the man is forced to examine his own more deeply.

In stanza two the question arises only as a feeling within the man. In stanza three, however (still scene two), the horse acts. He gives his harness bells a shake. "What's wrong?" he seems to say. "What are we waiting for?"

By now, obviously, the horse—without losing its identity as horse—has also become a symbol. A symbol is something that stands for something else. Whatever that something else may be, it certainly begins as that order of life that does not understand why a man stops in the wintry middle of nowhere to watch the snow come down. (Can one fail to sense by now that the dark and the snowfall symbolize a death wish, however momentary, *i.e.*, that hunger for final rest and surrender that a man may feel, but not a beast?)

So by the end of scene two the performance has given dramatic force to three elements that work upon the man. There is his relation to the world of the owner. There is his relation to the brute world of the horse. And there is also that third presence of the unownable world, the movement of the all-engulfing snow across all the orders of life, the man's, the owner's, and the horse's—with the difference that the man knows of that second dark-within-the-dark of which the horse cannot, and the owner will not, know.

The man ends scene two with all these forces working upon him simultaneously. He feels himself moved to a decision. And he feels a last call from the darkness: "the sweep/Of easy wind and downy flake." It would be so easy and so downy to go into the woods and let himself be covered over.

But scene three (stanza four) produces a fourth force. This fourth force can be given many names. It is certainly better, in fact, to give it many names than to attempt to limit it to one. It is social obligation, or personal commitment, or duty, or just the realization that a man cannot indulge a mood forever. All of these and more. But, finally, he has a simple decision to make. He may go into the woods and let the darkness and the snow swallow him from the world of beast and man. Or he must move on. And unless he is going to stop here forever, it is time to remember that he has a long way to go and that he had best be getting there. (So there is something to be said for the horse, too.)

Then and only then, his question driven more and more deeply into himself by these cross-forces, does the man venture a comment on what attracted him: "The woods are lovely, dark and deep." His mood lingers over the thought of that lovely dark-and-deep (as do the very syllables in which he phrases the thought), but the final decision is to put off the mood and move on. He has his man's way to go and his man's obligations to tend to before he can yield. He has miles to go before his sleep. He repeats that thought and the performance ends.

But why the repetition? The first time Frost says "And miles to go before I sleep," there can be little doubt that the primary meaning is: "I have a long way to go before I get to bed tonight." The second time he says it, however, "miles to go" and "sleep" are suddenly transformed into symbols. What are those "something-elses" the symbols stand for? Hundreds of people have tried to ask Mr. Frost that question and he has always turned it away. He has turned it away *because he cannot answer it.* He could answer some part of it. But some part is not enough.

For a symbol is like a rock dropped into a pool: it sends out ripples in all directions, and the ripples are in motion. Who can say where the last ripple disappears? One may have a sense that he knows the approximate center point of the ripples, the point at which the stone struck the water. Yet even then he has trouble marking it surely. How does one make a mark on water? Oh very well—the center point of that second "miles to go" is probably approximately in the neighborhood of being close to meaning, perhaps, "the road of life"; and the second "before I sleep" is maybe that close to meaning "before I take my final rest," the rest in darkness that seemed so temptingly dark-and-deep for the moment of the mood. But the ripples continue to move and the light to change on the water, and the longer one watches the more changes he sees. Such shifting-and-being-at-the-same-instant is of the very sparkle and life of poetry. One experiences it as one experiences life, for every time he looks at an experience he sees something new, and he sees it change as he watches it. And that sense of continuity in fluidity is one of the primary kinds of knowledge, one of man's basic ways of knowing, and one that only the arts can teach, poetry foremost among them.

Frost himself certainly did not ask what that repeated last line meant. It came to him and he received it. He "felt right" about it. And what he "felt right" about was in no sense a "meaning" that, say, an essay could apprehend, but an act of experience that could be fully presented only by the dramatic enactment of forces which is the performance of the poem.

Now look at the poem in another way. Did Frost know what he was going to do when he began? Considering the poem simply as an act of skill, as a piece of juggling, one cannot fail to respond to the magnificent turn at the end where, with one flip, seven of the simplest words in the language suddenly dazzle full of never-ending waves of thought and feeling. Or, more precisely, of felt-thought. Certainly an equivalent stunt by a juggler—could there be an equivalent—would bring the house down. Was it to cap his performance with that grand stunt that Frost wrote the poem?

Far from it. The obvious fact is that *Frost could not have known he was going to write those lines until he wrote them*. Then a second fact must be registered: *he wrote them because, for the fun of it, he had got himself into trouble*.

Frost, like every good poet, began by playing a game with himself. The most usual way of writing a four-line stanza with four feet to the line is to rhyme the third line with the first, and the fourth line with the second. Even that much rhyme is so difficult in English that many poets and almost all of the anonymous ballad makers do not bother to rhyme the first and third lines at all, settling for two rhymes in four lines as good enough. For English is a rhyme-poor language. In Italian and in French, for example, so many words end with the same sounds that rhyming is relatively easy— so easy that many modern French and Italian poets do not bother to rhyme at all. English, being a more agglomerate language, has far more final sounds, hence fewer of them rhyme. When an Italian poet writes a line ending with "vita"[1] (life) he has literally hundreds of rhyme choices available. When an English poet writes "life" at the end of a line he can summon "strife, wife, knife, fife, rife," and then he is in trouble. Now "life-strife" and "life-rife" and "life-wife" seem to offer a combination of possible ideas that can be related by more than just the rhyme. Inevitably, therefore, the poets have had to work and rework these combinations until the sparkle has gone out of them. The reader is normally tired of such rhyme-led associations. When he encounters "life-strife" he is certainly entitled to suspect that the poet did not really want to say "strife"—that had there been in English such a word as, say, "hife," meaning "infinite peace

---

[1] As Dante does in the first line of Canto I ("The Dark Wood") of *The Inferno*.

and harmony," the poet would as gladly have used that word instead of "strife." Thus, the reader feels that the writing is haphazard, that the rhyme is making the poet say things he does not really feel, and which, therefore, the reader does not feel except as boredom. One likes to see the rhymes fall into place, but he must end with the belief that it is the poet who is deciding what is said and not the rhyme scheme that is forcing the saying.

So rhyme is a kind of game, and an especially difficult one in English. As in every game, the fun of the rhyme is to set one's difficulties high and then to meet them skilfully. As Frost himself once defined it, freedom consists of "moving easy in harness."

In "Stopping by Woods on a Snowy Evening" Frost took a long chance. He decided to rhyme not two lines in each stanza, but three. Not even Frost could have sustained that much rhyme in a long poem (as Dante, for example, with the advantage of writing in Italian, sustained triple rhyme for thousands of lines in *The Divine Comedy*). Frost would have known instantly, therefore, when he took the original chance, that he was going to write a short poem. He would have had that much foretaste of it.

So the first stanza emerged rhymed a-a-b-a. And with the sure sense that this was to be a short poem, Frost decided to take an additional chance and to redouble: in English three rhymes in four lines is more than enough; there is no need to rhyme the fourth line. For the fun of it, however, Frost set himself to pick up that loose rhyme and to weave it into the pattern, thereby accepting the all but impossible burden of quadruple rhyme.

The miracle is that it worked. Despite the enormous freight of rhyme, the poem not only came out as a neat pattern, but managed to do so with no sense of strain. Every word and every rhyme falls into place as naturally and as inevitably as if there were no rhyme restricting the poet's choices.

That ease-in-difficulty is certainly inseparable from the success of the poem's performance. One watches the skill-man juggle three balls, then four, then five, and every addition makes the trick more wonderful. But unless he makes the hard trick seem as easy as an easy trick, then all is lost.

The real point, however, is not only that Frost took on a hard rhyme-trick and made it seem easy. It is rather as if the juggler, carried away, had tossed up one more ball than he could really handle, and then amazed himself by actually handling it. So with the real triumph of this poem. Frost could not have known what a stunning effect his repetition of the last line was going to produce. He could not even know he was going to repeat the last line. He simply found himself up against a difficulty he almost certainly had not foreseen and he had to improvise to meet it. For in picking up the rhyme from the third line of stanza one and carrying it over into stanza two, he had created an endless chain-link form within which each stanza left a hook sticking out for the next stanza to hang on. So by stanza four, feeling the poem rounding to its end, Frost had to do something about that extra rhyme.

He might have tucked it back into a third line rhyming with the *know-though-snow* of stanza one. He could thus have rounded the poem out to the mathematical symmetry of using each rhyme four times. But though such a device might be defensible in theory, a rhyme repeated after eleven lines is so far from its original rhyme sound that its feeling as rhyme must certainly be lost. And what good is theory if the reader is not moved by the writing?

It must have been in some such quandary that the final repetition suggested itself—a suggestion born of the very difficulties the poet had let himself in for. So there is that point beoynd mere ease in handling a hard thing, the point at which the very difficulty offers the poet the opportunity to do better than he knew he could. What, aside from having that happen to oneself, could be more self-delighting than to participate in its happening by one's reader-identification with the poem?

And by now a further point will have suggested itself: that the human insight of the poem and the technicalities of its poetic artifice are inseparable. Each feeds the other. That interplay is the poem's meaning, a matter not of WHAT DOES IT MEAN, for no one can ever say entirely what a good poem means, but of HOW DOES IT MEAN, a process one can come much closer to discussing.

There is a necessary epilogue. Mr. Frost has often discussed this poem on the platform, or more usually in the course of a long evening after a talk. Time and again I have heard him say that he just wrote it off, that it just came to him, and that he set it down as it came.

Once at Bread Loaf, however, I heard him add one very essential piece to the discussion of how it "just came." One night, he said, he had sat down after supper to work at a long piece of blank verse. The piece never worked out, but Mr. Frost found himself so absorbed in it that, when next he looked up, dawn was at his window. He rose, crossed to the window, stood looking out for a few minutes, and *then* it was that "Stopping by Woods" suddenly "just came," so that all he had to do was cross the room and write it down.

Robert Frost is the sort of artist who hides his traces. I know of no Frost work sheets anywhere. If someone has raided his wastebasket in secret, it is possible that such work sheets exist somewhere, but Frost would not willingly allow anything but the finished product to leave him. Almost certainly, therefore, no one will ever know what was in that piece of unsuccessful blank verse he had been working at with such concentration, but I for one would stake my life that could that work sheet be uncovered, it would be found to contain the germinal stuff of "Stopping by Woods"; that what was a-simmer in him all night without finding its proper form, suddenly, when he let his still-occupied mind look away, came at him from a different direction, offered itself in a different form, and that finding that form exactly right the impulse proceeded to marry itself to the new shape in one of the most miraculous performances of English lyricism.

And that, too—whether or not one can accept so hypothetical a discussion—is part of HOW the poem means. It means that marriage to the perfect form, the poem's shapen declaration of itself, its moment's monument fixed beyond all possibility of change. And thus, finally, in every truly good poem, "How does it mean?" must always be answered "Triumphantly." Whatever the poem "is about," *how* it means is always how Genesis means: the word become a form, and the form become a thing, and—when the becoming is true—the thing become a part of the knowledge and experience of the race forever.

REFLECTIONS (19)

REFLECTIONS

Granting that much may be learned by reading a poem (or story) closely, as John Ciardi does, are there also real advantages to *not* reading closely?

How is it possible to distinguish between a meaning that a writer probably intended and a meaning that someone "reads in"? Can you cite an example or two?

*Here is one more illustration of a discovery
by a reader—the sort of small discovery
which, though not very important in itself,
bolsters another more important discovery or
takes it a step further. Columbus, we know,
did not discover the New World all by
himself, nor did Neil Armstrong tell us
everything about the moon. Every voyager,
in whatever realm, adds his own discoveries
to the store of human knowledge.*

JAMES ARMSTRONG

The "Death Wish" in "Stopping by Woods"

Six years ago John Ciardi inadvertently unsettled a great many poetry-lovers with his analysis of Robert Frost's poem, "Stopping By Woods on a Snowy Evening" (*Saturday Review,* April 12, 1958). Mr. Ciardi's thesis was that practically all good poems are metaphorical, or symbolic, and that Frost's poem, in particular, "ends by suggesting meanings far beyond anything specifically referred to in the narrative." His attempt to elucidate some of those meanings led him to propose that "the dark and the snowfall symbolize a death wish, however momentary."

The response from readers was phenomenal. For weeks *Saturday Review's* letters page was filled with denunciations of Mr. Ciardi's critical ability and with general protests against "probing, poking, and picking" at poems, as one reader put it. There were letters of appreciation and congratulation as well, but the anti-analysis and anti-Ciardi responses were clearly in the majority. Mr. Ciardi defended himself and the name of Criticism with grace and good humor in a short follow-up article, and the furor, after a few more sputters, gradually subsided.

The issue was far from dead, however, as I soon began to discover. Resentment was still smoldering among Frost's admirers. What surprised me most was that where I expected to find the most sympathy for Mr. Ciardi's position—among college English teachers—I found more often displeasure. It was not the process of analysis that they objected to, as I soon learned, but the suggestion that Frost's poem expressed a "death-wish." To find such a feeling in a poem by Robert Frost, of all people, was apparently to them literary Freudianism at its worst. I began to suspect that it was really this point of interpretation, rather than criticism in general, at which most *Saturday Review* readers had taken offense. When I heard Mr. Frost himself at a public lecture pooh-pooh the death-wish interpretation, to the obvious and audible delight of the audience, my suspicions were confirmed.

If we feel obligated to accept Frost's disavowal as the final word, then there is no more to be said; but we need not do so. Many a poet has publicly refused to admit in his work the presence of an intention or meaning that to any discerning reader is clearly there. It may be that he justly regards his poem as his best and final statement of the matter and dislikes having it diluted or distorted by paraphrase. Or it may be that he resents having his thoughts and feelings pried at by morbid admirers who are not satisfied with the exceptional frankness about himself with which he has already complimented them in his work. For example, for Frost to admit that his poem embodies a "death-wish" would inevitably have called forth from countless well-meaning and naive admirers the question, "But for goodness' sake—why?" Few men would willingly put themselves in the position of having to answer such a question.

What is it about the idea of a "death-wish" in a Frost poem that is so disturbing? Can the impulse itself—"that hunger for final rest and surrender that a man may feel," as Mr. Ciardi described it—be so unfamiliar to us? I find it hard to think so. And even those who have never recognized it in themselves can hardly pretend that it is uncommon in literature. More than one poet has "been half in love with easeful Death." Perhaps it is hard to believe that Robert Frost ever entertained the feeling, much less gave it public expression. Yet we have only to read his poems.

I think of one, for example, called "The Onset," which begins,

Always the same, when on a fated night
At last the gathered snow lets down as white
As may be in dark woods, and with a song
It shall not make again all winter long
Of hissing on the yet uncovered ground,
I almost stumble looking up and round,
As one who overtaken by the end
Gives up his errand, and lets death descend
Upon him where he is, with nothing done
To evil, no important triumph won,
More than if life had never been begun. . . .

This is not so very different a poem, in setting and mood, from "Stopping
By Woods"; and the poet says, "I almost stumble . . . ,/As one who . . .
/*Gives up* his errand, and *lets* death descend. . . ." The inclination, the
temptation, to stop and rest is clearly there.

Nor is the association of death with dark, with winter, and with snow
an unnatural or a novel one. Thomas Mann, to recall a famous instance,
relies heavily on this traditional symbolic significance of snow in *The
Magic Mountain,* particularly in the chapter called "Snow," in which Hans
Castorp becomes lost in a mountain snowstorm while skiing. Like the speak-
ers in Frost's poems, he recognizes the temptation and resists it.

The resistance, of course, is important. The "death-wish" is not so much
a wish as a temptation, a brief flirtation with the possibility. Frost's final
word is always an affirmation, a turning back from death to life ("But I
have promises to keep . . .") and a postponement of the rendezvous with
the dark woods and the snow.

Others have recognized the compelling attraction that the woods exer-
cised upon Frost. Mr. J. M. Cox, writing in the *Virginia Quarterly Review*
(Winter 1959), says, "Confronting these desert places of his landscape,
Frost needs all the restraint at his command, for the dark woods possess a
magnetic attraction drawing him spellbound into them." And in "Stopping
By Woods," Mr. Cox sees "the powerful fascination the woods have upon
the lonely traveler . . ." who is "transfixed by the compelling invitation of
the forest." Whether the whispered invitation comes from the darkness,
the woods, the snow, or all three together, it is a strangely appealing one,
and many men have heard it.

No one, perhaps, has heard it more clearly than the nineteenth-century
English poet, Thomas Lovell Beddoes. The "death-wish"—the whispered
invitation of death—is the theme of many of his poems. In "The Phantom-

271

Wooer," there is not only a remarkable similarity of mood and theme to "Stopping By Woods," but a line occurring at a crucial point that is all but identical to a line in Frost's poem.

A "ghost" woos a lady as she sleeps. His identity is not specified, but his voice is the voice of "the little snakes of silver throat" that inhabit "mossy skulls" and whisper "die, oh! die." The poem gives us no alternative but to suppose that the voice comes from the sleeping lady's own subconscious mind. It is a persuasive voice, and a comforting one.

> Young soul put off your flesh, and come
> With me into the quiet tomb,
>   Our bed is lovely, dark, and sweet;
> The earth will swing us, as she goes,
> Beneath our coverlid of snows,
>   And the warm leaden sheet.

The "coverlid of snows" reveals a kinship at least of season with Frost's poem, but what really arrests the reader is that startling line: "Our bed is lovely, dark, and sweet. . . ." Is it unreasonable to suppose that this line was running through the head of the poet who wrote "The woods are lovely, dark and deep . . ."? Without insisting any further upon the likeness of the ideas embodied in the two poems, I will only point out that these two lines resemble each other not only in sound, but in tone and implication.

It is possible, of course, to dismiss this near-identity of line as mere coincidence, but it seems to me that to do so requires more audacity than to recognize the probability of a relationship. If we do recognize such a relationship, what does it mean? It means only that Robert Frost shared with the rest of us the common thoughts, fears, and dreams of humanity—something we knew all the time—and that he sometimes told us things about himself, and about ourselves, that we hadn't thought of before. It means, too, that a new interpretation of a familiar and favorite poem need not outrage us merely because it upsets our comfortable belief that we had it all figured out. The new idea ought to lead us instead to look at the poem again, and freshly, if we can. And if we are capable of being honest with the poem and with ourselves, we may see not only woods that are "lovely, dark and deep," but the promises that we must fulfill before we sleep.

*Here is Robert Frost himself, in one of his
rare prose statements about making poems,
dropping puns left and right, flinging metaphors about with apparent abandon, but
always—in his usual duplicity—with deadly
purpose, the purpose being* clarification—
*"a momentary stay against confusion." And
what Frost clarifies here is the nature of that
paradoxical synthesis that requires in the
making of a poem both order and freedom,
both plan and discovery.*

ROBERT FROST

The Figure a Poem Makes

Abstraction is an old story with the philosophers, but it has been like a new toy in the hands of the artists of our day. Why can't we have any one quality of poetry we choose by itself? We can have in thought. Then it will go hard if we can't in practice. Our lives for it.

Granted no one but a humanist much cares how sound a poem is if it is only *a* sound. The sound is the gold in the ore. Then we will have the sound out alone and dispense with the inessential. We do till we make the discovery that the object in writing poetry is to make all poems sound as different as possible from each other, and the resources for that of vowels, consonants, punctuation, syntax, words, sentences, meter are not enough. We need the help of context—meaning—subject matter. That is the greatest help towards variety. All that can be done with words is soon told. So also with meters—particularly in our language where there are virtually but two, strict iambic and loose iambic. The ancients with many

From SELECTED PROSE OF ROBERT FROST edited by Hyde Cox and Edward Connery Lathem. Copyright 1939, © 1967 by Holt, Rinehart and Winston, Inc. Reprinted by permission of Holt, Rinehart and Winston, Inc.

were still poor if they depended on meters for all tune. It is painful to watch our sprung-rhythmists straining at the point of omitting one short from a foot for relief from monotony. The possibilities for tune from the dramatic tones of meaning struck across the rigidity of a limited meter are endless. And we are back in poetry as merely one more art of having something to say, sound or unsound. Probably better if sound, because deeper and from wider experience.

Then there is this wildness whereof it is spoken. Granted again that it has an equal claim with sound to being a poem's better half. If it is a wild tune, it is a poem. Our problem then is, as modern abstractionists, to have the wildness pure; to be wild with nothing to be wild about. We bring up as aberrationists, giving way to undirected associations and kicking ourselves from one chance suggestion to another in all directions as of a hot afternoon in the life of a grasshopper. Theme alone can steady us down. Just as the first mystery was how a poem could have a tune in such a straightness as meter, so the second mystery is how a poem can have wildness and at the same time a subject that shall be fulfilled.

It should be of the pleasure of a poem itself to tell how it can. The figure a poem makes. It begins in delight and ends in wisdom. The figure is the same as for love. No one can really hold that the ecstasy should be static and stand still in one place. It begins in delight, it inclines to the impulse, it assumes direction with the first line laid down, it runs a course of lucky events, and ends in a clarification of life—not necessarily a great clarification, such as sects and cults are founded on, but in a momentary stay against confusion. It has denouement. It has an outcome that though unforeseen was predestined from the first image of the original mood—and indeed from the very mood. It is but a trick poem and no poem at all if the best of it was thought of first and saved for the last. It finds its own name as it goes and discovers the best waiting for it in some final phrase at once wise and sad—the happy-sad blend of the drinking song.

No tears in the writer, no tears in the reader. No surprise for the writer, no surprise for the reader. For me the initial delight is in the surprise of remembering something I didn't know I knew. I am in a place, in a situation, as if I had materialized from cloud or risen out of the ground. There is a glad recognition of the long lost and the rest follows. Step by step the wonder of unexpected supply keeps growing. The impressions most useful to my purpose seem always those I was unaware of and so made no note of at the time when taken, and the conclusion is come to that like giants we are always hurling experience ahead of us to pave the future with against the day when we may want to strike a line of purpose across it for somewhere. The line will have the more charm for not being mechanically straight. We enjoy the straight crookedness of a good walking stick. Modern instruments of precision are being used to make things crooked as if by eye and hand in the old days.

I tell how there may be a better wildness of logic than of inconsequence. But the logic is backward, in retrospect, after the act. It must be more felt than seen ahead like prophecy. It must be a revelation, or a series of revelations, as much for the poet as for the reader. For it to be that there must have been the greatest freedom of the material to move about in it and to establish relations in it regardless of time and space, previous relation, and everything but affinity. We prate of freedom. We call our schools free because we are not free to stay away from them till we are sixteen years of age. I have given up my democratic prejudices and now willingly set the lower classes free to be completely taken care of by the upper classes. Political freedom is nothing to me. I bestow it right and left. All I would keep for myself is the freedom of my material—the condition of body and mind now and then to summons aptly from the vast chaos of all I have lived through.

Scholars and artists thrown together are often annoyed at the puzzle of where they differ. Both work from knowledge; but I suspect they differ most importantly in the way their knowledge is come by. Scholars get theirs from conscientious thoroughness along projected lines of logic; poets theirs cavalierly and as it happens in and out of books. They stick to nothing deliberately, but let what will stick to them like burrs where they walk in the fields. No acquirement is on assignment, or even self-assignment. Knowledge of the second kind is much more available in the wild free ways of wit and art. A schoolboy may be defined as one who can tell you what he knows in the order in which he learned it. The artist must value himself as he snatches a thing from some previous order in time and space into a new order with not so much as a ligature clinging to it of the old place where it was organic.

More than once I should have lost my soul to radicalism if it had been the originality it was mistaken for by its young converts. Originality and initiative are what I ask for my country. For myself the originality need be no more than the freshness of a poem run in the way I have described: from delight to wisdom. The figure is the same as for love. Like a piece of ice on a hot stove the poem must ride on its own melting. A poem may be worked over once it is in being, but may not be worried into being. Its most precious quality will remain its having run itself and carried away the poet with it. Read it a hundred times: it will forever keep its freshness as a metal keeps its fragrance. It can never lose its sense of a meaning that once unfolded by surprise as it went.

. . . think of writing in terms of discovery, which is to say that creation must take place between the pen and the paper, not before in thought or afterwards in a recasting. . . . It will come if it is there and if you will let it come. . . . So how can you know what it will be? What will be best in it is that you really do not know. If you knew it all it would not be creation but dictation.

—Gertrude Stein

It is to me the most exciting moment—when you have a blank canvas and a big brush full of wet color, and you plunge. It is just like diving into a pond—then you start to swim. . . . Once the instinct and intuition get into the brush tip, the picture happens, *if it is to be a picture at all.*

—D. H. Lawrence,
"Making Pictures"

"The Hunting of the Snark" is a classic voyage of its kind. What its kind is, however, is not so easy to say, and perhaps the cleverest dodge at the moment is to postpone that question until the poem is done, and let the author himself introduce his work. . .

LEWIS CARROLL

Preface to the Hunting of the Snark

If—and the thing is wildly possible—the charge of writing nonsense were ever brought against the author of this brief but instructive poem, it would be based, I feel convinced, on the line

"Then the bowsprit got mixed with the rudder sometimes:"

In view of this painful possibility, I will not (as I might) appeal indignantly to my other writings as a proof that I am incapable of such a deed: I will not (as I might) point to the strong moral purpose of this poem itself, to the arithmetical principles so cautiously inculcated in it, or to its noble teachings in Natural History—I will take the more prosaic course of simply explaining how it happened.

The Bellman, who was almost morbidly sensitive about appearances, used to have the bowsprit unshipped once or twice a week to be revarnished; and it more than once happened, when the time came for replacing it, that no one on board could remember which end of the ship it belonged to. They knew it was not of the slightest use to appeal to the Bellman about it—he would only refer to his Naval Code, and read out in pathetic tones Admiralty Instructions which none of them had ever been able to understand—

so it generally ended in its being fastened on, anyhow, across the rudder. The helmsman[1] used to stand by with tears in his eyes: *he* knew it was all wrong, but alas! Rule 42 of the Code, *"No one shall speak to the Man at the Helm,"* had been completed by the Bellman himself with the words *"and the Man at the Helm shall speak to no one."* So remonstrance was impossible, and no steering could be done till the next varnishing day. During these bewildering intervals the ship usually sailed backwards.

As this poem is to some extent connected with the lay of the Jabberwock,[2] let me take this opportunity of answering a question that has often been asked me, how to pronounce "slithy toves." The "i" in "slithy" is long, as in "writhe"; and "toves" is pronounced so as to rhyme with "groves". Again, the first "o" in "borogroves" is pronounced like the "o" in "borrow". I have head people try to give it the sound of the "o" in "worry". Such is Human Perversity.

This also seems a fitting occasion to notice the other hard words in that poem. Humpty-Dumpty's theory,[3] of two meanings packed into one word like a portmanteau, seems to me the right explanation for all.

For instance, take the two words "fuming" and "furious". Make up your mind that you will say both words, but leave it unsettled which you will say first. Now open your mouth and speak. If your thoughts incline ever so little towards "fuming", you will say "fuming-furious", if they turn, by even a hair's breadth, towards "furious", you will say "furious-fuming"; but if you have that rarest of gifts, a perfectly balanced mind, you will say "frumious".

Supposing that, when Pistol[4] uttered the well-known words—

"Under which king, Bezonian? Speak or die!"

Justice Shallow had felt certain that it was either William or Richard, but had not been able to settle which, so that he could not possibly say either name before the other, can it be doubted that, rather than die, he would have gasped out "Rilchiam!"

---

[1] This office was usually undertaken by the Boots, who found in it a refuge from the Baker's constant complaints about the insufficient blacking of his three pairs of boots. [Carroll]

[2] "Jabberwocky," in Chapter 1 of *Through the Looking Glass* by Carroll.

[3] *Through the Looking Glass,* Chapter 1.

[4] In Shakespeare's *Merry Wives of Windsor.*

The Hunting of the Snark
An Agony, in Eight Fits[5]

FIT THE FIRST

The Landing

'JUST the place for a Snark!' the Bellman[6] cried,
   As he landed his crew with care;
Supporting each man on the top of the tide
   By a finger entwined in his hair.

'Just the place for a Snark! I have said it twice:
   That alone should encourage the crew.
Just the place for a Snark! I have said it thrice:
   What I tell you three times is true.'

The crew was complete: it included a Boots[7]—
   A maker of Bonnets and Hoods—
A Barrister,[8] brought to arrange their disputes—
   And a Broker,[9] to value their goods.

A Billiard-marker,[10] whose skill was immense,
   Might perhaps have won more than his share—
But a Banker, engaged at enormous expense,
   Had the whole of their cash in his care.

There was also a Beaver, that paced on the deck,
   Or would sit making lace in the bow:
And had often (the Bellman said) saved them from wreck
   Though none of the sailors knew how.

There was one who was famed for the number of things
   He forgot when he entered the ship:
His umbrella, his watch, all his jewels and rings,
   And the clothes he had bought for the trip.

---

[5] Fits are both cantos (parts or divisions in a poem or song) and convulsions.
[6] The Bellman, ordinarily a town crier, is here captain of the ship and organizer of the Snark hunt.
[7] A hotel servant who blacks boots and does other menial tasks.
[8] A trial lawyer.
[9] Either a stockbroker or a pawnbroker.
[10] A billiard-parlor employee who keeps score ("marks" the points) for the players.

He had forty-two boxes, all carefully packed,
    With his name painted clearly on each:
But, since he omitted to mention the fact,
    They were all left behind on the beach.

The loss of his clothes hardly mattered, because
    He had seven coats on when he came,
With three pair of boots—but the worst of it was,
    He had wholly forgotten his name.

He would answer to 'Hi!' or to any loud cry,
    Such as 'Fry me!' or 'Fritter my wig!'
To 'What-you-may-call-um!' or 'What-was-his-name!'
    But especially 'Thing-um-a-jig!'

While, for those who preferred a more forcible word,
    He had different names from these:
His intimate friends called him 'Candle-ends',
    And his enemies 'Toasted-cheese'.

'His form is ungainly—his intellect small—'
    (So the Bellman would often remark)—
'But his courage is perfect! And that, after all,
    Is the thing that one needs with a Snark.'

He would joke with hyænas, returning their stare
    With an impudent wag of the head:
And he once went a walk, paw-in-paw, with a bear,
    'Just to keep up its spirits,' he said.

He came as a Baker: but owned, when too late—
    And it drove the poor Bellman half-mad—
He could only bake Bridecake[11]—for which, I may state
    No materials were to be had.

The last of the crew needs especial remark,
    Though he looked an incredible dunce:
He had just one idea—but, that one being 'Snark',
    The good Bellman engaged him at once.

[11] Wedding cake.

He came as a Butcher: but gravely declared,
 When the ship had been sailing a week,
He could only kill Beavers. The Bellman looked scared,
 And was almost too frightened to speak:

But at length he explained, in a tremulous tone,
 There was only one Beaver on board;
And that was a tame one he had of his own,
 Whose death would be deeply deplored.

The Beaver, who happened to hear the remark,
 Protested, with tears in its eyes,
That not even the rapture of hunting the Snark
 Could atone for that dismal surprise!

It strongly advised that the Butcher should be
 Conveyed in a separate ship:
But the Bellman declared that would never agree
 With the plans he had made for the trip:

Navigation was always a difficult art,
 Though with only one ship and one bell:
And he feared he must really decline, for his part,
 Undertaking another as well.

The Beaver's best course was, no doubt, to procure
 A second-hand dagger-proof coat—
So the Baker advised it—and next, to insure
 Its life in some Office[12] of note:

This the Baker suggested, and offered for hire
 (On moderate terms), or for sale,
Two excellent Policies, one Against Fire
 And one Against Damage From Hail.

Yet still, ever after that sorrowful day,
 Whenever the Butcher was by,
The Beaver kept looking the opposite way,
 And appeared unaccountably shy.

[12] A life insurance company.

FIT THE SECOND

The Bellman's Speech

THE Bellman himself they all praised to the skies—
    Such a carriage, such ease and such grace!
Such solemnity, too! One could see he was wise,
    The moment one looked in his face!

He had bought a large map representing the sea,
    Without the least vestige of land:
And the crew were much pleased when they found it to be
    A map they could all understand.

'What's the good of Mercator's[13] North Poles and Equators,
    Tropics, Zones, and Meridian Lines?'
So the Bellman would cry: and the crew would reply
    'They are merely conventional signs!

'Other maps are such shapes, with their islands and capes!
    But we've got our brave Captain to thank!
(So the crew would protest) 'that he's bought *us* the best—
    A perfect and absolute blank!'

This was charming, no doubt: but they shortly found out
    That the Captain they trusted so well
Had only one notion for crossing the ocean,
    And that was to tingle his bell.

He was thoughtful and grave—but the orders he gave
    Were enough to bewilder a crew.
When he cried 'Steer to starboard, but keep her head larboard!'
    What on earth was the helmsman to do?

Then the bowsprit got mixed with the rudder sometimes:
    A thing, as the Bellman remarked,
That frequently happens in tropical climes,
    When a vessel is, so to speak, 'snarked'.

[13] Mercator was the sixteenth-century cartographer who devised the method for projecting a map of the globe on a flat surface.

But the principal failing occurred in the sailing,
    And the Bellman, perplexed and distressed,
Said he *had* hoped, at least, when the wind blew due East,
    That the ship would *not* travel due West!

But the danger was past—they had landed at last,
    With their boxes, portmanteaus, and bags:
Yet at first sight the crew were not pleased with the view
    Which consisted of chasms and crags.

The Bellman perceived that their spirits were low,
    And repeated in musical tone
Some jokes he had kept for a season of woe—
    But the crew would do nothing but groan.

He served out some grog[14] with a liberal hand,
    And bade them sit down on the beach:
And they could not but own that their Captain looked grand,
    As he stood and delivered his speech.

'Friends, Romans, and countrymen, lend me your ears!'
    (They were all of them fond of quotations:
So they drank to his health, and they gave him three cheers,
    While he served out additional rations).

'We have sailed many months, we have sailed many weeks,
    (Four weeks to the month you may mark),
But never as yet ('tis your Captain who speaks)
    Have we caught the least glimpse of a Snark!

'We have sailed many weeks, we have sailed many days,
    (Seven days to the week I allow),
But a snark, on the which we might lovingly gaze,
    We have never beheld till now!

'Come, listen, my men, while I tell you again
    The five unmistakable marks
By which you may know, wheresoever you go,
    The warranted genuine Snarks.

14 A mixture of liquor and water.

'Let us take them in order. The first is the taste,
  Which is meagre and hollow, but crisp:
Like a coat that is rather too tight in the waist,
  With a flavour of Will-o'-the-Wisp.

'Its habit of getting up late you'll agree
  That it carries too far, when I say
That it frequently breakfasts at five-o'clock tea,
  And dines on the following day.

'The third is its slowness in taking a jest.
  Should you happen to venture on one,
It will sigh like a thing that is deeply distressed:
  And it always looks grave at a pun.

'The fourth is its fondness for bathing-machines,[15]
  Which it constantly carries about,
And believes that they add to the beauty of scenes—
  A sentiment open to doubt.

'The fifth is ambition. It next will be right
  To describe each particular batch:
Distinguishing those that have feathers, and bite,
  From those that have whiskers, and scratch.

'For, although common Snarks do no manner of harm,
  Yet I feel it my duty to say
Some are Boojums—' The Bellman broke off in alarm,
  For the Baker had fainted away.

FIT THE THIRD

The Baker's Tale

THEY roused him with muffins—they roused him with ice—
  They roused him with mustard and cress—
They roused him with jam and judicious advice—
  They set him conundrums to guess.

---

[15] Individual wooden locker rooms on wheels, which could be drawn by horses into the ocean, to a depth of several feet.

When at length he sat up and was able to speak,
   His sad story he offered to tell;
And the Bellman cried 'Silence! Not even a shriek!'
   And excitedly tingled his bell.

There was silence supreme! Not a shriek, not a scream,
   Scarcely even a howl or a groan,
As the man they called 'Ho!' told his story of woe
   In an antediluvian tone.

'My father and mother were honest, though poor—'
   'Skip all that!' cried the Bellman in haste.
'If it once becomes dark, there's no chance of a Snark—
   We have hardly a minute to waste!'

'I skip forty years,' said the Baker in tears,
   'And proceed without further remark
To the day when you took me aboard of your ship
   To help you in hunting the Snark.

'A dear uncle of mine (after whom I was named)
   Remarked, when I bade him farewell—'
'Oh, skip your dear uncle!' the Bellman exclaimed,
   As he angrily tingled his bell.

'He remarked to me then,' said the mildest of men,
   ' "If your Snark be a Snark, that is right:
Fetch it home by all means—you may serve it with greens
   And it's handy for striking a light.

' "You may seek it with thimbles—and seek it with care—
   You may hunt it with forks and hope;
You may threaten its life with a railway-share;
   You may charm it with smiles and soap—" '

('That's exactly the method,' the Bellman bold
   In a hasty parenthesis cried,
'That's exactly the way I have always been told
   That the capture of Snarks should be tried!')

' "But oh, beamish nephew, beware of the day,
   If your Snark be a Boojum! For then
You will softly and suddenly vanish away,
   And never be met with again!"

'It is this, it is this that oppresses my soul,
  When I think of my uncle's last words:
And my heart is like nothing so much as a bowl
  Brimming over with quivering curds!

'It is this, it is this—' 'We have had that before!'
  The Bellman indignantly said.
And the Baker replied 'Let me say it once more,
  It is this, it is this that I dread!

'I engage with the Snark—every night after dark—
  In a dreamy delirious fight:
I serve it with greens in those shadowy scenes,
  And I use it for striking a light:

'But if ever I meet with a Boojum, that day,
  In a moment (of this I am sure),
I shall softly and suddenly vanish away—
  And the notion I cannot endure!'

FIT THE FOURTH

The Hunting

THE Bellman looked uffish,[16] and wrinkled his brow.
  'If only you'd spoken before!
It's excessively awkward to mention it now,
  With the Snark, so to speak, at the door!

'We should all of us grieve, as you well may believe,
  If you never were met with again—
But surely, my man, when the voyage began,
  You might have suggested it then?

'It's excessively awkward to mention it now—
  As I think I've already remarked.'
And the man they called 'Hi!' replied, with a sigh,
  'I informed you the day we embarked.

---

[16] Carroll elsewhere speculates that the word suggests "a state of mind when the voice is gruffish, the manner roughish, and the temper huffish."

'You may charge me with murder—or want of sense—
 (We are all of us weak at times):
But the slightest approach to a false pretence
 Was never among my crimes!

'I said it in Hebrew—I said it in Dutch—
 I said it in German and Greek:
But I wholly forgot (and it vexes me much)
 That English is what you speak!'

' 'Tis a pitiful tale,' said the Bellman, whose face
 Had grown longer at every word:
'But, now that you've stated the whole of your case,
 More debate would be simply absurd.

'The rest of my speech' (he exclaimed to his men)
 'You shall hear when I've leisure to speak it.
But the Snark is at hand, let me tell you again!
 'Tis your glorious duty to seek it!

'To seek it with thimbles, to seek it with care;
 To pursue it with forks and hope;
To threaten its life with a railway-share;
 To charm it with smiles and soap!

'For the Snark's a peculiar creature, that wo'n't
 Be caught in a commonplace way.
Do all that you know, and try all that you don't:
 Not a chance must be wasted to-day!

'For England expects[17]—I forbear to proceed:
 'Tis a maxim tremendous, but trite:
And you'd best be unpacking the things that you need
 To rig yourselves out for the fight.'

Then the Banker endorsed a blank cheque (which he crossed),[18]
 And changed his loose silver for notes:
The Baker with care combined his whiskers and hair,
 And shook the dust out of his coats:

---

[17] "England expects every man to do his duty." (Flag signal sent by Admiral Nelson to his fleet at the battle of Trafalgar in 1805.)
[18] Made payable only to the payee's bank account (a British practice).

The Boots and the Broker were sharpening a spade—
 Each working the grindstone in turn:
But the Beaver went on making lace, and displayed
 No interest in the concern:

Through the Barrister tried to appeal to its pride,
 And vainly proceeded to cite
A number of cases, in which making laces
 Had been proved an infringement of right.

The maker of Bonnets ferociously planned
 A novel arrangement of bows:
While the Billiard-marker with quivering hand
 Was chalking the tip of his nose.

But the Butcher turned nervous, and dressed himself fine,
 With yellow kid gloves and a ruff—
Said he felt it exactly like going to dine,
 Which the Bellman declared was all 'stuff'.

'Introduce me, now there's a good fellow,' he said,
 'If we happen to meet it together!'
And the Bellman, sagaciously nodding his head,
 Said 'That must depend on the weather.'

The Beaver went simply galumphing[19] about,
 At seeing the Butcher so shy:
And even the Baker, though stupid and stout,
 Made an effort to wink with one eye.

'Be a man!' said the Bellman in wrath, as he heard
 The Butcher beginning to sob.
'Should we meet with a Jubjub, that desperate bird,
 We shall need all our strength for the job!'

[19] Another of Carroll's portmanteau words, a blend of "galloping" and "triumphantly."

FIT THE FIFTH

The Beaver's Lesson

THEY sought it with thimbles, they sought it with care:
  They pursued it with forks and hope;
They threatened its life with a railway-share;
  They charmed it with smiles and soap.[20]

Then the Butcher contrived an ingenious plan
  For making a separate sally;
And had fixed on a spot unfrequented by man,
  A dismal and desolate valley.

But the very same plan to the Beaver occurred:
  It had chosen the very same place:
Yet neither betrayed, by a sign or a word,
  The disgust that appeared in his face.

Each thought he was thinking of nothing but 'Snark'
  And the glorious work of the day;
And each tried to pretend that he did not remark
  That the other was going that way.

But the valley grew narrower and narrower still,
  And the evening got darker and colder,
Till (merely from nervousness, not from good will)
  They marched along shoulder to shoulder.

Then a scream, shrill and high, rent the shuddering sky
  And they knew that some danger was near:
The Beaver turned pale to the tip of its tail,
  And even the Butcher felt queer.

He thought of his childhood, left far behind—
  That blissful and innocent state—
The sound so exactly recalled to his mind
  A pencil that squeaks on a slate!

[20] According to Martin Gardner in *The Annotated Snark,* "thimbles, forks, a railway share, smiles, and soap are connected with the Snark's five unmistakable marks mentioned in Fit 2. The forks are for eating crisp snark meat. The railway share appeals to the Snark's ambition to become wealthy and so can be used for baiting a death trap. Smiles are to let the Snark know when a pun has been perpetrated. The soap is of course for the bathing machines that the Snark carries about, and the thimble is used for thumping the side of the creature's head to wake him in time for five-o'clock tea."

' 'Tis the voice of the Jubjub!' he suddenly cried.
(This man, that they used to call 'Dunce'.)
'As the Bellman would tell you,' he added with pride,
   'I have uttered that sentiment once.

' 'Tis the note of the Jubjub! Keep count, I entreat.
   You will find I have told it you twice.
'Tis the song of the Jubjub! The proof is complete.
   If only I've stated it thrice.'

The Beaver had counted with scrupulous care,
   Attending to every word:
But it fairly lost heart, and outgrabe[21] in despair,
   When the third repetition occurred.

It felt that, in spite of all possible pains,
   It had somehow contrived to lose count,
And the only thing now was to rack its poor brains
   By reckoning up the amount.

'Two added to one—if that could but be done,'
   It said, 'with one's fingers and thumbs!'
Recollecting with tears how, in earlier years,
   It had taken no pains with its sums.

'The thing can be done,' said the Butcher, 'I think.
   The thing must be done, I am sure.
The thing shall be done! Bring me paper and ink,
   The best there is time to procure.'

The Beaver brought paper, portfolio, pens,
   And ink in unfailing supplies:
While strange creepy creatures came out of their dens,
   And watched them with wondering eyes.

So engrossed was the Butcher, he heeded them not,
   As he wrote with a pen in each hand,
And explained all the while in a popular style
   Which the Beaver could well understand.

---

[21] In the first chapter of *Through the Looking Glass*, Humpty Dumpty explains that *outgribing* "is something between bellowing and whistling, with a kind of sneeze in the middle. . . ."

'Taking Three as the subject to reason about—
  A convenient number to state—
We add Seven, and Ten, and then multiply out
  By One Thousand diminished by Eight.

'The result we proceed to divide, as you see,
  By Nine Hundred and Ninety and Two:
Then subtract Seventeen, and the answer must be
  Exactly and perfectly true.[22]

'The method employed I would gladly explain,
  While I have it so clear in my head,
If I had but the time and you had but the brain—
  But much yet remains to be said.

'In one moment I've seen what has hitherto been
  Enveloped in absolute mystery,
And without extra charge I will give you at large
  A Lesson in Natural History.'

In his genial way he proceeded to say
  (Forgetting all laws of propriety,
And that giving instruction, without introduction,
  Would have caused quite a thrill in Society),

'As to temper the Jubjub's a desperate bird.
  Since it lives in perpetual passion:
Its taste in costume is entirely absurd—
  It is ages ahead of the fashion:

'But it knows any friend it has met once before:
  It never will look at a bribe:
And in charity-meetings it stands at the door,
  And collects—though it does not subscribe.

'Its flavour when cooked is more exquisite far
  Than mutton, or oysters, or eggs:
(Some think it keeps best in an ivory jar,
  And some, in mahogany kegs:)

[22] Carroll under his real name, Charles Lutwidge Dodgson, was a mathematician, and so it is not surprising that the Butcher's fantastic method works, even though it proves nothing; it only produces the number he began with, three:

$$\frac{(3+7+10)\ (1000-8)}{992} - 17 = 3$$

'You boil it in sawdust: you salt it in glue:
    You condense it with locusts and tape:
Still keeping one principal object in view—
    To preserve its symmetrical shape.'

The Butcher would gladly have talked till next day,
    But he felt that the Lesson must end,
And he wept with delight in attempting to say
    He considered the Beaver his friend:

While the Beaver confessed with affectionate looks
    More eloquent even than tears,
It had learned in ten minutes far more than all books
    Would have taught it in seventy years.

They returned hand-in-hand, and the Bellman, unmanned
    (For a moment) with noble emotion,
Said 'This amply repays all the wearisome days
    We have spent on the billowy ocean!'

Such friends, as the Beaver and Butcher became,
    Have seldom if ever been known;
In winter or summer, 'twas always the same—
    You could never meet either alone.

And when quarrels arose—as one frequently finds
    Quarrels will, spite of every endeavour—
The song of the Jubjub recurred to their minds,
    And cemented their friendship for ever!

FIT THE SIXTH

The Barrister's Dream

THEY sought it with thimbles, they sought it with care;
    They pursued it with forks and hope;
They threatened its life with a railway-share;
    They charmed it with smiles and soap.

But the Barrister, weary of proving in vain
    That the Beaver's lace-making was wrong,
Fell asleep, and in dreams saw the creature quite plain
    That his fancy had dwelt on so long.

He dreamed that he stood in a shadowy Court,
  Where the Snark, with a glass in its eye,
Dressed in gown, bands, and wig, was defending a pig
  On the charge of deserting its sty.

The Witnesses proved, without error or flaw,
  That the sty was deserted when found:
And the Judge kept explaining the state of the law
  In a soft under-current of sound.

The indictment had never been clearly expressed,
  And it seemed that the Snark had begun,
And had spoken three hours, before any one guessed
  What the pig was supposed to have done.

The Jury had each formed a different view
  (Long before the indictment was read),
And they all spoke at once, so that none of them knew
  One word that the others had said.

'You must know—' said the Judge: but the Snark exclaimed
  That statute is obsolete quite!   ['Fudge!
Let me tell you, my friends, the whole question depends
  On an ancient manorial right.

'In the matter of Treason the pig would appear
  To have aided, but scarcely abetted:
While the charge of Insolvency fails, it is clear,
  If you grant the plea 'never indebted'.

'The fact of Desertion I will not dispute:
  But its guilt, as I trust, is removed
(So far as relates to the costs of this suit)
  By the Alibi which has been proved.

'My poor client's fate now depends on your votes.'
  Here the speaker sat down in his place,
And directed the Judge to refer to his notes
  And briefly to sum up the case.

But the Judge said he never had summed up before;
  So the Snark undertook it instead,
And summed it so well that it came to far more
  Then the Witnesses ever had said!

When the verdict was called for, the Jury declined,
  As the word was so puzzling to spell;
But they ventured to hope that the Snark wouldn't mind
  Undertaking that duty as well.

So the Snark found the verdict, although, as it owned,
  It was spent with the toils of the day:
When it said the word 'GUILTY!' the Jury all groaned
  And some of them fainted away.

Then the Snark pronounced sentence, the Judge being quite
  Too nervous to utter a word:
When it rose to its feet, there was silence like night,
  And the fall of a pin might be heard.

'Transportation for life' was the sentence it gave,
  'And *then* to be fined forty pound.'
The Jury all cheered, though the Judge said he feared
  That the phrase was not legally sound.

But their wild exultation was suddenly checked
  When the jailer informed them, with tears,
Such a sentence would have not the slightest effect,
  As the pig had been dead for some years.

The Judge left the Court, looking deeply disgusted
  But the Snark, though a little aghast,
As the lawyer to whom the defence was intrusted,
  Went bellowing on to the last.

Thus the Barrister dreamed, while the bellowing seemed
  To grow every moment more clear:
Till he woke to the knell of a furious bell,
  Which the Bellman rang close at his ear.

FIT THE SEVENTH

The Banker's Fate

THEY sought it with thimbles, they sought it with care;
  The pursued it with forks and hope;
They threatened its life with a railway-share;
  They charmed it with smiles and soap.

And the Banker, inspired with a courage so new
  It was matter for general remark,
Rushed madly ahead and was lost to their view
  In his zeal to discover the Snark.

But while he was seeking with thimbles and care,
  A Bandersnatch swiftly drew nigh
And grabbed at the Banker, who shrieked in despair,
  For he knew it was useless to fly.

He offered large discount—he offered a cheque
  (Drawn 'to bearer') for seven-pounds-ten:
But the Bandersnatch merely extended its neck
  And grabbed at the Banker again.

Without rest or pause—while those frumious[23] jaws
  Went savagely snapping around—
He skipped and he hopped, and he floundered and flopped,
  Till fainting he fell to the ground.

The Bandersnatch fled as the others appeared
  Led on by that fear-stricken yell:
And the Bellman remarked 'It is just as I feared!'
  And solemnly tolled on his bell.

He was black in the face, and they scarcely could trace
  The least likeness to what he had been:
While so great was his fright that his waistcoat turned white—
  A wonderful thing to be seen!

To the horror of all who were present that day,
  He uprose in full evening dress,
And with senseless grimaces endeavoured to say
  What his tongue could no longer express.

Down he sank in a chair—ran his hands through his hair—
  And chanted in mimsiest[24] tones
Words whose utter inanity proved his insanity,
  While he rattled a couple of bones.

---

23 See Carroll's Preface.
24 Another portmanteau word combining "miserable" and "flimsy."

'Leave him here to his fate—it is getting so late!'
    The Bellman exclaimed in a fright.
'We have lost half the day. Any further delay,
    And we sha'n't catch a Snark before night!'

FIT THE EIGHTH

The Vanishing

THEY sought it with thimbles, they sought it with care;
    They pursued it with forks and hope;
They threatened its life with a railway-share;
    They charmed it with smiles and soap.

They shuddered to think that the chase might fail,
    And the Beaver, excited at last,
Went bounding along on the tip of its tail,
    For the daylight was nearly past.

'There is Thingumbob shouting!' the Bellman said.
    'He is shouting like mad, only hark!
He is waving his hands, he is wagging his head,
    He has certainly found a Snark!'

They gazed in delight, while the Butcher exclaimed
    'He was always a desperate wag!'
They beheld him—their Baker—their hero unnamed—
    On the top of a neighbouring crag,

Erect and sublime, for one moment of time.
    In the next, that wild figure they saw
(As if stung by a spasm) plunge into a chasm,
    While they waited and listened in awe.

'It's a Snark!' was the sound that first came to their ears,
    And seemed almost too good to be true.
Then followed a torrent of laughter and cheers:
    Then the ominous words 'It's a Boo—'

Then, silence. Some fancied they heard in the air
    A weary and wandering sigh
That sounded like '—jum!' but the others declare
    It was only a breeze that went by.

They hunted till darkness came on, but they found
    Not a button, or feather, or mark,
By which they could tell that they stood on the ground
    Where the Baker had met with the Snark.

In the midst of the word he was trying to say,
    In the midst of his laughter and glee,
He had softly and suddenly vanished away—
    For the Snark *was* a Boojum, you see.

REFLECTIONS (20)

REFLECTIONS

According to Sidney Williams and Falconer Madan, the fore-going poem describes "with infinite humor the impossible voy-age of an improbable crew to find an inconceivable creature" (*Handbook of the Literature of the Rev. C. L. Dodgson*). And that about sums it up. But the question of the meaning of the poem persists, and it may be that we are no nearer to a solution of that problem than the original fans of Lewis Carroll were when it was first published. Carroll himself responded to in-quiries about the meaning of the poem at least five times in writing. Here is one of his answers in a letter written to some children:

> As to the meaning of the *Snark?* I'm very much afraid I didn't mean anything but nonsense! Still, you know, words mean more than we mean to express when we use them: so a whole book ought to mean a great deal more than the writer meant. So, whatever good meanings there are in the book, I'm very glad to accept as the meaning of the book. The best that I've seen is by a lady (she published it in a letter to a newspaper) —that the whole book is an allegory on the search after hap-piness. I think this fits beautifully in many ways—particularly about the bathing-machines: when the people get weary of life, and can't find happiness in town or in books, then they rush off to the seaside to see what bathing machines will do for them.

Carroll seems good-naturedly to recognize the need of many readers for *some* definite interpretation, and apparently feels that the "allegory on the search after happiness" is at least a fairly harmless one. Considering the way the poem ends, however, it may be that what it says about the possibility of finding happi-ness is not very encouraging.

Readers have offered many other interpretations over the years: the Snark represents material wealth; the poem is a satire on the craving for social advancement, or a satire on an unsound

298

business venture, or a satire on the Hegelian philosopher's search for the Absolute; and (more recently) the poem is about the modern condition of existential anxiety—the fear of death, of nothingness, of non-being. Martin Gardner, who edited *The Annotated Snark,* writes in his introduction:

> The *Snark* is a poem about being and nonbeing, an existential poem, a poem of existential agony. The Bellman's map is the map that charts the course of humanity; blank because we possess no information about where we are or whither we drift. The ship's bowsprit gets mixed with its rudder and when we think we sail west we sail east. The Snark is, in Paul Tillich's fashionable phrase, every man's ultimate concern. This is the great search motif of the poem, the quest for an ultimate good. But this motif is submerged in a stronger motif, the dread, the agonizing dread, of ultimate failure. The Boojum is more than death. It is the end of all searching. It is final, absolute extinction. In a literal sense, Carroll's Boojum means nothing at all. It is the void, the great blank emptiness out of which we miraculously emerged; by which we will ultimately be devoured; through which the absurd galaxies spiral and drift endlessly on their nonsense voyages from nowhere to nowhere.

Mr. Gardner is so eloquent it is almost tempting to believe he is serious. Certainly it is an interpretation that must be considered long and thoughtfully before daring to offer another. But that others will be offered there is little doubt. Why, when you stop to think of it. . .

299

Voyages of Discovery

Landfalls and Discoveries

*And therefore I have sailed the seas and come
To the holy city of Byzantium.*

—W. B. Yeats
"Sailing to Byzantium"

*An introduction to Columbus may seem
superfluous; he is one of those semi-legendary
heroes we have all known since we were five
or six. Yet anyone who begins reading in
the literature of his voyages (there were
four) is soon surprised to find how much
more to the story there is than he learned
in school. For example, the idea that the
earth is round was not original with
Columbus, nor even a product of his times,
and there were others who had already
thought of reaching the Indies by sailing
west.*

*The belief that the earth is round goes
back at least to the sixth century B.C., when
it was taught by Pythagoras of Samos, a
Greek living in southern Italy. During the
Middle Ages, however, the theories of
Pythagoras and other geographers and
astronomers were generally forgotten, and
only gradually revived. As early as the third
century B.C. another Greek, Eratosthenes,
estimated the circumference of the earth
with amazing accuracy at 250,000 stadia, or
27,750 miles; actually it is about 25,000
miles. Eratosthenes believed it should be
possible to sail westward from Spain to India,
if the Atlantic Ocean were not so for-
biddingly vast. He estimated the distance at
14,400 miles; actually it is about 12,200
miles from Portugal to Japan. Had Columbus
not mistakenly calculated the distance to be
much less—about 2,750 miles—he would
probably never have set out at all. Fortunately
for him, the unsuspected New World loomed
where he expected to find Japan, or Cipangu,
as it was then known.*

*The European desire to get to "the East"
perhaps originated in medieval legends of an
Earthly Paradise existing far to the east of
Jerusalem and unreachable by man "except
by the special grace of God." The desire was
stimulated by reports of a few, very few,
overland adventurers, such as Marco Polo,*

302

who, with his father and uncle, returned
from Cathay (China) in 1269 with tales of a
truly wondrous civilization in the East. As
European and Oriental traders began to
establish contact on overland routes, India
and the (East) Indies became known as
lands of spices, gold, and precious stones.
The trickle of real treasures from the East
gave credence to the rumors of incalculable
riches. Portuguese navigators sought a passage to India by sailing around Africa, and
eventually they succeeded. Vasco de Gama
reached India in 1498.

In the meantime, Columbus had made two
voyages to his "Indies" and was about to
embark on a third. The background of
Columbus is not well known, but he had had
considerable experience at sea in the Mediterranean, down the west coast of Africa, and
north to the British Isles. From Toscanelli,
a physician and scientist living in Florence,
he had obtained a map that Toscanelli had
constructed from statements of earlier
"authorities" (including Marco Polo), showing Cipangu and Cathay about 6,500 miles
across the ocean from Spain. Toscanelli had
failed to interest King Alfonso V of Portugal
in sending an expedition in that direction,
and Columbus had no better luck with
Alfonso's son, John II, in 1483 or 1484,
even though he was arguing by then that
Toscanelli's estimate of the distance was
too great.

Columbus then appealed to Ferdinand
and Ysabel for support, and when they put
him off, sent his brother Bartolomeo to
Henry VII of England and Charles VIII of
France to seek assistance, which was declined.
When Ferdinand and Ysabel successfully
concluded their conquest of Moorish
Granada, they listened more seriously to
Columbus, but were reluctant to agree to his
bold demands that he not only receive the
title of Don Cristóbal Colón and the rank of

Admiral of the Ocean, but that he be
appointed Viceroy and Governor of the
Indies and receive one-tenth of all the wealth
he discovered. Finally, however, the king's
treasurer apparently persuaded Ysabel to
reconsider, possibly because Columbus had
revealed to him his secret plan of sailing first
south, then west, in order to avoid the
westerly trade winds that had prevented
Portuguese sailors from going farther west
than the Azores, and to take advantage of
the easterly trade winds that blew off the
coast of Africa.
At any rate, Columbus finally received the
necessary financial support for his expedition,
which amounted possibly to as much as
2,000,000 maravedis—the cost of a thousand
head of cattle. Three ships were secured, of
which the Santa Maria was the largest, with
an estimated keel of 82 feet and a beam
(width) of 28 feet. (This is larger than the
Mayflower, which had a keel of only 58 feet
and a beam of 25.) After months of prepara-
tion, the tiny fleet sailed from the river port
of Palos into the Gulf of Cadiz on
August 3, 1492.
The journal kept by Columbus was addressed
to Ferdinand and Ysabel; two copies were
later made of it, but eventually both copies
and the original were lost. Fortunately,
Bishop Bartolomeo de las Casas had made a
careful summary from one of the copies, in-
cluding many passages word for word. It is
the Bishop who introduces the journal
passages that follow. They show Columbus
greatly impressed with the beauty of the
islands and the temperate climate, and with
the handsomeness and friendliness of the
natives, Ariwak Indians of the Taino culture,
whose descendants still live in Guiana. But
Columbus is always eager to press on, hoping
to find gold, hoping to reach Cipangu. After
three more voyages, during which he ex-
plored the coasts of Central and South

304

CHRISTOPHER COLUMBUS

Columbus in the Indies

Sunday, October 7th He kept on his course to the west; they made twelve miles an hour for two hours, and afterwards eight miles an hour; and up to an hour after sunrise he went twenty-three leagues.[1] He reckoned eighteen to his men.[2] On this day, at sunrise, the caravel *Niña,* which went ahead as she was a fast sailer, and they all went as quickly as they could in order to be the first to sight land and secure the reward which the Sovereigns[3] had promised to whomsoever should first sight it, hoisted a standard at the mast-head and fired a lombard,[4] as a sign that they saw land; for so the admiral had ordered. He had also ordered that, at sunrise and at sunset, all the ships should join him, since these are the two periods when it is most possible to see for a distance, the mists clearing. In the evening the land, which those in the *Niña* thought they had seen, was not sighted, and a great flock of birds passed from the direction of the north to the south-west, which led him to believe that they were going to sleep on land or

---

[1] Sixty-nine nautical miles. (A league is equivalent to three nautical miles; a nautical mile is 1.15 statute miles.)

[2] Columbus consistently misrepresented to his crew the distance they had traveled, in case Cipangu should be farther than he had told them.

[3] Ferdinand and Ysabel.

[4] A Spanish gun of the 15th and 16th centuries.

were, perhaps, flying from the winter which was about to come to the lands whence they came. As the admiral knew that most of the islands which the Portuguese held had been discovered through birds, on this account the admiral decided to abandon the westward course and to steer west-south-west, with the resolve to proceed in that direction for two days. He began to do so one hour before sunset. They made in the whole night a matter of five leagues, and twenty-three in the day; in the night and day together, they went in all twenty-eight leagues.

Monday, October 8th He navigated west-south-west, and day and night together they went about eleven and a half or twelve leagues, and it seems that at times in the night they made fifteen miles an hour, if the text be not corrupt. They had a sea like the river of Seville. "Thanks be to God," says the admiral, "the breezes were softer than in April at Seville, so that it is a pleasure to be in them: they are so laden with scent." The vegetation seemed to be very fresh; there were many land birds, and they took one, and they were flying to the south-west, terns and ducks and a booby.

Tuesday, October 9th He sailed south-westward; he made five leagues. The wind changed and he ran to the west by north, and went four leagues. Afterwards, in all, he made eleven leagues in the day and in the night twenty and a half leagues; he reckoned seventeen leagues to the men. All night they heard birds passing.

Wednesday, October 10th He navigated west-south-west; they made ten miles an hour and at times twelve and sometimes seven, and in the day and night together they went fifty-nine leagues; he reckoned to the men forty-four leagues, no more. Here the men could now bear no more; they complained of the long voyage. But the admiral heartened them as best he could, holding out to them bright hopes of the gains which they could make, and he added that it was vain for them to complain, since he was going to the Indies and must pursue his course until, with the help of Our Lord, he found them.

Thursday, October 11th He navigated to the west-south-west; they had a rougher sea than they had experienced during the whole voyage. They saw petrels and a green reed near the ship. Those in the caravel *Pinta* saw a cane and a stick, and they secured another small stick, carved, as it appeared, with iron, and a piece of cane, and other vegetation which grows on land, and a small board. Those in the caravel *Niña* also saw other indications of land and a stick loaded with barnacles. At these signs, all breathed again and rejoiced. On this day, to sunset, they went twenty-seven leagues. After sunset, he steered his former course to the west; they made twelve miles an hour, and up to two hours before midnight they had made ninety miles, which are twenty-two leagues and a half.[5] And since the caravel *Pinta* was swifter and went ahead of the admiral, she found land and made the signals which the admiral had commanded. This land was first sighted by a sailor called Rodrigo de Triana, although the admiral, at ten o'clock in the night, being on the sterncastle, saw a light. It was, however, so obscured that he would not affirm that it was land, but called Pedro Gutierrez, butler of the King's dais, and told him that there seemed to be a light, and that he should watch for it. He did so, and saw it. He said the same also to Rodrigo Sanchez de Segovia, whom the King and Queen had sent in the fleet as *veedor*,[6] and he saw nothing since he was not in a position from which it could be seen. After the admiral had so spoken, it was seen once or twice, and it was like a small wax candle, which was raised and lowered. Few thought that this was an indication of land, but the admiral was certain that they were near land. Accordingly, when they had said the *Salve*, which all sailors are accustomed to say and chant in their manner, and when they had all been gathered together, the admiral asked and urged them to keep a good look out from the forecastle and to watch carefully for land, and to him who should say first that he saw land, he would give at once a silk doublet apart from the other rewards which the Sovereigns had promised, which were ten thousand maravedis[7] annually to him who first sighted it. Two hours after midnight land appeared, at a distance of about two leagues from them. They took in all sail, remaining with the mainsail, which is the great sail without bonnets, and kept jogging, waiting for day, a Friday, on which they reached a small island of the Lucayos, which is called in the language of the Indians "Guanahaní."[8] Immediately they saw naked people, and the admiral went ashore in the armed boat, and Martin Alonso Pinzón and Vicente Yañez, his brother, who was captain of the *Niña*. The admiral brought out the royal standard, and the captains went with two banners of the Green Cross, which the admiral flew on all the ships as a flag, with an F and a Y,[9] and over each letter their crown, one being on one side of the cross and the other on the other. When they had landed, they saw very green trees and much water and fruit of various

[5] Bartolomeo, like Columbus, uses Roman miles, four to a league.
[6] An official appointed by the Sovereigns to keep track of all discovered riches, making sure the Crown was not cheated.
[7] Copper coins. The modern equivalent of this amount is difficult to calculate; a cow would cost about 2,000 *maravedis,* a pig 400.
[8] Probably what is now called Watling's Island in the Bahamas. Columbus named it San Salvador.
[9] For Ferdinand and Ysabel.

kinds. The admiral called the two captains and the others who had landed, and Rodrigo de Escobedo, secretary of the whole fleet, and Rodrigo Sanchez de Segovia, and said that they should bear witness and testimony how he, before them all, took possession of the island, as in fact he did, for the King and Queen, his Sovereigns, making the declarations which are required, as is contained more at length in the testimonies which were there made in writing. Soon many people of the island gathered there. What follows are the actual words of the admiral, in his book of his first voyage and discovery of these Indies.

"I," he says, "in order that they might feel great amity towards us, because I knew that they were a people to be delivered and converted to our holy faith rather by love than by force, gave to some among them some red caps and some glass beads, which they hung round their necks, and many other things of little value. At this they were greatly pleased and became so entirely our friends that it was a wonder to see. Afterwards they came swimming to the ships' boats, where we were, and brought us parrots and cotton thread in balls, and spears and many other things, and we exchanged for them other things, such as small glass beads and hawks' bells, which we gave to them. In fact, they took all and gave all, such as they had, with good will, but it seemed to me that they were a people very deficient in everything. They all go naked as their mothers bore them, and the women also, although I saw only one very young girl. And all those whom I did see were youths, so that I did not see one who was over thirty years of age; they were very well built, with very handsome bodies and very good faces. Their hair is coarse almost like the hairs of a horse's tail and short; they wear their hair down over their eyebrows, except for a few strands behind, which they wear long and never cut. Some of them are painted black, and they are the colour of the people of the Canaries, neither black nor white, and some of them are painted white and some red and some in any colour that they find. Some of them paint their faces, some their whole bodies, some only the eyes, and some only the nose. They do not bear arms or know them, for I showed to them swords and they took them by the blade and cut themselves through ignorance. They have no iron. Their spears are certain reeds, without iron, and some of these have a fish tooth at the end, while others are pointed in various ways. They are all generally fairly tall, good looking and well proportioned. I saw some who bore marks of wounds on their bodies, and I made signs to them to ask how this came about, and they indicated to me that people came from other islands, which are near, and wished to capture them, and they defended themselves. And I believed and still believe that they come here from the mainland to take them for slaves. They should be good servants and of quick intelligence, since I see that they very soon say all that is said to them, and I believe that they would easily be made Christians, for it appeared to me that they had no creed. Our Lord willing, at the time of my departure I will bring back six of them to Your Highnesses, that they may learn to talk. I saw no beast of any kind in this island, except parrots." All these are the words of the admiral.

"Saturday, October 13th   As soon as day broke, there came to the shore many of these men, all youths, as I have said, and all of a good height, very handsome people. Their hair is not curly, but loose and coarse as the hair of a horse; all have very broad foreheads and heads, more so than has any people that I have seen up to now. Their eyes are very lovely and not small. They are not at all black, but the colour of Canarians, and nothing else could be expected, since this is in one line from east to west with the island of Hierro in the Canaries. Their legs are very straight, all alike; they have no bellies but very good figures. They came to the ship in boats, which are made of a treetrunk like a long boat and all of one piece. They are very wonderfully carved, considering the country, and large, so that in some forty or forty-five men came. Others are smaller, so that in some only a solitary man came. They row them with a paddle, like a baker's peel, and they travel wonderfully fast. If one capsizes, all at once begin to swim and right it, baling it out with gourds which they carry with them. They brought balls of spun cotton and parrots and spears and other trifles, which it would be tedious to write down, and they gave all for anything that was given to them. And I was attentive and laboured to know if they had gold, and I saw that some of them wore a small piece hanging from a hole which they have in the nose, and from signs I was able to understand that, going to the south or going round the island to the south, there was a king who had large vessels of it and possessed much gold. I endeavoured to make them go there, and afterwards saw that they were not inclined for the journey. I resolved to wait until the afternoon of the following day, and after that to leave for the south-west, for, as many of them indicated to me, they said that there was land to the south and to the south-west and to the north-west, and that those of the north-west often came to attack them. So I resolved to go to the south-west, to seek the gold and precious stones. This island is fairly large and very flat; the trees are very green and there is much water. In the centre of it, there is a very large lake; there is no mountain, and all is so green that it is a pleasure to gaze upon it. The people also are very gentle and, since they long to possess something of ours and fear that nothing will be given to them unless they give something, when they have nothing, they take what they can and immediately

throw themselves into the water and swim. But all that they do possess, they give for anything which is given to them, so that they exchange things even for pieces of broken dishes and bits of broken glass cups. I even saw one give sixteen balls of cotton for three *ceotis* of Portugal, which are a Castilian *blanca,* and in these balls there was more than an *arroba* of spun cotton.[10] I should forbid this and should not allow anything to be taken, unless it be that I command all, if there be a quantity, to be taken for Your Highnesses. It grows here in this island, but owing to lack of time, I can give no definite account; and here is also produced that gold which they wear hanging from the nose. But, in order not to lose time, I wish to go and see if I can make the island of Cipangu. Now, as it was night, they all went to land in their boats." [Columbus next sailed to the north end of the island and explored a harbor there, "large enough for all the ships of Christendom." Seeing numerous islands on the horizon and hearing from the natives of "more than a hundred" others, he then sailed southeast about 25 miles to an island he named Santa Maria de la Concepción, the present-day Rum Cay. He encountered other Indians and bartered with them, trying to make a good impression on them and hoping to learn where he would find gold. Fernandina, as he named the next island (now Long Island) is another 25 miles away.]

"Tuesday and Wednesday, October 16th I departed from the islands of Santa Maria de Concepción where it was already about midday for that of Fernandina, which loomed very large to the westward, and I navigated all that day in a calm. I could not arrive in time to be able to see the bottom in order to anchor in a clear place, for it is necessary to exercise great care in this matter so as not to lose the anchors, and accordingly I stood off and on all that night until day when I came to a village, where I anchored and from which had come the man whom I had found the day before in that canoe in the middle of the channel. He had given so good a report of us that all that night there was no lack of canoes alongside the ship; they brought us water and what they had. I ordered something to be given to each of them, that is to say, some small beads, ten or a dozen of glass on a string, and some brass timbrels, of the kind which are worth a maravedi each in Castile, and some leather thongs; all these things they regarded as most excellent. When they came on board the ship, I also commanded molasses to be given to them to eat. And afterwards, at the hour of terce,[11] I sent the ship's boat ashore for water, and they with good will showed my

[10] About 25 pounds.
[11] Nine a.m.

310

people where the water was and themselves carried the full casks to the boat, and they were delighted to give us pleasure. This island is very large, and I am resolved to round it, because, as far as I can understand, there is in it or near it a gold mine. This island is distant from that of Santa Maria about eight leagues, almost from east to west, and this point, where I came, and all this coast runs north-north-west and south-south-west; I saw quite twenty leagues of it, but it did not end there. Now, as this is being written, I have set sail with a south wind in order to try to round the whole island and go on until I find Samoet, which is the island or city where there is gold, for so say all those who came on board the ship here, and so those from the island of San Salvador and from that of Santa Maria have told us. These people are like those of the said islands and have the same speech and manners, except that these here seem to me to be somewhat more domesticated and tractable, and more intelligent, because I see that they have brought here cotton to the ship and other trifles for which they know better how to bargain than the others did. And in this land also I saw cotton cloths made like mantillas, and the people are better disposed and the women wear in front of their bodies a small piece of cotton, which scarcely hides their secret parts. This island is very green and flat and very fertile, and I have no doubt that all the year they sow and reap Indian corn, and equally other things. I saw many trees very unlike ours, and many of them had many branches of different kinds, and all coming from one root; one branch is of one kind and one of another, and they are so unlike each other that it is the greatest wonder in the world. How great is the difference between one and another! For example: one branch has leaves like those of a cane and another leaves like those of a mastic tree, and thus, on a single tree, there are five or six different kinds all so diverse from each other. They are not grafted, for it might be said that it is the result of grafting; on the contrary, they are wild and these people do not cultivate them. No creed is known to them and I believe that they would be speedily converted to Christianity, for they have a very good understanding. There are here fish, so unlike ours that it is a marvel; there are some shaped like dories, of the finest colours in the world, blue, yellow, red and of all colours, and others painted in a thousand ways, and the colours are so fine that no man would not wonder at them or be anything but delighted to see them. There are also whales. I saw no land animals of any kind, except parrots and lizards. A boy told me that he saw a large snake. I did not see any sheep or goats or other animals, but I have been here a very short while, as it is now midday. None the less, if there had been any I could not have failed to see one. I will describe the circuit of this island when I have rounded it."
[Rounding Fernandina to the north, Columbus landed near a river mouth

to get fresh water, and there, he says, "I walked among the trees, and they were the loveliest sight that I have yet seen; they seemed to be as green as those of Andalusia in the month of May. . . ." Then when the wind changed to the northwest, he abandoned his plan to sail around Fernandina, and headed southeast instead.]

"Friday, October 19th At dawn I weighed anchor and sent the caravel *Pinta* to the east-south-east, and the caravel *Niña* to the south-south-east, while I in the ship went to the south-east. I gave orders that they should follow these courses until midday, and that both should then change their course and rejoin me. And presently, before we had sailed for three hours, we saw an island to the east, towards which we steered, and all the three vessels reached it before midday, at its northern point, where there is an islet and a reef of rocks on its seaward side to the north and another between it and the main island. These men from San Salvador, whom I have with me, called this island 'Samoet,' and I named it *Isabella*.[12] There was a north wind, and the said islet lay on the course from the island of Fernandina, from which I had navigated from east to west. Afterwards the coast ran from that islet to the west and extends for twelve leagues to a cape, which I named *Cape Hermoso*. It is on the west coast and it is indeed lovely, round and in deep water, with no shoals off it. At first the shore is stony and low, and further on there is a sandy beach which is characteristic of most of that coast, and there I anchored this night, Friday, until morning. All this coast, and the part of the island which I saw, is mainly a beach; the island is the loveliest thing that I have seen, for, if the others are very lovely, this is more so. It has many trees, very green and tall, and this land is higher than the other islands which have been discovered. There is in it one elevation, which cannot be called a mountain, but which serves to beautify the rest of the island, and it seems that there is much water there in the centre of the island. On this north-eastern side, the coast curves sharply, and is very thickly wooded with very large trees. I wished to go to anchor there, in order to land and to see such beauty, but the water was of little depth and I could only anchor at a distance from the shore, and the wind was very favourable for reaching this point where I am now lying at anchor, and which I have named Cape Hermoso, because such it is. So I did not anchor within that curve and also because I saw this cape, so green and lovely, at a distance. All the other things and lands of these islands are so lovely that I do not know where to go first, and my eyes never weary of looking at such lovely verdure so different from that of our own land.

[12] Now Crooked Island.

I believe, moreover, that here there are many herbs and many trees which will be of great value in Spain for dyes and as medicinal spices, but I do not recognize them and this causes me much sorrow. When I arrived here at this cape, there came from the land the scent of flowers or trees, so delicious and sweet, that it was the most delightful thing in the world. In the morning, before I go from here, I will land to see what there is here at this point. There is no village, except further inland, where these men, whom I have with me, say that there is a king and that he wears much gold. To-morrow I wish to go so far inland to find the village and to see or have speech with this king, who, according to the signs which these men make, rules all these neighbouring islands and is clothed and wears on his person much gold, although I do not put much trust in what they say, both because I do not understand them well and because they are so poor in gold that any small amount which this king may wear would seem to be much to them. This point here I call Cape Hermoso. I believe that it is an island separated from that of Samoet, and even that there is another small island between them. I make no attempt to examine so much in detail, since I could not do that in fifty years, because I wish to see and discover as much as I can, in order to return to Your Highnesses in April, if it please Our Lord. It is true that, if I arrive anywhere where there is gold or spices in quantity, I shall wait until I have collected as much as I am able. Accordingly I do nothing but go forward in the hope of finding these." [On Saturday, Columbus sails back to the north end of Isabella.]

"Sunday, October 21st   At ten o'clock I arrived here at this *Cape del Isleo* and anchored, as did the caravels. After having eaten, I went ashore, and there was there no village but only a single house, in which I found no one, so that I believe that they had fled in terror, because in the house were all their household goods. I allowed nothing to be touched, but only went with these captains and people to examine the island. If the others, which have been already seen, are very lovely and green and fertile, this is much more so, and has large and very green trees. There are here very extensive lagoons, and by them and around them there are wonderful woods, and here and in the whole island all is as green and the vegetation is as that of Andalusia in April. The singing of little birds is such that it seems that a man could never wish to leave this place; the flocks of parrots darken the sun, and there are large and small birds of so many different kinds and so unlike ours, that it is a marvel. There are, moreover, trees of a thousand types, all with their various fruits and all scented, so that it is a wonder. I am the saddest man in the world because I do not recognise them, for I am very sure that all are of some value, and I am bringing specimens of them

and also of the herbs. As I was thus going round one of these lagoons, I saw a snake, which we killed, and I am bringing its skin to Your Highnesses. When it saw us, it threw itself into the lagoon and we went in after it, for the water was not very deep, until we killed it with our spears. It is seven palms in length;[13] I believe that there are many similar snakes here in these lagoons. Here I recognised the aloe,[14] and to-morrow I am resolved to have ten quintals[15] brought to the ship, since they tell me that it is very valuable. Further, going in search of very good water, we arrived at a village near here, half a league from where I am anchored. The inhabitants, when they saw us, all fled and left their houses and hid their clothing and whatever they had in the undergrowth. I did not allow anything to be taken, even the value of a pin. Afterwards, some of the men among them came towards us and one came quite close. I gave him some hawks' bells and some little glass beads, and he was well content and very joyful. And that this friendly feeling might grow stronger and to make some request of them, I asked him for water; and, after I had returned to the ship, they came presently to the beach with their gourds full, and were delighted to give it to us, and I commanded that another string of small glass beads should be given to them, and they said that they would come here to-morrow. I was anxious to fill all the ships' casks with water here; accordingly, if the weather permit, I shall presently set out to go round the island, until I have had speech with this king and have seen whether I can obtain from him the gold which I hear that he wears. After that I wish to leave for another very large island, which I believe must be Cipangu, according to the signs which these Indians whom I have with me make; they call it 'Colba.'[16] They say that there are ships and many very good sailors there. Beyond this island, there is another which they call 'Bofio,'[17] which they say is also very large. The others, which lie between them, we shall see in passing, and according to whether I shall find a quantity of gold or spices, I shall decide what is to be done. But I am still determined to proceed to the mainland and to the city of Quisay[18] and to give the letters of Your Highnesses to the Grand Khan, and to request a reply and return with it."

[13] A *palmo* is eight inches.
[14] Actually an agave.
[15] A quintal is about 100 pounds.
[16] Cuba.
[17] Santo Domingo.
[18] Or Quinsay, the name given by Marco Polo to the capital of the Grand Khan.

REFLECTIONS (21)

REFLECTIONS

Does the attitude of Columbus toward the Indians seem typical of the Spanish explorers in the New World? How is it shown? How would you describe it?

As an observer, would you rate Columbus good, fair, or poor? What does he especially notice, and what does he seem not to notice? Is his observation influenced by any obvious factors?

Does Columbus really deserve credit for discovering the New World?

O, wonder!
How many goodly creatures are there here!
How beauteous mankind is! O brave new world
That has such people in't!

—Miranda, in Shakespeare's
The Tempest

He gave us this eternal spring
Which here enamels everything,
And sends the fowls to us in care,——
On daily visits through the air;
He hangs in shades the orange bright,
Like golden lamps in a green night,
And does in the pomegranates close
Jewels more rich than Ormus shows ...

—from Andrew Marvell's
"Bermudas"

*Charles Darwin had no idea what he was
looking for when he set out at the age of 23
for a five-year round-the-world cruise aboard
HMS* Beagle. *In one sense, he was not looking for anything at all; he had been invited,
upon completion of his studies at Cambridge
University, to serve as naturalist on the*
Beagle's *surveying cruise, and he was excited
at the prospect of adventure and gratified
by the opportunity to broaden his biological
knowledge by sampling plant and animal life
around the globe. In another sense, he was
looking for whatever he might see; his
powers of observation were trained and
whetted, and he had a driving curiosity that
impelled him to wonder* why *things were as
they were and to find his own answers rather
than accept someone else's. The* Beagle
*cruised down the coast of South America,
touching at Brazil, Argentina, and Tierra del
Fuego, then sailed north along the coast of
Chile and Peru to the Galapagos Islands, and
west across the Pacific to Tahiti, New
Zealand, and Australia. Darwin went ashore
at every opportunity, sometimes for periods
of several weeks, and crammed page after
page of his journal with detailed notes on his
observations of everything that came within
his range. The immediate consequence of
this copious journal was its publication, in
revised form, three years after Darwin's
return to England in 1836. But the long-
range consequences were still fermenting in
his brain, and 23 years after his return, the
conclusions to questions he had asked himself
during the* Beagle's *voyage burst forth on the
world in his famous book,* On the Origin of
Species *(1859). The Galapagos Islands were
a key landfall for Darwin. There he encountered a unique biological situation: an
environment in which hundreds of plant and
animal species had developed for perhaps
hundreds of thousands of years in isolation,
with the result that there were creatures*

317

living there unlike those anywhere else on earth. Darwin was fully aware of the uniqueness of the situation and the peculiar consequences it produced, but his published journal gives little indication of the tremendous implications he was beginning to suspect. In the following chapter from Darwin and the Beagle, *Alan Moorehead retells the story of Darwin's discoveries in the Galapagos.*

ALAN MOOREHEAD

Darwin in the Galapagos

After Tahiti the Galapagos were the most famous of all the tropical islands in the Pacific. They had been discovered in 1535 by Fray Tomas de Berlanga, Bishop of Panama, and were now owned by Ecuador, 500 odd miles away. Already in the 1830s some sixty or seventy whalers, mostly American, called there every year for 'refreshments'. They replenished their water tanks from the springs, they captured tortoises for meat, (*galapagos* is the Spanish word for giant tortoises), and they called for mail at Post Office Bay where a box was set up on the beach. Every whaling captain took from it any letters which he thought he might be able to forward. Herman Melville called in at the Galapagos aboard the *Acushnet* not long after the *Beagle's* visit, and the 'blighted Encantadas' are a part of the saga of the white whale. 'Little but reptile life is here found', wrote Melville, 'the chief sound of life is a hiss'.

Apart from their practical uses there was nothing much to recommend the Galapagos; they were not lush and beautiful islands like the Tahiti group, they were (and still are) far off the usual maritime routes, circled by capricious currents, and nobody lived in them then except for a handful of political prisoners who had been stranded there by the Ecuador government. The fame of the islands was founded upon one thing; they were infinitely strange, unlike any other islands in the world. No one who went there ever forgot them. For the *Beagle* this was just another port of call in a very long voyage, but for Darwin it was much more than that, for it was here, in the most unexpected way—just as a man might have a sudden inspiration while he is travelling in a car or a train—that he began to form a coherent view of the evolution of life on this planet. To put it into his own words: 'Here, both in space and time, we seem to be brought somewhat near to that great fact—that mystery of mysteries—the first appearance of new beings on this earth.'

For the *Beagle's* crew, however, the islands at first were not earthly at all; they looked more like hell. The ship came up to Chatham Island, the most easterly of the group, in a fresh breeze and they saw a shore of hideous black lava that had been twisted and buckled and tossed about as though it were a petrified stormy sea. Hardly a green thing grew; the thin skeletal brushwood looked as if it had been blasted by lightning, and on the crumbling rocks repulsive lizards crawled about. Even the coconut palm, that emblem of the Pacific, was missing. A lowering sultry sky hung overhead and a forest of little volcanic cones that stuck up like chimney pots reminded Darwin of the iron foundries of his native Staffordshire. There was even a smell of burning. 'A shore fit for pandemonium', was FitzRoy's[1] comment. 'The Infernal Regions . . .'

Yet they had good sport when the *Beagle* came to anchor in St Stephen's Harbour on 15 September 1835. Sharks, turtles and tropical fish popped up all around them, and it did not take the sailors long to get their lines over the side. 'This sport', Darwin noted, 'makes all hands very merry; loud laughter and the heavy flapping of fish (on the deck) are heard on every side'. There were several American whalers about, and one of them in particular, the *Science,* a big vessel carrying no less than nine whale boats, caught FitzRoy's expert eye. He thought her 'remarkably fine' as she came sailing majestically by.

A party landed on the black sand which was so hot that it burnt their feet through their thick boots. They found the shore littered with small barrows which the men from the whalers used to carry the huge tortoises down to the boats, and the great quantity of tortoise shells lying about were clear evidence of the massacres that went on. FitzRoy saw large

---

[1] Robert Fitzroy is the young captain of the *Beagle,* three years older than Darwin.

terrapin shells used to cover young plants in a crude garden, instead of flower pots. Mr Stokes observed some tortoises which seemed to be enjoying themselves, 'snuffling and waddling about in the soft clayey soil near a spring'. Some of these were so large that when standing on their four elephantine legs they could reach the breast of a man with their heads. These tortoises weighed up to and over 500 lbs, and one that Darwin measured was 96 inches round the waist, and 53 inches down the length of its back. The peculiar lizards (actually they were iguanas) ran clumsily out of the men's way and shuffled into their burrows.

The *Beagle* cruised for just over a month in the Galapagos, and whenever they reached an interesting point FitzRoy dropped off a boatload of men to explore. On Narborough Island the turtles were coming in at night to lay their eggs in the sand, thousands of them; they laid six eggs in each hole. On Charles Island there was a penal settlement of two hundred convicts, who cultivated sugar-cane, bananas and corn on the high ground. But the group that concerns us is the one that was put ashore on James Island. Here Darwin, Covington, Bynoe and two sailors were landed with a tent and provisions, and FitzRoy promised to come back and pick them up at the end of a week. Darwin visited other islands as well, but they did not differ very much from James Island, and so we can conveniently group all his experiences into this one extraordinary week. They set up their tent on the beach, laid out their bedding and their stores, and then began to look around them.

The marine lizards, on closer inspection, turned out to be miniature dragons, several feet in length, and they had great gaping mouths with pouches under them and long flat tails; 'imps of darkness', Darwin called them. They swarmed in thousands; everywhere Darwin went they scuttled away before him, and they were even blacker than the forbidding black rocks on which they lived. Everything about these iguanas was odd. They never went more than ten yards inland; either they sunned themselves on the shore or dived into the sea where at once they became expert swimmers, holding their webbed feet close to their sides and propelling themselves along with strong swift strokes of their tails. Through the clear water one could see them cruising close to the bottom, and they could stay submerged for a very long time; a sailor threw one into the sea with a heavy weight attached to it, and when he fished it up an hour later it was still alive and kicking. They fed on seaweed, a fact that Darwin and Bynoe ascertained when with Bynoe's surgical instruments they opened one up and examined the contents of its stomach. And yet, like some sailors, these marine beasts hated the sea. Darwin took one by the tail and hurled it into a big pool that had been left in the rocks by the ebb-tide. At once it swam back to the land. Again Darwin caught it and threw it back, and again it returned. No matter what he did the animal simply would not stay in the sea, and Darwin was forced to conclude that it feared the sharks there and instinctively, when threatened by anything, came ashore where it had no enemies. Their breeding season was November, when they put on their courting colours and surrounded themselves with their harems.

The other creatures on the coast were also strange in different ways; flightless cormorants, penguins and seals, both cold-sea creatures, unpredictably living here in these tropical waters, and a scarlet crab that scuttled over the lizards' backs, hunting for ticks. Walking inland with Covington, Darwin arrived among some scattered cactuses, and here two enormous tortoises were feeding. They were quite deaf and did not notice the two men until they had drawn level with their eyes. Then they hissed loudly and drew in their heads. These animals were so big and heavy that it was impossible to lift them or even turn them over on their sides— Darwin and Covington tried—and they could easily bear the weight of a man. Darwin got aboard and found it a very wobbly seat, but he in no way impeded the tortoise's progress; he calculated that it managed 60 yards in ten minutes, or 360 yards an hour, which would be roughly four miles a day—'allowing a little time for it to eat on the road'.

The tortoises were headed towards a freshwater spring on higher ground, and from many directions broad paths converged upon the spot. Darwin and Covington soon found themselves in the midst of a strange two-way procession, some of the animals going up, others coming down, all of them pacing deliberately along and occasionally pausing to browse on the cactus along the way. This procession continued all through the day and night, and appeared to have been going on for countless ages.

As they went higher the two men found themselves in quite different country; clouds filled the air with moisture and there were tall trees covered with ferns, orchids, lichens and mosses. At the spring itself one line of tortoises were quietly leaving, having drunk their fill, and another line were eagerly travelling towards the water, with outstretched necks. 'Quite regardless of any spectator, the tortoise buries his head in the water above his eyes, and greedily swallows great mouthfuls, at the rate of about ten in a minute.' They drank and drank as though they were not drinking for one day but for a month, as indeed they were.

The males were easily distinguished from the females by their greater size and their longer tails; during the mating season the male utters a hoarse bellow which can be heard a hundred yards away. 'The female', says Darwin briskly, 'never uses her voice'.

The huge beasts were quite defenceless. Whalers were taking them by the hundred to provision their ships, and Darwin himself had no difficulty in catching three young ones which were later put on board the *Beagle* and taken back alive to England. Natural hazards beset them too, of course; the carrion-feeding buzzards swooped on the young tortoises as soon as they were hatched, and occasionally Darwin would come upon the body of some monster who in his old age had missed his footing and fallen down a precipice. Everywhere through the islands discarded shells lay about. Roast tortoise, Darwin discovered, was good eating, especially if you cooked it as he had seen the gauchos cook the armadillos—in the shell.

Another phenomenon was the land iguana. These were almost as big as the marine iguana—a 4-foot specimen was nothing unusual—and even uglier; they had a ridge of spines along the back and a Joseph's coat of orange-yellow and brick-red that looked as though it had been splashed upon them in blotches by a clumsy hand. They fed upon the 30-foot cactus trees, climbing up quite high to get at the more succulent bits, and always seemed to be ravenous; when Darwin threw a group of them a branch one day they fell upon it, pulling and tugging it away from one another like dogs quarrelling over a bone. Their burrows were so numerous that Darwin was constantly putting his foot into them as he walked along, and they could shift the earth with astonishing rapidity, one quick scrape with the front paws and then another with the back. They had sharp teeth and a general air that was menacing, yet they never seemed to want to bite. 'Essentially mild and torpid monsters', they crawled slowly along, tails and bellies dragging on the ground, and often stopped for a short doze. Once Darwin waited until one of them had got himself fairly underground and then pulled him by the tail. Surprised rather than angry the animal whipped round and eyed Darwin indignantly as if it were saying, 'What did you pull my tail for?' But it did not attack. Its meat when cooked was white and not too bad, not at any rate as Darwin says 'for those whose stomachs soar above all prejudices'.

On James Island Darwin counted twenty-six species of land birds, all unique. 'I paid also much attention to the Birds', he wrote to Henslow,[2] 'which I suspect are very curious'. They were incredibly tame. Having never learned to fear man they regarded Darwin simply as another large harmless animal, and they sat unmoved in the bushes whenever he passed by. He brushed a hawk off a bough with the end of his gun. A mockingbird came down to drink from a pitcher of water he was holding in his hand, and at the pools in the rocks he knocked off with a stick or even with his hat as many doves and finches as he wanted. He quotes a paradisial

---

[2] Darwin's teacher, Professor of Botany at Cambridge.

description from Cowley, written in the year 1684: 'Turtle-doves were so tame that they would often alight upon our hats and arms . . . they not fearing man'. Alas that Cowley goes on to say that 'such times as some of our company did fire at them . . . they were rendered more shy'. In the same year Dampier remarked that a man in a morning's walk might kill six or seven dozen of these doves. On Charles Island Darwin saw a boy sitting by a well with a switch in his hand, with which he killed the doves and finches as they came in to drink; the boy told him that he was in the habit of getting his dinner this simple way. The birds never seemed to realise their danger. 'We may infer', wrote Darwin, 'what havoc the introduction of any new beast of prey must cause in a country, before the instincts of the indigenous inhabitants have become adapted to the stranger's craft or power'.

But still at that time most of the inhabitants of the Galapagos islands lived in peace together. Darwin saw a finch unconcernedly eating one end of a bit of cactus while a lizard ate the other, and in the upper, greener regions lizards and tortoises fed together on the same bush of berries.

And so an enchanted week went by, and Darwin's jars were filled with plants, seashells, insects, lizards and snakes. The Garden of Eden presumably was not quite like this, nevertheless the island had a quality of timelessness and innocence, nature was in a state of balance with itself, and the only real intruder here was man. One day they walked around the coast to a crater which contained a perfectly circular lake. The water was only a few inches deep, and it rested on a floor of sparkling white salt. The shore was covered with a fringe of bright green plants. In this idyllic spot the mutinous crew of a whaling ship had murdered their captain a short time before, and the dead man's skull was still lying on the ground.

The whalers, however, were not all as ferocious as this, and indeed Darwin and Bynoe were very grateful when an American vessel visited the island and provided them with three casks of water which they needed badly, and a welcome bucket of onions. 'Extraordinary kindness of Yankeys', Darwin noted in his diary.

But the *Beagle* could not linger, much as Darwin longed to. It is the fate of most voyagers, no sooner to discover what is most interest in any locality, than they are hurried from it.' Back on board he began to sort out his specimens, and was soon struck by an important fact: the majority of them were unique species which were to be found in these islands and nowhere else, and this applied to the plants as well as to the reptiles, birds, fish, shells and insects. It was true that they resembled other species in South America, but at the same time they were very different. 'It was most striking', Darwin wrote later, 'to be surrounded by new birds, new reptiles, new shells, new insects, new plants, and yet by innumerable trifling details of structure, and even by the tones of voice and plumage of the birds, to have the temperate plains of . . . Patagonia, or the hot dry deserts of northern Chile, vividly brought before my eyes'.

He made another discovery: the species differed from island to island, even though many of the islands were only fifty or sixty miles apart. His attention was first drawn to this by comparing the mocking-thrushes shot on various islands, but then Mr. Lawson, an Englishman who was acting as vice-governor of the archipelago, remarked that he could tell by one look at a tortoise which island it came from. Thus the tortoises of Albemarle Island had a different sort of shell from those on Chatham, and both differed again from those on James.

With the little finches these effects were still more marked. The finches were dull to look at, and made dreary unmusical sounds; all had short tails, built nests with roofs, and laid white eggs spotted with pink, four to a clutch. Their plumage varied within limits: it ranged from lava black to green, according to their habitat. (It was not only the finches that were so dully feathered; with the exception of a yellow-breasted wren and a scarlet-tufted flycatcher none of the birds had the usual gaudy colouring of the tropics.) But it was the number of different species of finch, and the variety of their beaks, that so amazed Darwin. On one island they had developed strong thick beaks for cracking nuts and seeds, on another the beak was smaller to enable the bird to catch insects, on another again the beak was adjusted to feeding on fruits and flowers. There was even a bird that had learned how to use a cactus spine to probe grubs out of holes.

Clearly the birds had found different foods available on different islands, and through successive generations had adjusted themselves accordingly. The fact that they differed so much among themselves as compared with other birds suggested that they had got to the Galapagos islands first; for a period, possibly quite a long one, they were probably without competitors for food and territory, and this had allowed them to evolve in directions which would otherwise have been closed to them. For instance, finches do not normally evolve into woodpecker-like types because there are already efficient woodpeckers at work, and had a small mainland woodpecker already been established in the Galapagos it is most unlikely that the woodpecker finch would ever have evolved. Similarly the finch which ate nuts, the finch which ate insects, and the finch which fed on fruit and flowers, had been left in peace to evolve their best method of approach. Isolation had encouraged the origin of new species.

Somewhere here a great principle was involved. Naturally Darwin did not grasp the full implications of it all at once; for instance, he makes little mention of the finches in the first published edition of his Journal, yet the subject of their diversity and modification later became one of the great arguments in his theory of natural selection. But by this time he must have realised that he was on the edge of a remarkable and disturbing discovery. Until this point he had never openly objected to the current belief in the creation of unchangeable species, though he may well have had secret doubts. But now here on the Galapagos, faced with the existence of different forms of mocking-birds, tortoises and finches on different islands, different forms of the same species, he was forced to question the most fundamental contemporary theories. Indeed, it was more than that; if the ideas that were now buzzing round in his head were proved correct then all the accepted theories of the origin of life on this earth would have to be revised, and the Book of Genesis itself—the story of Adam and Eve and the Flood—would be exposed as nothing more than a superstitious myth. It might take years of research and investigation to prove anything, but in theory at least all the pieces of the jig-saw seemed to be coming together.

He can hardly have failed to have put his ideas to FitzRoy if only in a tentative, speculative way; and if we follow the two men's later writings it is not impossible to reproduce their argument, not impossible to envisage them here in their narrow cabin, or, if you like, out on the poop deck on a calm night as they sailed away from the Galapagos, putting forth their ideas with all the force of young men who passionately want to persuade one another and to get to the absolute truth.

Darwin's thesis was simply this: the world as we know it was not just 'created' in a single instant of time; it had evolved from something infinitely primitive and it was changing still. There was a wonderful illustration of what had happened here in these islands. Quite recently they had been pushed up out of the sea by a volcanic eruption such as they had seen in Chile, and at first there was no life at all upon them. Then birds arrived, and they deposited seeds from their droppings, possibly even from mud clinging to their feet. Other seeds which were resistant to seawater floated across from the South American mainland. Floating logs may have transported the first lizards across. The tortoises may have come from the sea itself and have developed into land animals. And each species as it arrived adjusted itself to the food—the plant and animal life—that it found in the islands. Those that failed to do so, and those that could not defend themselves from other species, became extinct. That is what had happened to the huge creatures whose bones they had discovered in Patagonia; they had been set upon by enemies and destroyed. All living things had been submitted to this process. Man himself had survived and triumphed because he was more skilful and aggressive than his competitors, even though in the beginning he was a very primitive creature, more primitive than the Fuegians, more primitive even than the apes. Indeed, it was possible that all forms of life on earth had started from one common ancestor.

FitzRoy must have thought that all this was blasphemous rubbish, since it was in flat contradiction to the Bible; man, it was definitely stated there, was created perfect, the image of God Himself, and all the different species, plants as well as animals, were created separately and had not changed. Some had simply died out, that was all. He even went so far as to turn the question of the finches' beaks to support his own theories: 'This appears to be one of those admirable provisions of Infinite Wisdom by which each created thing is adapted to the place for which it was intended'.

FitzRoy as the voyage progressed had become more and more rigid in his biblical views. He believed that there were some things that we were not meant to understand; the explanation of the original source of the universe must remain a mystery which defied all of scientific investigations. But by now Darwin had gone too far to be able to accept this; he could not stop short at the Bible, he had to go beyond it. Civilised man was bound to go on asking that most vital of all questions, 'Where have I come from?', and to follow his enquiries wherever they took him. Perhaps they would lead him nearer to God than any act of blind faith could ever do.

There was to be no end to this argument. It was, in fact, an anticipation of that clash of opposite opinions, the one scientific and exploratory and the other religious and conservative, that was to take place at the bitter meeting in Oxford twenty-five years later. For the moment, however, the two men could not do more than agree to disagree; Darwin certainly did not push his ideas too hard, and there still remained a great deal of personal liking between the two young men. The future was to carry them far apart, but just now they were together and still dependent on one another. The voyage itself conspired to put aside their differences.

I have called this principle, by which each slight varia-tion, if useful, is preserved, by the name of Natural Selection.

—Charles Darwin
On the Origin of Species

It was Darwin sauntering among the burnt-out chimney stacks and sprawling reptiles of an enchanted forge, the forge of life, who saw most clearly life's inner power to transform itself.

—Loren Eiseley
in Eliot Porter's
Galapagos: the Flow of Wildness

REFLECTIONS (22)

REFLECTIONS

Darwin's theory of Natural Selection grew mainly not from the similarities but from the differences he observed in various related species of plant and animal life. Recently, an eminent child psychologist remarked that he can detect exceptionally bright youngsters by the fact that they tend to notice differences rather than similarities in a series of experiences. Why is it that most of us tend rather to concentrate on the similarities?

Darwin and FitzRoy use two fundamentally different methods of reasoning about their observations in the Galapagos. How does each man proceed? Is agreement possible between men reasoning in such different ways?

Does Darwin's idea of Natural Selection apply to areas other than the origin of species?

While some explorers search beyond the seas and far out into space, Dr. L. S. B. Leakey and his wife Mary have been making amazing discoveries beneath their feet. The prehistory of man is their specialty, and Africa's Olduvai Gorge their chief focus of study. There in the past 30 years they have unearthed fossil remains that have revolutionized our thinking about human origins. Here Dr. Leakey describes their method of work and some of their most important discoveries.

L. S. B. LEAKEY

Leakey's Diggings: Olduvai Gorge

"I've got him! I've got him! I've got him!" Mary's voice called it over and over as the Land-Rover rattled up to our African camp and she jumped out. "Got what? Are you hurt?" I asked my wife.

"Him, the man. Our man!" Mary said. "The one we've been looking for. Come quick. I've found his teeth!"

The headache that had kept me in camp that morning of July 17, 1959, departed magically. We bounced down the gorge trail in the car, then covered the last half mile at a run. Mary led me to a cairn, and we knelt to examine her treasure.

The teeth projected from a rock face. To us these shining bits of fossilized matter represented the end of a 28-year search. For there, in Tanganyika's remote Olduvai Gorge, lay the remains of the earliest man ever found.

We almost cried with joy. After all our hoping and hardship and sacrifice, we had reached our goal.

Gingerly we began the work of uncovering the find. Our method of search is simple and, to say the least, uncomfortable. It consists of crawling up and down the slopes of the gorge with eyes barely inches from the ground, stopping at the slightest fragment of a fossil bone and delicately investigating the clue with a fine brush or a dental pick. All this in heat that sometimes reaches 110° F.

We found that expansion and contraction of the soft rock had cracked our new-found skull into 400 fragments. In order not to lose a single precious scrap we sifted tons of scree below the find. After 19 days we recovered the nearly complete skull, minus only the lower jaw. From the fact that the wisdom teeth, the third molars, show no wear, I put the age of our specimen at 18. I call him Zinjanthropus, or "East Africa Man."

What does the Zinjanthropus skull tell us? Its flat cranium housed a brain probably less than half the size of ours. There is also a bony ridge crowning the skull which is found in some near-men. Clearly, Zinjanthropus stands a long way from the state of development seen in Homo sapiens of the present day. But I have counted at least 20 features in which he is more like modern man than are the near-men discovered in South Africa. . . .

"Leakey Luck," my colleagues tease, when we make an important discovery. I readily admit that luck often plays a part. But then so has 35 years' striving and digging and never giving up.

We had cleared more than a hundred sites on Rusinga Island in Lake Victoria before Mary made her great discovery there in 1948. We were scanning a slope when she suddenly spotted a tooth, just a speck of gray fossilized matter. As we cleared the rock we found another tooth, and something more. After several days we put our jigsaw puzzle together. It was a nearly complete skull of Proconsul africanus, a creature some 25 million years old! Many scientists believe it represents the common stock leading to both man and the apes. It was the first time anyone had found so nearly complete a specimen of an early fossil apelike skull. A new door in the study of man's past had opened. . . .

One other mystery appeared at Olduvai in 1962, and to me it is the most intriguing of all. In the very lowest level, well below the site of Zinjanthropus, we unearthed wide circles made of stones, some actually resting on top of others. No such stones existed on the site naturally when it was lakeshore two million years ago.

How did they get there? What forces arranged them in those unmistakable circles, and why? Could they be the remains of primitive dwellings or windbreaks?

Somewhere in Olduvai, the answers to such questions await us. It is this kind of detective work that makes our job so fascinating. I have often heard archeology referred to as a dry and boring science. Mary and I can tell you that it is nothing of the kind. The cleverest mystery story ever written cannot match our job for sheer excitement and suspense.

*To the sea voyager, a colorful port in an
exotic land is irresistibly fascinating. Not
only is it a welcome relief from the sameness
of weeks or months at sea, but it promises
strange new costumes and customs, food and
merchandise available nowhere else, people
who are interesting simply because they are
different, perhaps even . . . the possibility of
romance? Novelist John Steinbeck and his
friend Ed Ricketts, a marine biologist,
cruising the Gulf of California to collect
specimens of marine life, find the Mexican
port city of La Paz one of their most
memorable ports of call.*

JOHN STEINBECK

The Fascination of La Paz

March 21

It would not have done to sail for La Paz harbor that night, for the pilot has
short hours and any boat calling for him out of his regular hours must pay
double. But we wanted very much to get to La Paz; we were out of beer and
already the water in our tanks was stale-tasting. It had seemed to us that it
was stale when we put it in and time did not improve it. It isn't likely that
we would have died of thirst. The second or third day would undoubtedly
have seen us drinking the unpleasant stuff. But there were other reasons why

we longed for La Paz. Cape San Lucas had not really been a town, and our crew had convinced itself that it had been a very long time out of touch with civilization. In civilization we think they included some items which, if anything, are attenuated in highly civilized groups. In addition, there is the genuine fascination of the city of La Paz. Everyone in the area knows the greatness of La Paz. You can get anything in the world there, they say. It is a huge place—not of course so monstrous as Guaymas or Mazatlán, but beautiful out of all comparison. The Indians paddle hundreds of miles to be at La Paz on a feast day. It is a proud thing to have been born in La Paz, and a cloud of delight hangs over the distant city from the time when it was the great pearl center of the world. The robes of the Spanish kings and the stoles of bishops in Rome were stiff with the pearls from La Paz. There's a magic-carpet sound to the name, anyway. And it is an old city, as cities in the West are old, and very venerable in the eyes of Indians of the Gulf. Guaymas is busier, they say, and Mazatlán gayer perhaps, but La Paz is *antigua.*

The Gulf and Gulf ports have always been unfriendly to colonization. Again and again attempts were made before a settlement would stick. Humans are not much wanted on the Peninsula. But at La Paz the pearl oysters drew men from all over the world. And, as in all concentrations of natural wealth, the terrors of greed were let loose on the city again and again. An event which happened at La Paz in recent years is typical of such places. An Indian boy by accident found a pearl of great size, an unbelievable pearl. He knew its value was so great that he need never work again. In his one pearl he had the ability to be drunk as long as he wished, to marry any one of a number of girls, and to make many more a little happy too. In his great pearl lay salvation, for he could in advance purchase masses sufficient to pop him out of Purgatory like a squeezed watermelon seed. In addition he could shift a number of dead relatives a little nearer to Paradise. He went to La Paz with his pearl in his hand and his future clear into eternity in his heart. He took his pearl to a broker and was offered so little that he grew angry, for he knew he was cheated. Then he carried his pearl to another broker and was offered the same amount. After a few more visits he came to know that the brokers were only the many hands of one head and that he could not sell his pearl for more. He took it to the beach and hid it under a stone, and that night he was clubbed into unconsciousness and his clothing was searched. The next night he slept at the house of a friend and his friend and he were injured and bound and the whole house searched. Then he went inland to lose his pursuers and he was waylaid and tortured. But he was very angry now and he knew what he must do. Hurt as he was he crept back to La Paz in the night and he skulked like a hunted fox to the beach and took out his pearl from under the stone. Then he cursed it and threw it as far as he could into the channel. He was a free man again with his soul in danger and his food and shelter insecure. And he laughed a great deal about it.[1]

This seems to be a true story, but it is so much like a parable that it almost can't be. This Indian boy is too heroic, too wise. He knows too much and acts on his knowledge. In every way, he goes contrary to human direction. The story is probably true, but we don't believe it; it is far too reasonable to be true.

La Paz, the great city, was only a little way from us now, we could almost see its towers and smell its perfume. And it was right that it should be so hidden here out of the world, inaccessible except to the galleons of a small boy's imagination.

While we were anchored at Espíritu Santo Island a black yacht went by swiftly, and on her awninged after-deck ladies and gentlemen in white clothing sat comfortably. We saw they had tall cool drinks beside them and we hated them a little, for we were out of beer. And Tiny said fiercely, "Nobody but a pansy'd sail on a thing like that." And then more gently, "But I've never been sure I ain't queer." The yacht went down over the horizon, and up over the horizon climbed an old horror of a cargo ship, dirty and staggering. And she stumbled on toward the channel of La Paz; her pumps must have been going wide open. Later, at La Paz, we saw her very low in the water in the channel. We said to a man on the beach, "She is sinking." And he replied calmly, "She always sinks."

On the *Western Flyer*, vanity had set in. Clothing was washed unmercifully. The white tops of caps were laundered, and jeans washed and patted smooth while wet and hung from the stays to dry. Shoes were even polished and the shaving and bathing were deafening. The sweet smell of unguents and hair oils, of deodorants and lotions, filled the air. Hair was cut and combed; the mirror over the washstand behind the deckhouse was in constant use. We regarded ourselves in the mirror with the long contemplative coy looks of chorus girls about to go on stage. What we found was not good, but it was the best we had. Heaven knows what we expected to find in La Paz, but we wanted to be beautiful for it.

And in the morning, when we got under way, we washed the fish blood off the decks and put away the equipment. We coiled the lines in lovely spirals and washed all the dishes. It seemed to us we made a rather gallant show, and we hoped that no beautiful yacht was anchored in La Paz. If there were a yacht, we would be tough and seafaring, but if no such con-

[1] This is the story Steinbeck later elaborated as *The Pearl*.

trast was available some of us at least proposed to be not a little jaunty. Even the least naïve of us expected Spanish ladies in high combs and mantillas to be promenading along the beach. It would be rather like the opening scene of a Hollywood production of *Life in Latin America*, with dancers in the foreground and cabaret tables upstage from which would rise a male chorus to sing "I met my love in La Paz—satin and Latin she was."

We assembled on top of the deckhouse, the *Coast Pilot* open in front of us. Even Tony[2] had succumbed; he wore a gaudy white seaman's cap with a gold ornament on the front of it which seemed to be a combination of field artillery and submarine service, except that it had an arrow-pierced heart superimposed on it.

• • •

We ran happily up under Prieta Point as suggested,[3] and dropped anchor and put up the American flag and under it the yellow quarantine flag. We would have liked to fire a gun, but we had only the ten-gauge shotgun, and its hammer was rusted down. It was only for a show of force anyway; we had never intended it for warlike purposes. And then we sat and waited. The site was beautiful—the highland of Prieta Point and a tower on the hillside. In the distance we could see the beach of La Paz, and it really looked like a Hollywood production, the fine, low buildings close down to the water and trees flanking them and a colored bandstand on the water's edge. The little canoes of Nayarit sailed by, and the sea was ruffled with a fair breeze. We took some color motion pictures of the scene, but they didn't come out either.

After what seemed a very long time, the little launch mentioned in the *Coast Pilot* started for us. But it had no white flag with the letter "P." Like the municipal pier, that was gone. The pilot, an elderly man in a business suit and a dark hat, came stiffly aboard. He had great dignity. He refused a drink, accepted cigarettes, took his position at the wheel, and ordered us on grandly. He looked like an admiral in civilian clothes. He governed Tex with a sensitive hand—a gentle push forward against the air meant "ahead." A flattened hand patting downward signified "slow." A quick thumb over the shoulder, "reverse." He was not a talkative man, and he ran us through the channel with ease, hardly scraping us at all, and signaled our anchor down 250 yards westward of the municipal pier—if there had been one— the choicest place in the harbor.

---

[2] The boat's owner and captain, who "was known as a cautious man who would not indulge in nonsense."
[3] In the *Coast Pilot*, which describes the characteristics of the harbor and tells seamen what to expect when landing.

335

La Paz grew in fascination as we approached. The square, iron-shuttered colonial houses stood up right in back of the beach with rows of beautiful trees in front of them. It is a lovely place. There is a broad promenade along the water lined with benches, named for dead residents of the city, where one may rest oneself.

Soon after we had anchored, the port captain, customs man, and agent came aboard. The captain read our papers, which complimented us rather highly, and was so impressed that he immediately assigned us an armed guard—or, rather, three shifts of armed guards—to protect us from theft. At first we did not like this, since we had to pay these men, but we soon found the wisdom of it. For we swarmed with visitors from morning to night; little boys clustered on us like flies, in the rigging and on the deck. And although we were infested and crawling with very poor people and children, we lost nothing; and this in spite of the fact that there were little gadgets lying about that any one of us would have stolen if we had had the chance. The guards simply kept our visitors out of the galley and out of the cabin. But we do not think they prevented theft, for in other ports where we had no guard nothing was stolen.

The guards, big pleasant men armed with heavy automatics, wore uniforms that were starched and clean, and they were helpful and sociable. They ate with us and drank coffee with us and told us many valuable things about the town. And in the end we gave each of them a carton of cigarettes, which seemed valuable to them. But they were the reverse of what is usually thought and written of Mexican soldiers—they were clean, efficient, and friendly.

With the port captain came the agent, probably the finest invention of all. He did everything for us, provisioned us, escorted us, took us to dinner, argued prices for us in local stores, warned us about some places and recommended others. His fee was so small that we doubled it out of pure gratitude.

As soon as we were cleared, Sparky and Tiny and Tex[4] went ashore and disappeared, and we did not see them until late that night, when they came back with the usual presents: shawls and carved cow-horns and colored handkerchiefs. They were so delighted with the exchange(which was then six pesos for a dollar) that we were very soon deeply laden with curios. There were five huge stuffed sea-turtles in one bunk alone, and Japanese toys, combs from New England, Spanish shawls from New Jersey, machetes from Sheffield and New York; but all of them, from having merely lived a while in La Paz, had taken on a definite Mexican flavor. Tony, who does not trust foreigners, stayed aboard, but later even he went ashore for a while.

[4] The rest of the boat's crew.

. . .

No doubt we were badly cheated in La Paz. Perhaps the boatmen cheated us and maybe we paid too much for supplies—it is very hard to know. And besides, we were so incredibly rich that we couldn't tell, and we had no instinct for knowing when we were cheated. Here we were rich, but in our own country it was not so. The very rich develop an instinct which tells them when they are cheated. We knew a rich man who owned several large office buildings. Once in reading his reports he found that two electric-light bulbs had been stolen from one of the toilets in one of his office buildings. It hurt him; he brooded for weeks about it. "Civilization is dying," he said. "Whom can you trust any more? This little theft is an indication that the whole people is morally rotten."

But we were so newly rich that we didn't know, and besides we were a little flattered. The boatmen raised their price as soon as they saw the Sea-Cow[5] wouldn't work, but as they said, times are very hard and there is no money.

. . .

March 22

On the water's edge of La Paz a new hotel was going up, and it looked very expensive. Probably the airplanes will bring week-enders from Los Angeles before long, and the beautiful poor bedraggled town will bloom with a Floridian ugliness.

Hearing a burst of chicken voices, we looked over a mud wall and saw that there were indeed chickens in the yard behind it. We asked then of a woman if we might buy several. They could be sold, she said, but they were not what one calls "for sale." We entered her yard. One of the proofs that they were not for sale was that we had to catch them ourselves. We picked out two which looked a little less muscular than the others, and went for them. Whatever has been said, true or not, of the indolence of the Lower Californian is entirely untrue of his chickens. They were athletes, highly trained both in speed and in methods of escape. They could run, fly, and, when cornered, disappear entirely and re-materialize in another part of the yard. If the owner did not want to catch them, that hesitancy was not shared by the rest of La Paz. People and children came from everywhere; a mob collected, first to give excited advice and then to help. A pillar of dust arose

[5] Steinbeck's name for their consistently unreliable outboard motor, sometimes used to power their skiff.

out of that yard. Small boys hurled themselves at the chickens like football-players. We were bound to catch them sooner or later, for as one group became exhausted, another took up the chase. If we had played fair and given those chickens rest periods, we would never have caught them. But by keeping at them, we finally wore them down and they were caught, completely exhausted and almost shorn of their feathers. Everyone in the mob felt good and happy then and we paid for the chickens and left.

On board it was Sparky's job to kill them, and he hated it. But finally he cut their heads off and was sick. He hung them over the side to bleed and a boat came along and mashed them flat against our side. But even then they were tough. They had the most highly developed muscles we have ever seen. Their legs were like those of ballet dancers and there was no softness in their breasts. We stewed them for many hours and it did no good whatever. We were sorry to kill them, for they were gallant, fast chickens. In our country they could easily have got scholarships in one of our great universities and had collegiate careers, for they had spirit and fight and, for all we know, loyalty.

$$\bullet \quad \bullet \quad \bullet$$

In the evening Tiny returned to the *Western Flyer*, having collected some specimens of *Phthirius pubis*,[6] but since he made no notes in the field, he was unable or unwilling to designate the exact collecting station. His items seemed to have no unusual qualities but to be members of the common species so widely distributed throughout the world.

We were to sail in the early morning, and that night we walked a little in the dim-lighted streets of La Paz. And we wondered why so much of the Gulf was familiar to us, why this town had a "home" feeling. We had never seen a town which even looked like La Paz, and yet coming to it was like returning rather than visiting. Some quality there is in the whole Gulf that trips a trigger of recognition so that in fantastic and exotic scenery one finds oneself nodding and saying inwardly, "Yes, I know." And on the shore the wild doves mourn in the evening and then there comes a pang, some kind of emotional jar, and a longing. And if one followed his whispering impulse he would walk away slowly into the thorny brush following the call of the doves. Trying to remember the Gulf is like trying to re-create a dream. This is by no means a sentimental thing, it has little to do with beauty or even conscious liking. But the Gulf does draw one, and we have talked to rich men who own boats, who can go where they will. Regularly they find themselves sucked into the Gulf. And since we have returned,

[6] Pubic lice, commonly called "crabs."

there is always in the backs of our minds the positive drive to go back again. If it were lush and rich, one could understand the pull, but it is fierce and hostile and sullen. The stone mountains pile up to the sky and there is little fresh water. But we know we must go back if we live, and we don't know why.

Late at night we sat on the deck. They were pumping water out of the hold of the trading boat, preparing her to float and flounder away to Guaymas for more merchandise. But La Paz was asleep; not a soul moved in the streets. The tide turned and swung us around, and in the channel the ebbing tide whispered against our hull and we heard the dogs of La Paz barking in the night.

We were curious. Our curiosity was not limited, but was as wide and horizonless as that of Darwin or Agassiz or Linnaeus or Pliny. We wanted to see everything our eyes would accommodate, to think what we could, and, out of our seeing and thinking, to build some kind of structure in modeled imitation of the observed reality.

—John Steinbeck
The Log from the Sea of Cortez

REFLECTIONS (23)

REFLECTIONS

John Steinbeck's humor is both subtle and frequently directed at himself, or, in this case, at himself and his companions. Consider the various resources of humor—exaggeration, understatement, incongruous juxtaposition, etc. What method or methods does Steinbeck tend to favor?

In describing La Paz as a port of call, Steinbeck is characterizing a place rather than a person. His description is both objective and subjective; that is, he describes how things appear to him and how they affect him emotionally. Is there any necessary relationship between these two kinds of description, or is it possible to have one without the other?

In describing what a place is like, what kinds of impressions can a writer use besides visual ones? Does Steinbeck use more of one sort of detail than another?

*No stranger, more fascinating, or more
frightening world exists for most teenagers
than the unexplored territory of sex. It makes
it no easier to know that nearly everyone
older has already been there; the tales of
these travelers are unreliable, contradictory,
and at best incomplete. Each one of us must
make this journey himself, perhaps with the
help of a more experienced guide, perhaps in
the company of another equally innocent
explorer. Maya Angelou's frank relation of
her confused and fearful wanderings may
strike chords of sympathetic recognition in
voyagers who have taken this trip or are
still en route.*

MAYA ANGELOU

The Strange New World of Sex

The Well of Loneliness[1] was my introduction to lesbianism and what
I thought of as pornography. For months the book was both a treat and a
threat. It allowed me to see a little of the mysterious world of the pervert. It
stimulated my libido and I told myself that it was educational because it

[1] A novel by Radclyffe Hall, published in 1928. The book was an early and somewhat
sentimental attempt to deal seriously with the problems of homosexuality. It created
a considerable stir and was banned in England.

informed me of the difficulties in the secret world of the pervert. I was certain that I didn't know any perverts. Of course I ruled out the jolly sissies who sometimes stayed at our house and cooked whopping eight-course dinners while the perspiration made paths down their made-up faces. Since everyone accepted them, and more particularly since they accepted themselves, I knew that their laughter was real and that their lives were cheerful comedies, interrupted only by costume changes and freshening of make-up.

But true freaks, the "women lovers," captured yet strained my imagination. They were, according to the book, disowned by their families, snubbed by their friends and ostracized from every society. This bitter punishment was inflicted upon them because of a physical condition over which they had no control.

After my third reading of *The Well of Loneliness* I became a bleeding heart for the downtrodden misunderstood lesbians. I thought "lesbian" was synonymous with hermaphrodite, and when I wasn't actively aching over their pitiful state, I was wondering how they managed simpler body functions. Did they have a choice of organs to use, and if so, did they alternate or play favorite? Or I tried to imagine how two hermaphrodites made love, and the more I pondered the more confused I became. It seemed that having two of everything other people had, and four where ordinary people just had two, would complicate matters to the point of giving up the idea of making love at all.

It was during this reflective time that I noticed how heavy my own voice had become. It droned and drummed two or three whole tones lower than my schoolmates' voices. My hands and feet were also far from being feminine and dainty. In front of the mirror I detachedly examined my body. For a sixteen-year-old my breasts were sadly undeveloped. They could only be called skin swellings, even by the kindest critic. The line from my rib cage to my knees fell straight without even a ridge to disturb its direction. Younger girls than I boasted of having to shave under their arms, but my armpits were as smooth as my face. There was also a mysterious growth developing on my body that defied explanation. It looked totally useless.

Then the question began to live under my blankets: How did lesbianism begin? What were the symptoms? The public library gave information on the finished lesbian—and that woefully sketchy—but on the growth of a lesbian, there was nothing. I did discover the difference between hermaphrodites and lesbians was that hermaphrodites were "born that way." It was impossible to determine whether lesbians budded gradually, or burst into being with a suddenness that dismayed them as much as it repelled society.

I had gnawed into the unsatisfying books and into my own unstocked mind without finding a morsel of peace or understanding. And meantime, my voice refused to stay up in the higher registers where I consciously pitched it, and I had to buy my shoes in the "old lady's comfort" section of the shoe stores.

I asked Mother.

Daddy Clidell was at the club one evening, so I sat down on the side of Mother's bed. As usual she woke completely and at once. (There is never any yawning or stretching with Vivian Baxter. She's either awake or asleep.)

"Mother, I've got to talk to you . . ." It was going to kill me to have to ask her, for in the asking wouldn't it be possible that suspicion would fall on my own normality? I knew her well enough to know that if I committed almost any crime and told her the truth about it she not only wouldn't disown me but would give me her protection. But just suppose I was developing into a lesbian, how would she react? And then there was Bailey[2] to worry about too.

"Ask me, and pass me a cigarette." Her calmness didn't fool me for a minute. She used to say that her secret to life was that she "hoped for the best, was prepared for the worst, so anything in between didn't come as a surprise." That was all well and good for most things but if her only daughter was developing into a . . .

She moved over and patted the bed, "Come on, baby, get in the bed. You'll freeze before you get your question out."

It was better to remain where I was for the time being.

"Mother . . . my pocketbook . . ."

"Ritie, do you mean your vagina? Don't use those Southern terms. There's nothing wrong with the word 'vagina.' It's a clinical description. Now, what's wrong with it?"

The smoke collected under the bed lamp, then floated out to be free in the room. I was deathly sorry that I had begun to ask her anything.

"Well? . . . Well? Have you got crabs?"

Since I didn't know what they were, that puzzled me. I thought I might have them and it wouldn't go well for my side if I said I didn't. On the other hand, I just might not have them, and suppose I lied and said I did?

"I don't know, Mother."

"Do you itch? Does your vagina itch?" She leaned on one elbow and jabbed out her cigarette.

"No, Mother."

"Then you don't have crabs. If you had them, you'd tell the world."

[2] Maya's older brother.

344

I wasn't sorry or glad not to have them, but made a mental note to look up "crabs" in the library on my next trip.

She looked at me closely, and only a person who knew her face well could have perceived the muscles relaxing and interpreted this as an indication of concern.

"You don't have a venereal disease, do you?"

The question wasn't asked seriously, but knowing Mother I was shocked at the idea. "Why, Mother, of course not. That's a terrible question." I was ready to go back to my room and wrestle alone with my worries.

"Sit down, Ritie. Pass me another cigarette." For a second it looked as if she was thinking about laughing. That would really do it. If she laughed, I'd never tell her anything else. Her laughter would make it easier to accept my social isolation and human freakishness. But she wasn't even smiling. Just slowly pulling in the smoke and holding it in puffed cheeks before blowing it out.

"Mother, something is growing on my vagina."

There, it was out. I'd soon know whether I was to be her ex-daughter or if she'd put me in hospital for an operation.

"Where on your vagina, Marguerite?"

Uh-huh. It was bad all right. Not "Ritie" or "Maya" or "Baby." "Marguerite."

"On both sides. Inside." I couldn't add that they were fleshy skin flaps that had been growing for months down there. She'd have to pull that out of me.

"Ritie, go get me that big *Webster's* and then bring me a bottle of beer."

Suddenly, it wasn't all that serious. I was "Ritie" again, and she just asked for beer. If it had been as awful as I anticipated, she'd have ordered Scotch and water. I took her the huge dictionary that she had bought as a birthday gift for Daddy Clidell and laid it on the bed. The weight forced a side of the mattress down and Mother twisted her bed lamp to beam down on the book.

When I returned from the kitchen and poured her beer, as she had taught Bailey and me beer should be poured, she patted the bed.

"Sit down, baby. Read this." Her fingers guided my eyes to VULVA. I began to read. She said, "Read it out loud."

It was all very clear and normal-sounding. She drank the beer as I read, and when I had finished she explained it in every-day terms. My relief melted the fears and they liquidly stole down my face.

Mother shot up and put her arms around me.

"There's nothing to worry about, baby. It happens to every woman. It's just human nature."

It was all right then to unburden my heavy, heavy heart. I cried into the crook of my arm. "I thought maybe I was turning into a lesbian."

Her patting of my shoulder slowed to a still and she leaned away from me.

"A lesbian? Where the hell did you get that idea?"

"Those things growing on my . . . vagina, and my voice is too deep and my feet are big, and I have no hips or breasts or anything. And my legs are so skinny."

Then she did laugh. I knew immediately that she wasn't laughing at me. Or rather that she was laughing at me, but it was something about me that pleased her. The laugh choked a little on the smoke in its way, but finally broke through cleanly. I had to give a small laugh too, although I wasn't tickled at all. But it's mean to watch someone enjoy something and not show your understanding of their enjoyment.

When she finished with the laughter, she laid it down a peal at a time and turned to me, wiping her eyes.

"I made arrangements, a long time ago, to have a boy and a girl. Bailey is my boy and you are my girl. The Man upstairs, He don't make mistakes. He gave you to me to be my girl and that's just what you are. Now, go wash your face, have a glass of milk and go back to bed."

I did as she said but I soon discovered my new assurance wasn't large enough to fill the gap left by my old uneasiness. It rattled around in my mind like a dime in a tin cup. I hoarded it preciously, but less than two weeks later it became totally worthless.

A classmate of mine, whose mother had rooms for herself and her daughter in a ladies' residence, had stayed out beyond closing time. She telephoned me to ask if she could sleep at my house. Mother gave her permission, providing my friend telephoned her mother from our house.

When she arrived, I got out of bed and we went to the upstairs kitchen to make hot chocolate. In my room we shared mean gossip about our friends, giggled over boys and whined about school and the tedium of life. The unusualness of having someone sleep in my bed (I'd never slept with anyone except my grandmothers) and the frivolous laughter in the middle of the night made me forget simple courtesies. My friend had to remind me that she had nothing to sleep in. I gave her one of my gowns, and without curiosity or interest I watched her pull off her clothes. At none of the early stages of undressing was I in the least conscious of her body. And then suddenly, for the briefest eye span, I saw her breasts. I was stunned.

They were shaped like light-brown falsies in the five-and-ten-cent store, but they were real. They made all the nude paintings I had seen in museums come to life. In a word they were beautiful. A universe divided what she had from what I had. She was a woman.

346

My gown was too snug for her and much too long, and when she wanted to laugh at her ridiculous image I found that humor had left me without a promise to return.

Had I been older I might have thought that I was moved by both an esthetic sense of beauty and the pure emotion of envy. But those possibilities did not occur to me when I needed them. All I knew was that I had been moved by looking at a woman's breasts. So all the calm and casual words of Mother's explanation a few weeks earlier and the clinical terms of Noah Webster did not alter the fact that in a fundamental way there was something queer about me.

I somersaulted deeper into my snuggery of misery. After a thorough self-examination, in the light of all I had read and heard about dykes and bull-daggers, I reasoned that I had none of the obvious traits—I didn't wear trousers, or have big shoulders or go in for sports, or walk like a man or even want to touch a woman. I wanted to be a woman, but that seemed to me to be a world to which I was to be eternally refused entrance.

What I needed was a boyfriend. A boyfriend would clarify my position to the world and, even more important, to myself. A boyfriend's acceptance of me would guide me into that strange and exotic land of frills and femininity.

Among my associates, there were no takers. Understandably the boys of my age and social group were captivated by the yellow- or light-brown-skinned girls, with hairy legs and smooth little lips, and whose hair "hung down like horses' manes." And even those sought-after girls were asked to "give it up or tell where it is." They were reminded in a popular song of the times, "If you can't smile and say yes, please don't cry and say no." If the pretties were expected to make the supreme sacrifice in order to "belong," what could the unattractive female do? She who had been skimming along on life's turning but never-changing periphery had to be ready to be a "buddy" by day and maybe by night. She was called upon to be generous only if the pretty girls were unavailable.

I believe most plain girls are virtuous because of the scarcity of opportunity to be otherwise. They shield themselves with an aura of unavailableness (for which after a time they begin to take credit) largely as a defense tactic.

In my particular case, I could not hide behind the curtain of voluntary goodness. I was being crushed by two unrelenting forces: the uneasy suspicion that I might not be a normal female and my newly awakening sexual appetite.

I decided to take matters into my own hands. (An unfortunate but apt phrase.)

Up the hill from our house, and on the same side of the street, lived two handsome brothers. They were easily the most eligible young men in the neighborhood. If I was going to venture into sex, I saw no reason why I shouldn't make my experiment with the best of the lot. I didn't really expect to capture either brother on a permanent basis, but I thought if I could hook one temporarily I might be able to work the relationship into something more lasting.

I planned a chart for seduction with surprise as my opening ploy. One evening as I walked up the hill suffering from youth's vague malaise (there was simply nothing to do), the brother I had chosen came walking directly into my trap.

"Hello, Marguerite." He nearly passed me.

I put the plan into action. "Hey." I plunged, "Would you like to have a sexual intercourse with me?" Things were going according to the chart. His mouth hung open like a garden gate. I had the advantage and so I pressed it.

"Take me somewhere."

His response lacked dignity, but in fairness to him I admit that I had left him little chance to be suave.

He asked, "You mean, you're going to give me some trim?"

I assured him that that was exactly what I was about to give him. Even as the scene was being enacted I realized the imbalance in his values. He thought I was giving him something, and the fact of the matter was that it was my intention to take something from him. His good looks and popularity had made him so inordinately conceited that they blinded him to that possibility.

We went to a furnished room occupied by one of his friends, who understood the situation immediately and got his coat and left us alone. The seductee quickly turned off the lights. I would have preferred them left on, but didn't want to appear more aggressive than I had been already. If that was possible.

I was excited rather than nervous, and hopeful instead of frightened. I had not considered how physical an act of seduction would be. I had anticipated long soulful tongued kisses and gentle caresses. But there was no romance in the knee which forced my legs, nor in the rub of hairy skin on my chest.

Unredeemed by shared tenderness, the time was spent in laborious gropings, pullings, yankings and jerkings.

Not one word was spoken.

My partner showed that our experience had reached its climax by getting up abruptly, and my main concern was how to get home quickly. He may have sensed that he had been used, or his disinterest may have been an indication that I was less than gratifying. Neither possibility bothered me.

Outside on the street we left each other with little more than "Okay, see you around."

Thanks to Mr. Freeman nine years before, I had had no pain of entry to endure, and because of the absence of romantic involvement neither of us felt much had happened.

At home I reviewed the failure and tried to evaluate my new position. I had had a man. I had been had. I not only didn't enjoy it, but my normalcy was still a question.

What happened to the moonlight-on-the-prairie feeling? Was there something so wrong with me that I couldn't share a sensation that made poets gush out rhyme after rhyme, that made Richard Arlen brave the Arctic wastes and Veronica Lake betray the entire free world?

There seemed to be no explanation for my private infirmity, but being a product (is "victim" a better word?) of the Southern Negro upbringing, I decided that I "would understand it all better by-and-by." I went to sleep.

Three weeks later, having thought very little of the strange and strangely empty night, I found myself pregnant.

•   •   •

The world had ended, and I was the only person who knew it. People walked along the streets as if the pavements hadn't all crumbled beneath their feet. They pretended to breathe in and out while all the time I knew the air had been sucked away in a monstrous inhalation from God Himself. I alone was suffocating in the nightmare.

The little pleasure I was able to take from the fact that if I could have a baby I obviously wasn't a lesbian was crowded into my mind's tiniest corner by the massive pushing in of fear, guilt, and self-revulsion.

For eons, it seemed, I had accepted my plight as the hapless, put-upon victim of fate and the Furies, but this time I had to face the fact that I had brought my new catastrophe upon myself. How was I to blame the innocent man whom I had lured into making love to me? In order to be profoundly dishonest, a person must have one of two qualities: either he is unscrupulously ambitious, or he is unswervingly egocentric. He must believe that for his ends to be served all things and people can justifiably be shifted about, or that he is the center not only of his own world but of the worlds which others inhabit. I had neither element in my personality, so I hefted the burden of pregnancy at sixteen onto my own shoulders where it belonged. Admittedly, I staggered under the weight.

I finally sent a letter to Bailey, who was at sea with the merchant marine. He wrote back, and he cautioned me against telling Mother of my condition. We both knew her to be violently opposed to abortions, and she would

349

very likely order me to quit school. Bailey suggested that if I quit school before getting my high school diploma I'd find it nearly impossible to return.

The first three months, while I was adapting myself to the fact of pregnancy (I didn't really link pregnancy to the possibility of my having a baby until weeks before my confinement), were a hazy period in which days seemed to lie just below the water level, never emerging fully.

Fortunately, Mother was tied up tighter than Dick's hatband in the weave of her own life. She noticed me, as usual, out of the corner of her existence. As long as I was healthy, clothed and smiling she felt no need to focus her attention on me. As always, her major concern was to live the life given to her, and her children were expected to do the same. And to do it without too much brouhaha.

Under her loose scrutiny I grew more buxom, and my brown skin smoothed and tight-pored, like pancakes fried on an unoiled skillet. And still she didn't suspect. Some years before, I had established a code which never varied. I didn't lie. It was understood that I didn't lie because I was too proud to be caught and forced to admit that I was capable of a less than Olympian action. Mother must have concluded that since I was above out-and-out lying I was also beyond deceit. She was deceived.

All my motions focalized on pretending to be that guileless schoolgirl who had nothing more wearying to think about than mid-term exams. Strangely enough, I very nearly caught the essence of teenage capriciousness as I played the role. Except that there were times when physically I couldn't deny to myself that something very important was taking place in my body.

Mornings, I never knew if I would have to jump off the streetcar one step ahead of the warm sea of nausea that threatened to sweep me away. On solid ground, away from the ship-motioned vehicle and the smell of hands coated with recent breakfasts, I regained my balance and waited for the next trolley.

School recovered its lost magic. For the first time since Stamps, information was exciting for itself alone. I burrowed myself into caves of facts, and found delight in the logical resolutions of mathematics.

I credit my new reactions (although I didn't know at the time that I had learned anything from them) to the fact that during what surely must have been a critical period I was not dragged down by hopelessness. Life had a conveyor-belt quality. It went on unpursued and unpursuing, and my only thought was to remain erect, and keep my secret along with my balance.

Midway along to delivery, Bailey came home and brought me a spun-silver bracelet from South America, Thomas Wolfe's *Look Homeward, Angel,* and a slew of new dirty jokes.

As my sixth month approached, Mother left San Francisco for Alaska. She was to open a night club and planned to stay three or four months until it got on its feet. Daddy Clidell was to look after me but I was more or less left on my own recognizance and under the unsteady gaze of our lady roomers.

Mother left the city amid a happy and cheerful sendoff party (after all how many Negros were in Alaska?), and I felt treacherous allowing her to go without informing her that she was soon to be a grandmother.

Two days after V-Day, I stood with the San Francisco Summer School class at Mission High School and received my diploma. That evening, in the bosom of the now-dear family home I uncoiled my fearful secret and in a brave gesture left a note on Daddy Clidell's bed. It read: *Dear Parents, I am sorry to bring this disgrace on the family, but I am pregnant. Marguerite.*

The confusion that ensued when I explained to my stepfather that I expected to deliver the baby in three weeks, more or less, was reminiscent of a Molière comedy. Except that it was funny only years later. Daddy Clidell told Mother that I was "three weeks gone." Mother, regarding me as a woman for the first time, said indignantly, "She's more than any three weeks." They both accepted the fact that I was further along than they had first been told but found it nearly impossible to believe that I had carried a baby, eight months and one week, without their being any the wiser.

Mother asked, "Who is the boy?" I told her. She recalled him, faintly.

"Do you want to marry him?"

"No."

"Does he want to marry you?" The father had stopped speaking to me during my fourth month.

"No."

"Well, that's that. No use ruining three lives." There was no overt or subtle condemnation. She was Vivian Baxter Jackson. Hoping for the best, prepared for the worst, and unsurprised by anything in between.

Daddy Clidell assured me that I had nothing to worry about. That "women been gittin' pregnant ever since Eve ate that apple." He sent one of his waitresses to I. Magnin's to buy maternity dresses for me. For the next two weeks I whirled around the city going to doctors, taking vitamin shots and pills, buying clothes for the baby, and except for the rare moments alone, enjoying the imminent blessed event.

After a short labor, and without too much pain (I decided that the pain of delivery was overrated), my son was born. Just as gratefulness was confused in my mind with love, so possession became mixed up with motherhood. I had a baby. He was beautiful and mine. Totally mine. No one had bought him for me. No one had helped me endure the sickly gray months. I had had help in the child's conception, but no one could deny that I had had an immaculate pregnancy.

Totally my possession, and I was afraid to touch him. Home from the hospital, I sat for hours by his bassinet and absorbed his mysterious perfection. His extremities were so dainty they appeared unfinished. Mother handled him easily with the casual confidence of a baby nurse, but I dreaded being forced to change his diapers. Wasn't I famous for awkwardness? Suppose I let him slip, or put my fingers on that throbbing pulse on the top of his head?

Mother came to my bed one night bringing my three-week-old baby. She pulled the cover back and told me to get up and hold him while she put rubber sheets on my bed. She explained that he was going to sleep with me.

I begged in vain. I was sure to roll over and crush out his life or break those fragile bones. She wouldn't hear of it, and within minutes the pretty golden baby was lying on his back on the center of my bed, laughing at me.

I lay on the edge of the bed, stiff with fear, and vowed not to sleep all night long. But the eat-sleep routine I had begun in the hospital, and kept up under Mother's dictatorial command, got the better of me. I dropped off.

My shoulder was shaken gently. Mother whispered, "Maya, wake up. But don't move."

I knew immediately that the awakening had to do with the baby. I tensed. "I'm awake."

She turned the light on and said, "Look at the baby." My fears were so powerful I couldn't move to look at the center of the bed. She said again, "Look at the baby." I didn't hear sadness in her voice, and that helped me to break the bonds of terror. The baby was no longer in the center of the bed. At first I thought he had moved. But after closer investigation I found that I was lying on my stomach with my arm bent at a right angle. Under the tent of blanket, which was poled by my elbow and forearm, the baby slept touching my side.

Mother whispered, "See, you don't have to think about doing the right thing. If you're for the right thing, then you do it without thinking."

She turned out the light and I patted my son's body lightly and went back to sleep.

REFLECTIONS (24)

REFLECTIONS

Were the sources of your own adolescent doubts and discoveries about sex similar to Maya Angelou's, or of a different order?

"I believe most plain girls are virtuous because of the scarcity of opportunity to be otherwise," writes Maya Angelou. Since she includes herself in this group, her candid estimation carries a certain weight. Are there also other factors that strongly discourage early sexual experimentation?

Maya Angelou's greatest fear was that she was "different," her greatest discovery that she was quite normal. (Her honesty and frankness stem from the knowledge.) Does fear of this kind exist significantly in areas other than sex? How can it be overcome?

Most of us are in the uncomfortable position of knowing more about what occurs 238,000 miles away on the surface of the moon than what happens six inches below our own navels.

—David Reuben
*Everything You've Always
Wanted to know About Sex*

We read that the traveller asked the boy if the swamp before him had a hard bottom. The boy replied that it had. But presently the traveller's horse sank in up to the girths, and he observed to the boy, "I thought you said that this bog had a hard bottom." "So it has," answered the latter, "but you have not got half way to it yet."

—Henry David Thoreau
"Conclusion," *Walden*

Voyages of Discovery

~~~~~~

Seas of the Soul

Soto! Explore thyself!
Therein thyself shall find
The "Undiscovered Continent"—
No Settler had the Mind.

—Emily Dickinson

Sail forth—steer for the deep waters only
Reckless O soul, exploring, I with thee, and thou with me,
For we are bound where mariner has not yet dared to go,
And we will risk the ship, ourselves and all.

—Walt Whitman
"Passage to India"

In the concluding chapter of Walden, *the fruit of one of the most profitable inner voyages ever undertaken, Henry David Thoreau reminds himself and us of the value of kicking ourselves free of the restraints that bind us to security and routine, and setting out to learn more of the world and of ourselves. Thoreau insisted that it was not necessary to go to the ends of the earth to make the most important discoveries. ("I have traveled a good deal in Concord," he wrote.) The wilderness still least explored lies within ourselves.*

HENRY DAVID THOREAU

Explore Thyself

To the sick the doctors wisely recommend a change of air and scenery. Thank Heaven, here is not all the world. The buckeye does not grow in New England, and the mocking-bird is rarely heard here. The wild-goose is more of a cosmopolite than we; he breaks his fast in Canada, takes a luncheon in the Ohio, and plumes himself for the night in a southern bayou. Even the bison, to some extent, keeps pace with the seasons, cropping the pastures of the Colorado only till a greener and sweeter grass awaits him by the Yellowstone. Yet we think that if rail-fences are pulled down, and stone-walls piled up on our farms, bounds are henceforth set to our lives and our fates decided. If you are chosen town-clerk, forsooth, you cannot go to Tierra del Fuego this summer: but you may go to the land of infernal fire nevertheless. The universe is wider than our views of it.

Yet we should oftener look over the tafferel of our craft, like curious passengers, and not make the voyage like stupid sailors picking oakum.[1]

---

[1] Untwisting fibers of worn hemp rope, to be used for caulking the seams of a ship.

356

The other side of the globe is but the home of our correspondent. Our voyaging is only great-circle sailing,[2] and the doctors prescribe for diseases of the skin merely. One hastens to Southern Africa to chase the giraffe; but surely that is not the game he would be after. How long, pray, would a man hunt giraffes if he could? Snipes and woodcocks also may afford rare sport; but I trust it would be nobler game to shoot one's self.—

> "Direct your eye right inward, and you'll find
> A thousand regions in your mind
> Yet undiscovered. Travel them, and be
> Expert in home-cosmography."[3]

What does Africa,—what does the West stand for? Is not our own interior white on the chart? black though it may prove, like the coast, when discovered. Is it the source of the Nile, or the Niger, or the Mississippi, or a North-West Passage around this continent, that we would find? Are these the problems which most concern mankind? Is Franklin the only man who is lost, that his wife should be so earnest to find him? Does Mr. Grinnell know where he himself is? Be rather the Mungo Park, the Lewis and Clarke and Frobisher, of your own streams and oceans; explore your own higher latitudes,—with shiploads of preserved meats to support you, if they be necessary; and pile the empty cans sky-high for a sign. Were preserved meats invented to preserve meat merely? Nay, be a Columbus to whole new continents and worlds within you, opening new channels, not of trade, but of thought. Every man is the lord of a realm beside which the earthly empire of the Czar is but a petty state, a hummock left by the ice. Yet some can be patriotic who have no *self*-respect, and sacrifice the greater to the less. They love the soil which makes their graves, but have no sympathy with the spirit which may still animate their clay. Patriotism is a maggot in their heads. What was the meaning of that South-Sea Exploring Expedition, with all its parade and expense, but an indirect recognition of the fact, that there are continents and seas in the moral world, to which every man is an isthmus or an inlet, yet unexplored by him, but that it is easier to sail many thousand miles through cold and storm and cannibals, in a government ship, with five hundred men and boys to assist one, than it is to explore the private sea, the Atlantic and Pacific Ocean of one's being alone.—

> "Erret, et extremos alter scrutetur Iberos.
> Plus habet hic vitæ, plus habet ille viæ."

[2] Sailing along an arc of a circle whose center is the center of the earth.

[3] Thoreau's adaptation of a poem by William Habbington (1605–1664).

Let them wander and scrutinize the outlandish Australians.
I have more of God, they more of the road.[4]

It is not worth the while to go round the world to count the cats in Zanzibar.[5] Yet do this even till you can do better, and you may perhaps find some "Symmes' Hole"[6] by which to get at the inside at last. England and France, Spain and Portugal, Gold Coast and Slave Coast, all front on this private sea; but no bark from them has ventured out of sight of land, though it is without doubt the direct way to India. If you would learn to speak all tongues and conform to the customs of all nations, if you would travel farther than all travellers, be naturalized in all climes, and cause the Sphinx to dash her head against a stone, even obey the precept of the old philosopher, and Explore thyself. Herein are demanded the eye and the nerve. Only the defeated and deserters go to the wars, cowards that run away and enlist. Start now on that farthest western way, which does not pause at the Mississippi or the Pacific, nor conduct toward a worn-out China or Japan, but leads on direct a tangent to this sphere, summer and winter, day and night, sun down, moon down, and at last earth down too.

[4] Bringing up to date his translation of these lines by Claudian (fl 400 A.D.), Thoreau substitutes "Australians" for "Iberians."

[5] As Charles Pickering did (among other things) on his world tour reported in *The Races of Man* (1851).

[6] According to John Symmes, a retired Army officer, "the earth is hollow and habitable within."

REFLECTIONS (25)

REFLECTIONS

It's easy to say, "Explore yourself," or "Know yourself," and equally easy to assent to the wisdom of such advice. But what does it really mean? What can a person discover about himself that he doesn't already know? Does self-discovery come only accidentally, or can it be deliberately pursued?

Suppose you suddenly felt an overwhelming need to know yourself better than you do, and you had an entire summer vacation, with no other commitments, in which to take an "inward voyage." How would you go about it? What would you hope to learn?

Nikos Kazantzakis, author of Zorba the
Greek, *is not only one of the two or three
greatest authors of the twentieth century, but
one of our most courageous and tireless
voyagers of the spirit. His life was a perpetual odyssey in search of something greater,
something more, than he had ever known
or achieved. To aid him in his quest, he
apprenticed himself to more than a dozen
masters—Buddha, Jesus, Dante, Don
Quixote, St. Francis, Nietzsche, Lenin, and
Zorba, to name a few—not to serve them as
a disciple, but to learn what they could teach
him, and then to go beyond them. Of all his
avowed teachers, the only one he felt he
never outgrew was Odysseus. Because of the
passionate intensity with which Kazantzakis
at one time or another followed these various
masters, he has been called "atheist," "com-
munist," "nihilist," and "existentialist." But
these convenient labels, suggesting as they do
something negative, the personality of a nay-
sayer, only betray an ignorance of Kazantzakis' life and work, for he was more an
affirmer than a denier, and he was never a
dogmatist or ideologue. Paradox was for him
the nearest one could come to the expression
of truth, and his works are nearly all concerned with violent conflicts between powerful opposing forces, physical or spiritual,
neither of which is completely good or bad.
"Struggle" is one of the key words in
Kazantzakis' concept of life; another is
"ascent." He was an evolutionist, but like his
contemporary, the French Jesuit anthropologist and philosopher, Pierre Teilhard de
Chardin, he was more concerned with man's
spiritual than physical evolution. Growth,
progress, ascent, life itself, were for him a
process of "transforming flesh into spirit,"
by which he meant not only creating art and
joy, but consuming himself so thoroughly in
the process of creation that Death would find
little left to claim. Kazantzakis' concept of*

360

God was not anthropomorphic; it might
more aptly be called anthropocentric, for he
believed that God is not "out there" some-
where, but within man, and that as man
grows and changes and becomes better and
greater, so does God, the spirit that both
sustains him and depends on him. The
Saviors of God, then, are those mortal men
in whose own heroic development lies the
further spiritual evolution of God.

NIKOS KAZANTZAKIS
Translated by Kimon Friar

The Saviors of God:
Spiritual Exercises

Prologue

We come from a dark abyss, we end in a dark abyss, and we call the luminous interval life. As soon as we are born the return begins, at once the setting forth and the coming back; we die in every moment. Because of this many have cried out: The goal of life is death! But as soon as we are born we begin the struggle to create, to compose, to turn matter into life; we are born in every moment. Because of this many have cried out: The goal of ephemeral life is immortality! In the temporary living organism these two streams collide: (a) the ascent toward composition, toward life, toward immortality; (b) the descent toward decomposition, toward matter, toward death. Both streams well up from the depths of primordial essence. Life startles us at first; it seems somewhat beyond the law, somewhat contrary to nature, somewhat like a transitory counteraction to the dark eternal fountains; but deeper down we feel that Life is itself without beginning, an indestructible force of the Universe. Otherwise, from where did that superhuman strength come which hurls us from the unborn to the born and gives us—plants, animals, men—courage for the struggle? But both opposing forces are holy. It is our duty, therefore, to grasp that vision which can embrace and harmonize these two enormous, timeless, and indestructible forces, and with this vision to modulate our thinking and our action.

The Preparation

First Duty

With clarity and quiet, I look upon the world and say: All that I see, hear, taste, smell, and touch are the creations of my mind.

2. The sun comes up and the sun goes down in my skull. Out of one of my temples the sun rises, and into the other the sun sets.

3. The stars shine in my brain; ideas, men, animals browse in my temporal head; songs and weeping fill the twisted shells of my ears and storm the air for a moment.

4. My brain blots out, and all, the heavens and the earth, vanish.

5. The mind shouts: "Only I exist!

6. "Deep in my subterranean cells my five senses labor; they weave and unweave space and time, joy and sorrow, matter and spirit.

7. "All swirl about me like a river, dancing and whirling; faces tumble like water, and chaos howls.

8. "But I, the Mind, continue to ascend patiently, manfully, sober in the vertigo. That I may not stumble and fall, I erect landmarks over this vertigo; I sling bridges, open roads, and build over the abyss.

9. "Struggling slowly, I move among the phenomena which I create, I distinguish between them for my convenience, I unite them with laws and yoke them to my heavy practical needs.

10. "I impose order on disorder and give a face—my face—to chaos.

11. "I do not know whether behind appearances there lives and moves a secret essence superior to me. Nor do I ask; I do not care. I create phenomena in swarms, and paint with a full palette a gigantic and gaudy cur-

tain before the abyss. Do not say, 'Draw the curtain that I may see the painting.' The curtain *is* the painting.

12. "This kingdom is my child, a transitory, a human work. But it's a solid work, nothing more solid exists, and only within its boundaries can I remain fruitful, happy, and at work.

13. "I am the worker of the abyss. I am the spectator of the abyss. I am both theory and practice. I am the law. Nothing beyond me exists."

14. To see and accept the boundaries of the human mind without vain rebellion, and in these severe limitations to work ceaselessly without protest —this is where man's first duty lies.

15. Build over the unsteady abyss, with manliness and austerity, the fully round and luminous arena of the mind where you may thresh and winnow the universe like a lord of the land.

16. Distinguish clearly these bitter yet fertile human truths, flesh of our flesh, and admit them heroically: (a) the mind of man can perceive appearances only, and never the essence of things; (b) and not all appearances but only the appearances of matter; (c) and more narrowly still: not even these appearances of matter, but only relationships between them; (d) and these relationships are not real and independent of man, for even these are his creations; (e) and they are not the only ones humanly possible, but simply the most convenient for his practical and perceptive needs.

17. Within these limitations the mind is the legal and absolute monarch. No other power reigns within its kingdom.

18. I recognize these limitations, I accept them with resignation, bravery, and love, and I struggle at ease in their enclosure, as though I were free.

19. I subdue matter and force it to become my mind's good medium. I rejoice in plants, in animals, in man and in gods, as though they were my children. I feel all the universe nestling about me and following me as though it were my own body.

20. In sudden dreadful moments a thought flashes through me: "This is all a cruel and futile game, without beginning, without end, without meaning." But again I yoke myself swiftly to the wheels of necessity, and all the universe begins to revolve around me once more.

21. Discipline is the highest of all virtues. Only so may strength and desire be counterbalanced and the endeavors of man bear fruit.

22. This is how, with clarity and austerity, you may determine the omnipotence of the mind amid appearances and the incapacity of the mind beyond appearances—before you set out for salvation. You may not otherwise be saved.

Second Duty

I will not accept boundaries; appearances cannot contain me; I choke! To bleed in this agony, and to live it profoundly, is the second duty.

2. The mind is patient and adjusts itself, it likes to play; but the heart grows savage and will not condescend to play; it stifles and rushes to tear apart the nets of necessity.

3. What is the value of subduing the earth, the waters, the air, of conquering space and time, of understanding what laws govern the mirages that rise from the burning deserts of the mind, their appearance and reappearance?

4. I have one longing only: to grasp what is hidden behind appearances, to ferret out that mystery which brings me to birth and then kills me, to discover if behind the visible and unceasing stream of the world an invisible and immutable presence is hiding.

5. If the mind cannot, if it was not made to attempt the heroic and desperate breach beyond frontiers, then if only the heart could!

6. Beyond! Beyond! Beyond! Beyond man I seek the invisible whip which strikes him and drives him into the struggle. I lie in ambush to find out what primordial face struggles beyond animals to imprint itself on the fleeting flesh by creating, smashing, and remolding innumerable masks. I struggle to make out beyond plants the first stumbling steps of the Invisible in the mud.

7. A command rings out within me: "Dig! What do you see?"
"Men and birds, water and stones."
"Dig deeper! What do you see?"
"Ideas and dreams, fantasies and lightning flashes!"
"Dig deeper! What do you see?"
"I see nothing! A mute Night, as thick as death. It must be death."
"Dig deeper!"
"Ah! I cannot penetrate the dark partition! I hear voices and weeping. I hear the flutter of wings on the other shore."
"Don't weep! Don't weep! They are not on the other shore. The voices, the weeping, and the wings are your own heart."

8. Beyond the mind, on the edge of the heart's holy precipice, I proceed, trembling. One foot grips the secure soil, the other gropes in the darkness above the abyss.

9. Behind all appearances, I divine a struggling essence. I want to merge with it.

10. I feel that behind appearances this struggling essence is also striving

to merge with my heart. But the body stands between us and separates us. The mind stands between us and separates us.

11. What is my duty? To shatter the body, to rush and merge with the Invisible. To let the mind fall silent that I may hear the Invisible calling.

12. I walk on the rim of the abyss, and I tremble. Two voices contend within me.

13. The mind: "Why waste ourselves by pursuing the impossible? Within the holy enclosure of our five senses it is our duty to acknowledge the limitations of man."

14. But another voice within me—call it the Sixth Power, call it the heart—resists and shouts: "No! No! Never acknowledge the limitations of man. Smash all boundaries! Deny whatever your eyes see. Die every moment, but say: 'Death does not exist.' "

15. The mind: "My eye is without hope or illusion and gazes on all things clearly. Life is a game, a performance given by the five actors of my body.

16. "I look on avidly, with inexpressible curiosity, but I am not like the naïve peasant to believe what I see, clambering on the stage to meddle with the blood-drenched comedy.

17. "I am the wonder-working fakir who sits unmoving at the crossroads of the senses and watches the world being born and destroyed, watches the mob as it surges and shouts in the multicolored paths of vanity.

18. "Heart, naïve heart, become serene, and surrender!"

19. But the heart leaps up and shouts: "I am the peasant who jumps on the stage to meddle with the course of the world!"

20. I don't keep checks and balances, I don't seek to adjust myself. I follow the deep throbbing of my heart.

21. I ask and ask again, beating on chaos: "Who plants us on this earth without asking our permission? Who uproots us from this earth without asking our permission?"

22. I am a weak, ephemeral creature made of mud and dream. But I feel all the powers of the universe whirling within me.

23. Before they crush me, I want to open my eyes for a moment and to see them. I set my life no other purpose.

24. I want to find a single justification that I may live and bear this dreadful daily spectacle of disease, of ugliness, of injustice, of death.

25. I once set out from a dark point, the Womb, and now I proceed to another dark point, the Tomb. A power hurls me out of the dark pit and another power drags me irrevocably toward the dark pit.

26. I am not like the condemned man whose mind has been deadened

with drink. Stone sober, with a clear head, I stride along a narrow path between two cliffs.

27. And I strive to discover how to signal my companions before I die, how to give them a hand, how to spell out for them in time one complete word at least, to tell them what I think this procession is, and toward what we go. And how necessary it is for all of us together to put our steps and hearts in harmony.

28. To say in time a simple word to my companions, a password, like conspirators.

29. Yes, the purpose of Earth is not life, it is not man. Earth has existed without these, and it will live on without them. They are but the ephemeral sparks of its violent whirling.

30. Let us unite, let us hold each other tightly, let us merge our hearts, let us create—so long as the warmth of this earth endures, so long as no earthquakes, cataclysms, icebergs or comets come to destroy us—let us create for Earth a brain and a heart, let us give a human meaning to the superhuman struggle.

31. This anguish is our second duty.

Third Duty

The mind adjusts itself. It wants to fill its dungeon, the skull, with great works, to engrave on the walls heroic mottoes, to paint on its shackles the wings of freedom.

2. The heart cannot adjust itself. Hands beat on the wall outside its dungeon, it listens to erotic cries that fill the air. Then, swollen with hope, the heart responds by rattling its chains; for a brief moment it believes that its chains have turned to wings.

3. But swiftly the heart falls wounded again, it loses all hope, and is gripped once more by the Great Fear.

4. The moment is ripe: leave the heart and the mind behind you, go forward, take the third step.

5. Free yourself from the simple complacency of the mind that thinks to put all things in order and hopes to subdue phenomena. Free yourself from the terror of the heart that seeks and hopes to find the essence of things.

6. Conquer the last, the greatest temptation of all: Hope. This is the third duty.

7. We fight because we like fighting, we sing even though there is no ear to hear us. We work even though there is no master to pay us our wages when night falls. We do not work for others, we are the masters. This vineyard of earth is ours, our own flesh and blood.

8. We cultivate and prune it, we gather its grapes and tread them, we drink its wine, we sing and we weep, ideas and visions rise in our heads.

9. In what season of the vineyard has it fallen your lot to work? In the digging? In the vintage? In the feasting? All these are one.

10. I dig and rejoice in the grapes' entire cycle. I sing as I thirst and toil, drunk with the wine to come.

11. I hold the brimming wineglass and relive the toils of my grandfathers and great-grandfathers. The sweat of my labor runs down like a fountain from my tall, intoxicated brow.

12. I am a sack filled with meat and bones, blood, sweat, and tears, desires and visions.

13. I revolve for a moment in air, I breathe, my heart beats, my mind glows, and suddenly the earth opens, and I vanish.

14. In my ephemeral backbone the two eternal streams rise and fall. In my vitals a man and woman embrace. They love and hate each other, they fight.

15. The man is smothering, and he cries out: "I am the shuttle that longs to tear apart the warp and woof, to leap out of the loom of necessity.

16. "To go beyond the law, to smash bodies, to conquer death. I am the Seed!"

17. And the other, profound voice, alluring and womanly, replies with serenity and surety: "I sit cross-legged on the ground and spread my roots deep under the tombs. Motionless, I receive the seed and nourish it. I am all milk and necessity.

18. "And I long to turn back, to descend into the beast, to descend even lower, into the tree, within the roots and the soil, and there never to move.

19. "I hold back the Spirit to enslave it, I won't let it escape, for I hate the flame which rises ever upward. I am the Womb!"

20. And I listen to the two voices; they are both mine; I rejoice in them and deny neither one. My heart is a dance of the five senses; my heart is a counterdance in denial of the five senses.

21. Innumerable powers, visible and invisible, rejoice and follow me when, fighting against the almighty current, I ascend with agony.

22. Innumerable powers, visible and invisible, are relieved and grow calm again when I descend and return to earth.

23. My heart streams on. I do not seek the beginning and the end of the world. I follow my heart's dread rhythm and plod on!

24. Say farewell to all things at every moment. Fix your eyes slowly, passionately, on all things and say: "Never again!"

25. Look about you: All these bodies that you see shall rot. There is no salvation.

26. Look at them well: They live, work, love, hope. Look again: Nothing exists!

27. The generations of man rise from the earth and fall into the earth again.

28. The endeavors and virtues of man accumulate, increase, and mount to the sky.

29. Where are we going? Do not ask! Ascend, descend. There is no beginning and no end. Only this present moment exists, full of bitterness, full of sweetness, and I rejoice in it all.

30. Life is good and death is good; the earth is round and firm in the experienced palms of my hands like the breast of a woman.

31. I surrender myself to everything. I love, I feel pain, I struggle. The world seems to me wider than the mind, my heart a dark and almighty mystery.

32. If you can, Spirit, rise up over the roaring waves and take in all the sea with an encircling glance. Hold the mind fast, don't let it be shaken. Then plunge suddenly into the waves once more and continue the struggle.

33. Our body is a ship that sails on deep blue waters. What is our goal? To be shipwrecked!

34. Because the Atlantic is a cataract, the new Earth exists only in the heart of man, and suddenly, in a silent whirlpool, you will sink into the cataract of death, you and the whole world's galleon.

35. Without hope, but with bravery, it is your duty to set your prow calmly toward the abyss. And to say: "Nothing exists!"

36. Nothing exists! Neither life nor death. I watch mind and matter hunting each other like two nonexistent erotic phantasms—merging, begetting, disappearing—and I say: "This is what I want!"

37. I know now: I do not hope for anything. I do not fear anything, I have freed myself from both the mind and the heart. I have mounted much higher, I am free. This is what I want. I want nothing more. I have been seeking freedom.

The March

But suddenly a convulsive cry tears through me: "Help me!" Who calls?

2. Gather your strength and listen; the whole heart of man is a single outcry. Lean against your breast to hear it; someone is struggling and shouting within you.

3. It is your duty every moment, day and night, in joy or in sorrow, amid

all daily necessities, to discern this Cry with vehemence or restraint, according to your nature, with laughter or with weeping, in action or in thought, striving to find out who is imperiled and cries out.

4. And how we may all be mobilized together to free him.

5. Amidst our greatest happiness someone within us cries out: "I am in pain! I want to escape your happiness! I am stifling!"

6. Amidst our deepest despair someone within us cries out: "I do not despair! I fight on! I grasp at your head, I unsheathe myself from your body, I detach myself from the earth, I cannot be contained in brains, in names, in deeds!"

7. Out of our most ample virtue someone rises up in despair and cries out: "Virtue is narrow, I cannot breathe! Paradise is small and cannot contain me! Your God resembles a man, I do not want him!"

8. I hear the savage cry, and I shudder. The agony that ascends within me composes itself, for the first time, into an integral human voice; it turns full face toward me and calls me clearly, with my own name, with the name of my father and my race.

9. This is the moment of greatest crisis. This is the signal for the March to begin. If you do not hear this Cry tearing at your entrails, do not set out.

10. Continue, with patience and submission, your sacred military service in the first, second, and third rank of preparation.

11. And listen: In sleep, in an act of love or of creation, in a proud and disinterested act of yours, or in a profound despairing silence, you may suddenly hear the Cry and set forth.

12. Until that moment my heart streams on, it rises and falls with the Universe. But when I hear the Cry, my emotions and the Universe are divided into two camps.

13. Someone within me is in danger, he raises his hands and shouts: "Save me!" Someone within me climbs, stumbles, and shouts: "Help me!"

14. Which of the two eternal roads shall I choose? Suddenly I know that my whole life hangs on this decision—the life of the entire Universe.

15. Of the two, I choose the ascending path. Why? For no intelligible reason, without any certainty; I know how ineffectual the mind and all the small certainties of man can be in this moment of crisis.

16. I choose the ascending path because my heart drives me toward it. "Upward! Upward! Upward!" my heart shouts, and I follow it trustingly.

17. I feel this is what the dread primordial cry asks of me. I leap to its side. I cast in my lot with its own.

18. Someone within me is struggling to lift a great weight, to cast off the mind and flesh by overcoming habit, laziness, necessity.

19. I do not know from where he comes or where he goes. I clutch at his onward march in my ephemeral breast, I listen to his panting struggle, I shudder when I touch him.

20. Who is he? I prick up my ears. I set up various signs, I sniff the air. I ascend, groping upwards, panting and struggling. The dread and mystical March begins.

First Step, The Ego

I am not good, I am not innocent, I am not serene. My happiness and un-happiness are both unbearable; I am full of inarticulate voices and dark-nesses; I wallow, all blood and tears, in this warm trough of my flesh.

2. I am afraid to talk. I adorn myself with false wings; I shout, I sing and I weep to drown out the inexorable cry of my heart.

3. I am not the light, I am the night; but a flame stabs through my en-trails and consumes me. I am the night devoured by light.

4. Imperiled, moaning and staggering in darkness, I strive to shake my-self free from sleep and to stand erect for a while, for as long as I can bear.

5. A small but undaunted breath within me struggles desperately to van-quish happiness, weariness, death.

6. I put my body through its paces like a war horse; I keep it lean, sturdy, prepared. I harden it and I pity it. I have no other steed.

7. I keep my brain wide awake, lucid, unmerciful. I unleash it to battle relentlessly so that, all light, it may devour the darkness of the flesh. I have no other workshop where I may transform darkness into light.

8. I keep my heart flaming, courageous, restless. I feel in my heart all commotions and all contradictions, the joys and sorrows of life. But I struggle to subdue them to a rhythm superior to that of the mind, harsher than that of my heart—to the ascending rhythm of the Universe.

9. The Cry within me is a call to arms. It shouts: "I, the Cry, am the Lord your God! I am not an asylum. I am not hope and a home. I am not the Father nor the Son nor the Holy Ghost. I am your General!

10. "You are not my slave, nor a plaything in my hands. You are not my friend, you are not my child. You are my comrade-in-arms!

11. "Hold courageously the passes which I entrusted to you; do not be-tray them. You are in duty bound, and you may act heroically by remaining at your own battle station.

12. "Love danger. What is most difficult? That is what I want! Which road should you take? The most craggy ascent! It is the one I also take: follow me!

13. "Learn to obey. Only he who obeys a rhythm superior to his own is free.

14. "Learn to command. Only he who can give commands may represent me here on earth.

15. "Love responsibility. Say: 'It is my duty, and mine alone, to save the earth. If it is not saved, then I alone am to blame.'

16. "Love each man according to his contribution in the struggle. Do not seek friends; seek comrades-in-arms.

17. "Be always restless, unsatisfied, unconforming. Whenever a habit becomes convenient, smash it! The greatest sin of all is satisfaction.

18. "Where are we going? Shall we ever win? What is the purpose of all this fighting? Be silent! Soldiers never question!"

18. I stoop and listen to this war cry within me. I begin to discern the face of my leader, to distinguish his voice, to accept harsh commands with joy and terror.

20. Yes, yes, I am *not* nothing! A vaporous phosphorescence on a damp meadow, a miserable worm that crawls and loves, that shouts and talks about wings for an hour or two until his mouth is blocked with earth. The dark powers give no other answer.

21. But within me a deathless Cry, superior to me, continues to shout. For whether I want to or not, I am also, without doubt, a part of the visible and the invisible Universe. We are one. The powers which labor within me, the powers which goad me on to live, the powers which goad me on to die are, without doubt, its own powers also.

22. I am not a suspended, rootless thing in the world. I am earth of its earth and breath of its breath.

23. I am not alone in my fear, nor alone in my hope, nor alone in my shouting. A tremendous host, an onrush of the Universe fears, hopes, and shouts with me.

24. I am an improvised bridge, and when Someone passes over me, I crumble away behind Him. A Combatant passes through me, eats my flesh and brain to open up roads, to free himself from me at last. It is not I but He who shouts.

Second Step, The Race

The cry is not yours. It is not you talking, but innumerable ancestors talking with your mouth. It is not you who desire, but innumerable generations of descendants longing with your heart.

2. Your dead do not lie in the ground. They have become birds, tre

air. You sit under their shade, you are nourished by their flesh, you inhale their breathing. They have become ideas and passions, they determine your will and your actions.

3. Future generations do not move far from you in an uncertain time. They live, desire, and act in your loins and your heart.

4. In this lightning moment when you walk the earth, your first duty, by enlarging your ego, is to live through the endless march, both visible and invisible, of your own being.

5. You are not one; you are a body of troops. One of your faces lights up for a moment under the sun. Then suddenly it vanishes, and another, a younger one, lights up behind you.

6. The race of men from which you come is the huge body of the past, the present, and the future. It is the face itself; you are a passing expression. You are the shadow; it is the meat.

7. You are not free. Myriad invisible hands hold your hands and direct them. When you rise in anger, a great-grandfather froths at your mouth; when you make love, an ancestral caveman growls with lust; when you sleep, tombs open in your memory till your skull brims with ghosts.

8. Your skull is a pit of blood round which the shades of the dead gather in myriad flocks to drink of you and be revived.

9. "Do not die that we may not die," the dead cry out within you. "We had no time to enjoy the women we desired; be in time, sleep with them! We had no time to turn our thoughts into deeds; turn them into deeds! We had no time to grasp and to crystallize the face of our hope; make it firm!

10. "Finish our work! Finish our work! All day and all night we come and go through your body, and we cry out. No, we have not gone, we have not detached ourselves from you, we have not descended into the earth. Deep in your entrails we continue the struggle. Deliver us!"

11. It is not enough to hear the tumult of ancestors within you. It is not enough to feel them battling at the threshold of your mind. All rush to clutch your warm brain and to climb once more into the light of day.

12. But you must choose with care whom to hurl down again into the chasms of your blood, and whom you shall permit to mount once more into the light and the earth.

13. Do not pity them. Keep vigil over the bottomless gulf of your heart, and choose. You shall say: "This shade is humble, dark, like a beast: send him away! This one is silent and flaming, more living than I: let him drink all my blood!"

14. Enlighten the dark blood of your ancestors, shape their cries into

speech, purify their will, widen their narrow, unmerciful brows. This is your second duty.

15. For you are not only a slave. As soon as you were born, a new possibility was born with you, a free heartbeat stormed through the great sunless heart of your race.

16. Whether you would or not, you brought a new rhythm, a new desire, a new idea, a fresh sorrow. Whether you would or not, you enriched your ancestral body.

17. Where are you going? How shall you confront life and death, virtue and fear? All the race takes refuge in your breast; it asks questions there and lies waiting in agony.

18. You have a great responsibility. You do not govern now only your own small, insignificant existence. You are a throw of the dice on which, for a moment, the entire fate of your race is gambled.

19. Everything you do reverberates throughout a thousand destinies. As you walk, you cut open and create that river bed into which the stream of your descendants shall enter and flow.

20. When you shake with fear, your terror branches out into innumerable generations, and you degrade innumerable souls before and behind you. When you rise to a valorous deed, all of your race rises with you and turns valorous.

21. "I am not alone! I am not alone!" Let this vision inflame you at every moment.

22. You are not a miserable and momentary body; behind your fleeting mask of clay, a thousand-year-old face lies in ambush. Your passions and your thoughts are older than your heart or brain.

23. Your invisible body is your dread ancestors and your unborn descendants. Your visible body is the living men, women, and children of your own race.

24. Only he has been freed from the inferno of his ego who feels deep pangs of hunger when a child of his race has nothing to eat, who feels his heart throbbing with joy when a man and a woman of his race embrace and kiss one another.

25. All these are limbs of your larger, visible body. You suffer and rejoice, scattered to the ends of the earth in a thousand bodies, blood of your blood.

26. Fight on behalf of your larger body just as you fight on behalf of your smaller body. Fight that all of your bodies may become strong, lean, prepared, that their minds may become enlightened, that their flaming, manly, and restless hearts may throb.

27. How can you become strong, enlightened, manly, if all these virtues do not storm throughout your entire larger body? How can you be saved unless all your blood is saved? If but one of your race is lost, he drags you down with him to destruction. A limb of your body and your mind rots.

28. Be deeply alive to this identity, not as theory, but as flesh and blood.

29. You are a leaf on the great tree of your race. Feel the earth mounting from dark roots and spreading out into branches and leaves.

30. What is your goal? To struggle and to cling firmly to a branch, either as a leaf or flower or fruit, so that within you the entire tree may move and breathe and be renewed.

31. Your first duty, in completing your service to your race, is to feel within you all your ancestors. Your second duty is to throw light on their onrush and to continue their work. Your third duty is to pass on to your son the great mandate to surpass you.

32. Agony within you! Someone is fighting to escape you, to tear himself away from your flesh, to be freed of you. A seed in your loins, a seed in your brains, does not want to remain with you any more. It cannot be contained in your entrails any longer; it fights for freedom.

33. "Father, I cannot be contained in your heart! I want to smash it and pass through! Father, I hate your body, I am ashamed to be glued to you, I want to leave you.

34. "You are nothing now but a sluggish horse, your feet can no longer follow the rhythm of my heart. I am in haste, Father. I shall dismount, I shall mount another body, and I shall leave you on the road."

35. And you, the father, rejoice to hear the contemptuous voice of your child. "All, all for my son!" you shout. "I am nothing. I am the Ape, he is the Man. I am the Man, he is the Son of Man!"

36. A power greater than you passes through you, smashing your body and mind, shouting: "Gamble the present and all things certain, gamble them for the future and all things uncertain!

37. "Hold nothing in reserve. I love danger! We may be lost, we may be saved. Do not ask. Place the whole world in the hands of danger every single moment. I, the seed of the unborn, eat at the entrails of your race, and I shout!"

Third Step, Mankind

It is not you talking. Nor is it your race only which shouts within you, for all the innumerable races of mankind shout and rush within you: white, yellow, black.

2. Free yourself from race also; fight to live through the whole struggle of man. See how he has detached himself from the animal, how he struggles to stand upright, to co-ordinate his inarticulate cries, to feed the flame between his hearthstones, to feed his mind amid the bones of his skull.

3. Let pity overwhelm you for this creature who one morning detached himself from the ape, naked, defenseless, without teeth or horns, with only a spark of fire in his soft skull.

4. He does not know from where he comes or where he goes. But by loving, toiling, and killing, he wants to conquer the earth.

5. Look upon men and pity them. Look at yourself amid all men and pity yourself. In the obscure dusk of life we touch and fumble at each other, we ask questions, we listen, we shout for help.

6. We run. We know that we are running to die, but we cannot stop. We run.

7. We carry a torch and run. Our faces light up for a moment, but hurriedly we surrender the torch to our son, and then suddenly vanish and descend into Hades.

8. The mother looks ahead, toward her daughter; the daughter in turn looks ahead, beyond the body of her husband, toward her son—this is how the Invisible proceeds on earth.

9. We all look directly before us, ruthlessly, driven by dark, enormous, infallible powers behind us.

10. Rise above the improvised bastion of your body, look at the centuries behind you. What do you see? Hairy, blood-splattered beasts rising in tumult out of the mud. Hairy, blood-splattered beasts descending in tumult from the mountain summits.

11. The two bellowing armies meet like a man and a woman and become a lump of mud, blood, and brain.

12. Behold: multitudes ascend like grass out of the soil and fall into the soil again, fertile manure for future offspring. And the earth grows fat from the ashes, the blood, and the brains of man.

13. Numbers without end vanish in mid-journey; they are born, but they die barren. Huge pits suddenly gape in the darkness, multitudes tumble and fall, disorderly commands are heard in confused clamor, and the human herd stampedes and scatters.

14. Below and about us and within the abyss of our hearts we suddenly become aware of blind, heartless, brainless, ravenous powers.

15. We sail on a storm-tossed sea, and in a yellow lightning flash we feel we've entrusted our wealth, our children, and our gods to an eggshell.

16. The centuries are thick, dark waves that rise and fall, steeped in blood. Every moment is a gaping abyss.

17. Gaze on the dark sea without staggering, confront the abyss every moment without illusion or impudence or fear.

18. Without illusion, impudence, or fear. But this is not enough; take a further step: battle to give meaning to the confused struggles of man.

19. Train your heart to govern as spacious an arena as it can. Encompass through one century, then through two centuries, through three, through ten, through as many centuries as you can bear, the onward march of mankind. Train your eye to gaze on people moving in great stretches of time.

20. Immerse yourself in this vision with patience, with love and high disinterestedness, until slowly the world begins to breathe within you, the embattled begin to be enlightened, to unite in our heart and to acknowledge themselves as brothers.

21. The heart unites whatever the mind separates, pushes on beyond the arena of necessity and transmutes the struggle into love.

22. Walk tiptoe on the edge of the insatiable precipice and struggle to give order to your vision. Raise the multicolored trap door of the mystery—the stars, the sea, men and ideas; give form and meaning to the formless, the mindless infinitude.

23. Gather together in your heart all terrors, recompose all details. Salvation is a circle; close it!

24. What is meant by happiness? To live every unhappiness. What is meant by light? To gaze with undimmed eyes on all darknesses.

25. We are a humble letter, a single syllable, one word out of a gigantic Odyssey. We are immersed in an enormous song and we shine like humble pebbles as long as they remain immersed in the sea.

26. What is our duty? To raise our heads from the text a moment, as long as our lungs can bear it, and to breathe in the transoceanic song.

27. To bring together all our adventures, to give meaning to our voyage, to battle undauntedly with men, with gods, with animals, and then slowly, patiently, to erect in our brains, marrow of our marrow, our Ithaca.

28. Out of an ocean of nothingness, with fearful struggle, the work of man rises slowly like a small island.

29. Within this arena, which grows more stable night after day, generations work and love and hope and vanish. New generations tread on the corpses of their fathers, continue the work above the abyss and struggle to tame the dread mystery. How? By cultivating a single field, by kissing a woman, by studying a stone, an animal, an idea.

30. Earthquakes come, the island sways, a corner crumbles away, another rises out of the sunless waves.

31. The mind is a seafaring laborer whose work is to build a seawall in chaos.

32. From all these generations, from all these joys and sorrows, from this lovemaking, these battles, these ideas, a single voice rings out, pure and serene. Pure and serene because, though it contains all the sins and disquietudes of struggling man, it yet flies beyond them all and mounts higher still.

33. Amidst all this human material Someone clambers up on his hands and knees, drowned in tears and blood, struggling to save himself.

34. To save himself from whom? From the body which entwines him, from the people who support him, from the flesh, from the heart and the brains of man.

35. "Lord, who are you? You loom before me like a Centaur, his hands stretched toward the sky, his feet transfixed in mud."

"I am He who eternally ascends."

"Why do you ascend? You strain every muscle, you struggle and fight to emerge from the beast. From the beast, and from man. Do not leave me!"

"I fight and ascend that I may not drown. I stretch out my hands, I clutch at every warm body, I raise my head above my brains that I may breathe. I drown everywhere and can nowhere be contained."

"Lord, why do you tremble?"

"I am afraid! This dark ascent has no ending. My head is a flame that tries eternally to detach itself, but the breath of night blows eternally to put me out. My struggle is endangered every moment. My struggle is endangered in every body. I walk and stumble in the flesh like a traveler overtaken by night, and I call out: 'Help me!'"

Fourth Step, The Earth

It is not you who call. It is not your voice calling from within your ephemeral breast. It is not only the white, yellow, and black generations of man calling in your heart. The entire Earth, with her trees and her waters, with her animals, with her men and her gods, calls from within your breast.

2. Earth rises up in your brains and sees her entire body for the first time.

3. She shudders; she is a beast that eats, begets, moves, remembers. She hungers, she devours her children—plants, animals, men, thoughts—she grinds them in her dark jaws, passes them through her body once more, then casts them again into the soil.

4. She recalls her passions and broods upon them. Her memory unfolds within my heart, it spreads everywhere and conquers time.

5. It is not the heart which leaps and throbs in the blood. It is the entire Earth. She turns her gaze backward and relives her dread ascent through chaos.

6. I recall an endless desert of infinite and flaming matter. I am burning!

I pass through immeasurable, unorganized time, completely alone, despairing, crying in the wilderness.

7. And slowly the flame subsides, the womb of matter grows cool, the stone comes alive, breaks open, and a small green leaf uncurls into the air, trembling. It clutches the soil, steadies itself, raises its head and hands, grasps the air, the water, the light, and sucks at the Universe.

8. It sucks at the Universe and wants to pass it through its body—thin as a thread—to turn it into flower, fruit, seed. To make it deathless.

9. The sea shudders and is torn in two; out of its muddy depths a voracious, restless, and eyeless worm ascends.

10. The weight of matter is conquered, the slab of death heaves high, and armies of trees and beasts emerge filled with lust and hunger.

11. I gaze upon Earth with her muddy brain, and I shudder as I relive the peril. I might have sunk and vanished amid these roots that suck at the mud blissfully; I might have smothered in this tough and many-wrinkled hide; or I might have twitched eternally within the bloody, dark skull of the primordial ancestor.

12. But I was saved. I passed beyond the thick-leaved plants, I passed beyond the fishes, the birds, the beasts, the apes. I created man.

13. I created man, and now I struggle to be rid of him.

14. "I am cramped and crushed! I want to escape!" This cry destroys and fructifies the bowels of the earth eternally. It leaps from body to body, from generation to generation, from species to species, becoming always stronger and more carnivorous. All parents shout: "I want to give birth to a son greater than I!"

15. During those fearful moments when the Cry passes through our bodies, we feel a prehuman power driving us ruthlessly. Behind us a muddy torrent roars, full of blood, tears, and sweat, filled with squeals of joy, of lust, of death.

16. An erotic wind blows over Earth, a giddiness overpowers all living creatures till they unite in the sea, in caves, in the air, under the ground, transferring from body to body a great, incomprehensible message.

17. Only now, as we feel the onslaught behind us, do we begin dimly to apprehend why the animals fought, begot, and died; and behind them the plants; and behind these the huge reserve of inorganic forces.

18. We are moved by pity, gratitude, and esteem for our old comrades-in-arms. They toiled, loved, and died to open a road for our coming.

19. We also toil with the same delight, agony, and exaltation for the sake of Someone Else who with every courageous deed of ours proceeds one step farther.

20. All our struggle once more will have a purpose much greater than

we, wherein our toils, our miseries, and our crimes will have become useful and holy.

21. This is an onslaught! A Spirit rushes, storms through matter and fructifies it, passes beyond the animals, creates man, digs its claws into his head like a vulture, and shrieks.

22. It is our turn now. It molds us, pummels matter within us and turns it into spirit, tramples on our brains, mounts astride our sperm, kicks our bodies behind it, and struggles to escape.

23. It is as though the whole of life were the visible, eternal pursuit of an invisible Bridegroom who from body to body hunts down his untamed Bride, Eternity.

24. And we, all the guests of the wedding procession—plants, animals, men—rush trembling toward the mystical nuptial chamber. We each carry with awe the sacred symbols of marriage—one the *Phallos,* another the Womb.

The Vision

You heard the Cry and set forth. From battle to battle you passed through all the war service of militant man.

2. You fought within the small tent of your body, but behold, the battle arena seemed too narrow; you felt stifled and rushed out to escape.

3. You pitched your camp on your race, you brimmed with hands and hearts as with your blood you first revived the dread ancestors and then set forth with the dead, the living, and the unborn to give battle.

4. Suddenly all races moved with you, the holy army of man was arranged for battle behind you, and all earth resounded like a military encampment.

5. You climbed to a high peak from which the plan of battle branched out amid the coils of your brain, and all opposing expeditions united in the secret encampment of your heart.

6. Behind you the plants and animals were organized like supply troops for the front-line battling armies of man.

7. Now entire Earth clings to you, becomes flesh of your flesh, and cries out of chaos.

8. How can I besiege this dread vision with words? I stoop over chaos and listen. Someone is groaning and climbing up a secret, dangerous slope.

9. He struggles and agonizes stubbornly to ascend. But he finds a contrary force that impedes him: Someone is hurriedly climbing down a secret and easy downward slope.

10. Within the descending sluggish stream the Spirit is dismembered and whirled about, and for a moment—the duration of every life—the two opposing desires are balanced.

11. This is how bodies are born, how the world is created, how among living things the two antithetical powers find equilibrium.

12. For a moment the One ascending is entwined by a beloved body—his own body—and is retarded in his climbing. But quickly, with love, with death, he escapes it, and then continues to plod on.

13. He tramples on inorganic matter, he shapes the plant and fills it. He encamps in it with his whole being. By "his whole being" is meant together with the longing and the power to escape.

14. He emerges a little, breathes with difficulty, chokes. He abandons to the plants as much heaviness, as much stupor and immobility as he can and, thus disburdened, leaps, with his whole being again, farther and higher still, creating the animals and encamping in their loins.

15. Again, "with his whole being" means together with the longing and the power to escape.

16. The bodies breathe, feed, store up strength, and then in an erotic moment are shattered, are spent and drained utterly, that they may bequeath their spirit to their sons. What spirit? The drive upward!

17. He purifies himself slowly by struggling amid their bodies, and abandons to the animals as much passion, as much slavishness, as much impotence and darkness as he can.

18. Then once more he rises slightly, a bit lighter, and rushes to escape. It is this drive toward freedom, this strife with matter, which slowly creates the head of man.

19. And now we feel with terror that he is again struggling to escape beyond us, to cast us off with plants and animals, and to leap farther. The moment has come—O great joy and bitterness!—when we, the vanquished, must also be cast away among the reserve troops.

20. Behind the stream of my mind and body, behind the stream of my race and all mankind, behind the stream of plants and animals, I watch with trembling the Invisible, treading on all visible things and ascending.

21. Behind his heavy and blood-splattered feet I hear all living things being trampled on and crushed.

22. His face is without laughter, dark and silent, beyond joy and sorrow, beyond hope.

23. I tremble. Are *you* my God? Your body is steeped in memory. Like one locked up in dungeons for many years, you have adorned your arms and chest with strange trees and hairy dragons, with gory adventures, with cries and chronologies.

24. Lord, my Lord, you growl like a wild beast! Your feet are covered with blood and mire, your jaws are heavy millstones that grind slowly.

25. You clutch at trees and animals, you tread on man, you shout. You climb up the endless black precipice of death, and you tremble.

26. Where are you going? Pain increases, the light and the darkness increase. You weep, you hook onto me, you feed on my blood, you grow huge and strong, and then you kick at my heart. I press you to my breast, and I fear you and pity you.

27. It is as though we had buried Someone we thought dead, and now hear him calling in the night: Help me! Heaving and panting, he raises the gravestone of our soul and body higher and still higher, breathing more freely at every moment.

28. Every word, every deed, every thought is the heavy gravestone he is forever trying to lift. And my own body and all the visible world, all heaven and earth, are the gravestone which God is struggling to heave upward.

29. Trees shout, animals and stars: "We are doomed!" Every living creature flings two huge hands as high as the heavens to seek help.

30. With his knees doubled up under his chin, with his hands spread toward the light, with the soles of his feet turned toward his back, God huddles in a knot in every cell of flesh.

31. When I break a fruit open, this is how every seed is revealed to me. When I speak to men, this what I discern in their thick and muddy brains.

32. God struggles in every thing, his hands flung upward toward the light. What light? Beyond and above every thing!

33. Pain is not the only essence of our God, nor is hope in a future life or a life on this earth, neither joy nor victory. Every religion that holds up to worship one of these primordial aspects of God narrows our hearts and our minds.

34. The essence of our God is *struggle*. Pain, joy, and hope unfold and labor within this struggle, world without end.

35. It is this ascension, the battle with the descending countercurrent, which gives birth to pain. But pain is not the absolute monarch. Every victory, every momentary balance on the ascent fills with joy every living thing that breathes, grows, loves, and gives birth.

36. But from every joy and pain a hope leaps out eternally to escape this pain and to widen joy.

37. And again the ascent begins—which is pain—and joy is reborn and new hope springs up once more. The circle never closes. It is not a circle, but a spiral which ascends eternally, ever widening, enfolding and unfolding the triune struggle.

38. What is the purpose of this struggle? This is what the wretched self-seeking mind of man is always asking, forgetting that the Great Spirit does not toil within the bounds of human time, place, or casualty.

39. The Great Spirit is superior to these human questionings. It teems with many rich and wandering drives which to our shallow minds seem contradictory; but in the essence of divinity they fraternize and struggle together, faithful comrades-in-arms.

40. The primordial Spirit branches out, overflows, struggles, fails, succeeds, trains itself. It is the Rose of the Winds.

41. Whether we want to or not, we also sail on and voyage, consciously or unconsciously, amid divine endeavors. Indeed, even our march has eternal elements, without beginning or end, assisting God and sharing His perils.

42. Which is that one force amid all of God's forces which man is able to grasp? Only this: We discern a crimson line on this earth, a red, blood-splattered line which ascends, struggling, from matter to plants, from plants to animals, from animals to man.

43. This indestructible prehuman rhythm is the only visible journey of the Invisible on this earth. Plants, animals, and men are the steps which God creates on which to tread and to mount upward.

44. Difficult, dreadful, unending ascension! Shall God conquer or be conquered in this onslaught? Does victory exist? Does defeat exist? Our bodies shall rot and turn to dust, but what will become of Him who for a moment passed beyond the body?

45. Yet these are all lesser concerns, for all hopes and despairs vanish in the voracious, funneling whirlwind of God. God laughs, wails, kills, sets us on fire, and then leaves us in the middle of the way, charred embers.

46. And I rejoice to feel between my temples, in the flicker of an eyelid, the beginning and the end of the world.

47. I condense into a lightning moment the seeding, sprouting, blossoming, fructifying, and the disappearance of every tree, animal, man, star, and god.

48. All Earth is a seed planted in the coils of my mind. Whatever struggles for numberless years to unfold and fructify in the dark womb of matter bursts in my head like a small and silent lightning flash.

49. Ah! let us gaze intently on this lightning flash, let us hold it for a moment, let us arrange it into human speech.

50. Let us transfix this momentary eternity which encloses everything, past and future, but without losing in the immobility of language any of its gigantic erotic whirling.

51. Every word is an Ark of the Covenant around which we dance and shudder, divining God to be its dreadful inhabitant.

52. You shall never be able to establish in words that you live in ecstasy. But struggle unceasingly to establish it in words. Battle with myths, with comparisons, with allegories, with rare and common words, with exclamations and rhymes, to embody it in flesh, to transfix it!

53. God, the Great Ecstatic, works in the same way. He speaks and struggles to speak in every way He can, with seas and with fires, with colors, with wings, with horns, with claws, with constellations and butterflies, that he may establish His ecstasy.

54. Like every other living thing, I also am in the center of the Cosmic whirlpool. I am the eye of monstrous rivers where everything dances about me as the circle continually narrows with greater vehemence till the heavens and earth plunge into the red pit of my heart.

55. Then God confronts me with terror and love—for I am His only hope—and says: "This Ecstatic, who gives birth to all things, who rejoices in them all and yet destroys them, this Ecstatic is my Son!"

The Action

The Relationship between God and Man

The ultimate most holy form of theory is action.

2. Not to look on passively while the spark leaps from generation to generation, but to leap and to burn with it!

3. Action is the widest gate of deliverance. It alone can answer the questionings of the heart. Amid the labyrinthine complexities of the mind it finds the shortest route. No, it does not "find"—it creates its way, hewing to right and left through resistances of logic and matter.

4. Why did you struggle behind phenomena to track down the Invisible? What was the purpose of all your warlike, your erotic march through flesh, race, man, plants, and animals? Why the mystic marriage beyond these labors, the perfect embracement, the bacchic and raging contact in darkness and in light?

5. That you might reach the point from which you began—the ephemeral, palpitating, mysterious point of your existence—with new eyes, with new ears ,with a new sense of taste, smell, touch, with new brains.

6. Our profound human duty is not to interpret or to cast light on the

rhythm of God's march, but to adjust, as much as we can, the rhythm of our small and fleeting life to his.

7. Only thus may we mortals succeed in achieving something immortal, because then we collaborate with One who is Deathless.

8. Only thus may we conquer mortal sin, the concentration on details, the narrowness of our brains; only thus may we transubstantiate into freedom the slavery of earthen matter given us to mold.

9. Amid all these things, beyond all these things every man and nation, every plant and animal, every god and demon, charges upward like an army inflamed by an incomprehensible, unconquerable Spirit.

10. We struggle to make this Spirit visible, to give it a face, to encase it in words, in allegories and thoughts and incantations, that it may not escape us.

11. But it cannot be contained in the twenty-six letters of an alphabet which we string out in rows; we know that all these words, these allegories, these thoughts, and these incantations are, once more, but a new mask with which to conceal the Abyss.

12. Yet only in this manner, by confining immensity, may we labor within the newly incised circle of humanity.

13. What do we mean by "labor"? To fill up this circle with desires, with anxieties, and with deeds; to spread out and reach frontiers until, no longer able to contain us, they crack and collapse. By thus working with appearances, we widen and increase the essence.

14. For this reason our return to appearances, after our contact with essence, possesses an incalculable worth.

15. We have seen the highest circle of spiraling powers. We have named this circle God. We might have given it any other name we wished: Abyss, Mystery, Absolute Darkness, Absolute Light, Matter, Spirit, Ultimate Hope, Ultimate Despair, Silence.

16. But we have named it God because only this name, for primordial reasons, can stir our heart profoundly. And this deeply felt emotion is indispensable if we are to touch, body with body, the dread essence beyond logic.

17. Within this gigantic circle of divinity we are in duty bound to separate and perceive clearly the small, burning arc of our epoch.

18. On this barely perceptible flaming curve, feeling the onrush of the entire circle profoundly and mystically, we travel in harmony with the Universe, we gain impetus and dash into battle.

19. Thus, by consciously following the onrush of the Universe, our ephemeral action does not die with us.

20. It does not become lost in a mystical and passive contemplation of the entire circle; it does not scorn holy, humble, and daily necessity.

21. Within its narrow and blood-drenched ditch it stoops and labors steadfastly, conquering easily both space and time within a small point of space and time—for this point follows the divine onrush of the entire circle.

22. I do not care what face other ages and other people have given to the enormous, faceless essence. They have crammed it with human virtues, with rewards and punishments, with certainties. They have given a face to their hopes and fears, they have submitted their anarchy to a rhythm, they have found a higher justification by which to live and labor. They have fulfilled their duty.

23. But today we have gone beyond these needs; we have shattered this particular mask of the Abyss; our God no longer fits under the old features.

24. Our hearts have overbrimmed with new agonies, with new luster and silence. The mystery has grown savage, and God has grown greater. The dark powers ascend, for they have also grown greater, and the entire human island quakes.

25. Let us stoop down to our hearts and confront the Abyss valiantly. Let us try to mold once more, with our flesh and blood, the new, contemporary face of God.

26. For our God is not an abstract thought, a logical necessity, a high and harmonious structure made of deductions and speculations.

27. He is not an immaculate, neutral, odorless, distilled product of our brains, neither male nor female.

28. He is both man and woman, mortal and immortal, dung and spirit. He gives birth, fecundates, slaughters—death and eros in one—and then he begets and slays once more, dancing spaciously beyond the boundaries of a logic which cannot contain the antinomies.

29. My God is not Almighty. He struggles, for he is in peril every moment; he trembles and stumbles in every living thing, and he cries out. He is defeated incessantly, but rises again, full of blood and earth, to throw himself into battle once more.

30. He is full of wounds, his eyes are filled with fear and stubbornness, his jawbones and temples are splintered. But he does not surrender, he ascends; he ascends with his feet, with his hands, biting his lips, undaunted.

31. My God is not All-holy. He is full of cruelty and savage justice, and he chooses the best mercilessly. He is without compassion; he does not trouble himself about men or animals; nor does he care for virtues and ideas. He loves all these things for a moment, then smashes them eternally and passes on.

32. He is a power that contains all things, that begets all things. He begets them, loves them, and destroys them. And if we say, "Our God is an erotic wind and shatters all bodies that he may drive on," and if we remem-

ber that eros always works through blood and tears, destroying every individual without mercy—then we shall approach his dread face a little closer.

33. My God is not All-knowing. His brain is a tangled skein of light and darkness which he strives to unravel in the labyrinth of the flesh.

34. He stumbles and fumbles. He gropes to the right and turns back; swings to the left and sniffs the air. He struggles above chaos in anguish. Crawling, straining, groping for unnumbered centuries, he feels the muddy coils of his brain being slowly suffused with light.

35. On the surface of his heavy, pitch-black head he begins with an indescribable struggle to create eyes by which to see, ears by which to hear.

36. My God struggles on without certainty. Will he conquer? Will he be conquered? Nothing in the Universe is certain. He flings himself into uncertainty; he gambles all his destiny at every moment.

37. He clings to warm bodies; he has no other bulwark. He shouts for help; he proclaims a mobilization throughout the Universe.

38. It is our duty, on hearing his Cry, to run under his flag, to fight by his side, to be lost or to be saved with him.

39. God is imperiled. He is not almighty, that we may cross our hands, waiting for certain victory. He is not all-holy, that we may wait trustingly for him to pity and to save us.

40. Within the province of our ephemeral flesh all of God is imperiled. He cannot be saved unless we save him with our own struggles; nor can we be saved unless he is saved.

41. We are one. From the blind worm in the depths of the ocean to the endless arena of the Galaxy, only one person struggles and is imperiled: You. And within your small and earthen breast only one thing struggles and is imperiled: the Universe.

42. We must understand well that we do not proceed from a unity of God to the same unity of God again. We do not proceed from one chaos to another chaos, neither from one light to another light, nor from one darkness to another darkness. What would be the value of our life then? What would be the value of all life?

43. But we set out from an almighty chaos, from a thick abyss of light and darkness tangled. And we struggle—plants, animals, men, ideas—in this momentary passage of individual life, to put in order the Chaos within us, to cleanse the abyss, to work upon as much darkness as we can within our bodies and to transmute it into light.

44. We do not struggle for ourselves, nor for our race, not even for humanity.

45. We do not struggle for Earth, nor for ideas. All these are the precious yet provisional stairs of our ascending God, and they crumble away as soon as he steps upon them in his ascent.

46. In the smallest lightning flash of our lives, we feel all of God treading upon us, and suddenly we understand: if we all desire it intensely, if we organize all the visible and invisible powers of earth and fling them upward, if we all battle together like fellow combatants eternally vigilant—then the Universe might possibly be saved.

47. It is not God who will save us—it is we who will save God, by battling, by creating, and by transmuting matter into spirit.

48. But all our struggle may go lost. If we tire, if we grow faint of spirit, if we fall into panic, then the entire Universe becomes imperiled.

49. Life is a crusade in the service of God. Whether we wished to or not, we set out as crusaders to free—not the Holy Sepulchre—but that God buried in matter and in our souls.

50. Every body, every soul is a Holy Sepulchre. Every seed of grain is a Holy Sepulchre; let us free it! The brain is a Holy Sepulchre, God sprawls within it and battles with death; let us run to his assistance!

51. God gives the signal for battle, and I, too, rush to the attack, trembling.

52. Whether I straggle behind as a deserter or battle valiantly, I know that I shall always fall in battle. But on the first occasion my death would be sterile, for with the destruction of my body my soul would also be lost and scattered to the winds.

53. On the second occasion, I would descend into earth like a fruit brimming with seed. Though my breath abandon my body to rot, it would organize new bodies and continue the battle.

54. My prayer is not the whimpering of a beggar nor a confession of love. Nor is it the trivial reckoning of a small tradesman: Give me and I shall give you.

55. My prayer is the report of a soldier to his general: This is what I did today, this is how I fought to save the entire battle in my own sector, these are the obstacles I found, this is how I plan to fight tomorrow.

56. My God and I are horsemen galloping in the burning sun or under drizzling rain. Pale, starving, but unsubdued, we ride and converse.

57. "Leader!" I cry. He turns his face toward me, and I shudder to confront his anguish.

58. Our love for each other is rough and ready, we sit at the same table, we drink the same wine in this low tavern of life.

59. As we clink our glasses, swords clash and resound, loves and hates

spring up. We get drunk, visions of slaughter ascend before our eyes, cities crumble and fall in our brains, and though we are both wounded and screaming with pain, we plunder a huge Palace.

The Relationship between Man and Man

What is the essence of our God? The struggle for freedom. In the indestructible darkness a flaming line ascends and emblazons the march of the Invisible. What is our duty? To ascend with this blood-drenched line.

2. Whatever rushes upward and helps God to ascend is good. Whatever drags downward and impedes God from ascending is evil.

3. All virtues and all evils take on a new value. They are freed from the moment and from earth, they exist completely within man, before and after man, eternally.

4. For the essence of our ethic is not the salvation of man, who varies within time and space, but the salvation of God, who within a wide variety of flowing human forms and adventures is always the same, the indestructible rhythm which battles for freedom.

5. We, as human beings, are all miserable persons, heartless, small, insignificant. But within us a superior essence drives us ruthlessly upward.

6. From within this human mire divine songs have welled up, great ideas, violent loves, an unsleeping assault full of mystery, without beginning or end, without purpose, beyond every purpose.

7. Humanity is such a lump of mud, each one of us is such a lump of mud. What is our duty? To struggle so that a small flower may blossom from the dunghill of our flesh and mind.

8. Out of things and flesh, out of hunger, out of fear, out of virtue and sin, struggle continually to create God.

9. How does the light of a star set out and plunge into black eternity in its immortal course? The star dies, but the light never dies; such also is the cry of freedom.

10. Out of the transient encounter of contrary forces which constitute your existence, strive to create whatever immortal thing a mortal may create in this world—a Cry.

11. And this Cry, abandoning to the earth the body which gave it birth, proceeds and labors eternally.

12. A vehement eros runs through the Universe. It is like the ether: harder than steel, softer than air.

13. It cuts through and passes beyond all things, it flees and escapes. It does not repose in warm detail nor enslave itself in the beloved body. It is a Militant Eros. Behind the shoulders of its beloved it perceives mankind

surging and roaring like waves, it perceives animals and plants uniting and dying, it perceives the Lord imperiled and shouting to it: "Save me!"

14. Eros? What other name may we give that impetus which becomes enchanted as soon as it casts its glance on matter and then longs to impress its features upon it? It confronts the body and longs to pass beyond it, to merge with the other erotic cry hidden in that body, to become one till both may vanish and become deathless by begetting sons.

15. It approaches the soul and wishes to merge with it inseparably so that "you" and "I" may no longer exist; it blows on the mass of mankind and wishes, by smashing the resistances of mind and body, to merge all breaths into one violent gale that may lift the earth!

16. In moments of crisis this Erotic Love swoops down on men and joins them together by force—friends and foes, good and evil. It is a breath superior to all of them, independent of their desires and deeds. It is the spirit, the breathing of God on earth.

17. It descends on men in whatever form it wishes—as dance, as eros, as hunger, as religion, as slaughter. It does not ask our permission.

18. In these hours of crisis God struggles to knead flesh and brains together in the trough of earth, to cast all this mass of dough into the merciless whirlwind of his rotation and to give it a face—his face.

19. He does not choke with disgust, he does not despair in the dark, earthen entrails of men. He toils, proceeds, and devours the flesh; he clings to the belly, the heart, the mind and the *phallos* of man.

20. He is not the upright head of a family; he does not portion out either bread or brains equally to his children. Injustice, Cruelty, Longing, and Hunger are the four steeds that drive his chariot on this rough-hewn earth of ours.

21. God is never created out of happiness or comfort or glory, but out of shame and hunger and tears.

22. At every moment of crisis an array of men risk their lives in the front ranks as standard-bearers of God to fight and take upon themselves the whole responsibility of the battle.

23. Once long ago it was the priests, the kings, the noblemen, or the burghers who created civilizations and set divinity free.

24. Today God is the common worker made savage by toil and rage and hunger. He stinks of smoke and wine and meat. He swears and hungers and begets children; he cannot sleep; he shouts and threatens in the cellars and garrets of earth.

25. The air has changed, and we breathe in deeply a spring laden and filled with seed. Cries rise up on every side. Who shouts? It is we who

shout—the living, the dead, and the unborn. But at once we are crushed by fear, and we fall silent.

26. And then we forget—out of laziness, out of habit, out of cowardice. But suddenly the Cry tears at our entrails once more, like an eagle.

27. For the Cry is not outside us, it does not come from a great distance that we may escape it. It sits on the center of our hearts, and cries out.

28. God shouts: "Burn your houses! I am coming! Whoever has a house cannot receive me!

29. "Burn your ideas, smash your thoughts! Whoever has found the solution cannot find me.

30. "I love the hungry, the restless, the vagabonds. They are the ones who brood eternally on hunger, on rebellion, on the endless road—on ME!

31. "I am coming! Leave your wives, your children, your ideas, and follow me. I am the great Vagabond.

32. "Follow! Stride over joy and sorrow, over peace and justice and virtue! Forward! Smash these idols, smash them all, they cannot contain me. Smash even yourself that I may pass."

33. Set fire! This is our great duty today amid such immortal and hopeless chaos.

34. War against the unbelievers! The unbelievers are the satisfied, the satiated, the sterile.

35. Our hate is uncompromising because it knows that it works for love better and more profoundly than any weak-hearted kindness.

36. We hate, we are never content, we are unjust, we are cruel and filled with restlessness and faith; we seek the impossible, like lovers.

37. Sow fire to purify the earth! Let a more dreadful abyss open up between good and evil, let injustice increase, let Hunger descend to thresh our bowels, for we may not otherwise be saved.

38. We are living in a critical, violent moment of history; an entire world is crashing down, another has not yet been born. Our epoch is not a moment of equilibrium in which refinement, reconciliation, peace, and love might be fruitful virtues.

39. We live in a moment of dread assault, we stride over our enemies, we stride over our lagging friends, we are imperiled in the midst of chaos, we drown. We can no longer fit into old virtues and hopes, into old theories and actions.

40. The wind of devastation is blowing; this is the breath of our God today; let us be carried away in its tide! The wind of devastation is the first dancing surge of the creative rotation. It blows over every head and every city, it knocks down houses and ideas, it passes over desolate wastes, and it shouts: "Prepare yourselves! War! It's War!"

41. This is our epoch, good or bad, beautiful or ugly, rich or poor—we did not choose it. This is our epoch, the air we breathe, the mud given us, the bread, the fire, the spirit!

42. Let us accept Necessity courageously. It is our lot to have fallen on fighting times. Let us tighten our belts, let us arm our hearts, our minds, and our bodies. Let us take our place in battle!

43. War is the lawful sovereign of our age. Today the only complete and virtuous man is the warrior. For only he, faithful to the great pulse of our time, smashing, hating, desiring, follows the present command of our God.

44. This identification of ourselves with the Universe begets the two superior virtues of our ethics: responsibility and sacrifice.

45. It is our duty to help liberate that God who is stifling in us, in mankind, in masses of people living in darkness.

46. We must be ready at any moment to give up our lives for his sake. For life is not a goal; it is also an instrument, like death, like beauty, like virtue, like knowledge. Whose instrument? Of that God who fights for freedom.

47. We are all one, we are all an imperiled essence. If at the far end of the world a spirit degenerates, it drags down our spirit into its own degradation. If one mind at the far end of the world sinks into idiocy, our own temples overbrim with darkness.

48. For it is only One who struggles at the far end of earth and sky. One. And if He goes lost, it is we who must bear the responsibility. If He goes lost, then we go lost.

49. This is why the salvation of the Universe is also our salvation, why solidarity among men is no longer a tenderhearted luxury but a deep necessity and self-preservation, as much a necessity as, in an army under fire, the salvation of your comrade-in-arms.

50. But our morality ascends even higher. We are all one army under fire. Yet we have no certain knowledge that we shall conquer, we have no certain knowledge that we shall be conquered.

51. Does salvation exist, does a purpose exist which we serve and in the service of which we shall find deliverance?

52. Or is there no salvation, is there no purpose, are all things in vain and our contribution of no value at all?

53. Neither one nor the other. Our God is not almighty, he is not all-holy, he is not certain that he will conquer, he is not certain that he will be conquered.

54. The essence of our God is obscure. It ripens continuously; perhaps victory is strengthened with our every valorous deed, but perhaps even all

these agonizing struggles toward deliverance and victory are inferior to the nature of divinity.

55. Whatever it might be, we fight on without certainty, and our virtue, uncertain of any rewards, acquires a profound nobility.

56. All the commandments are put to rout. We do not see, we do not hear, we do not hate, we do not love as once we did. Earth takes on a new virginity. Bread and water and women take on a new flavor. Action takes on a new, incalculable value.

57. All acquire an unexpected holiness—beauty, knowledge, hope, the economic struggle, daily and seemingly meaningless cares. Shuddering, we feel everywhere about us the same gigantic, enslaved Spirit striving for freedom.

58. Everyone has his own particular road which leads him to liberation —one the road of virtue, another the road of evil.

59. If the road leading you to your liberation is that of disease, of lies, of dishonor, it is then your duty to plunge into disease, into lies, into dishonor, that you may conquer them. You may not otherwise be saved.

60. If the road which leads you to your liberation is the road of virtue, of joy, of truth, it is then your duty to plunge into virtue, into joy, into truth, that you may conquer them and leave them behind you. You may not otherwise be saved.

61. We do not fight our dark passions with a sober, bloodless, neutral virtue which rises above passion, but with other, more violent passions.

62. We leave our door open to sin. We do not plug up our ears with wax that we may not listen to the Sirens. We do not bind ourselves, out of fear, to the mast of a great idea; nor by hearing and by embracing the Sirens do we abandon our ship, and perish.

63. On the contrary, we seize the Sirens and pitch them into our boat so that even they may voyage with us; and we continue on our way. This, my comrades, is our new Asceticism, our Spiritual Exercises!

64. God cries to my heart: "Save me!"

65. God cries to men, to animals, to plants, to matter: "Save me!"

66. Listen to your heart and follow him. Shatter your body and awake: We are all one.

67. Love man because you are he.

68. Love animals and plants because you were they, and now they follow you like faithful co-workers and slaves.

69. Love your body; only with it may you fight on this earth and turn matter into spirit.

70. Love matter. God clings to it tooth and nail, and fights. Fight with him.

71. Die every day. Be born every day. Deny everything you have every day. The superior virtue is not to be free but to fight for freedom.

72. Do not condescend to ask: "Shall we conquer? Shall we be conquered?" Fight on!

73. So may the enterprise of the Universe, for an ephemeral moment, for as long as you are alive, become your own enterprise. This. Comrades, is our new Decalogue.

The Relationship between Man and Nature

All this world, all this rich, endless flow of appearances is not a deception, a multicolored phantasmagoria of our mirroring mind. Nor is it absolute reality which lives and evolves freely, independent of our mind's power.

2. It is not the resplendent robe which arrays the mystic body of God. Nor the obscurely translucent partition between man and mystery.

3. All this world that we see, hear, and touch is that accessible to the human senses, a condensation of the two enormous powers of the Universe permeated with all of God.

4. One power descends and wants to scatter, to come to a standstill, to die. The other power ascends and strives for freedom, for immortality.

5. These two armies, the dark and the light, the armies of life and of death, collide eternally. The visible signs of this collision are, for us, plants, animals, men.

6. The antithetical powers collide eternally; they meet, fight, conquer and are conquered, become reconciled for a brief moment, and then begin to battle again throughout the Universe—from the invisible whirlpool in a drop of water to the endless cataclysm of stars in the Galaxy.

7. Even the most humble insect and the most insignificant idea are the military encampments of God. Within them, all of God is arranged in fighting position for a critical battle.

8. Even in the most meaningless particle of earth and sky I hear God crying out: "Help me!"

9. Everything is an egg in which God's sperm labors without rest, ceaselessly. Innumerable forces within and without it range themselves to defend it.

10. With the light of the brain, with the flame of the heart, I besiege every cell where God is jailed, seeking, trying, hammering to open a gate in

the fortress of matter, to create a gap through which God may issue in heroic attack.

11. Lie in ambush behind appearances, patiently, and strive to subject them to laws. Thus may you open up roads through chaos and help the spirit on its course.

12. Impose order, the order of your brain, on the flowing anarchy of the world. Incise your plan of battle clearly on the face of the abyss.

13. Contend with the powers of nature, force them to the yoke of superior purpose. Free that spirit which struggles within them and longs to mingle with that spirit which struggles within you.

14. When a man fighting with chaos subdues a series of appearances to the laws of his mind and strictly confines these laws within the boundaries of reason, then the world breathes, the voices are ranged in order, the future becomes clarified, and all the dark and endless quantities of numbers are freed by submitting to mystical quality.

15. With the help of our minds we compel matter to come with us. We divert the direction of descending powers, we alter the course of the current, we transform slavery into freedom.

16. We do not only free God by battling and subduing the visible world about us; we also create God.

17. "Open your eyes," God shouts; "I want to see! Prick up your ears, I want to hear! March in the front ranks: you are my head!"

18. A stone is saved if we lift it from the mire and build it into a house, or if we chisel the spirit upon it.

19. The seed is saved—what do we mean by "saved"? It frees the God within it by blossoming, by bearing friut, by returning to earth once more. Let us help the seed to save itself.

20. Every man has his own circle composed of trees, animals, men, ideas, and he is in duty bound to save this circle. He, and no one else. If he does not save it, he cannot be saved.

21. These are the labors each man is given and is in duty bound to complete before he dies. He may not otherwise be saved. For his own soul is scattered and enslaved in these things about him, in trees, in animals, in men, in ideas, and it is his own soul he saves by completing these labors.

22. If you are a laborer, then till the earth, help it to bear fruit. The seeds in the earth cry out, and God cries out within the seeds. Set him free! A field awaits its deliverance at your hands, a machine awaits its soul. You may never be saved unless you save them.

23. If you are a warrior, be pitiless; compassion is not in the periphery of your duty. Kill the foe mercilessly. Hear how God cries out in the body

of the enemy: "Kill this body, it obstructs me! Kill it that I may pass!"

24. If you are a man of learning, fight in the skull, kill ideas and create new ones. God hides in every idea as in every cell of flesh. Smash the idea, set him free; Give him another, a more spacious idea in which to dwell.

25. If you are a woman, then love. Choose austerely among all men the father of your children. It is not you who make the choice, but the indestructible, merciless, infinite, masculine God within you. Fulfill all your duty, so overbrimming with bitterness, love, and valor. Give up all your body, so filled with blood and milk.

26. Say: "This child, which I hold suckling at my breast, shall save God. Let me give him all my blood and milk."

27. Profound and incommensurable is the worth of this flowing world: God clings to it and ascends, God feeds upon it and increases.

28. My heart breaks open, my mind is flooded with light, and all at once this world's dread battlefield is revealed to me as an erotic arena.

29. Two violent contrary winds, one masculine and the other feminine, met and clashed at a crossroads. For a moment they counterbalanced each other, thickened, and became visible.

30. This crossroads is the Universe. This crossroads is my heart.

31. This dance of the gigantic erotic collision is transmitted from the darkest particle of matter to the most spacious thought.

32. The wife of my God is matter; they wrestle with each other, they laugh and weep, they cry out in the nuptial bed of flesh.

33. They spawn and are dismembered. They fill sea, land and air with species of plants, animals, men, and spirits. This primordial pair embraces, is dismembered, and multiplies in every living creature.

34. All the concentrated agony of the Universe bursts out in every living thing. God is imperiled in the sweet ecstasy and bitterness of flesh.

35. But he shakes himself free, he leaps out of brains and loins, then clings to new brains and new loins until the struggle for liberation again breaks out from the beginning.

36. For the first time on this earth, from within our hearts and our minds, God gazes on his own struggle.

37. Joy! Joy! I did not know that all this world is so much part of me, that we are all one army, that windflowers and stars struggle to right and left of me and do not know me; but I turn to them and hail them.

38. The Universe is warm, beloved, familiar, and it smells like my own body. It is Love and War both, a raging restlessness, persistence and uncertainty.

39. Uncertainty and terror. In a violent flash of lightning I discern on

the highest peak of power the final, the most fearful pair embracing: Terror and Silence. And between them, a Flame.

The Silence

The soul of man is a flame, a bird of fire that leaps from bough to bough, from head to head, and that shouts: "I cannot stand still, I cannot be consumed, no one can quench me!"

2. All at once the Universe becomes a tree of fire. Amidst the smoke and the flames, reposing on the peak of conflagration, immaculate, cool, and serene, I hold that final fruit of fire, the Light.

3. From this lofty summit I look on the crimson line which ascends—a tremulous, blood-stained phosphorescence that drags itself like a lovesick insect through the raincool coils of my brain.

4. The ego, race, mankind, earth, theory and action, God—all these are phantasms made of loam and brain, good only for those simple hearts that live in fear, good only for those flatulent souls that imagine they are pregnant.

5. Where do we come from? Where are we going? What is the meaning of this life? That is what every heart is shouting, what every head is asking as it beats on chaos.

6. And a fire within me leaps up to answer: "Fire will surely come one day to purify the earth. Fire will surely come one day to obliterate the earth. This is the Second Coming.

7. "The soul is a flaming tongue that licks and struggles to set the black bulk of the world on fire. One day the entire Universe will become a single conflagration.

8. "Fire is the first and final mask of my God. We dance and weep between two enormous pyres."

9. Our thoughts and our bodies flash and glitter with reflected light. Between the two pyres I stand serenely, my brain unshaken amid the vertigo, and I say:

10. "Time is most short and space most narrow between these two pyres, the rhythm of this life is most sluggish, and I have no time, nor a place to dance in. I cannot wait."

11. Then all at once the rhythm of the earth becomes a vertigo, time disappears, the moment whirls, becomes eternity, and every point in space—insect or star or idea—turns into dance.

12. It was a jail, and the jail was smashed, the dreadful powers within it were freed, and that point of space no longer exists!

13. This ultimate stage of our spiritual exercise is called Silence. Not because its contents are the ultimate inexpressible despair or the ultimate inexpressible joy and hope. Nor because it is the ultimate knowledge which does not condescend to speak, or the ultimate ignorance which cannot.

14. Silence means: Every person, after completing his service in all labors, reaches finally the highest summit of endeavor, beyond every labor, where he no longer struggles or shouts, where he ripens fully in silence, indestructibly, eternally, with the entire Universe.

15. There he merges with the Abyss and nestles within it like the seed of man in the womb of woman.

16. The Abyss is now his wife, he plows her, he opens and devours her vitals, he transmutes her blood, he laughs and weeps, he ascends and descends with her, and he never leaves her.

17. How can you reach the womb of the Abyss to make it fruitful? This cannot be expressed, cannot be narrowed into words, cannot be subjected to laws; every man is completely free and has his own special liberation.

18. No form of instruction exists, no Savior exists to open up the road. No road exists to be opened.

19. Every person ascending above and beyond his own head, escapes from his small brain, so crammed with perplexities.

20. Within profound Silence, erect, fearless, in pain, and in play, ascending ceaselessly from peak to peak, knowing that the height has no ending, sing this proud and magical incantation as you hang over the Abyss:

I believe in one God, defender of the borders, of double descent, militant, suffering, or mighty but not of omnipotent powers, a warrior at the farthest frontiers, commander-in-chief of all the luminous powers, the visible and the invisible.

2. I believe in the innumerable, the ephemeral masks which God has assumed throughout the centuries, and behind his ceaseless flux I discern an indestructible unity.

3. I believe in his sleepless and violent struggle which tames and fructifies the earth as the life-giving fountain of plants, animals, and men.

4. I believe in man's heart, that earthen threshing-floor where night and day the defender of the borders fights with death.

5. O Lord, you shout: "Help me! Help me!" You shout, O Lord, and I hear.

6. Within me all forefathers and all descendants, all races and all earth hear your cry with joy and terror.

7. Blessed be all those who hear and rush to free you, Lord, and who say: "Only you and I exist."

8. *Blessed be all those who free you and become united with you, Lord, and who say: "You and I are one."*

9. *And thrice blessed be those who bear on their shoulders and do not buckle under this great, sublime, and terrifying secret:*

THAT EVEN THIS ONE
DOES NOT EXIST!

The stronger the soul and the flesh, the more fruitful the struggle and the richer the final harmony. God does not love weak souls and flabby flesh. The spirit desires to wrestle with flesh which is strong and full of resistance.

—Nikos Kazantzakis
Report to Greco

Abyss *is the name we give to whatever we cannot bridge. There is no abyss, no end of the road; there is only the soul of man, which names everything in keeping with its own bravery or cowardice. Christ, Buddha, and Moses all found abysses. But they erected bridges and crossed over.*

—Nikos Kazantzakis
Report to Greco

No religious dogma, no political ideology may claim Nikos Kazantzakis. His works will always be a heresy to any political or religious faith which exists today, or which may be formulated in the future, for in the heart of his Spiritual Exercise lies a bomb timed to explode all visions which are betrayed into the petrifaction of ritual, constitution, or dogma.

—Kimon Friar
Introduction to *Spiritual Exercises*

Without Contraries is no progression.

—William Blake
The Marriage of Heaven and Hell

REFLECTIONS (26)

REFLECTIONS

Why does Kazantzakis number the paragraphs of *The Saviors of God?* What impression does this make on you?

The translator, Kimon Friar, points out in the notes to his translation that the original subtitle of the work was a word which might be translated "Ascetic" or "Asceticism." Yet he decided, with Kazantzakis' permission, to render this as "Spiritual Exercises." In what sense are these dramatic statements "spiritual exercises"?

Is Kazantzakis writing here an account of his personal evolution, or the evolution of mankind?

The Saviors of God is perhaps closer to poetry than to philosophy, and yet it contains many statements of belief about the nature of man, God, and life. Are there statements you find it impossible to accept or agree with? If so, are these statements more acceptable in the context of the whole work than when taken alone, or not?

If you were to take a single sentence or paragraph from *The Saviors of God* as the theme around which to develop an exposition of your personal credo, which would you choose?

*Some voyages and journeys are begun unwill-
ingly. The black slaves who made the
notorious Middle Passage had no choice, and
even free men are sometimes forced to set
forth on paths that terrify them. Nuñez
Cabeza de Vaca, a sixteenth-century Spaniard
in the New World, was such a man, and his
terrible eight-year trek across the continent,
from Florida to Mexico City, led him and
his three companions through almost unen-
durable suffering and the constant threat of
death. But Cabeza de Vaca not only endured,
he prevailed, and his physical journey became
the stimulus to a simultaneous spiritual
journey that transformed his personality and
his view of life into something resembling
saintliness. Coronado and many other Spaniards, driven by a lust for gold and power,
could no longer understand his motives or
even believe him when he told them what
he had seen. Nor, perhaps, could his King,
the Emperor Charles V, to whom he sent an
account of his incredible journey.*

HANIEL LONG

The Power within Us

Note I

Along in late November, 1528, a handful of Spaniards, survivors of an ill-starred expedition to Florida, were washed ashore in the Gulf of Mexico, some think near the present site of Galveston. One of these men was Nuñez Cabeza de Vaca, thirty-eight years old, the lieutenant of the expedition, an adaptable man with some secret of growth in him. Despite the privations he had endured, this Nuñez led two other Spaniards and a Moor on a journey across the entire continent, barefoot and naked, which occupied them eight years.

After he reached Mexico City, Nuñez wrote a letter to his King, relating what had befallen him. It begins as the usual story of a European adventurer who leaves home to exploit people. But Nuñez little by little finds out that people are his brothers and sisters, and feels genuine concern for them. Stories require the right audience, and he seems afraid that His Majesty might not be interested in what he has to say, for it is the story of a disaster in Spanish colonial history and in the King's personal finances. In the world of the individual, nonetheless, it is a story of triumph, however lackadaisical the manner of its telling.

My account of Nuñez is not the account he sent the King, apart of course from the actual facts. But I believe it to be the account he wished to send the King. I preserve the core of his narrative, as translated by Fanny Bandelier, and I try to show what, quite plainly, was happening to the spirit of the man. That is, I allow him to speak as though unafraid of his King and his times. I wish him to address us four hundred years later, in this world of ours where human relation is still the difficult problem, and exploitation the cancer.

Nuñez found the limitless within the narrowly limited. He helped when he had no means of helping, and gave when he had nothing to give. So, what is interesting is that at a certain point he ceases to be a historical personage and becomes a symbol. If he were alive today, he would be free to bring into the open the inwardness of his adventure. Thus he would greatly concern the present western world and our entire human world, for we are his proper audience.

In his emergency Nuñez slides out of theories and prejudices which unfit one to live on. Possibly the capacity to survive depends upon courage of spirit to accept one's fate. Possibly also, danger can be a real benefit to the physical man. Nuñez was remarkably flexible; he had what seems unlimited courage, unlimited strength. To him life itself was not different from hardship and danger, life *was* these things, and they are what makes life good. His plight was hopeless, but he set in motion a train of thought and action which saved him. My attention wanders from the perfunctory narrative to the thing he refrains from confiding to the royal ear. That thing is a mystical feeling about the increase of life in a man from effort and from taking thought of his fellows. The weather-beaten explorer of the XVIth century, lost in a thorny land among copper-colored savages and facing a blank future, discovered religion to be a reality of which he had never dreamt. His effort, his feeling for others, take novel paths; but underneath, quite apparently, lies an ageless and universal experience.

Note II

The *Naufragios* ("Shipwrecks") of Nuñez Cabeza de Vaca first appeared at Zamora in 1542. It was this rare first edition which Mrs. Bandelier translated as one of the volumes of the "Trail Makers" series (*The Journey of Alvar Nuñez Cabeza de Vaca and His Companions from Florida to the Pacific 1528-1536*. Tr. Fanny Bandelier with Introduction by Ad. F. Bandelier. New York. A. S. Barnes and Co. 1905). In 1555 the *Naufragios*, reprinted with minor changes, was included in the first edition of the *Comentarios*, a narrative in which Nuñez relates the events of his South American expedition. This edition of the "Shipwrecks" was translated into English in 1851 by T. Buckingham Smith, under the title *The Narrative of Alvar Nuñez Cabeca de Vaca*. An edition of Smith's translation, with many additions, appeared in New York in 1871, with John Gilmary Shea as editor. This annotated edition of the Narrative under the editorial supervision of Frederick W. Hodge of the Bureau of American Ethnology is included in the series "Original Narratives of Early American History" (*Spanish Explorers in the Southern United States 1528-1543*. Charles Scribner's Sons. New York. 1907). Morris Bishop's *The Odyssey of Cabeza de Vaca* (Century Co., 1933) is a biographical account of Nuñez, as drawn from the "Shipwrecks," the "Commentaries," and other sources, such as the records of the trial which clouded the last years of the explorer.

Your Majesty, I am that Nuñez Cabeza de Vaca who lately sent you a Relation of his shipwrecks and mischances during the eight years he was absent from your dominions. In painful doubt whether my words were clear enough, I write again. My meanings being new to your Majesty and at a hasty glance unconcerned with your prestige, you might consider my narrative a poor occasion for exercising your serene power of understanding. The fault would then lie in me, not in what I have to say. Be my forgiving reader, your Majesty. Grant me your grace.

I was at the battle of Ravenna in 1512. Between dawn and sunset that day perished a thousand score. Young as I was, Ravenna taught me something of how easy to tear asunder and destroy a man is, body and spirit. In the days that followed, in my desolation first confronted with slaughter, I saw a far off light, heard a far off strain of music. Such words serve as well as any: what can describe a happening in the shadows of the soul?

Again that far off flicker of music came to me in the disorders at Sevilla in 1521, when I fought under the Duke of Medina-Sidonia.

Seven years passed without that flash of inward fire and I forgot about it. Sevilla was then a marvellous, disturbing world. I saw the heretics burning in the arms of the iron prophets. I saw Columbus as an old man, Magellan as a young man. The sailors came ashore with parrots and gold ingots and Indian girls.

Then I too sailed acronss the seas, Lord Treasurer of the expedition of Pámfilo Narvaez.

All that day when we were in sight of Teneriffe[1] I thought of my grandfather, the conqueror of the Grand Canary. In my childhood I was surrounded by the natives of that island, the Guanches, whom he brought home as slaves. I listened to their vague and melancholy singing, learned to be at ease with inarticulate people.

For the money to conquer the Grand Canary, perhaps your Majesty will remember, Pedro de Vera Mendoza had pawned to the Moor his two sons, my father and my uncle.

As I told your Majesty in my account of that journey, never had expedition more calamities than ours. Some of our ships foundered from hurricanes in the harbors of Cuba. The others we left behind deliberately in the lagoons of Florida.

---

[1] Largest of the Canary Islands, Spanish possessions in the Atlantic off the north-western coast of Africa.

Our greatest misfortune, aside from our greed and ignorance, lay in our commander, Pámfilo Narvaez himself. Pámfilo believed himself born under a lucky star, though nothing justified such a belief. Before Hernán Cortés he could have marched to Tenochtitlan.[2] But he did not. When Cortés and his soldiers were richly quartered in the palaces of Montezuma, he could have replaced him in command. For that purpose was he dispatched from Havana by Velásquez. But Cortés came flying on horseback all the way to Vera Cruz, and talked Pámfilo's soldiers away from under his very nose. Pámfilo was not without a magnetism. But he was cocksure, a braggart, and what was worse, uncertain of the line between dream and reality. He forgot that Cortés burnt his ships only after studying the jewelled emissaries of Montezuma, and becoming sure of the value of the quarry. Pámfilo had nothing to be sure of. And yet he pictured himself another Cortés, he pictured another Tenochtitlan concealed in the fronds of Florida. Having pictured these things he was as certain that they existed as of the vein in his neck.

Your Majesty is at liberty to picture *us* under this aging, adipose, credulous commander. Across that steaming land we marched with our armor glittering and our horses covered with gaudy trappings, 578 of us, towards utter ruin. Believing that on the page of history we would share the glory of Cortés and his murderous band . . .

Pámfilo would summon the copper-colored natives and tell them with gestures that he was searching for a city of the size and value of Tenochtitlan. The Indians had never heard of Tenochtitlan nor of Montezuma. But they had heard of a big town and pointed northward exclaiming, "Apaláchee!"

We marched and we marched, and had fevers and fevers. Yes, your Majesty is at liberty to picture us.

Apaláchee was no Tetnochtitlan . . . We found it. It was in an immense swamp, a large impoverished settlement of thatched huts, a place of unbearable squalor.

There was nothing for it but seek the sea again and sail back to Cuba. Our arms and armor made us feel like dolts, and we wished we had pierced the jungle carrying carpenter's tools. For now, without axe, adze, or hammer, we had to build ourselves boats.

This is the tale of what men can and cannot do when they must do something or die. We built nine open boats. During the weeks it required, some of us went with scant food, and those whose palates allowed it devoured the horses.

---

[2] Ancient capital of the Aztec empire, on the site now occupied by Mexico City.

Our 580 men had become 400 when at last we set sail and left behind us the Indian marksmen and the snakes, neither of which in Florida err when they strike.

Day after day tide and wind washed us out to sea and then washed us in to land, along a dazzling and uncertain coast. From thirst, and from the exposure to the frightful sun, our 400 became 40.

Who knows what was lost in these boats? Another Magellan, another Camoens, another Cervantes, another St. John of the Cross . . .

No one has so sympathetic an imagination as your Majesty. You will understand what I am not telling you; that I saw men jump overboard, mad from thirst and sun. That I saw them swell and die slowly in delirium, heard their words and songs pour out the pitiful contents of their minds. That I saw men gnaw at corpses. And that these were Spanish gentlemen.

It is curious to have so graphic a lesson in what life may become. We had been a proud band, relying on our united strength, our armor, and our horses. Slowly our strength disunited, until nothing that we had in common remained to help any of us.

As I say, it is curious when one has nobody and nothing to rely upon outside of oneself.

Yet again that music, that fitful run and flash of brightness I first heard on the battlefield of Ravenna. Your Majesty is renowned as a patron of music; here was a music it is possible you may never have heard.

Somewhere on that coast a handful of us crawled ashore, and were fed and tended by kindly Indians till we regathered nervous vitality for the hopeless voyage to Cuba. We stript and launched the boat, first putting our clothes aboard her. But a great comber capsized the rotten heavy hulk, imprisoning and drowning three of us. The others emerged mother-naked on the beach, shivering in the November wind of that overcast afternoon.

The Indians came back and found us as naked as they were, and our barge gone, and in tears. They sat down beside us and cried, too. I cried all the harder, to think people so miserable had pity for us. I have informed your Majesty of their tears and mine. These simple Indians were the first relenting of nature to us in months and months. That evening, for fear we might die on the way, the Indians made fires at intervals along the path to their village, warming us at each fire. That night and many nights after we slept beside them on the oyster shells which floor their huts, wrapt in hides against the cold winds from the sea.

While we were subjects of your Majesty, we had everything life offers, and now we had nothing. To understand what it means to have nothing one must have nothing. No clothing against the weather might appear the worst. But for us poor skeletons who survived it, it was not.

The worst lay in parting little by little with the thoughts that clothe the soul of a European, and most of all the idea that a man attains strength through dirk and dagger, and serving in your Majesty's guard. We had to surrender such fantasies till our inward nakedness was the nakedness of an unborn babe, starting life anew in a womb of sensations which in themselves can mysteriously nourish. Several years went by before I could relax in that living plexus for which even now I have no name; but only when at last I relaxed, could I see the possibilities of a life in which to be deprived of Europe was not to be deprived of too much.

Tempests came, we could pull no more roots from the sea-channels, the canebrake yielded no more fish. People died in the flimsy lodges. News came that five Spaniards further down the coast, men from another barge, had eaten one another up till but one remained. This deed startled the innocence of our Indians. They debated whether to kill us, to be rid of us. Instead, they made us their beasts of burden.

In April the Indians went down to the sea taking us with them; for a whole month we ate the blackberries of the sand dunes. The Indians danced incessantly. They asked us to cure their sick. When we said we did not know how to cure, they withheld our food from us. We began to watch the procedure of their medicine men. It seemed to us both irreligious and uninstructed. Besides, we found the notion of healing Indians somewhat repellent, as your Majesty will understand. But we had to heal them or die. So we prayed for strength. We prayed on bended knees and in an agony of hunger. Then over each ailing Indian we made the sign of the Cross, and recited the Ave María and a Pater noster. To our amazement the ailing said they were well. And not only they but the whole tribe went without food so that we might have it. Yet so great was the lack of food for us all, it seemed impossible that life could last.

Truly, it was to our amazement that the ailing said they were well. Being Europeans, we thought we had given away to doctors and priests our ability to heal. But here it was, still in our possession, even if we had only Indians to exercise it upon. It was ours after all, we were more than we had thought we were.

I am putting my words together for whatever intelligence there may be in the world. There is no other reality among men than this intelligence; Sire, it is greatly to your glory that you can incarnate it.

To be more than I thought I was—a sensation utterly new to me . . .

Starvation, nakedness, slavery: sensations utterly new to me, also . . . The last of my fellow Spaniards on the island dies . . . Nothing to eat after the sea-roots sprouted but the blackberries of the sand dunes. Nothing to protect me from the attack of the terrible frost, or the terrible sun. No one who

knew my language . . . And it endured for months, for years maybe . . .
Everyone I saw as starved as I was. The human body emaciated, the lean
cheek, the burning eye—the ribs showing, each rib distinct—the taut skin,
the weak loins, the shrunken haunch and pap. In the whole world there
can be no poverty like the poverty of these people. I could not stand it.
I ran away . . .

At this time, as I remember it, I began to think of Indians as fellow
human beings. If I introduce this idea it is to prepare your Majesty for other
ideas which came to me later, in consequence.

These were days when I reassorted the pictures of my childhood, as a
child turns his kaleidoscope. I saw the Guanche slaves anew, and as though
I were one of them. I saw my grandfather through the eyes of his slaves.
I remembered, now without laughing, how he had tricked the Gaunches
into slavery. He pretended to enlist them to sail from the Grand Canary
to conquer Teneriffe, and when he had them below decks he battened down
the hatches and set sail for Cádiz . . .

My grandfather's brutality earned him the public denunciation of Bishop
Juan de Frías. This too I remembered.

In this wilderness I became a trader, and went to and fro on the coast and
a little inland. I went inland with seashells and cockles, and a certain shell
used to cut beans, which the natives value. I came out with hides, and red
ochre for the face and hair, flint for arrow points, and tassels of deerhide. I
came to be well known among the tribes, and found out the lay of the land.

One day I heard someone calling me by name, "Alvar Nuñez, Alvar
Nuñez!" It was Alonso del Castillo, one of the captains of the expedition.
He said that Pámfilo's barge had drifted ashore among unfriendly Indians,
and left of its occupants were only himself and Captain Andrés Dorantes,
and Dorantes' blackamoor, Estevanico. We hid ourselves in a thicket and
laid our plans.

That summer, when the coast tribes came together for the summer orgies,
we four made good our escape westward.

Thus our 580 had become 400, our 400, forty, and our forty, four.

Certain natives came to Castillo. From ribs to cleft they were having
spasms, and they begged him to cure them. He prayed, and required us
anxiously to pray with him. When he had done praying he made the sign of
the Cross over the Indians, and their spasms left off. We knelt down to give
thanks for this new amazement.

Through this region there are no trails, and I lost my way. I found a
burning tree to spend that very cold night beside. In the morning I loaded
myself with dry wood, and took two burning sticks. Thus with fuel and fire,
I went on for five days, seeing nobody, but having the sun with me by day

and Mazzaroth and Arcturus by night. These five days I felt a numbness of those organs which keep one aware of the misery of existence. When curing sick Indians, I have struggled to shut out the thought of Andrés and Alonso (for we are self-conscious, knowing one another's sins); and in the effort of praying I have felt as though something in me had broken, to give me the power of healing. But alone in this wilderness no tissue of the body hindered the mysterious power.

Nothing of me, your Majesty, existed then outside of that music I first heard at Ravenna.

The sixth day I found my companions, who had concluded that a snake must have bitten me. I told them we ought not to be self-conscious with one another. That power we had felt flowing in us and through us could not, in the nature of things, be acutely conscious of us as individuals. It must come rather as wind comes to the trees of a forest, or as the ocean continues to murmur in the seashell it has thrown ashore.

A gulf deeper than ocean yawns between the old world and new; and what by now I was accustomed to, would startle a burgher of Madrid or of Salamanca.

At Sevilla in my youth, as I have said, I saw the heretics burning in the arms of the iron prophets. This picture was with me often. Perhaps, like me, those heretics had had to pick up their notions of the Invisible as they went through life, and without the assistance of book or priest. What I myself was learning, came from many blinding days in an open boat, while men died beside me crying for their mothers; and from living among these simple Indians, who insisted on our curing them of their ills. And so my notions of the Invisible may differ from what the books say. I mention it in passing, your Majesty.

When he assailed my grandfather openly in his cathedral, calling him coward and fiend, did Juan de Frías follow a lesson he had learned by rote? That good bishop had a heart and mind to which life itself could speak, and speak forcibly.

Indians came bringing five persons shrivelled and paralysed and very ill. Each of the five offered Castillo silently his bows and arrows. Castillo prayed, we with him; in the morning the five were cured . . .

Indians came from many places. But Castillo was always afraid his sins would interfere with his working miracles. The Indians turned to me. I told Castillo it was no moment for indulging the idea of being sinful, and then I followed the Indians to their ranch. The dying man was dead; Dorantes and I found him with eyes upturned, and no pulse. I removed the mat that covered him and prayed. At last the something in me like a membrane broke, and I was confident the old man would rise up again. As he did.

During the night the natives came to tell us he had talked, eaten and walked about. They gave us many presents, and we left them the happiest people on earth, for they had given away their very best.

Your Majesty may by now have had enough of our cures and curing, exertions outside of Holy Church, and for the sole benefit of miserable Indians. Yet so profound is your courtesy, I know, that you will let me reveal all that is within my heart. We found ourselves so pressed that Dorantes and the Moor, who had little taste for it, had to become medicine men, too. Boys and girls, men and women, old men and women, human bodies deformed, starved, wasted by affliction (only rarely one sound and firm) . . . Their eyes followed us every moment. I do not forget those eyes . . . Your Majesty, since I addressed you first, you have become more mysterious to me and more majestic, and this increases my sense of freedom in speaking to you. To the understanding of such days and events this additional narrative becomes necessary, like a real figure to walk beside a ghost. Those eyes . . . they thrust me out of myself, into a world where nothing, if done for another, seems impossible.

Months went by as in a dream. The nerve of vision no longer rendered plausible that European world of which we had been a part. That world grew fantastic, and fantastic our countrymen there. We ourselves were only too real. From lack of clothing we had big sores and deep skin fissures on our backs and shoulders, and it hurst us to carry the hides we slept in. And it hurt us to find firewood among the cactus. My thighs and arms bled so much I stood it only by remembering—and yet whom or what did I remember? Was it a Person—was it a quality of life—was it an emotion? Was it even a remembering, was it not perhaps a listening?

Often for a time it rained gently at dusk, soothing our thighs and arms. In one such dusk we encountered squinting women in an opening. They were afraid to run away from the three pale figures and the shadowy blackamoor, for they us took to be gods floating about in the mist and rain. They led us to a village of fifty huts. Here we cured, and cured . . .

Our journey westward was but a long series of encounters. Your Majesty, encounters have become my meditation. The moment one accosts a stranger or is accosted by him is above all in this life the moment of drama. The eyes of Indians who crossed my trail have searched me to the very depths to estimate my *power*. It is true the world over. It is true of a Spaniard meeting another on the road between Toledo and Salamanca. Whoever we meet watches us intently at the quick strange moment of meeting, to see whether we are disposed to be friendly.

Seeing our bodies, seeing my own, and Alonso's, and Andrés', and the black Moor's, sometimes I think how once I was different, and we all were. What would Doña Alonza Maldonado and her husband Dr. Castillo of

410

Salamanca think, if they could see their little boy Alonso today, striding here ahead of me, lashed by starvation, scorched and baked by the sun, his hair and beard unkempt, small about the flanks, his body shrivelled like a mummy?

In youth the human body drew me and was the object of my secret and natural dreams. But body after body has taken away from me that sensual phosphorescence which my youth delighted in. Within me is no disturbing interplay now, but only the steady currents of adaptation and of sympathy.

Your Majesty's piercing mind glides pliantly through what is interstitial and hidden. But upon me it was dawning only slowly that I had it in my discretion to grant life and health to others . . . Imagine me then perturbed; you are aware of what my training had been as one of your Majesty's soldiers.

Dark clouds rise to the south. To the west a great rainbow spreads its double arc. Alonso strides sturdily towards it. After him comes the Arab negro from Azamor, whose black limbs endure every privation and still shine with superfluous sweat. For this blackamoor am I specially grateful. His reflections on our suffering do not reduce him to apathy. No adverse heats and chills deprive his loins of their strength. He is a sight to see, carrying a copper rattle in his hand, and on his shoulder a green and orange parrot.

There was the afternoon we crossed a big river, more than waist deep, as wide as the Guadalquivir at Sevilla, and with a swift current. I speak of it again because I loved it.

There was the village where each Indian wished to be the first to touch us, and we were squeezed almost to death in the sweating crowd . . .

. . . the village so solicitous to be blest that Alonso fainted of exhaustion . . .

. . . the village where a new custom began: the Indians who came with us took from the villagers all their bows, arrows, shoes and beads. From that time on, those who accompanied us took tribute of those to whom they brought us. It made us uneasy, but the victims reassured us. They said they were too glad to see us to feel the loss of their property—and besides, they could make good their losses at the next village, who were very rich Indians . . .

. . . the plain where first we saw mountains, very low, like white sheep lying down . . .

. . . the village where they were so pertinacious about touching us all over that in three hours we could not get through with them . . .

. . . the village where many had one eye clouded, and others were totally blind from the same cause: which amazed us . . .

To clarify the same occurrences, words can be arranged differently, as no

411

one knows better than your Majesty. It was a drunkenness, this feeling I began to have of power to render life and happiness to others. Yet I was concerned about it. The concern was the important thing—not the wondering about the nature of the power, how widespread it might be, how deep, whether Andrés or Alonso or Estevanico had it in equal measure with me. What occupied me was whether I myself knew how to use it, whether I could master it, whether indeed it was for me to master—perhaps being a self-directing power that came through me. But after one accustoms oneself to the idea, it is good to be able to give out health and joy whether one man have it, or whether we all have it. Had this thought occurred to your Majesty? Never before had it occurred to me.

I said to Andrés, "If we reach Spain I shall petition His Majesty to return me to this land, with a troop of soldiers. And I shall teach the world how to conquer by gentleness, not by slaughter." "Why then a troop of soldiers?" asked Dorantes, smiling. "Soldiers look for Indian girls and gold." "Perhaps I could teach them otherwise." "They would kill you, or tie you to a tree and leave you. What a dunce you are, Alvar Nuñez!"

"And what will *you* do if we reach Spain again?" I asked Andrés. "It will be enough to reach Mexico," he answered. "I may look about for a rich widow, and spend the rest of my life as a rancher." "I could not care for such a life," I said. "To each his adventure," replied Andrés.

It occurred to me that Andrés might be afraid of the great power at this period within us. I inquired of him. "Yes, I am afraid—who would not be?" he answered, earnestly.

Another day, after he had been silent a long time, Andrés said to us: "If I could always heal these people and help them, I might be willing to stay among them. I don't know. But our present relation to them is caused by our novelty, our transiency, and the surprise at our good works. That state of things would wear off. Besides, it is not miracles these people need. They need everything fate has stript us of in bringing us amongst them naked and on equal terms. Yet not quite equal. We can remember childhood and youth in a land where people live in stone houses, till the same fields year after year, build barns to store the harvests in. The towns are related to one another and support the mutual good. Each nobleman and alcalde is an avenue leading to the king; and king, alcalde, thief, and villager all bow to the will of God through Holy Church."

I take my time thinking these words over. They are true and yet I cannot assent to them. Then I answer Andrés: "When these Indians call upon us to have mercy and heal them, is the power they feel in us derived from stone houses, barns and tilled fields—from alcalde or nobleman, or from Holy Church, for that matter? Let the truth be said, Andrés: All that we learned across the water we have had to throw away. Only what we learned as babes in our mothers' arms has stayed with us to help others." "And what did we learn in our mothers' arms, good dunce?" asked Andrés, putting his arm round my shoulder.

. . . a mountain seven leagues long, the stones of which were iron slags . . .

. . . a night when the moon was round, and in its light a multitude of dwellings beside an unexpected and charming river . . .

. . . a man who some years since had been shot through the left side of the back with an arrow. He told me the wound made him feel sick all the while. I observed that the head of the arrow lay in the cartilage. I prayed for an hour, and then grasped the very sharp thin stone which served me as a knife, and cut open the breast. Feeling for the arrowhead, I thrust my hand into the palpitating tissue of the body. Your Majesty, that we human beings should be made of limp wet meat appeared to me as strange as that we should be also air and spirit; and in that hour nausea and a quick curiosity mingled with my pity. . . .

This cure was a misfortune to us; it gained us fame in every direction. We soon had with us three or four thousand persons. It went past human endurance to breathe on and make the sign of the Cross over every morsel they ate. In these parts mountain deer, quail, birds, rabbits abounded, and what they killed the Indians set before us. They would not touch it and would have died of hunger had we not yielded the blessing they asked for. Besides, they asked our permission for various things they felt like doing, and it soon wore us out. Even doing good, it appears, can lead to ennui, even the sight of the happiness one causes can satiate. And yet your Majesty will rejoice that heaven vouchsafed us a weariness such as this, perhaps never before experienced by a European.

Tribe after tribe, language after language . . . nobody's memory could recall them all. Always they robbed one another, but those who lost and those who gained were equally content.

Estevanico, the good black, the good link between the aloofness of white men and the warm spermatic life of the Indians. Men, women and children joked and played with him. What matter what he did, he was not wearied of it. What matter what he did, the mystery failed not to act through him to heal and restore.

. . . fifty leagues through a land of desert, with nothing to eat and little to drink. Through villages where the women dressed in white deerskin and people lived in real houses . . . people the best formed we had seen, the liveliest and most capable, and those who best understood us . . .

. . . moonlight in another adobe village, and we four alternately standing or lying down in the center of the plaza, and the Indians running to us from all the houses with gifts, touching us and running back to their houses for more gifts, running to us again and touching us—a living glistening cobweb of runners in the moon—keeping up for hours this naked flash to and fro from center to periphery, periphery to center.

Your Majesty, such were the scenes in which I found myself treating all human beings alike. I screw up my courage to confess it. Perhaps it is the secret thing which life has it in itself to become—a long, long march on the road, meeting people, thrown into relations with them, having to meet demands often terrible and without the aid of mysterious power impossible: demands of healing and understanding and constantly the exorcism of fear.

With a reasonable man and a timorous man and a carnal man as my companions and even part of me. And who is any of us, that without starvation he can go through the kingdoms of starvation?

And seventeen successive days of starvation.

And a sunset, on a plain between very high mountains, with a people who for four months of the year eat only powdered straw . . .

And more starvation . . .

And permanent houses once more, where maize is harvested, and where they gave us brightly decorated blankets. For a hundred leagues good houses and harvested crops, the women better treated than anywhere else. They wear shoes, and blouses open in front and tied with deer string. At sunrise these people lift their clasped hands to the horizon and pass them over their bodies. At sunset they repeat the gesture. As I watched them at these devotions, I recalled a youngster from Cadiz, one of those who died of thirst beside me in the open boat. That boy drank in the beauty of Florida, watched palm and headland along the coast even in his final delirium. I was sorry he had not lived on to see these natives laving their golden figures in the gold of dawn.

At last we found a sign of our countrymen—what through months and years we had been praying for. On the neck of an Indian a little silver buckle from a sword belt, with a horseshoe nail sewed inside it. . . . We questioned him. He said that men with beards like ours had come from heaven to that river; that they had horses, lances, and swords, and had lanced two Indians.

The country grew more and more doleful. The natives had fled to the mountains, leaving their fields. The land was fertile and full of streams, but the people were wan. They told us our countrymen had burnt all the villages, taking with them half the men and all the women and children . . .

Then a day when Indians said that on the night before they had watched the Christians from behind some trees. They saw them take along many persons in chains.

Our countrymen, these slave-catchers, were startled when they saw us approaching. Yet almost with their first words they began to recite their troubles. For many days they had been unable to find Indians to capture. They did not know what to do, and were on the point of starvation. The idea of enslaving our Indians occurred to them in due course, and they were vexed at us for preventing it. They had their interpreter make a fine speech. He told our Indians that we were as a matter of fact Christians too, but had gone astray for a long while, and were people of no luck and little heart. But the Christians on horseback were real Christians, and the lords of the land to be obeyed and served. Our Indians considered this point of view. They answered that the real Christians apparently lied, that we could not possibly be Christians. For we appeared out of sunrise, they out of sunset; we cured the sick, while they killed even the healthy; we went naked and barefoot, while they wore clothes, and rode horseback and stuck people with lances; we asked for nothing and gave away all we were given, while they never gave anybody anything and had no other aim than to steal.

Your Majesty will remember my indignation in my first narrative, that Christians should be so wicked, especially such as had the advantages of being your subjects. I did not at the time understand the true source of my indignation. I do now, and I will explain it. In facing these marauders I was compelled to face the Spanish gentleman I myself had been eight years before. It was not easy to think of it. Andrés and Alonso agreed that it was not easy. What, your Majesty, is so melancholy as to confront one's former unthinking and unfeeling self?

It was many days before I could endure the touch of clothing, many a night before I could sleep in a bed.

Shoes were the worst. In the Spanish settlements I dared not go barefoot, for provincials are the most easily shocked of Spaniards. I had not valued enough the pressure of earth on my naked feet, while permitted that refreshment.

At first I did not notice other ways in which our ancient civilisation was affecting me. Yet soon I observed a certain reluctance in me to do good to others. I would say to myself, Need I exert what is left of me, I who have undergone tortures in an open boat and every privation and humiliation among the Indians, when there are strong healthy men about me, fresh from Holy Church and from school, who know their Christian duty? We Europeans all talk this way to ourselves. It has become second nature to us. Each nobleman and alcalde and villager is an avenue that leads us to this way of talking; we can admit it privately, your Majesty, can we not? If a man need a cloak, we do not give it to him if we have our wits about us; nor are we to be caught stretching out our finger in aid of a miserable

415

woman. Someone else will do it, we say. Our communal life dries up our milk: we are barren as the fields of Castile. We regard our native land as a power which acts of itself, and relieves us each of exertion. While with them I thought only about doing the Indians good. But back among my fellow countrymen, I had to be on my guard not to do them positive harm. If one lives where all suffer and starve, one acts on one's own impulse to help. But where plenty abounds, we surrender our generosity, believing that our country replaces us each and several. This is not so, and indeed a delusion. On the contrary the power of maintaining life in others, lives within each of us, and from each of us does it recede when unused. It is a concentrated power. If you are not acquainted with it, your Majesty can have no inkling of what it is like, what it portends, or the ways in which it slips from one. In the name of God, your Majesty, *Farewell*.

Then came the story of Cabeza de Vaca, of the miracles he accomplished not only for himself but for others. It was the first bright spot I encountered in the bloody legend created by the conquistadores.

—Henry Miller

I believe that it expresses best the key idea of all my writing, namely: that each of us has, in a degree, the power of giving health and happiness to others.

—Haniel Long

417

REFLECTIONS (27)

REFLECTIONS

Considering what Cabeza de Vaca learned about himself, about life, about human nature and human possibilities, what were his most important discoveries?

"In suffering learn wisdom" is a saying that occurs frequently in ancient Greek drama. Could Cabeza de Vaca have learned what he did *without* suffering?

Haniel Long adapted Cabeza de Vaca's original narrative, as he explains in Note I, because he believed the story had great relevance to our own times. Aside from the *general* significance of the story, what *specific* applications or examples do you see of this?

WALT WHITMAN

A Noiseless Patient Spider

A noiseless patient spider,
I mark'd where on a little promontory it stood isolated,
Mark'd how to explore the vacant vast surrounding,
It launch'd forth filament, filament, filament, out of itself,
Ever unreeling them, ever tirelessly speeding them.

And you O my soul where you stand,
Surrounded, detached, in measureless oceans of space,
Ceaselessly musing, venturing, throwing, seeking the spheres to
    connect them,
Till the bridge you will need be form'd, till the ductile anchor hold,
Till the gossamer thread you fling catch somewhere, O my soul.

Voyages of Discovery

~~~~~~

Journey's End

We shall not cease from exploration
And the end of all our exploring
Will be to arrive where we started
And know the place for the first time

T. S. Eliot
"Little Gidding"
Four Quartets

*The home port. What echoes of comfort
and relief that has for all of us, whether we
have ever been to sea or not. The voyage was
good, but the homecoming is better—or just
as good, at any rate, in its own way. To find
ourselves among familiar places and people
once more, to relax our vigilance and slide
comfortably into another and slower
rhythm . . .; let no one ask us when we mean
to put to sea again. With characteristic
modesty and understatement, Joshua Slocum
assesses the meaning of his voyage. He claims
little, but the deep satisfaction is there, the
quiet pride of accomplishment. He did what
he set out to do, what someone had said
couldn't be done—what no one, in fact, had
ever done before. He had sailed around the
world alone, and now he was home.*

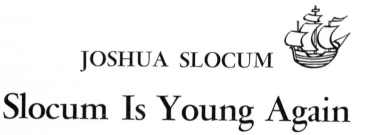

JOSHUA SLOCUM

Slocum Is Young Again

The experiences of the voyage of the *Spray,* reaching over three years, had been to me like reading a book, and one that was more and more interesting as I turned the pages, till I had come now to the last page of all, and the one more interesting than any of the rest.

When daylight came I saw that the sea had changed color from dark green to light. I threw the lead and got soundings in thirteen fathoms. I made the land soon after, some miles east of Fire Island, and sailing thence before a pleasant breeze along the coast, made for Newport. The weather

from SAILING ALONE AROUND THE WORLD by Capt. Joshua Slocum, Dover Publications, Inc.

after the furious gale was remarkably fine. The *Spray* rounded Montauk Point early in the afternoon; Point Judith was abeam at dark; she fetched in at Beavertail next. Sailing on, she had one more danger to pass—Newport harbor was mined.[1] The *Spray* hugged the rocks along where neither friend nor foe could come if drawing much water, and where she would not disturb the guard-ship in the channel. It was close work, but it was safe enough so long as she hugged the rocks close, and not the mines. Flitting by a low point abreast of the guard-ship, the dear old *Dexter,* which I knew well, some one on board of her sang out, "There goes a craft!" I threw up a light at once and heard the hail, *"Spray,* ahoy!" It was the voice of a friend, and I knew that a friend would not fire on the *Spray.* I eased off the mainsheet now, and the *Spray* swung off for the beacon-lights of the inner harbor. At last she reached port in safety, and there at 1 A.M. on June 27, 1898, cast anchor, after the cruise of more than forty-six thousand miles around the world, during an absence of three years and two months, with two days over for coming up.

Was the crew well? Was I not? I had profited in many ways by the voyage. I had even gained flesh, and actually weighed a pound more than when I sailed from Boston. As for aging, why, the dial of my life was turned back till my friends all said, "Slocum is young again." And so I was, at least ten years younger than the day I felled the first tree for the construction of the *Spray.*

My ship was also in better condition than when she sailed from Boston on her long voyage. She was still as sound as a nut, and as tight as the best ship afloat. She did not leak a drop—not one drop! The pump, which had been little used before reaching Australia, had not been rigged since that at all.

The first name on the *Spray's* visitors' book in the home port was written by the one who always said, "The *Spray* will come back." The *Spray* was not quite satisfied till I sailed her around to her birthplace, Fairhaven, Massachusetts, farther along. I had myself a desire to return to the place of the very beginning whence I had, as I have said, renewed my age. So on July 3, with a fair wind, she waltzed beautifully round the coast and up the Acushnet River to Fairhaven, where I secured her to the cedar spile driven in the bank to hold her when she was launched. I could bring her no nearer home.

If the *Spray* discovered no continents on her voyage, it may be that there were no more continents to be discovered; she did not seek new worlds, or sail to powwow about the dangers of the seas. The sea has been much maligned. To find one's way to lands already discovered is a good thing, and

[1] Because of the Spanish-American War (1898).

423

the *Spray* made the discovery that even the worst sea is not so terrible to a well-appointed ship. No king, no country, no treasury at all, was taxed for the voyage of the *Spray,* and she accomplished all that she undertook to do.

To succeed, however, in anything at all, one should go understandingly about his work and be prepared for every emergency. I see, as I look back over my own small achievement, a kit of not too elaborate carpenters' tools, a tin clock, and some carpet-tacks, not a great many, to facilitate the enterprise as already mentioned in the story. But above all to be taken into account were some years of schooling, where I studied with diligence Neptune's laws, and these laws I tried to obey when I sailed overseas; it was worth the while.

And now, without having wearied my friends, I hope, with detailed scientific accounts, theories, or deductions, I will only say that I have endeavored to tell just the story of the adventure itself. This, in my own poor way, having been done, I now moor ship, weather-bitt cables, and leave the sloop *Spray,* for the present, safe in port.

REFLECTIONS (28)

REFLECTIONS

Assessing your own voyage—through this book or through this course—what changes do you notice in yourself? Did you accomplish as much as you expected to? Or more, or less?

What have been the highlights of your voyage? Were there discoveries that still seem important? If you were to tell the story in a book, what episodes would you emphasize?

*The homecoming of Ulysses (Odysseus) is
one of the most dramatic in all literature, but
unfortunately that part of his story is too
long and too complex to be included here.
Since most readers, however, know the story
at least in general outline, a brief review may
help to put the following poem into perspective. During the last three or four years of
Ulysses' 20-year absence from his kingdom,
a throng of over a hundred young noblemen
has paid court to Ulysses' queen, Penelope,
telling her that Ulysses is undoubtedly dead
by now, and insisting that she choose one of
them to be her new husband. Penelope has
put them off by various ruses, the most
successful one being to tell them that she will
make her choice when she finishes weaving
a shroud for her father-in-law. But all that
she weaves by day, she unravels again by
night. In the meantime, the suitors virtually
move in to the great hall of the palace, taking
advantage of the laws of hospitality to eat
and drink daily at the expense of Ulysses'
household. Landing secretly on Ithaca and
meeting with his son, Telemachus, Ulysses
learns of these abuses to his honor and his
wealth. Disguised as an old beggar, he enters
the great hall, and at the appropriate moment
throws off his disguise, unleashes his great
bow, and with the help of Telemachus,
mercilessly slaughters the suitors to the last
man. Peace and honor restored, Ulysses
reclaims his throne, his wife, and his royal
bed. Reflecting on the justice of Ulysses'
terrible vengeance, Alastair Reid confronts a
nagging doubt. Could Ulysses' motives have
been as simple as Homer makes them seem?
Considering his sexual affairs with Circe,
Calypso, and Nausicaa, might something
deeper be troubling Ulysses?*

426

ALASTAIR REID

A Homecoming

Landfall in Ithaca. And so, Ulysses,
the will to win was all, all wandering done.
It did not matter what the past had cost
as now in your great bed you drowned again.
Gone were the various trials by sea, and gone
the trials by women—nights of sweated lust
in Circe's bed, the Sirens' dreamed-of kisses,
white-limbed Nausicaa—all past, all lost.
The Suitors? Who could expect you to be just?
Outside, the heaped-up bodies of the slain
slopped in their blood. But at your side lay she,
your virtuous weeping queen, Penelope.
She was good, she was true. Why then did you choose to carve
so cruel a way back to your marriage-bed?
What was there to avenge? Not faithlessness,
as all your baffling arrows found their dead?
Yet did her weaving and unweaving ask
so liberal a testament of blood?
What then? Was she too good to be true?
Did it come back, the phantom of your lust,
to haunt the restless edges of your sleep,
whispering "Are these faithful tears for you,
or in the web of darkness does she weep
for silent bloodstained lips, for the still thighs
of all the dead, for silver-tongued Eurymachus,
for Antinous, your arrow in his throat,
for Polybus, whose spilt blood fills his eyes?"
Was it this, Ulysses? And from some remote
lost island in the dark, did you cry at last
"O doubt, O doubt, O all the bitter past!"

*Hilaire Belloc, the author of numerous
volumes of prose and verse, including several
works of history, was also a devoted and
experienced amateur seaman. Having "picked
up moorings" in many places over the years,
he explains in this essay why he preferred
dropping anchor and describes his ideal
image of a final anchorage, such as every
sailor, perhaps, longs for at last.*

HILAIRE BELLOC

On Dropping Anchor

The best noise in all the world is the rattle of the anchor chain when one comes into harbour at last, and lets it go over the bows.

You may say that one does nothing of the sort, that one picks up moorings, and that letting go so heavy a thing as an anchor is no business for you and me. If you say that you are wrong. Men go from inhabited place to inhabited place, and for pleasure from station to station, then pick up moorings as best they can, usually craning over the side and grabbing as they pass, and cursing the man astern for leaving such way on her[1] and for passing so wide. Yes, I know that. You are not the only man who has picked up moorings. Not by many many thousands. Many moorings have I picked up in many places, none without some sort of misfortune; therefore do I still prefer the rattle of the anchor chain.

Once—to be accurate, seventeen years ago—I had been out all night by myself in a boat called the *Silver Star*. She was a very small boat. She had only one sail; she was black inside and out, and I think about one hundred years old. I had hired her of a poor man, and she was his only possession.

[1] Permitting the boat to go so fast.

428

It was a rough night in the late summer when the rich are compelled in their detestable grind to go to the Solent.[2] When I say it was night I mean it was the early morning, just late enough for the rich to be asleep aboard their boats, and the dawn was silent upon the sea. There was a strong tide running up the Medina. I was tired to death. I had passed the Royal Yacht Squadron grounds, and the first thing I saw was a very fine and noble buoy —new-painted, gay, lordly—moorings worthy of a man!

I let go the halyard very briskly, and I nipped forward and got my hand upon that great buoy—there was no hauling of it inboard; I took the little painter of my boat and made it fast to this noble buoy, and then immediately I fell asleep. In this sleep of mine I heard, as in a pleasant dream, the exact motion of many oars rowed by strong men, and very soon afterwards I heard a voice with a Colonial accent swearing in an abominable manner, and I woke up and looked—and there was a man of prodigious wealth, all dressed in white, and with an extremely new cap on his head. His whiskers also were white and his face bright red, and he was in a great passion. He was evidently the owner or master of the buoy, and on either side of the fine boat in which he rowed were the rowers, his slaves. He could not conceive why I had tied the *Silver Star* to his magnificent great imperial moorings, to which he had decided to tie his own expensive ship, on which, no doubt, a dozen as rich as himself were sailing the seas.

I told him that I was sorry I had picked up his moorings, but that, in this country, it was the common courtesy of the sea to pick up any spare moorings one could find. I also asked him the name of his expensive ship, but he only answered with curses. I told him the name of my ship was the *Silver Star*.

Then, when I had cast off, I put out the sweeps and I rowed gently, for it was now slack water at the top of the tide, and I stood by while he tied his magnificent yacht to the moorings. When he had done that I rowed under the stern of that ship and read her name. But I will not print it here, only let me tell you it was the name of a ship belonging to a fabulously rich man. Riches, I thought then and I think still, corrupt the heart.

Upon another occasion I came with one companion across the bar of Orford River, out of a very heavy wind outside and a very heavy sea. I just touched as I crossed that bar, though I was on the top of the highest tide of the year, for it was just this time in September, the highest springs[3] of the hunter's moon.

My companion and I sailed up Orford River, and when we came to Or-

---

[2] A strait between the Isle of Wight and Hampshire, England.
[3] Spring tides, high tides resulting from the combined influence of sun and moon.

ford Town we saw a buoy, and I said to my companion, "Let us pick up moorings."

Upon the bank of the river was a long line of men, all shouting and howling, and warning us not to touch that buoy. But we called out to them that we meant no harm. We only meant to pick up those moorings for a moment, so as to make everything snug on board, and that then we would take a line ashore and lie close to the wharf. Only the more did those numerous men (whom many others ran up to join as I called) forbid us with oaths to touch the buoy. Nevertheless, we picked up the little buoy (which was quite small and light) and we got it in-board, and held on, waiting for our boat to swing to it. But an astonishing thing happened! The boat paid no attention to the moorings, but went careering up river carrying the buoy with it, and apparently dragging the moorings along the bottom without the least difficulty. And this was no wonder, for we found out afterwards that the little buoy had only been set there to mark a racing point, and that the weights holding the line of it to the bottom were very light and few. So it was no wonder the men of Orford had been so angry. Soon it was dark, and we replaced the buoy stealthily, and when we came in to eat at the Inn we were not recognised.

It was on this occasion that was written the song:

> The men that lived in Orford stood
>   Upon the shore to meet me;
> Their faces were like carven wood,
>   They did not wish to greet me.
>   etc.

It has eighteen verses.

I say again, unless you have moorings of your own—an extravagant habit —picking up moorings is always a perilous and doubtful thing, fraught with accident and hatred and mischance. Give me the rattle of the anchor chain!

I love to consider a place which I have never yet seen, but which I shall reach at last, full of repose and marking the end of those voyages, and security from the tumble of the sea.

This place will be a cove set round with high hills on which there shall be no house or sign of men, and it shall be enfolded by quite deserted land; but the westering sun will shine pleasantly upon it under a warm air. It will be a proper place for sleep.

The fair-way into that haven shall lie behind a pleasant little beach of shingle,[4] which shall run out aslant into the sea from the steep hillside, and shall be a breakwater made by God. The tide shall run up behind it smoothly, and in a silent way, filling the quiet hollow of the hills, brimming it all up like a cup—a cup of refreshment and of quiet, a cup of ending.

Then with what pleasure shall I put my small boat round, just round the point of that shingle beach, noting the shoal water by the eddies and the deeps by the blue colour of them where the channel runs from the main into the fair-way. Up that fair-way shall I go, up into the cove, and the gates of it shall shut behind me, headland against headland, so that I shall not see the open sea any more, though I shall still hear its distant noise. But all around me, save for that distant echo of the surf from the high hills, will be silence; and the evening will be gathering already.

Under that falling light, all alone in such a place, I shall let go the anchor chain, and let it rattle for the last time. My anchor will go down into the clear salt water with a run, and when it touches I shall pay out four lengths or more so that she may swing easily and not drag, and then I shall tie up my canvas and fasten all for the night, and get me ready for sleep. And that will be the end of my sailing.

[4] Smooth pebbles.

Where lies the final harbor,
whence we unmoor no more?

—Herman Melville
Moby Dick

Here he lies where he longed to be
Home is the sailor, home from the sea
And the hunter home from the hill

—Robert Louis Stevenson
his epitaph

REFLECTIONS (29)

REFLECTIONS

Belloc says that "picking up moorings is always a perilous and doubtful thing, fraught with accident and hatred and mischance." Taking the statement metaphorically, does your own experience confirm its truth?

Belloc creates a sense of peace, rest, and finality in his closing paragraphs. How does he achieve this feeling?

Do you have an image of the sort of place where some day you would like to "drop anchor"?

Voyages of Discovery

~~~~~~

The Eternal Quest

But where is what I started for so long ago?
And why is it yet unfound?

—Walt Whitman
"Facing West from California's Shores"

I long ago lost a hound, a bay
horse, and a turtledove, and am
still on their trail. Many are the
travelers I have spoken concerning
them, describing their tracks and
what calls they answer to. I have
met one or two who had heard the
hound, and the tramp of the horse,
and even seen the dove disappear
behind a cloud, and they seemed
as anxious to recover them as if
they had lost them themselves.

—Henry David Thoreau
Walden

The voyage is ended; we have come home.
Or have we?

ROBERT FROST

Reluctance

Out through the fields and the woods
    And over the walls I have wended;
I have climbed the hills of view
    And looked at the world, and descended;
I have come by the highway home,
    And lo, it is ended.

The leaves are all dead on the ground,
    Save those that the oak is keeping
To ravel them one by one
    And let them go scraping and creeping
Out over the crusted snow,
    When others are sleeping.

And the dead leaves lie huddled and still,
    No longer blown hither and thither;
The last lone aster is gone;
    The flowers of the witch hazel wither;
The heart is still aching to seek,
    But the feet question "Whither?"

Ah, when to the heart of man
    Was it ever less than a treason
To go with the drift of things,
    To yield with a grace to reason,
And bow and accept the end
    Of a love or a season?

*Will it surprise you to find that perennial
voyager, Ulysses, restless again. It is dull
"to pause, to make an end . . ."*

ALFRED, LORD TENNYSON

Ulysses

IT little profits that an idle king,
By this still hearth, among these barren crags,
Match'd with an aged wife, I mete and dole
Unequal laws unto a savage race,
That hoard, and sleep, and feed, and know not me.
I cannot rest from travel: I will drink
Life to the lees: all times I have enjoy'd
Greatly, have suffer'd greatly, both with those
That loved me, and alone; on shore, and when
Thro' scudding drifts the rainy Hyades
Vext the dim sea: I am become a name;
For always roaming with a hungry heart
Much have I seen and known; cities of men
And manners, climates, councils, governments,
Myself not least, but honour'd of them all;
And drunk delight of battle with my peers,
Far on the ringing plains of windy Troy.
I am a part of all that I have met;
Yet all experience is an arch wherethro'
Gleams that untravell'd world, whose margin fades
For ever and for ever when I move.
How dull it is to pause, to make an end,
To rust unburnish'd, not to shine in use!
As tho' to breathe were life. Life piled on life
Were all too little, and of one to me
Little remains: but every hour is saved

From that eternal silence, something more,
A bringer of new things; and vile it were
For some three suns to store and hoard myself,
And this grey spirit yearning in desire
To follow knowledge, like a sinking star,
Beyond the utmost bound of human thought.
    This is my son, mine own Telemachus,
To whom I leave the sceptre and the isle—
Well-loved of me, discerning to fulfil
This labour, by slow prudence to make mild
A rugged people, and thro' soft degrees
Subdue them to the useful and the good.
Most blameless is he, centred in the sphere
Of common duties, decent not to fail
In offices of tenderness, and pay
Meet adoration to my household gods,
When I am gone. He works his work, I mine.
    There lies the port: the vessel puffs her sail:
There gloom the dark broad seas. My mariners,
Souls that have toil'd, and wrought, and thought with me—
That ever with a frolic welcome took
The thunder and the sunshine, and opposed
Free hearts, free foreheads—you and I are old;
Old age hath yet his honour and his toil;
Death closes all: but something ere the end,
Some work of noble note, may yet be done,
Not unbecoming men that strove with Gods.
The lights begin to twinkle from the rocks:
The long day wanes: the slow moon climbs: the deep
Moans round with many voices. Come, my friends,
'Tis not too late to seek a newer world.
Push off, and sitting well in order smite
The sounding furrows; for my purpose holds
To sail beyond the sunset, and the baths
Of all the western stars, until I die.

It may be that the gulfs will wash us down:
It may be we shall touch the Happy Isles,
And see the great Achilles, whom we knew.
Tho' much is taken, much abides; and tho'
We are not now that strength which in old days
Moved earth and heaven; that which we are, we are;
One equal temper of heroic hearts,
Made weak by time and fate, but strong in will
To strive, to seek, to find, and not to yield.

It's a wild call and a clear call that may
not be denied; and so we take
our leave once more . . .

ROBERT FROST

Away!

Now I out walking
The world desert,
And my shoe and my stocking
Do me no hurt.
I leave behind
Good friends in town.
Let them get well-wined
And go lie down.
Don't think I leave
For the outer dark
Like Adam and Eve
Put out of the Park.
Forget the myth.
There is no one I
Am put out with
Or put out by.
Unless I'm wrong
I but obey
The urge of a song:
"I'm—bound—away!"
And I may return
If dissatisfied
With what I learn
From having died.

Whatever it is we search for, the quest is endless.
What we find is never enough for long.
Old desires take new shapes, are reborn.

WILLIAM BUTLER YEATS

The Song of Wandering Aengus

I went out to the hazel wood,
Because a fire was in my head,
And cut and peeled a hazel wand,
And hooked a berry to a thread;
And when white moths were on the wing,
And moth-like stars were flickering out,
I dropped the berry in a stream
And caught a little silver trout.
When I had laid it on the floor
I went to blow the fire aflame,
But something rustled on the floor,
And some one called me by my name:
It had become a glimmering girl
With apple blossom in her hair
Who called me by my name and ran
And faded through the brightening air.
Though I am old with wandering
Through hollow lands and hilly lands,
I will find out where she has gone,
And kiss her lips and take her hands;
And walk among long dappled grass,
And pluck till time and times are done
The silver apples of the moon,
The golden apples of the sun.

Reprinted with permission of The Macmillan Company from COLLECTED POEMS by
William Butler Yeats. Copyright 1906 by The Macmillan Company, renewed 1934 by
William Butler Yeats.

SELDON OSTEEN

So as Not to Return

Here, there must be somewhere
   you're going
and it must include
in some order
a plain
foothills
a rocky mountain range
waterfalls, thick trees and wild
   grass
a desert
bright suns running down a
   riverbed
stumble stones, stepping stones,
   lifting stones
shades of light
patterns of darkness,
heartheat, hearttremble, heart-
   soar
mindstorms
and heavy calm
and it should tend upwards
so as not
to return.

Envoi

Why did I make this voyage? Dig deep enough, and you will find that it has been your dream also—even if you have never been to sea or your fathers before you. Sometime, perhaps long ages ago, they had this same dream, and it is still in your flesh and will always be—be you seventy or a hundred or a boy of twelve, for dreams never die.

But perhaps this explanation sounds too distant and too mystical to describe my urge for the solitude of the sea and unbroken horizons, and I will try to come a little closer to the subject: Ever since I was a child at my mother's knee, I heard her speak of the beauty of open fields and woods and the wide and endless sea. Truly a dreamer and seer she was, for then she had only known the sea from pictures. And so I am just walking her way.

—William Willis
Whom the Sea Has Taken

ENVOI by William Willis, copyright 1966, reprinted by permission of Hawthorn Books, Inc.

Index

Index